CHRISTIAN SPIRITUAL FORMATION

An Integrated Approach for Personal and Relational Wholeness

DIANE J. CHANDLER

IVP Academic
An imprint of InterVarsity Press
Downers Grove, Illinois

InterVarsity Press
P.O. Box 1400, Downers Grove, IL 60515-1426
ivpress.com
email@ivpress.com

InterVarsity Press® is the book-publishing division of InterVarsity Christian Fellowship/USA®, a movement of students and faculty active on campus at hundreds of universities, colleges and schools of nursing in the United States of America, and a member movement of the International Fellowship of Evangelical Students. For information about local and regional activities, visit intervarsity.org.

While all stories in this book are true, some names and identifying information in this book have been changed to protect the privacy of the individuals involved.

Cover design: Cindy Kiple
Interior design: Beth McGill
Images: blank paper: © Tolga_TEZCAN/iStockphoto
flames: © sbayram/iStockphoto

ISBN 978-0-8308-4042-7 (print)
ISBN 978-0-8308-8024-9 (digital)

Printed in the United States of America ♾

green press INITIATIVE *As a member of the Green Press Initiative, InterVarsity Press is committed to protecting the environment and to the responsible use of natural resources. To learn more, visit greenpressinitiative.org.*

Library of Congress Cataloging-in-Publication Data

Chandler, Diane J.
Christian spiritual formation : an integrated approach for personal and relational wholeness / Diane J. Chandler.
pages cm
Includes bibliographical references and index.
ISBN 978-0-8308-4042-7 (pbk. : alk. paper)
1. Spiritual formation. I. Title.
BV4511.C47 2014
253.5'3--dc23

2014005167

P 26 25 24 23 22 21 20 19 18 17 16 15 14 13 12 11 10 9 8 7 6 5 4

Y 38 37 36 35 34 33 32 31 30 29 28 27 26 25 24 23 22 21 20 19

To my husband, Doug,
who continues to teach me much about Christian spiritual formation.

And to all those who desire to become more like Jesus
in all dimensions of life.

Contents

List of Figures

Preface

Over the past nine years, I have collaborated in developing and teaching an approach to Christian spiritual formation that is holistic in nature. I have explored how the human person develops in seven primary dimensions, including the spirit (the most critical), emotions, relationships, intellect, vocation, physical health and stewardship of our resources—referring to how we handle God's creation, money, possessions and time—and how these seven dimensions interrelate as we mature as followers of Jesus. Since we are created in the image of God, I could think of no better starting place than creation for addressing why and how these seven dimensions characterize the human fabric across time, regardless of gender, ethnicity or culture. Further, my study confirmed that from creation to our eternal home and from Genesis to Revelation God creates, interacts and moves in people's lives through love—a love that is stronger than death.

From the onset of this research initiative, I have anchored the Christian spiritual formation approach from the perspective of divine love in solid biblical and theological scholarship, while at the same time drawing on other disciplines that bear on these seven formation dimensions. Few other publications explore human formation from a multidisciplinary approach that is both biblically and theologically grounded. Thus, various dialogue partners appearing in this book include not only biblical scholars and theologians but also ministry practitioners and leaders, historians, educators, psychologists, sociologists, medical doctors, nutritionists, other health care professionals, neuroscientists, environmentalists, philosophers, and ethicists. Sifting through their perspectives has enriched my understanding of how God fashions persons as integrated beings. Although we will never fully understand the mystery of God in creation, we are beginning to understand what it means to be made in the image and likeness of God, and how we are to live in order to reflect divine glory.

This book also offers a resource for deepening one's life in God, punctuated through real-world examples and personal vignettes. Those who desire academic challenge will find this book full of helpful resources that ground the work in relevant scholarship. Others will find this book anchored in biblical principles that prompt practical steps for growth in each of the seven formation dimensions. A blend of theory and praxis, this book encourages readers to deepen their relationship with God and others and become healthier, whole and fulfilled in the process. At the same time, this book becomes a guide in learning how to love God, others and oneself through the faithful stewardship of one's God-given resources, as demonstrated through godly character and ethical living.

Acknowledgments

Many people have played a significant role in this book's development. To those who reviewed the initial book proposal or one or a few sample chapters, I owe a debt of gratitude. Their constructive input has served to challenge my thinking and strengthen the respective chapters. They include Richard E. Averbeck, Dorothy C. Bass, Cornelius J. Bekker, Craig L. Blomberg, Steven Bouma-Prediger, James P. Bowers, Simon Chan, M. Gail Derrick, Elizabeth Lewis Hall, Lee Hardy, Antipas L. Harris, Lynne Marie Kohm, Vickey Macklin, J. Robert Mulholland, Gary W. Moon, Glendon L. Moriarty, Stephen E. Parker, Stephen G. Post, Jennifer S. Ripley, Magda Serrano, Caroline J. Simon, J. Lyle Story, Wolfgang Vondey, Jo Williams and Amos Yong. One anonymous reviewer likewise provided invaluable input for which I am grateful. For the final product, however, I take full responsibility.

I wish to thank Michael Palmer, the former dean of the Regent University School of Divinity, for supporting a one-semester sabbatical leave, which enabled me to complete the manuscript. I am humbled to be a member of such a fine divinity faculty and am especially grateful to Mara Crabtree and Kristina Chalfin, with whom I've collaborated in implementing an integrated approach to Christian formation within a master's-level curriculum. My sincere thanks likewise extend to interlibrary loan supervisor extraordinaire Patty Hughson and her staff, who have facilitated delivery of scores of books needed for this research initiative. Further, I appreciate graduate assistants Kellie Nitz Iseman, LaShawne Thomas,

Stephanie Holt, Beverly Lepski Taylor, Crystal Fleeger Wray and Grace Park, who have helped in various phases of this project. Furthermore, I am profoundly grateful to my current and former students who have helped me to anchor Christian spiritual formation in real-life application.

As for the terrific editorial, copyediting and production team at InterVarsity Press Academic, I extend sincere thanks. Sincere appreciation goes to my editor, Brannon Ellis, whose wisdom, expertise and sensibilities were rivaled only by his consistent support throughout this project.

I am grateful for friends and family members who have provided ongoing encouragement in both tangible and intangible ways. They include Maureen D'Amelio, Emily Duenke, Cheryl Fisher, Anita Foged, Marcie Thomas, Vanja Bule, Gladys Chandler, Sharon Masters, Scott McAfee, Uta Milewski, Linda D. Miller, Towera Nyirenda, Lisa Marie Otto, Cathy Reagan, Kevin Turpin, Graham and Barbara Twelftree, and Leta Van Meter.

Finally, I offer immense gratitude to my husband and best friend, Doug, whose loving support and many sacrifices have made this writing adventure possible.

To God be the glory.

1

Introduction

We are God's handiwork,
created in Christ Jesus to do good works,
which God prepared in advance for us to do.

Ephesians 2:10 NIV

The ceiling of the Sistine Chapel is one of the most spectacular artistic masterpieces in human history.[1] Composed of nine frescoes designed and painted by Michelangelo between 1508 and 1512, the ceiling depicts scenes from the book of Genesis, including the *Creation of Adam*, the most well known. This scene portrays the God of creation and giver of life reaching out to touch the finger of Adam. Seemingly timeless, the beauty and luster of this and the other frescoes, including the *Creation of Eve*, inevitably deteriorated.

Through the centuries, several restoration efforts have ensued to preserve these works of art. The most recent restoration took place between 1980 and 1994. Ceiling cracks, structural and water damage, the buildup of smoke and waxy residue from burning candles, automotive exhaust from the once-opened windows at the top of the structure, and the effects of thousands of annual visitors increasingly compromised the frescoes' unsustainable beauty. What took four years to create five centuries ago required almost fourteen years of restorative work. The renovated ceiling, however, drew both praise and criticism, with some bemoaning that the original color and vitality were lost because of the misaligned techniques utilized by the conservators. As well-intended as the conservators were in the restoration process, they could not exactly replicate Michelangelo's original work. Creation, whether in artwork or in human life, is left in the hands of its creator and is virtually impossible to duplicate.

Although Michelangelo intended to portray the moment when God infused life into Adam, he could not possibly depict the magnificent miracle of life that began at the moment of creation (Gen 1:26-28). The mystery of creation eludes even the most careful observer and researcher, such as those working on the thirteen-year Human Genome Project, completed in 2003.[2] Although scientists have been able to identify over twenty thousand genes in human DNA, the life-generating substance within cell nuclei, they are unable to actually produce human life and uncover all its corresponding intricacies, as diligently as they may try. Despite what is known about human anatomy and physiology, God-given human capability involving the multiple dimensions of the human person cannot be reduced to mere scientific discovery and evaluation alone.

For example, as we have exceeded the seven billion world population mark, we acknowledge that each human being is created in the image of God with unique DNA, and that all life directly derives from God. But like the conservators trying to restore the Sistine Chapel ceiling to its original condition, only God can perfectly restore fallen humanity into wholeness through the person of Jesus Christ, the Son of God. Only through the love and grace of God manifested by Christ's death on the cross can we be restored and begin a process of being conformed to Christ's image in order to bring God glory in every dimension of life. As Michelangelo's Sistine Chapel was created in beauty, experienced decay and was painstakingly restored, so too humankind was fashioned by God in beauty, experienced decay through sin and has been restored in Christ for those who believe. By responding to God's love and grace in the person of Jesus Christ, we are able to be conformed to Christ's image through the person and power of the Holy Spirit.

This book presents an integrated approach in which to view the formation and development of human persons from a distinctly biblical and theological perspective. Christian spiritual formation (CSF) describes the process of being restored into the image of God through Jesus Christ in its multidimensionality by the work of the Holy Spirit. The fall of Adam and Eve through the entrance of sin in the world corrupted the perfect image of God infused in humanity at creation. This corrupted image is restored through Jesus Christ.

As a result of divine intent, the love of God that infused creation is to be received and reciprocated (Ps 31:23; Mt 22:37-40) through fellowship with God (1 Cor 1:9) and others in the body of Christ (1 Jn 1:6-7) and through loving one's neighbor (Mt 22:39). We glorify God by stewarding through grace all life dimensions in order to be effective ambassadors in a deeply broken world (see Ps 34:3; 2 Cor 5:20; 1 Pet 4:10). This process begins by acknowledging that Jesus died for our sins and paid the price for our eternal salvation and by receiving him through faith as our personal Savior and Lord (Jn 1:12; Acts 4:12).[3] Then the restoration process of being conformed to the image of Jesus in order to glorify God begins in seven formational dimensions: (1) spirit, (2) emotions, (3) relationships, (4) intellect, (5) vocation, (6) physical health and wellness, and (7) resource stewardship. Each of these dimensions will be briefly explained in this chapter.

The purpose of this book is to (1) present an integrated approach to Christian spiritual formation in seven dimensions reflecting holistic integration; (2) biblically and theologically anchor CSF, beginning with an analysis of the *imago Dei* (Lat. "image of God"), as derived from the Genesis creation narrative and furthered by understanding how Christ became the image to whom we are conformed; (3) demonstrate that receiving the love of God, as expressed through the Father, Son and Holy Spirit, is the catalyzing motivation for CSF; and (4) examine the seven formation dimensions and encourage authentic growth in each of them in order to glorify God. By wise stewardship of these seven God-given human dimensions through grace, we both reflect the *imago Dei* through godly character and ethical living, and give God glory in the process. The CSF model, which unifies each chapter, is presented in figure 1.1.

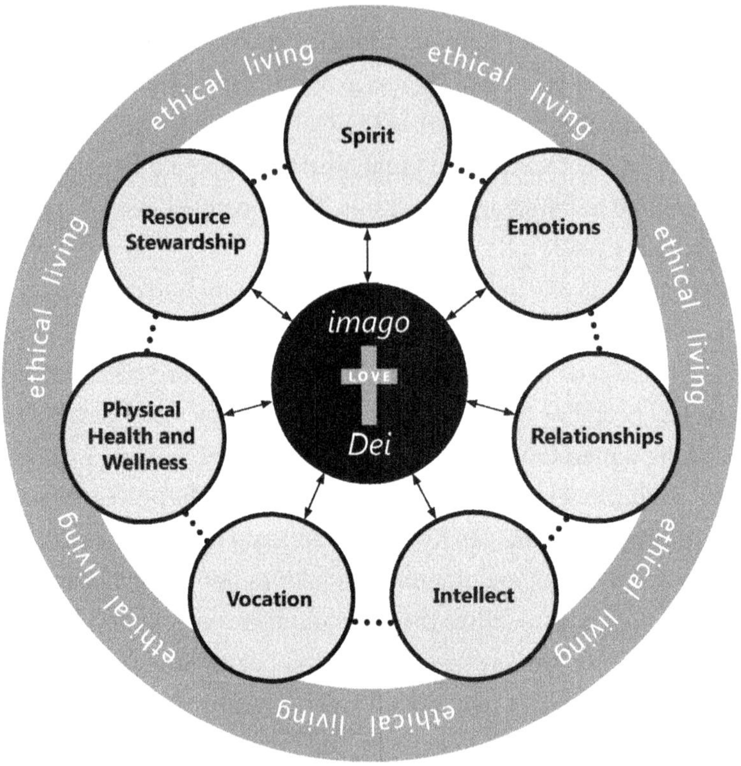

Figure 1.1. Christian spiritual formation model

WHAT IS CHRISTIAN SPIRITUAL FORMATION?

Throughout this book, CSF will be utilized for describing an integrated approach to human formation. The word *Christian* connotes that all personal formation flows from the person of God in Christ by the power of the Holy Spirit. For our purposes, the word *spiritual* relates to more than simply the nonphysical and mystical components of life lived in God; rather, it is utilized to describe *all dimensions of life* as influenced by the Spirit. *Formation* refers to both what is formed and the manner in which it is shaped.[4] In other words, CSF advances a whole-person theology.[5] Hence,

Christian spiritual formation connotes both the process and the result of this shaping process. For followers of Jesus, the CSF process is fostered by God, yet we must cooperate with God for holistic growth to occur.[6]

Therefore, CSF is defined as an interactive process by which God the Father fashions believers into the image of his Son, Jesus, through the empowerment of the Holy Spirit by fostering development in seven primary life dimensions (spirit, emotions, relationships, intellect, vocation, physical health and resource stewardship). Through refining the scope of CSF, I offer these seven life dimensions because they are universally shared across cultures as being those in which the human person is both inherently endowed and capable of exercising autonomy for personal growth and development.[7] Further, for believers to be Christ's ambassadors (2 Cor 5:20), I argue that these seven dimensions are intended by God to coalesce into an ethical lifestyle that witnesses to the unbelieving world of God's redeeming love.

CSF is predicated on believers receiving the abundant grace of God in salvation and throughout life as they are conformed into the image of Jesus (Eph 1:7-8; 2:4-5; 2 Pet 3:18). The *imago Dei,* being created in the image of God, fundamentally derives from God's love for humanity, indicated by the inner circle in figure 1.1. The CSF model offers a graphic illustration of various dimensions of formation, with the love of God as the primary catalyst, demonstrated by Jesus' death on the cross. Therefore, the center circle in figure 1.1 represents God's love as being the very core of CSF, with the cross of Christ reflecting what Stephen Seamands suggests as the visible manifestation of divine love: "Christ's death not only supremely reveals the nature of divine love, it also discloses what is eternally etched in the heart of the triune God."[8] Further, Jürgen Moltmann asserts, "The cross is the center of the Trinity. . . . Before the world was, the sacrifice was already in God. No Trinity is conceivable without the Lamb, without the sacrifice of love, without the crucified Son."[9]

Paul Fiddes simply states, "God creates out of love"; and as loving Creator without deficiency, God desires reciprocal love from humankind.[10] Accordingly in figure 1.1, the seven bidirectional arrows, which connect the center circle to the seven circles signifying the formation dimensions, represent reciprocal love: the love of God extended to humankind and humankind's love response to God. The larger dotted circle connecting each of the seven circles signifies the interrelatedness of each of the formation dimensions to one another. The solid outer circle, representing ethical living, conveys the outward demonstration of love to others, framed through one's godly character, for the glory of God.

From the onset, clarifying the definition of godly love is imperative, as love frames a central theme of this book. Therefore, I advance this definition: *Godly love is the essence of God's character and personality, proceeding from the Father as demonstrated by the Son through the work of the Holy Spirit, which unconditionally upholds the highest good of others and fosters the same altruism and benevolence in human relationships without regard for personal sacrifice.*[11] This definition frames love as deriving from God, the source of all love, who demonstrated cruciform love through the cross.[12] Godly love connotes being crucified with Christ, yet living for God's glory through losing oneself for Christ's sake and the sake of others (cf. Gal 2:20). In other words, godly love is the self-giving expression that results from divine initiative and human responsibility in serving God and others in relationality as evidenced by godly character and ethical living. Each of the seven formation dimensions derives from being created in the image of God, as predicated on the love of God most clearly revealed through Christ's sacrificial death on the cross, and is demonstrated as believers express their love to God and others through CSF, godly character and ethical living.

THE SEVEN CHRISTIAN SPIRITUAL FORMATION DIMENSIONS

God created man and woman holistically with inherent capacity in the seven life dimensions. Throughout time and across cultures, these seven dimensions characterize human life and capture the potentiality within the human person. Each formation dimension introduced will be further explained in subsequent chapters. The intrinsic flow of the chapters proceeds accordingly, with the priority of place given to formation of the spirit.

Formation of the spirit relates to our faith journey as the grace-based, interactive process of nurture and growth of the human spirit as it is conformed to the image of Jesus and overseen by the Father through the indwelling Holy Spirit in the context of the believing community.[13] All other formation dimensions predicate on the spiritual dimension.

Emotional formation refers to the process of understanding, expressing and reflecting on our feelings, passions, and desires in productive ways in order to reflect the image and character of Christ and come to terms with past hurts, wounds and bondages that stymie emotional freedom. Emotional formation is integrally tied to the spiritual dimension.

Relational formation relates to how we are conformed continuously into the image of Jesus through social interactions and the life of the church, which invariably are embedded within cultural contexts. Relational formation influences both spiritual and emotional formation, as well as the other dimensions.

Intellectual formation concerns the development of the mind to think, reason and discern truth consonant with the Word of God in order to nurture godly beliefs and a Christ-honoring worldview that reflects biblical knowledge, wisdom and understanding. Intellect develops in conjunction with the preceding three dimensions.

Vocational formation involves the process of being conformed into the image of Jesus in our life calling through the development of God-given giftings, talents, abilities and skills that reflect the grace and glory of God in life and work-related contexts. A sense of life purpose involves the spiritual, emotional, relational and intellectual life dimensions as they interact across time.

Physical health formation pertains to the care of our physical bodies, which Paul identifies as the temple of the Holy Spirit (1 Cor 6:19), in order to maximize our effectiveness in fulfilling our life purpose. Physical health underlies each of the preceding formation dimensions. We cannot be fully formed without taking into consideration the body, which sustains the other six dimensions.

Resource formation relates to the wise stewardship of the earth, finances, material possessions and time in order to bring maximum glory to God. Resource formation expresses a confluence of the other six dimensions.

Christian Spiritual Formation Integration

Interdisciplinary research reveals just how integrated our lives are across these seven vital dimensions. For example, spiritual growth is deeply affected by our emotions and formative interpersonal relationships. If we are angry with God, we would do well to explore whether we are also angry with others. Christian psychologists alert us to the synergistic relationship between the spiritual, emotional, relational and intellectual dimensions.[14] Furthermore, medical doctors continue to identify the interconnectedness between our physical health and spiritual life.[15] Our physical health and wellness influence the six other dimensions through life circumstances, personal choice or by default. For example, when we become sick or disabled, our physical condition may hinder life-giving interactions with others in relational formation. In addition, our vocational choices influence our relationships. Having a job that misaligns with our gifting and calling may prompt us to feel depressed and despondent toward God and others. Simon Chan emphasizes the holistic nature of our overall development: "Both body and mind have a part to play in spiritual development and must not be neglected in favor of the spirit."[16]

The integration of our formation across these seven dimensions especially came to light for me on three separate occasions. The first relates to a young woman I worked with who had a genuine spiritual hunger and passion for God, yet was deeply affected by debilitating emotional and mental illness. Her devotional life in God was active and growing, but she became continually sidelined by unresolved emotional and family issues, which turned into unpredictable behavioral patterns.

Second, a busy ministry leader once told me that he finally realized that his obsessive overeating and poor nutritional choices had created a significant weight problem. Facing critical warning signs of impending debilitation, he admitted that active stewardship of his physical health had to become a higher priority.

Third, a Christian couple moved into a new vocational venture in the real estate market to make "lots of money." When the venture began to crumble during an economic downturn, they realized their complete obsession with financial gain to the exclusion of other critical life dimensions. They eventually reprioritized their lives around biblical values. Each of these examples highlights that the seven formation dimensions are intricately interwoven and worthy of attention. The following account provides a historical example of how a life dedicated to Christ is expressed through CSF.

Christian Spiritual Formation Exemplified

John Newton's (1725–1807) life personifies the integration of the seven holistic dimensions identified in the CSF model. For Newton, receiving Christ as his personal Savior through forgiveness of sin was only the beginning of the multifaceted transformation in each of the seven formation dimensions that altered his life trajectory. While on board the British slave ship Greyhound *in 1748, Newton experienced deep transformation after reading* The Imitation of Christ *by Thomas à Kempis. Ironically that same night a violent storm lasting several days threatened to sink the ship. While at the helm Newton experienced a deep sense of conviction over his grievous wrongdoing and licentious lifestyle. Following a bout with poor health, his subsequent conversion to Christ led to his retirement from the slave trade.*

While Newton's transformation was spiritual, being reconciled to God through the forgiveness of sin, his transformation pervaded every dimension of his life. His emotions aligned with noble passions and desires. His social connections were recalibrated to honor Christ. For example, Newton's close relationship with William Wilberforce, a member of the British Parliament and ardent opponent of the slave trade, prompted Newton to publicly protest against slavery on biblical and moral grounds.[17] *His mind's focus shifted to Kingdom endeavors. His vocation changed from being a slave trader to becoming an author and rector of an Anglican church in London. His physical health improved when his behavioral habits changed. And Newton's resources of money, possessions and time were distilled into a Christ-honoring lifestyle. In glimpsing who Jesus was and the great price Jesus paid for his soul, Newton surrendered all dimensions of his life to God.*

Humans are made in the image of God with potential to develop, serve as stewards of and maximize God-given resources for God's glory. The CSF di-

mensions interdependently interact and frame our overall life and well-being. By growing in each formation dimension through grace, we bring God glory. God's glory relates to the beauty and majesty of God's very essence.[18] *To glorify God is to give God respect, awe and dignity, which correspond to God's supreme preeminence.*[19] *We give God glory when manifesting God's character and ways—in what we say, do, think, feel and love—just as John Newton did after conversion. We are to do everything for the glory of God (1 Cor 10:31). Hence, to bring God glory is to manifest something of God's essential nature and character in one's life and relationships.*

THE PROCESS

For Christians the ultimate goal of CSF is to become more like Jesus in order to reflect God's glory. Just as most parents want their children to resemble them, God also desires that we grow into the image of Jesus by becoming like him. Paul's injunction to the Ephesians to be imitators of God and to live in love succinctly sums up CSF (Eph 5:1-2). As Jason Hood explains, Paul's view of imitation with an emphasis on conformity to Christ through the Holy Spirit does not convey "rote mimicry" or mindless copying, but rather lies at the very heart of image bearing and the discipleship journey.[20] Human effort, however, is insufficient for the task. As Michael Gorman contends, imitation of Christ reflects "Christ's formation in believers," not the result of self-assertion but rather of the Spirit's working within to produce Christlike character.[21] This holistic transformation through God's redeeming grace is why Jesus came to rescue fallen humanity. As God's children we are nurtured by a loving Father through the person of Jesus by the power of the Holy Spirit, who in every way is dedicated to our overall growth and development. Affirming this developmental process into Christlikeness, the apostle John stated, "Beloved, we are God's children now; what we will be has not yet been revealed. What we do know is this: when he is revealed, we will be like him, for we will see him as he is" (1 Jn 3:2).

John R. Tyson acknowledges that this transformation process takes time: "There are few shortcuts in the journey from being a sin-dominated person to becoming a spiritually empowered, Christlike person; it is not a journey that is made quickly or easily."[22] Throughout the Gospels, Jesus beckons his disciples to follow him and become like him, which is exactly the focus of Thomas à Kempis's classic work *The Imitation of Christ.* In becoming more like Jesus, God works within us over time, but we also must respond to God's initiative. Observing God's divine action and human agency, Simon Chan argues, "The 'automatic' fruit accruing from God's action does not cancel out human will; rather, God acts within human activity."[23] We have an essential part to play in our own Christian formation.[24] At the same time, we must acknowledge the sublime mystery of God's Spirit working across the seven dimensions to fashion us into the image of Jesus. Transformation into the image of Jesus begins with surrender to God, which prompts the Holy Spirit to fashion us into Christlikeness. This way, Jesus becomes the primary model for the activity and change we desire.

The good news is that a loving God with abundant grace desires to meet us right where we are. Asking God for grace to intersect our motivations and desires is the entry point for deeper levels of transformation. Grace is the self-giving resource and gift from God that provides favor and enablement to fulfill one's Kingdom purpose.[25] This book addresses how God's grace engages the heart, will and actions in order to communicate divine love and thereby glorify God through each formation dimension as evidenced through godly character and an ethical lifestyle.

The various chapters in this book will appeal to Bible college and seminary students, Christian educators, ministry and pastoral leaders, spiritual directors, counselors and coaches, and those interested in fostering personal and corporate CSF growth within the family and various vocational contexts. Chapter two examines biblical and theological perspectives relative to the *imago Dei* in framing the CSF model. Chapter three focuses on the compelling incentive for CSF through an analysis of the Trinity, as characterized by the Father's love, the Son's model and the Holy Spirit's empowerment. Chapters four through ten respectively describe each of the seven formation dimensions in order to maximize personal growth in each area, beginning with the formation of the spirit in one's faith journey with God. Chapter eleven addresses ethical living through the seven CSF dimensions as critical for godly character and effective witness, with godly love presented as the highest virtue. Chapter twelve provides a summary of the CSF process and a call for a balanced approach.

Prior to painting the Sistine Chapel ceiling, Michelangelo resisted the invitation to enact this massive undertaking, insisting that he was a sculptor, not a painter. However, the nine frescoes detailing scenes from the book of Genesis are among his most notable work. Through them, Michelangelo graphically articulated the origin of God's grand narrative in an unsurpassed visual masterpiece. Our individual stories continue to be painted on the canvas of human history, as God invites us on a developmental journey of transformation for God's glory (see Jn 17:22; Rom 5:2; 2 Cor 3:18; 1 Thess 2:12; 2 Pet 1:3).

2

The Birthplace of Christian Spiritual Formation

The *Imago Dei*

What determines one's being is the image one adopts.

Abraham Heschel,
Who Is Man?

Anyone who has been a part of the childbirth process knows what an incredible miracle it is. I have had the privilege of playing a supportive role in the childbirth process of two dear friends. Even more important were their husbands who literally and figuratively stood by them, offering verbal encouragement, expressing their love, tending to their needs and praying for them in between labor pains. In both cases, the heart monitors indicated fetal distress prior to delivery, signaled by fading heartbeats. Both obstetricians recognized the importance of prompt delivery to avoid possible long-term consequences. Fortunately, both babies were delivered naturally into the world with searing screams to announce their healthy debuts.

As expected, the husbands quickly identified their baby's gender. Then they and their wives observed the baby's characteristics similar to their own, including hair color and facial features. Although physical features offer immediate sources of comparison, parents soon discover that their babies have personalities, dispositions, emotions, minds (and often strong ones at that!) and a capacity to form relationships with them and others.

Ideally, Christian parents desire that their children grow in all formational areas in order to ultimately become godly and responsible adults. The human birthing process demonstrates the result of creative genius in fashioning human life in God's image.

This chapter begins by focusing on God's making human persons in the *imago Dei,* as depicted in the shaded center of the Christian spiritual formation (CSF) model in figure 2.1. After reviewing the creation nar-

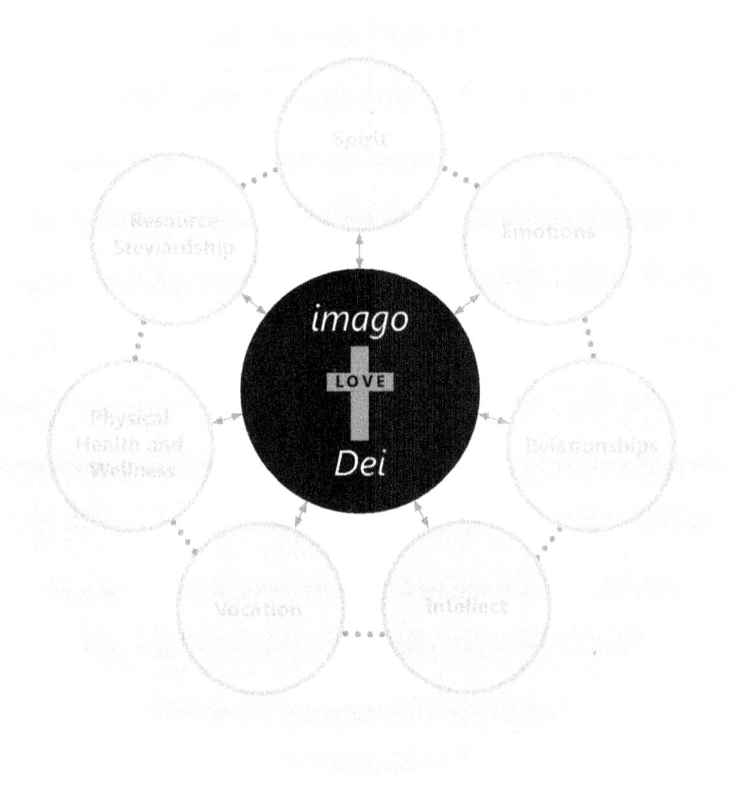

Figure 2.1. The *imago Dei*

rative relative to the *imago Dei,* I present four theological and historical perspectives, highlighting the nature of human creation and Jesus as the perfect *imago Dei,* which in turn informs the development of the CSF model. In summary, the origin of Christian spiritual formation derives from God's making humans in the *imago Dei*, followed by Christ's redeeming work on the cross as the ultimate expression of love for fallen humanity and the Holy Spirit's ongoing empowerment to live a godly life. We begin at the beginning.

THE *IMAGO DEI*

In Christian tradition humanness has as its origin God's making human persons in God's image, as reflected in the biblical creation narrative. Genesis 1:26-27 reveals that God made humankind in God's image, not as a random endeavor but as an intentionally creative demonstration of God's loving genius: "Then God said, 'Let us make humankind in our image, according to our likeness; and let them have dominion over the fish of the sea, and over the birds of the air, and over the cattle, and over all the wild animals of the earth, and over every creeping thing that creeps upon the earth.'"[1] God, as originator of life, spoke creation into existence. However, God deliberated before making humans, signified in Genesis 1:26 ("Let us make humankind in our image") and Genesis 2:7 ("then the LORD God formed the man from the dust of the ground, and breathed into his nostrils the breath of life; and the man became a living being"). Although all creation has its origin in God, only humankind is made in God's image.

Several biblical scholars and theologians comment on these passages. W. Lee Humphreys notes that "we first meet God as sovereign designer of a finely articulated cosmos, with its lines of authority, separations and distinctions, and its hierarchy fully defined (Gen 1:1–2:4a)."[2] Claus Westermann observes that God made a concerted decision to create human beings, which was neither casual nor haphazard.[3] Nothing existed before God, and all that was created was by God's initiative. Further, Gerhard von Rad concludes that the creation of humankind signifies the epitome of God's creativity over all nonhuman creation, evidenced by the trifold repetition of the word *make* in Genesis 1:27.[4] As Creator, God stands alone as the single initiator of all creation and its dynamism.[5]

In Genesis 1:26 we notice the plural grammatical construction of "let us" and "in our image," reflecting unity within God's inherent nature.[6] Some view this plurality as a description of the Trinity, whereas others ascribe this plurality to heavenly beings that surround God.[7] Although various interpretations have been offered to explain this plurality, Anthony Hoekema generally concludes that the plurality "brings out the uniqueness" of humankind, such that "in connection with no other creature is such a divine counsel mentioned."[8] Human beings are not to form God into their image but rather to conform to God's image.[9]

The exact meaning of the word *image* has been debated, with multiple interpretations offered. Gordon Wenham notes that the rarity of the word and the uncertainty of its etymology make the interpretation challenging.[10] Did God create humans to be an imitation of God's character and nature, God's representatives on earth, or God's counterpart? Raymond Van Leeuwen sees each as a valid interpretation, and Eugene Merrill notes that the word's meaning is determined by the interpretation of the prepositions *in* or *as* (i.e., "*in* his image" or "*as* his image").[11] Four primary perspectives on the interpretation of the image are offered later in this chapter.

Commentators note that a linguistic analysis of the words *image* and *likeness* makes little distinction between the terms but rather reinforces their parallelism.[12] For example, Derek Kidner comments, "The words *image* and *likeness* reinforce one another: there is no 'and' between the phrases, and Scripture does not use them as technically distinct expressions, as some theologians have done."[13] Hoekema observes only a slight nuance between both words in that the Hebrew word for image (*tselem*) derives from the root word that means "to carve" or "to cut." It can therefore mean a carved likeness of an original. The word for likeness (*demut*) derives from a Hebrew root meaning "to be like." How humanity is like God as "an image that is like us" is not specific or explicitly identified.[14] In essence, we learn that God exists in relationship through a plurality as Elohim and that we have been made in Elohim's image.

From the Genesis 1–3 narrative, general statements can be inferred in our attempt to understand what this image and likeness generally comprise.

First, man and woman are like God in that they are God's representatives on earth, having been made in God's image (Gen 1:26-27). Second, man and woman are like God in having dominion over the earth (Gen 1:26, 28-30). Third, they are like God in that being created in God's image entails being male and female, capable of companionship and procreation as social beings (Gen 1:27; 2:23-24). Fourth, humankind being fashioned in the image of God implies the capacity for relationship with and responsiveness to God (cf. Gen 2:15; 3:8-13).[15] Although some may assert that humankind lost the image of God as a consequence of the fall, the rest of Scripture, particularly the New Testament, indicates that although the image of God in humanity was corrupted during the fall, it was restored in Christ. I argue, therefore, that the creation of humankind in the *imago Dei* is holistic in nature, as presented in the next section.

Christian Formation in the *Imago Dei*

In Genesis 1–3 we can trace the foundations of all seven CSF dimensions. The formation of Adam and Eve, created in the image of God as integrated beings, entails a physical body, spiritual endowment, emotions, relational capacity, intelligence, vocational propensity for work, capability for physical health and wellness, and the ability to be stewards of themselves, God's creation and God-given resources. God did not assemble humankind in piecemeal fashion, incrementally adding to their physical bodies the capacity for spirit, emotions, relationships, intellect and stewardship. Rather, God created Adam and Eve by infusing them with an integrated, holistic capability.[16]

First and foundationally, God created humankind with spiritual capacity, as evidenced in Adam and Eve's intimate relationship with God in the Garden. This relationship radically changed as a result of the fall because of disobedience, which had profound consequences on the human spirit. Second, human emotion is also evident in the creation narrative, demonstrated when Adam and Eve felt completeness, pleasure, desire, fear, shame and suspicion. Their emotions were real, raw and observable. Third, the relational dimension of human formation is unmistakably apparent in that they were created to be in intimate relationship with God and each other. Fourth, intellectual formation is reflected in God's fashioning Adam and Eve with thinking, reasoning and decision-making abilities. For example, Adam named all the animals (Gen 2:20), Adam and Eve made the decision to eat the forbidden fruit (Gen 3:6-7), and both decided to hide from God (Gen 3:8). Fifth, God fashioned Adam and Eve vocationally to tend the Garden of Eden (Gen 2:15-16, 18). The boundary of their calling to work was the perimeter of the garden. Sixth, Adam and Eve had all necessary elements for physical health formation, as God abundantly provided everything they needed for wellness, giving them seed-bearing plants, fruit from trees and all the other resources found in animals (Gen 1:29-30). Last, their resource formation was likewise provided for in that they were to serve as stewards of the land, which offered provision for all their needs (Gen 2:15).

God made man and woman as integrated beings. G. C. Berkouwer contends, "Scripture's emphasis on the whole [person] an as the image of God has triumphed time and time again over all objections and opposing principles. Scripture never makes a distinction between [humankind's] spiritual and bodily attributes in order to limit the image of God to the spiritual, as furnishing the only possible analogy between [persons] and God."[17] The creation of man and woman reveals holistic dynamism. The next section presents four historical and theological perspectives on the *imago Dei* that inform the CSF model.

Four Perspectives on the *Imago Dei*

To better understand how formation derives from the creation narrative, four historical and theological perspectives of the *imago Dei* within the Christian tradition are offered as a concrete starting place.[18] Humankind's capacity in the dimensions of the spiritual, emotional, relational, intellectual, vocational, physical health and wellness, and resource stewardship are evidenced in these four perspectives, giving credence to their inclusion in the CSF model. The *imago Dei* reflects humankind's capacity for (1) thinking and reasoning, (2) interpersonal relationships, (3) dominion of the earth, and (4) becoming further restored into God's image through the sanctification process as not only a present reality but also a divine goal and destiny. Douglas John Hall asserts that the theme of the *imago Dei* points to "the mystery of human identity that must be rediscovered by each generation of the believing community."[19] While the contributions of church theologians inform our contemporary understanding of the *imago Dei* in historical perspective, I affirm Hall's call for an ongoing discovery of the unexamined dimensions of being created in God's image.[20] While each of the four perspectives identified presents a unique interpretation in the development of the *imago Dei* in Christian tradition, I argue that none of them presents a fully orbed understanding of the human person, as my subsequent analysis of each perspective attests.[21] Therefore, I contend for an integrated approach to understanding the *imago Dei* that advances a more robust consideration of the multidimensionality of human flourishing that is not limited to any single historical interpretation.

Perspective 1. The **imago Dei** ***as humankind's capacity to think and reason.*** This perspective is referred to as the structural view, with the *imago Dei* signifying humankind's qualities that reflect God's reasoning ability. Early church fathers such as Irenaeus (202), Clement of Alexandria (c. 150–c. 215), Athanasius (c. 296–373), Gregory of Nyssa (c. 335–c. 395) and Augustine of Hippo (354–430) framed their patristic theology around being made in God's image as the unique ability to reason, unlike non-human creation. Influenced by Greek philosophers such as Plato and Aristotle, Irenaeus primarily ascribed the image of God as human rationality. Irenaeus is credited with differentiating the image of God and the likeness of God, maintaining that humans retained God's image after the fall but lost God's likeness because of disobedience. Likewise, Clement primarily connected the *imago Dei* to human reason, and Athanasius viewed humanity in the *imago Dei* as being a rational soul, as did Gregory of Nyssa. David Cairns summarizes this view: "In all the Christian writers up to Aquinas we find the image of God conceived of as man's power of reason."[22]

Latin church father Augustine of Hippo developed an interpretation of this structural view of the *imago Dei* as being humankind's capacity for memory, intellect and will, corresponding to remembering, understanding and loving, which reflect the Trinity. Augustine argued that humankind was created with reason and intelligence to excel above all the creatures of the world, and that they have the capacity to know and love God.[23] Stanley Grenz observes, "For Augustine, then, the seat of the divine image in the human person is the soul in its intellectual dimension, insofar as the goal of the image is knowledge of God" in tandem with the love of God.[24] Supporting Augustine's position, Aquinas further linked the divine image to rationality or the intellectual capability of humanity. The intellectual dimension featured in the CSF model derives from this perspective.

However as important as the structural view of the *imago Dei* is, humankind's inherent potentiality goes beyond the intellectual dimension. Interestingly, Augustine's great influence in understanding the *imago Dei* came under criticism in the Reformation period, and with good reason. Humans are sufficiently complex in other dimensions. For example, human dimensionality and growth are tangibly demonstrated through human emotion. Therefore, limiting the *imago Dei* exclusively to the intellectual dimension is insufficient, as it ignores the multidimensionality of the human person, including the emotional domain, which is included in the CSF model.

Perspective 2. The* imago Dei *as humankind's capacity for relationship. Following the Middle Ages, the Reformation era offered a second perspective in understanding the *imago Dei*. Based on his proclamation of justification by faith alone for salvation, Martin Luther (1483–1546) challenged medieval thinking that humans could achieve knowledge of God on their own through rationality. Instead he asserted that all powers to know God are found outside of themselves—within God alone—through *relationship* with God. Luther argued that if humankind's inherent capacity to know God were true, then Satan was created in the image of God, since he has natural capacity for memory, intellect and will. Although Luther readily admitted that the endowments of reason, intellect and volition derive from God, he asserted that the image of and likeness to God were lost through sin and only could be restored in Christ through the vehicles of the Word of God and the Holy Spirit.[25] Some have suggested that Luther viewed the *imago Dei* as original righteousness that was lost in the fall.[26]

Other Reformers such as John Calvin (1509–1564) contributed to this relational view of the *imago Dei*. According to David Cairns, Calvin, more than anyone else since Augustine, developed the strongest perspective on the *imago Dei*.[27] Grenz highlights Calvin's central position: "In drawing out his central metaphor, Calvin emphasized the dynamic aspect of the *imago dei;* the divine image consists of the actual act of mirroring God."[28] For Calvin the fall destroyed the image of God in humanity, but restoration came in Christ as the second Adam and as the incarnate Word of God. Humans are to mirror or reflect the divine within their soul and body through God's grace by being in right relationship with God.

Karl Barth (1886–1968) likewise tied his understanding of the *imago Dei* to a relational view by highlighting the male-female dynamic in human creation as distinctive. Barth applies the relational I-Thou interpretation of Martin Buber's works and Dietrich Bonhoeffer's interpretation of Genesis 1:27 to the biblical reference of "male and female" in humankind's relationship with God and within all human existence. Barth encapsulates his perspective: "The relationship between the summoning I in God's being and the summoned divine Thou is reflected in the relationship of God to the man whom He has created, and also in the relationship between the I and the Thou between male and female, in human existence itself."[29] This relational view of the *imago Dei* dominated several other Protestant writers, such as Søren Kierkegaard, Paul Ramsey (a protégé of Kierkegaard) and Emil Brunner.[30] Further, human relationships bespeak social affections that involve emotions.[31] God created humankind with *relational* and *emotional* capacity, two of the seven identified formation dimensions.

The historical development of the *imago Dei* is indebted to Reformation and contemporary theologians who built upon the structural view of the *imago Dei* and highlighted humankind's relational capacity in mirroring the divine image. As critical as this relational view of humankind is, I argue that this sole interpretation fails to address a fully orbed perspective on human dimensionality. Although Luther and Calvin argued that the right ordering of reason would position the human person to know and love

God, and that the lost image can be restored in Christ by the Word of God and the Holy Spirit, the Reformers fell short of a robust understanding of the *imago Dei,* that is, the potential in all primary life dimensions universally shared across human history. God created humankind with capacity for vocation formation, physical health and wellness, and resource stewardship. This leads to the third perspective of the *imago Dei.*

Perspective 3. The* imago Dei *as humankind's dominion over the earth. A third perspective related to the *imago Dei* is referred to as the functional view, recognizing the empowerment of humankind to superintend the earth's resources and creatures, as evidenced in God's directive in Genesis 1:26-30. In Genesis 1:28, God said to Adam and Eve, "Be fruitful and multiply, and fill the earth and subdue it; and have *dominion* over the fish of the sea and over the birds of the air and over every living thing that moves upon the earth" (italics added). As espoused by many Old Testament scholars, the dominion perspective views humankind as superintending all of the nonhuman world, earthly life and its institutions, including politics, education and the arts.[32] In fact, Douglas John Hall applies this dominion interpretation to an ontological ethic for human stewardship of creation, positing that divine sovereignty in creation is to be met with human responsibility for its governance.[33] The dominion perspective correlates with the three formation dimensions of *vocational, physical health and wellness, and resource stewardship formation.* I argue that dominion, the responsibility of caring for the earth, implies vocational and resource stewardship within the context of physical health and wellness. Therefore vocational formation, physical health and wellness, and resource stewardship are included in the CSF model.

While the dominion perspective of the *imago Dei* is implicit in the Genesis creation narrative (Gen 1:26, 28) regarding God's intent for humankind to care responsibly for creation predicated on God's original mandate to work and care for the garden (Gen 2:15), other dimensions, including the spiritual dimension, remain unaddressed. Few would argue that humanity lacks spiritual capacity. From where is this spiritual dimension derived if not from God who made humankind to reflect God's image and glory in the world? The fourth perspective relates to spiritual dimension.

Perspective 4. The* imago Dei *as humankind's divine goal and destiny. Stanley Grenz views the *imago Dei* as a divinely given goal or destiny that anticipates present transformation for future eschatological fulfillment.[34] God, in Christ, is the ultimate model to whom we aspire; and through him, over time, we become increasingly conformed into God's likeness in the depths of our spiritual natures. God has created humans with capacity to desire God and with the potential to achieve the goal of becoming increasingly more like Jesus through a variety of factors as overseen by God's providence.

This divine goal was Paul's passion for the churches he planted. For example, Paul longed to see Christ formed in the lives of the Galatian believers ("My little children, for whom I am again in the pain of childbirth until Christ is formed in you" [Gal 4:19]) and spoke of this shaping process by the Spirit to the church in Rome ("For those whom he foreknew he also predestined to be conformed to the image of his Son, in order that he might be the firstborn within a large family" [Rom 8:29]). Paul spoke of the Corinthian believers being transformed into Christ's likeness with ever-increasing glory by the Spirit, which is an ongoing process over time (2 Cor 3:18). The word *transformed* (Gk. *metamorphoo*) comprises two Greek words: *meta*, meaning "with," "among" or "after," and *morphe*, meaning "form."[35] To be transformed into Christ's likeness is to be changed into another form, namely his. This perspective of the divine goal or destiny primarily relates to *formation of the spirit*, the foundational dimension, which gives purpose to the other six.

To summarize, through the centuries, the *imago Dei* has been seen in terms of humankind's capacity to (1) think and reason, the *intellectual* dimension, (2) forge *relationship* through *emotional* connectivity with God and others, (3) assume dominion over the earth through *vocational capacity, physical health and wellness, and resource stewardship*, and (4) become more like Jesus *spiritually* over time, which is humankind's goal and destiny. Rather than a single view of what it means to be made in the image of God, I argue for a multidimensional approach, which at first glance appears abstract and nonspecific. Each of the four perspectives of the *imago Dei* finds expression in the CSF model. As we shall see, the unique mission of Christ as the ultimate fulfillment of the *imago Dei* leads to our fractured identities being restored in fullness, as we receive Christ as Savior (Jn 1:12) and God's abundant grace (Eph 1:6-8). CSF, therefore, is clearly centered in our being made in the image of God in Christ.

Christ, the Perfect *Imago Dei*

Whereas the *imago Dei* was corrupted in the fall of humanity (Gen 3), the image was renewed through Christ's redemption.[36] Christ is clearly depicted as the perfect *imago Dei* in the New Testament.[37] Thus, Christ is the perfect image of the Father, given as a gift to believers who are redeemed through faith by his blood, and who are continuously conformed into Christ's image by grace (2 Cor 3:18). As a result, the image of Christ as renewed within believers moves from individual expression to that of a redeemed community of faith.[38] Through the church, the restoration of the *imago Dei* also has an ecclesial aspect.[39] The church, as the body of Christ, reflects Christ's image to the world. Exploring the concept of image in the New Testament links the *imago Dei* to Christ.

The New Testament counterpart of the Hebrew word *tselem,* which means "image," is *eikon.* The word *eikon* suggests "what completely corresponds to the 'prototype'" or the "perfect reflection of the prototype."[40] Several authors affirm this contention. For example, Robert Louis Wilken asserts that the *imago Dei* cannot be fully understood without reflecting on Christ, the perfect image of God.[41] In concert, Grenz states, "The New Testament writers declare that ultimately the *imago dei* is Christ and, by extension, the new humanity, consisting of those who through union with Christ share in Christ's relationship to God and consequently are being transformed into the image of God in Christ."[42] By this relationship to Christ, male and female become "the new humanity" in "relationality of persons in community."[43] Further, "the pathway between humankind as male and female and the *imago dei* leads inevitably through the church as the prolepsis of the new humanity, and the relational self is ultimately the ecclesial self."[44] We are formed through relationships with others, including those within the church. Christ, then, is the divine image to which human beings are to aspire individually and corporately, as members of the body of Christ. Because sin corrupted the perfect image of God in humanity, Christ provided the restoration of the image that was lost in the Garden and foreshadowed an eternal glory yet to come. We are to demonstrate the life of Christ through godly character and ethical living in holistic tandem.

Several New Testament passages directly associate Christ with the divine image of God. Romans 8:29 states, "For those whom he foreknew he also predestined to be conformed to the image of his Son, in order that he might be the firstborn within a large family." With Jesus being the perfect image of God the Father, Hoekema suggests that being conformed to the image of Jesus is "the purpose or goal for which God has predestined his chosen people," which will not be fully actualized until the life to come.[45] Grenz concludes, "The humankind created in the *imago dei* is none other than the new humanity conformed to the *imago Christi*."[46] In other words, Jesus is the perfect image that humankind lost during the fall but through whom humankind now is alive with potential for restoration through redemption and is capable of holistic growth into the image of Christ. All seven holistic formation life dimensions are to come under his lordship.

In 2 Corinthians 3:12-18, Paul contrasts the old covenant—in which Moses veiled his face to keep the Israelites from seeing the fading glory of God—to the unveiled glory of Christ reflected in believers' lives through the new covenant. Paul wrote, "And all of us, with unveiled faces, seeing the glory of the Lord as though reflected in a mirror, are being transformed into the same *image* from one degree of glory to another; for this comes from the Lord, the Spirit" (v. 18, italics added). According to Paul, the goal of our lives is transformation into Christ's likeness by the power of the Holy Spirit.

The concept of the image of God personified in Christ is explicit in 2 Corinthians 4:4 and Colossians 1:15. In 2 Corinthians 4:4-6, Paul defends his apostolic authority and explains why some rejected his message: "In their case the god of this world has blinded the minds of the unbelievers, to keep them from seeing the light of the gospel of the glory of Christ, who is the *image* of God" (italics added). In applying imagery of light shining out of darkness that links God's glory with Christ, Paul seems to harken back to the creation narrative (Gen 1:3-4) and possibly his own conversion experience (Acts 9:8-18).[47] C. K. Barrett further elaborates on Christ being the very image of God: "As the image of God he [Christ] is the place where God himself, the invisible, is known."[48]

In Colossians 1:15-17, Paul provides an apologetic for Christ being supreme above all creation as the perfect *imago Dei.*

> He is the *image* of the invisible God, the firstborn of all creation; for in him all things in heaven and on earth were created, things visible and invisible, whether thrones or dominions or rulers or powers—all things have been created through him and for him. He himself is before all things, and in him all things hold together.

Christ is clearly portrayed as preeminent over all creation as the "image of the invisible God." According to F. F. Bruce, "Christ is presented as the agent of God in the whole range of his gracious purpose towards the human race, from the primeval work of creation, through the redemption accomplished at history's mid-point, on to the new creation in which the divine purpose will be consummated."[49] Bruce further comments that "the very nature and being of God have been perfectly revealed—that in him [Christ] the invisible has become visible."[50] On the use of the Greek word *eikon* in Colossians 1:15, Arthur Patzia observes, "Christ participates in and with the nature of God, not merely copying, but visibly manifesting and perfectly revealing God in human form."[51] Christ is the perfect *imago Dei,* and we are to be conformed to his image.

In Colossians 1:19-20, Paul specifically addresses Gnostic heresies, contending that Christ is preeminent and adequate for salvation as the perfect *imago Dei:* "For in him all the fullness of God was pleased to dwell, and through him God was pleased to reconcile to himself all things, whether on earth or in heaven, by making peace through the blood of his cross." To Paul, having the fullness of Christ means having access to all of the Father's powers and attributes. In similar fashion, Paul writes to the Colossian believers: "For in him the whole fullness of deity dwells bodily, and you have come to fullness in him, who is the head of every ruler and authority" (Col 2:9-10). Paul makes clear that those who are in Christ have access to the fullness of God with all his resident power, which assists believers to put off the sinful nature, making them alive in Christ (vv. 11-14). In light of believers being created in the image of God, Paul exhorted the Colossian church to be mindful of their conduct one to the other: "Do not lie to one another, seeing that you have stripped off the old self with its practices and have clothed yourselves with the new self, which is being renewed in knowledge according to the *image* of its creator" (Col 3:9-10, italics added). In our renewed and restored selves in Christ, Paul affirmed that we retain the image of God (cf. Eph 4:24).

Likewise, Hebrews 1:3 affirms Christ as the perfect image of God: "He is the reflection of God's glory and the exact imprint [Gk. *charakter*] of God's very being, and he sustains all things by his powerful word." The Greek word *charakter* connotes a stamp or seal, "in which case the seal or die which makes an impression bears the image produced by it, and, vice versa, all the features of the image correspond respectively with those of the instrument producing it."[52] In Hebrews 1:3, *charakter* is used metaphorically to describe the Son of God. The Son of God not only bears the image of the Father but also is the exact impress of the Father's essence.[53] As Hoekema noted, "It is hard to imagine a stronger figure to convey the thought that Christ is a perfect reproduction of the Father. Every trait, every characteristic, every quality found in the Father is also found in the Son, who is the Father's exact representation."[54] Unlike sinful humanity, Christ is the perfect image of God without being tainted by sin.

Having briefly surveyed the *imago Dei* theme from the Genesis narrative, a historical perspective and the New Testament, we clearly observe the divine intent in making man and woman in God's image, the fractured image that resulted from the fall, and God's redeeming grace inviting all to be restored through faith in Christ, who is the perfect *imago Dei*. Chapter three describes the limitless love of God through the Father, Son and Holy Spirit as the impetus for understanding and enacting growth in CSF. The process occurs in each of the seven dimensions in order to glorify God through godly character in ethical congruence as ambassadors in the world.

3

The Love of God

The Starting Place

For love is given by God alone. . . .
Love is due to no one else but to God and for God.

Bernard of Clairvaux,
The Love of God and Spiritual Friendship

We have surveyed the origin of Christian spiritual formation by tracing the theme of the *imago Dei* as the genesis of true human dimensionality and identity. Now we turn to the fundamental impetus—the love of God, with love, set within the cross, as the core of the center circle. For if indeed we were made in the image of God and God has given us stewardship capacity through caring responsibility over ourselves and the created order, then the motivation to cooperate with God in our own CSF is reciprocal love. French abbot Bernard of Clairvaux (1090–1153) addressed the primary motivation for loving God as being God's very essence—love. Bernard affirmed, "These [believers] easily love God the most, because they understand how greatly they are loved; for he to whom less love is given will himself love less."[1]

If God created us and is loving, good and kind, then it behooves us to understand the love of God as expressed through the Father, the Son and the Holy Spirit. If God loves us (and God does!), then our response should be to love God in return (Mt 22:37-38) and serve as stewards of the God-given resources given to us, including our spirits, emotions, relationships, minds, vocational pursuits, physical bodies and material resources, in order to reflect God's love, grace, goodness and glory to others (Mt 22:39). As Emil Brunner asserts, God is the only one who wills a free response to divine love as "a response which gives back love for love, a living echo."[2] As John succinctly expressed, "We love because he first loved us" (1 Jn 4:19).

Healthy reciprocal human love between a parent and child provides a lens into the love of God. Reciprocal love is powerfully illustrated in the relationship between Heisman Trophy winner Tim Tebow and his parents, Bob and Pam Tebow. While serving in the Philippines as missionaries, this Christian couple discovered they were pregnant with Tim. Pam subsequently developed a life-threatening infection. To allay dysentery and coma, Pam was prescribed medication that threatened the life of her unborn child. Dismissing a physician's advice to abort, Pam delivered Tim, who grew up to be a strong Christian believer, gives God the glory for his life and football prowess, and reflects reciprocal love with his parents.[3] This human parental-child love is a microcosm of the limitless love of God. As C. S. Lewis notes, "God, who needs nothing, loves into existence, holy, superfluous creatures in order that He may love and perfect them."[4]

Love is the compelling motivation of God in the creation of humanity.[5] Love has been defined in different ways and through the lens of multiple disciplines and cultural contexts.[6] As mentioned in chapter one, I define godly love *as the essence of God's character and personality, proceeding from the Father as demonstrated by the Son through the work of the Holy Spirit, which unconditionally upholds the highest good of others and fosters the same altruism and benevolence in human relationships without regard for personal sacrifice.* This definition frames love as coming from God, the source of all love, as it reaches out in human relationships. The apostle John wrote, "Whoever does not love does not know God, for God is love" (1 Jn 4:8) and "So we have known and believe the love that God has for us. God is love, and those who abide in love abide in God, and God abides in them" (1 Jn 4:16). God the Father is the source of love, which he demonstrated by sending his Son into the world that we might have eternal life through him

(1 Jn 4:9-10). Tragically, our contemporary culture has adulterated the pure meaning of love and reduced it to self-indulgent pleasure and sexual fulfillment. In stark contrast, God dwells in holy, limitless love. Understanding how God the Father, Jesus the Son and the Holy Spirit interact in unity to fashion us into the *imago Dei* is foundational to understanding human existence. Without experientially receiving the love of God, CSF becomes a hollow endeavor, devoid of meaning and life.

This chapter focuses on the limitless trinitarian love of God—the Father who loves us, the Son who reflects the Father and the Holy Spirit—who transforms us into the image of Jesus. As represented by the word *love* within the cross in figure 3.1, love is God's motivation for creating hu-

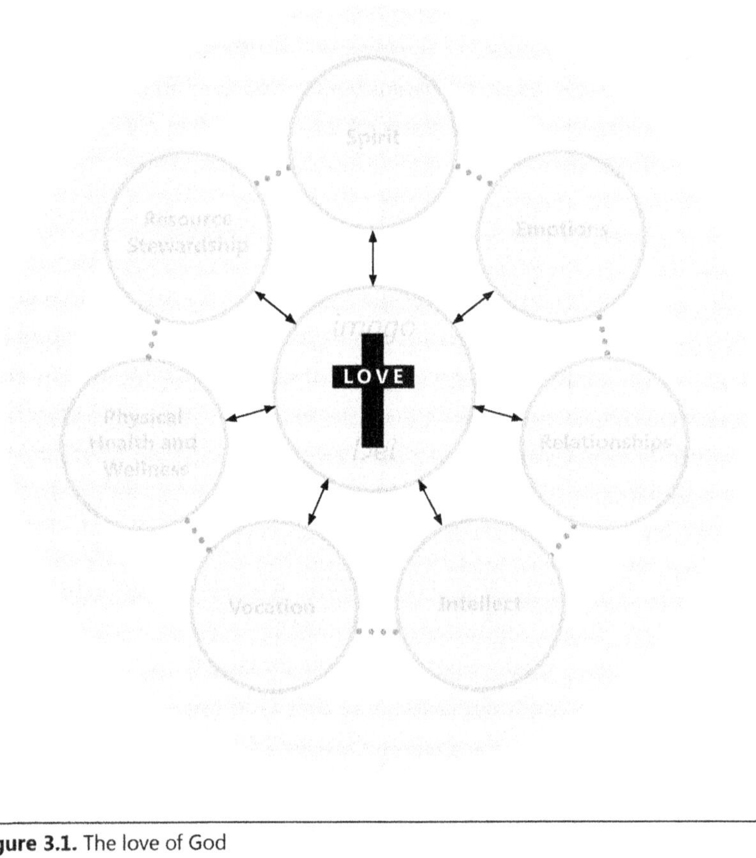

Figure 3.1. The love of God

mankind in the *imago Dei* and for redeeming humanity through Christ's death on the cross. In order to conform us into the *imago Christ* (image of Christ), God adopts us as sons and daughters in order to enjoy loving union (Jn 17:3), as we live to glorify Jesus as God's ambassadors.[7] God's limitless love prompts us to respond to grace by growth in each formation dimension.

Limitless Love

Being created in God's image intimately interweaves with God's love for us, so poignantly demonstrated in Christ's ultimate sacrifice on our behalf (Rom 5:8). Anthony Hoekema summarizes the response that our Creator intended us to offer as being "the kind of response of reverent and grateful love—a response that is to be given not just in words but by one's entire life."[8] Thus, our spirituality derives from our relationship with God and begins by first receiving God's love. As Donald Bloesch insists, "The focus of true spirituality is on God's holy love, not on humanity's spiritual fulfillment. But this divine love is celebrated not as a transcendent ideal but as a gracious act of God on behalf of a lost human race."[9]

An exposition of God's limitless love is found in the influential work of Augustine of Hippo. His great work *De Trinitate* (*The Trinity*) emphasizes God's essential nature as love. Proffering that the Trinity is the unity of three mutually related persons in equal essence, Augustine argued that the Trinity is imprinted within humanity as the mind, knowledge and love, which are reflected in memory, understanding and will. Augustine presented three elements of love (e.g., God that loves, that which is loved, and love itself), which also hints at the Trinity. According to Augustine, love is the reason for the incarnation, where the love between the Father and Son is mediated by the Holy Spirit.[10] Augustine called the Spirit the bond of love between the Father and the Son. His identification of God as love became a central point in Christian thought and deeply influenced theology for ensuing generations.

However, twelfth-century monastic Richard of St. Victor established a correction to Augustine's approach by highlighting the three persons of the Trinity in mutual relationship, including the Spirit, rather than love being primarily a bond between the Father and the Son.[11] Richard's proposed social understanding of the Trinity was significant, because it argued that mutual love must be shared by three persons of the Trinity, not only two; or as theologian Colin E. Gunton expresses, love is not a self-enclosed circle nor a duality between Father and Son, but a love that moves outward to others through the Spirit.[12] The Holy Spirit shares in mutual and reciprocal love within the Trinity.

Our entire lives are to be an expression of reverence and gratefulness to God for creating us, saving us and giving us a future with hope (Jer 29:11). Paul Fiddes comments, "A God of love, then, will gain much both in delight and in the values produced by creation, through drawing created persons into the fellowship of divine love."[13] By receiving the love of the Father through the Son by the person and power of the Holy Spirit, we are able to fulfill God's purpose for us through our adoption as children of God (Rom 8:15). As such, Fiddes continues, "The Christian image of God as Trinity affirms that love is relational and not simply attitudinal; the God who is love exists eternally in the relationships of Father, Son, and Spirit."[14] By its very nature, love is intended to be reciprocal.

The power of reciprocal love is profoundly observed in the account of Nicholas Winton, who in 1938 was a twenty-nine-year-old clerk serving at the London Stock Exchange. During World War II, he learned about the plight of Jewish children in Czechoslovakia. Acting with haste after hearing of *Kristallnacht*, the violent Nazi attack against German and Austrian Jews, Winton organized eight transports of over 660 Jewish children and arranged for English and Swedish foster families to care for them. In 2009 two dozen survivors, along with their family members, returned to London on the seventieth anniversary of their rescue in order to pay tribute to the man who saved them.[15] At the time, Winton was one hundred years old. Winton's life and actions reflect the love of God that unconditionally upholds the highest good of others and fosters altruism and benevolence in human relationships without regard for personal sacrifice. The survivors who honored Winton, the one who risked his life and livelihood to rescue them, mirror reciprocal love. Similarly, the love of God is to not only be received but also to be reciprocated in heartfelt gratitude.[16]

The Father, Son and Holy Spirit live in "limitless love," as Jürgen Moltmann suggests, and by their "reciprocal kenosis" dwell in relationship with one another and imprint all outward works of creation.[17] Kenosis refers to the self-emptying of one's will in support of God's divine will, most readily seen when Jesus emptied himself of divinity to become a servant in redeeming humanity on the cross (Phil 2:7-8). Because relationship is the very essence of the Trinity, God desired to "echo Trinitarian life on the finite level and to produce beings that will share in the life of the Father with the Son by the Spirit."[18] In order to know the one who fashions us in the *imago Dei*, it is important to identify each person of the Trinity—God the Father, God the Son and God the Holy Spirit—to more fully understand divine love, the way each member of the Godhead operates in that love and how we might more fully embrace this reciprocal love relationship through Christian formation in its seven dimensions. It all begins with the Father's love.

The Father Who Loves Us

During my high school years, I became very involved in music and theater. My emergent love for the musical arts resulted from my admiration for Mr. S. J. Starr ("Jerry"), who taught English, drama and speech. He directed the musical productions and fostered life-giving relationships with thousands of students throughout his teaching career. During my senior year, I was chosen to work alongside him as his student director of the high school's annual musical production. This experience was life changing. Not only was I chosen for this privileged student director's role from beginning to end, but I had a bird's-eye view of Mr. Starr's character, interactions with others and artful coordination of such a huge undertaking. Being affirmed, recognized and seen as an equal partner in the process did not negate the fact that Mr. Starr was the one in charge.

These early experiences fueled my love for music and the performing arts and prompted my considering a future music career. Along with other graduates, I was deeply influenced by Mr. Starr's consistent compassion and en-

couragement. He affirmed our gifts and was committed to our success. The relationships that were formed during rehearsals and many backstage conversations formed us into a nuclear family of sorts, which remains the highlight of my adolescent years. Mr. Starr set high expectations, was firm but supportive, and typified a tender role model that many of us had not experienced in our own homes. Participating in these musical productions under his leadership grew us emotionally, drew us together relationally and threw many of us into future vocations and avocations in the performing arts. His secret? He was like a loving father who desired that we grow holistically to our maximum potential.

God the Father is a loving father who nurtures relationship not only with the Son and Holy Spirit but also with us. Unfortunately, through various theological streams, focus on the Father has been neglected in favor of an exclusive focus on the Son or the Holy Spirit. Reflecting on the Father, who cannot be arbitrarily separated from the Son and the Holy Spirit, gives us insight into their complete unity, as well as the source of God's unfailing love. The Gospels attest to the Father as the source of everything in creation and in redemption, and to Jesus as the obedient Son of the Father (Jn 14:28; 15:1, 15).[19] What we learn about the Father emerges directly from our observations of his relationship with Jesus (Jn 10:30, 37).

Jesus' emerging identity as the Son of God the Father catalyzed when he remained in Jerusalem at age twelve during the Feast of the Passover. Rather than return with his parents to Nazareth, Jesus lingered in the temple courts and engaged in dialogue with the teachers of the law. His revealing reply to his parents' rebuke reinforces his growing self-awareness and calling as God's Son. "He said to them, 'Why were you searching for me? Did you not know that I must be in my Father's house?'" (Lk 2:49). The priority of his Father's business confirmed Jesus' identity as the Father's Son but also declared his complete unity with the Father, which would consume his life through unabashed obedience. Later, at Jesus' baptism, the voice of the Father proclaimed Jesus' sonship after the Holy Spirit descended on him,

"You are my Son, the Beloved; with you I am well pleased" (Lk 3:22), so reminiscent of the messianic proclamation in Psalm 2:7 and Isaiah 42:1. The Gospel of John especially highlights the relationship between the Father and Jesus. Jesus is not the originator of his teachings, creative miracles and relationships with the disciples and others. The originator is clearly the Father. A survey of John's Gospel reveals that Jesus unquestionably received his mandate from the Father. When Jesus cleared the temple courts of those polluting God's holiness, he exclaimed, "Take these things out of here! Stop making my Father's house a marketplace!" (Jn 2:16). Jesus' identity as God's Son caused him to defend the righteous expectations of the Father.

The love relationship between the Father and Jesus stands firm: "The Father loves the Son and has placed all things in his hands" (Jn 3:35). To address the Jews who persecuted him and to authenticate his mission, Jesus declared, "the very works that I am doing testify on my behalf that the Father has sent me. And the Father who has sent me has himself testified on my behalf" (Jn 5:36-37). Jesus explained that his teaching was not his own but rather came from the Father (Jn 7:16; 8:28). Furthermore, Jesus repeatedly emphasized that the Father had sent him (Jn 7:28; 8:16-18; 10:36; 11:41; 12:49), the Father loved him as he loved the Father (Jn 10:17; 15:9), the Father and he were one (Jn 10:38), and his main mission was to glorify the Father (Jn 12:28; 17:4, 24).

Because of Jesus' claim of being equal with God, the Jews sought ways to kill him (Jn 5:18). Jesus responded, "Very truly, I tell you, the Son can do nothing on his own, but only what he sees the Father doing; for whatever the Father does, the Son does likewise. The Father loves the Son and shows him all that he himself is doing" (Jn 5:19-20). Moreover, in pronouncing judgment on the cities that did not repent after his miracles, Jesus proclaimed praise to the Father for hiding truth of these things from the wise and learned and revealing them to children and affirmed, "All things have been handed over to me by my Father; and no one knows the Son except the Father, and no one knows the Father except the Son and anyone to whom the Son chooses to reveal him" (Mt 11:27).

Robert Hamerton-Kelly notes that Jesus employed the word *Father* or *Abba* in all of his recorded prayers, with one exception—Jesus' final cry to the Father on the cross: "My God, my God, why have you forsaken me?" (Mt 27:46; Mk 15:34). All of Jesus' authority was tied to his relationship with Abba Father. Hamerton-Kelly observes:

> It [the word *Abba*] is, in brief, a word from the everyday speech of the family; and while our evidence shows that the Jews of Jesus' world never addressed God as "Abba," Jesus always did! Therefore, "Abba" is an actual word of the historical Jesus. It reveals the heart of the relationship to God, and therefore, the essence of the kingdom. "Abba" holds the key to Jesus' authority and identity.[20]

To Jesus, Abba was his Father from whom everything flowed and around whom everything was to be given.

The apostle Paul confirmed the Father's role in our adoption as daughters and sons of God. Pronouncing that all who believe in Jesus Christ through faith are children of God, and severing the bondage that came from trying to fulfill the law, Paul applied this Abba cry to the Galatian believers: "Because you are children, God has sent the Spirit of his Son into our hearts, crying, 'Abba! Father!' So you are no longer a slave but a child, and if a child then also an heir, through God" (Gal 4:6-7). Paul exhorted the Galatians not to return to the former state of bondage in following legalistic Judaism from which they had been delivered, but rather to exercise their sonship as heirs of the Father, subject to receive all of the Father's blessed inheritance. In Philippians 2:6-11, Paul spoke to the Philippians about modeling attitudes of humility after the example of Christ, highlighting the role of the Father in the exultation of Jesus:

> And being found in human form,
> he humbled himself
> and became obedient to the point of death—
> even death on a cross.
> Therefore God also highly exalted him
> and gave him the name

that is above every name . . .
to the glory of God the Father. (vv. 7-9, 11)

According to Thomas Smail, the Father's role is to send the Son and the Spirit, and as Creator, the Father is understood through them.[21] Smail affirms, "The Father has his *identity* through and in his Son" and as such "defines the fatherhood of God in relation to the image of human fatherhood that he found in Israel."[22] Not surprisingly, human fatherhood affects our perceptions of God the Father.

Our experiences with earthly fathers or father figures and our perceptions of God are closely intertwined. Smail defends the Father's image against the backdrop of human fathers. He asserts, "God's fatherhood is not to be defined by projection either. . . . There is obviously a very close psychological connection between our experiences of human fatherhood and our approach to God's fatherhood. . . . It is surrounded by conscious memories, half-hidden loves, longings and resentments."[23] Effective fathering makes a significant impact in the lives of children. Similarly, knowing that we have a heavenly Father has multiple positive implications related to receiving God's unconditional love as sons and daughters of God. The cry for godly human fathers is glaringly apparent, while the consequences of fatherlessness continue to fill news headlines.[24]

Social problems such as drug and alcohol abuse, crime and incarceration have been directly linked to the instability and fracture of the nuclear family, while the epidemic of fatherlessness continues to rise. As such, the US Department of Health and Human Services affirms the positive outcome of healthy father engagement in children's lives: "Children with involved, loving fathers are significantly more likely to do well in school, have healthy self-esteem, exhibit empathy and pro-social behavior compared to children who have uninvolved fathers."[25] Healthy father involvement in the lives of children enhances a sense of security and psychosocial development.

Furthermore, children living with their biological fathers are two to three times more likely not to be poor; not to engage in drug use; not to experience educational, health, emotional and behavioral problems; and not to become victims of child abuse or engage in criminal behaviors, compared to their peers who live without married and biological (or adoptive) parents.[26] This is not to say that children who do not have fathers present in the home will be maladjusted or deficient. However, the data suggest that healthy and well-adjusted fathers who are positively involved in their children's lives model positive behaviors that assist children in their development.

Hence, a close emotional, psychological and relational connection exists between our experience with and perceptions of our earthly fathers (and father figures) and our conception of God as Father. Early human attachment to parents and caregivers, whether positive, benign or negative, influences one's concept of God. Researchers have found that people project onto God their image of God as being good, kind and loving; indifferent and unresponsive; or cruel and judgmental based on their attachment experiences with parental figures and caregivers.[27] Being loved by a human father or father figure contributes to overall well-being. Smail contends: "Unless the whole image of fatherhood is corrected or redeemed, we shall almost inevitably project onto God the father we have loved or missed, have desired or resented, so that our adult spiritual life will be secretly controlled by our reactions to our early family life."[28] Consequently, our Christian formation is influenced by our early childhood development involving our relationship with parents or parental figures—particularly human fathers or father figures.

Most would acknowledge the importance of having loving fathers or father figures in one's life, regardless of their own personal experiences. That is not to say that all problems that children encounter are caused by father issues.[29] Some problems emerge because of sinful, rebellious human nature, which is so readily expressed in the parable of the prodigal son. Regardless of our family history or past, our heavenly Father unconditionally loves us. The parable of the prodigal son provides a poignant illustration of the Father's love.

The compassionate father and the prodigal son. The parable of the prodigal son (Lk 15:11-32) reveals the heart of Father God. The father in the parable represents our loving heavenly Father. As Helmut Thielicke points out, Jesus' telling the parable makes the parable completely credible because Jesus essentially is saying, "He who sees me sees the Father."[30] Although the title of the parable focuses on the younger son, it is clear that the parable could easily be titled "The Compassionate or Perfect Father Based on Three Sons," rather than two: (1) the younger son, (2) the older son, and (3) the son (Jesus) telling the story. Although the younger son asserts his independence by leaving home and taking with him his requested inheritance, he essentially severs relationship with his father in a radical and seemingly final family and cultural breach. In effect, the younger son cuts off his true identity, which is then further compromised when he squanders his inheritance in licentious living and moves progressively from the humiliating work of feeding pigs to the humiliation of desiring to eat their food.

Out of desperation, the younger son finally comes to his senses in the midst of a severe famine; he is completely destitute and without resources. He remembers his father's home with plentiful provision and desires to return not as a son but as a future employee. Deep within his psyche he realizes that his original departure had severed the father-son relationship. Thus, the only way he can emotionally and psychologically reconcile his return is to view his father as his future employer who could offer him recompense like the other hired hands.

Miroslav Volf offers a poignant commentary on the parable. When the younger son came to himself, "he remembers the other whom he wanted to push out of his world but to whom he found himself still belonging" and "through departure he wanted to become a 'non-son'; his return begins not with repentance but with something that makes the repentance possible—the memory of sonship."[31] The son's return is actualized because of his awareness of true belonging to his father, which could never be severed. Volf reflects on the father:

> The most significant aspect of the story is, however, that the father who lets the son depart *does not let go of the relationship between them*. . . . Away from home, the son remained still in the father's heart. Against the force of the

> wrongdoing suffered and the shame endured that sought to push the son out, the father kept the son in his heart as an absence shaped by the memory of the former presence.[32]

Therefore when the son returns, the father is able to run to him, embrace and kiss him, as well as prepare a feast in celebration. Volf continues: "Without the father's having kept the son in his heart, the father would not have put his arms around the prodigal. No confession was necessary for the embrace to take place for the simple reason that the relationship did not rest on moral performance and therefore could not be destroyed by immoral acts."[33] Exclusion prompted the younger son to "un-father" the father. However, embrace never allowed the father to "un-son" this younger son. And so it is with us. The Father unconditionally loves us and beckons us to renewed and ongoing relationship despite our backgrounds and past actions.

Some of us can relate to the younger son's "un-soning" himself or to the older son's angst at his father's embrace of his younger brother. Volf observes that the older son also "un-fathers" his father by refusing to reinstate his younger brother and self-righteously believing that his goodness has been sorely overlooked. The father retains unconditional connections, however, which supersede moral failure and unmet expectations. The theme of exclusion and embrace relating to personal identity is ubiquitous within each of the characters in the parable. The identity of the two sons uniquely hinges on the father's unconditional love for each of them. Despite the turbulence of their identities and changing relationships, the father's consistent identity as their father provides the platform for reconciliation.

This parable contains an all-too-personal application for me. Over thirty years ago, one of my two stepbrothers left the family after the tragic death of his biological brother, my other stepbrother. Magnified by other unresolved issues, he surrendered his soul to the open swath of life that he hoped to experience in order to escape the pain of our brother's death. He has not yet returned. During these intervening years, the Father, filled with compassion and longing to embrace him when he returns home, has been waiting patiently at the door. Like the father in the parable, God is waiting for my stepbrother's return. The Father desires for each of us to receive divine love and to be reconciled to God and others. The love of the Father who sent Jesus, the perfect *imago Dei*, is our model and impetus for holistic growth in the seven formational dimensions, even in our deepest brokenness, in order to bring God glory. Jesus is the Son who reflects the Father.

The Son Who Reflects the Father

Biological sons may or may not physically resemble their fathers. This is especially true of Rick Hoyt, who was born in 1962 with cerebral palsy. For over thirty years his father, Dick, has taken his disabled son on over sixty-five marathons, twenty-nine duathlons, 216 triathlons and six Ironman competitions. Their secret lies in both the father's commitment to his son and the son's reflection of his father's love. When they run, Dick pushes his son in a special wheelchair. When they bike, Dick seats Rick in a special seat up front. When they swim, Dick pulls Rick in a special boat. Affectionately named "Team Hoyt," this father-son duo has crossed an estimated one thousand finish lines. With the assistance of a computer voice program, Rick once mused, "When my dad and I are out there on a run, a special bond forms between us. And it feels like there is nothing Dad and I cannot do."[34] This son reflects his father's unselfish love, commitment and self-sacrifice. Such is the love of the Father for Jesus who sacrificed himself for us. Although Rick is physically disabled, which affects physical health and wellness formation, he has been nurtured by his loving father in other formational dimensions, including emotional, relational, intellectual and vocational development. Having worked in the past with disabled children and young adults, I have come to understand that the greatest disability in life is being unloved.[35]

Without Rick's love for his father, we would have a partial understanding of the bond that connects them. Similarly, without Christ as the Son of the Father, we would have an eclipsed view of God. Jesus is the exact representation of the Father (Heb 1:3) and, as such, not only reflects the Father's personhood but also the Father's love. Employing descriptive metaphors, Jesus depicts himself as the Son of God who is the sower (Mt 13:3-23), the good shepherd (Jn 10:14), the bridegroom (Mt 25:5), the living bread of life (Jn 6:48, 51, 58), the living way (Jn 14:6; cf. Heb 10:20), and the Logos of God (John 1:1-16). Jesus also applies Old Testament passages to himself that further validate his sonship to the Father.[36]

James Dunn identifies how others viewed Jesus—as Messiah, more than a prophet, a teacher with authority, and as Josephus observed, the "doer of extraordinary deeds" through exorcism and healing.[37] From his study, Dunn makes several conclusions, namely that the first Christians affirmed Jesus as the Messiah, that the transfiguration elevated Jesus above Moses and Elijah as the paragon of the prophetic office, that Jesus had authority over evil spirits (Mk 1:27), and that Jesus' teaching resolutely supported his sonship. Dunn further notes how often Jesus referred to God as Father: thirty times in the Gospel of Matthew and one hundred in John's Gospel.[38] Even the miracles of Jesus point to his sonship and support his messiahship. As Graham Twelftree asserts, "Jesus was uniquely aware that he was God's anointed individual or Messiah, who was at the same time at the center of these eschatological events that were expressions of God's reign or powerful presence."[39] Although Jesus fulfilled all these roles, he was first and foremost God's Son, the divine reflection of the Father's love, and he personified this reciprocal love relationship with the Father to others. Through this love relationship we are able to respond by loving God and others.

David R. Bauer cites how Jesus understood his sonship through three emphases.[40] First, Jesus addressed the Father using the intimate term *Abba*, something early church historian Joachim Jeremias states was the first time a Jew addressed God in this way.[41] Second, what characterizes Jesus as the Son of God is his absolute surrender and obedience to the Father's will. Although the Father speaks at Jesus' baptism to affirm his sonship identity (cf. "You are my Son, the Beloved; with you I am well pleased" [Mk 1:11]), Jesus' obedience is no more clearly seen than in Gethsemane (Mk 14:32-42), where he pleaded with the Father to let the cup of suffering and death pass from him and yet remained obedient unto death (cf. Ps 2; Is 42:1; Phil 2:6-11). Third, because Jesus is the Son of God, he alone is able to bring his followers into divine relationship, highlighting his unique mediating relationship between the Father and his followers. Jesus, the model of perfect and obedient sonship, calls us as sons and daughters to be ambassadors of reconciliation and hope in a lost world.

As we look back in history, the Nicene Creed (A.D. 325) emphatically declared Jesus as the Son of God, which then became the key title for Christ from that point in time onward. The Nicene Creed affirms Christ's sonship: "We believe . . . in one Lord Jesus Christ, the Son of God, begotten from the Father, only begotten, that is, from the substance of the Father."[42]

In Philippians 2:6-8, Paul's hymn of praise particularly highlights the obedience of Jesus to the Father that so characterizes his sonship, even to the point of death. It is through Christ's obedience as the Son of God that we see with clarity the love of the Father. Jürgen Moltmann comments:

> The love of the Father which begets and brings forth the Son is therefore open for further response through creations which correspond to the Son, which enter into harmony with his responsive love and thereby fulfill the joy of the Father. It calls created beings into life, beings made in the image of the Son, who in fellowship with the Son return the Father's love.[43]

Moltmann views Jesus' obedience as emerging from this self-giving and mutual love with the Father. Similarly, Stanley Grenz views Jesus' love for the Father as his driving motivation in his love for humankind. Grenz comments, "The New Testament, in turn, elevates the story of Jesus as the supreme expression of the divine love."[44] The apostle Paul expresses Jesus' ultimate expression of love, "But God demonstrates his own love for us in this: While we were still sinners, Christ died for us" (Rom 5:8 NIV; cf. 1 Jn 4:10) as the embodiment of ultimate altruism and benevolence.

Grenz comments on the centrality of God's divine love evidenced throughout the Scriptures: "This grand narrative of the one who freely sacrificed his life for the sake of sinful humankind led the biblical writers to the previously obscure Greek word *agape* as the term that could best express the self-giving disposition of the God of the salvation story."[45] The agape of

God is fully personified in Jesus Christ. In John 17:26, Jesus prays for all believers and concludes his prayer to the Father acknowledging the Father's love: "'I made your name known to them, and I will make it known, so that the love with which you have loved me may be in them, and I in them.'" God's unending, pursuing, motivating and compelling love is what characterizes Jesus. Grenz summarizes the nature of God's love: "The New Testament presents Jesus as the unique Son of the Father, the one who lives in communion and acts in union with the Father. The Gospel writers present this unique Trinitarian relationship as one of mutual love, mutual self-giving, mutual testifying, and mutual glorifying."[46] This mutuality of self-giving love shared by the Father, Son and Holy Spirit is the foundational core of God's love for us and the motivation for CSF. Along with Bernard of Clairvaux we might exclaim, "So great a love, shown by so great a Lord, how can one pay it back?"[47] I argue that the way we express our reciprocal love to God is to first receive God's love and grace and cooperate with God in intentionally stewarding each of the seven formation dimensions as derived from the *imago Dei* in order to bring God glory and reflect godly character and moral consistency as God's witnesses in the world.

Drawing from the writings of John's Gospel and epistles, D. A. Carson observes that love provides the pattern from the Father to the Son and the Son to the Father in relationship one to the other: "Jesus is so uniquely and unqualifiedly the Son of God that the Father shows him *all* he does, *out of sheer love for him,* and the Son, however dependent on the Father, does *everything* the Father does."[48] Jesus only did what he saw the Father doing and is the perfect reflection of the Father's love. According to Emil Brunner, faith in Christ restores us to our true human identity because of the love of God. "Faith in Jesus is therefore the *restauratio imaginis* [restoration of the image], because he restores to us that existence in the Word of God which we had lost through sin. . . . True human existence is existence in the love of God."[49]

David Benner describes the trust process as "a surrender of my efforts to live my life outside of the grasp of God's love and surrender to God's will and gracious Spirit."[50] Like floating on water, we must offer the full weight of our present, past and future to Jesus, and let go of our own instincts to save ourselves. It is because of the Father's love for the Son, the Son's love for the Father and the magnificent work of the Holy Spirit that this love is available to us on the current of God's sustaining grace. Next, we turn to the Holy Spirit, who makes the Father's love through the Son a reality in our hearts and who empowers us in our CSF journey.

The Holy Spirit Who Transforms Us

On June 14, 2008, at age sixteen, Zac Sunderland set out to become the youngest person to sail solo around the world. Thirteen months and forty thousand miles later, Sunderland had successfully navigated his sailboat, the Intrepid, *from California to Hawaii, the Marshall Islands, Australia, Mauritius, South Africa, St. Helena, Trinidad and Panama before returning again to California. In one of Sunderland's videos, he bemoaned the lack of wind during one specific day of the journey. That day, the sailboat drifted backward for about twelve miles.*[51] *As all sailors well know, movement of the sailboat is contingent on the wind blowing, not the current.*

Similarly, the Holy Spirit is the source of movement and growth in CSF. No matter how hard we try, we cannot make the wind of the Holy Spirit blow. Our role is to prepare the sails of our lives in anticipation of the movement of the Holy Spirit (Jn 3:8; Eph 5:18) to move us forward. As the person of the Godhead who is the personal and dynamic source of our being moved along, the Holy Spirit fashions us into the image of Jesus in each of the seven formation dimensions.

As the Father loves us through the Son, so the Holy Spirit empowers us to be conformed to the image of Jesus, the perfect *imago Dei*. The renewal of the image of God is undertaken by the Holy Spirit through a lifelong process of sanctification in order to be holy and available for God's purposes. Anthony Hoekema defines sanctification as "that gracious and continuing operation of the Holy Spirit" involving our "responsible participation, by which the Spirit progressively delivers the regenerated person from the pollution of sin, and enables him or her to live to the praise of God."[52] Simply stated, the Holy Spirit empowers believers through an ongoing process of renewal into the image of Jesus.

Who is the Holy Spirit, and how does the Spirit conform us into the image of Jesus? The Holy Spirit is the person of the Trinity who proceeds from the Father and is the source of believers' sanctification, or the process of becoming holy through grace.[53] Gordon Fee argues that although we see the activity of the Holy Spirit in the New Testament, we also see the Spirit as the agent over and above impersonal influence or power.[54] Unlike Moltmann, who sees the identity of the Holy Spirit as a person being problematic, Fee affirms the personhood of the Holy Spirit. Similarly, Clark Pinnock views the Holy Spirit as not only God's presence in the world but also as the transcendent power of creation and the divine immanence.[55] Asserting that the Holy Spirit is God's presence, power and person who breathed forth in trinitarian life and also poured forth from Abba Father and the risen Christ, Ralph Del Colle posits, "By the Holy Spirit we presence ourselves in empowerment for others in a communion of love. The Spirit's inhumanation [indwelling] is gift; our being in-personed in the Spirit is the perfecting work of love."[56] The person of the Holy Spirit serves as divine (1) agent or envoy, (2) empowering presence, (3) energy of life and love, and (4) gift to believers to celebrate life and glorify Jesus in obedience to the Holy Scriptures. Let's look at these in more detail.

First, evidence of the Holy Spirit as God's very agent or envoy can be seen especially in Paul's writings.[57] For example, as a person of the Godhead, the Holy Spirit is the conduit for God's sanctifying work in the lives of believers (Rom 15:16; 1 Cor 6:11; 2 Thess 2:13), divine transforming love (Col 1:8; Gal 5:22), victory over the sinful nature (Rom 8:13; Gal 5:16), strengthening of the inner person (Eph 3:16), revelation of truth (Eph 3:5), joy and hope (Rom 15:13; 1 Thess 1:6), and power for gospel proclamation (1 Thess 1:5). The Spirit knows the mind of God (1 Cor 2:11), searches all things "even the depths of God" (1 Cor 2:10), gives life to believers (Jn 6:63), indwells us (1 Cor 3:16), testifies that we are children of God (Rom 8:16), and bears witness and calls out with our human spirit (Rom 8:16; Gal 4:6). Further, the Spirit intercedes for us (Rom 8:26-27) and is grieved when we sin (Eph

4:30). Hence, the Holy Spirit is an indispensable person of the Trinity who is distinctive in role and responsible for Christian formation.

Second, the Holy Spirit is God's empowering presence among the people of God. In examining Paul's writings, Fee concludes that Paul's theology of the Holy Spirit refers back to the Old Testament passages in Jeremiah and Ezekiel, whereby God himself promised to indwell the people of God. The temple is then no longer understood to be a dwelling place of brick and mortar, but a dwelling place in the very body of the believer. Believers become indwelt by the living God in the person of the Holy Spirit, who takes up residence within them. Fee comments, "As the personal presence of God, the Spirit is not merely some 'force' or 'influence.' The living God is a God of power; and by the Spirit the power of the living God is present with and for us."[58]

The Holy Spirit is God's very presence sent to indwell believers in order to fulfill God's purposes in and through them in the world (Jn 16:5-15). As a result, they become God's ambassadors, called to the ministry of reconciliation (2 Cor 5:19-20). Fee emphatically affirms that the Holy Spirit is *person*, personal *presence* and God's *empowering presence*, and as such God's presence is the distinguishing characteristic of the Christian faith.[59] Moltmann likewise sees the Spirit as the "efficacious presence of God," bringing divine energies to fullness.[60] The Holy Spirit enables us to do what we could not do on our own, such as yielding our wills to God without violating free will, receiving God's power for godly living, allowing God to bring transformation in every dimension of our lives—our spirits, emotions, relationships, minds, vocations, physical health and wellness, and stewardship of our material resources.[61] The Holy Spirit provides the grace through which we respond in obedience to a loving God who could not love us any more than God already does.

Third, the Holy Spirit is the divine energy of life and love through whom we experience God in relationship and transformation. Whereas God's Spirit in the Old Testament seemed to represent a life force, the Holy Spirit in the New Testament is a person outpoured after the resurrection to make our spirits eternally alive. Moltmann's perspective focuses on the Spirit's infusing life with vitality and love as the "wellspring of life," similar to the *ruah* (wind) of God.[62] "The indwelling of the Spirit brings the divine energies of life in Jesus to rapturous and overflowing fullness," demonstrated in the Spirit's work at Jesus' baptism (Mt 3:16-17), as well as Jesus' driving out demons (Lk 4:41), healing the sick (Mt 14:14), raising the dead (Jn 11:43-44) and loving others (Mt 5:44).[63]

Clark Pinnock notes that the Holy Spirit is humble yet efficacious in desiring to bless others: "The flame of love is humble and self-effacing in the presence of the beloved."[64] Lest we think that the Father-Son relationship is exclusive, the Holy Spirit is a witness of the love of the Father and Son, and fosters this love in, to and through God's children. Jesus experienced the Spirit in relationship to the Father and to others and invites us to do the same.

Fourth, the coming of the Holy Spirit at Pentecost, the gift and the fulfillment of a promise (Acts 2:38; cf. Jn 20:22), purposefully enables our CSF formation into the *imago Dei*. According to Tom Smail, the Holy Spirit is the giving gift since there is nothing one can do to earn the gift. The Holy Spirit exemplifies the giving and receiving in the relationship between Spirit, Father and Son, and also with those who receive him. The Holy Spirit is not only the "what" but also the "who" of God's gift. Smail describes the nature of the Spirit: "A gift is often an object that is passed from one to another. But here the Gift is a subject, living, acting, loving, sovereign and free."[65] Smail goes on to observe: "We are at the receiving end of a great movement of divine giving, first from Father to Son, and then from Son to us. It is the work of the Holy Spirit to see that we receive what God so graciously gives."[66] As gift, the Holy Spirit guides us into all truth, serves as counselor, convicts of sin, speaks only from the heart of the Father and Son, and brings glory to Jesus (Jn 16:5-15).

The Holy Spirit, then, is the gift who is the perfect and uninhibited reality of God's grace to us, which is reciprocally expressed through gratitude in a life surrendered to the crucified Christ (Gal 2:20) in all seven CSF dimensions. It is through the Spirit that Christ comes to us and through the Spirit that we can praise God and give thanks to the Father. As patristic scholar Peter Widdicombe asserts, "It is the reception of the Holy Spirit into our hearts that enables us to call God 'Father,' to become God's children; because we are creatures, becoming sons [and daughters] is not something we can do for ourselves."[67] In summary, the Holy Spirit is the person of the Trinity who is God's empowering presence, the divine energy of life and love, and a gift. The Holy Spirit is the source of conforming us into the image of Jesus, such that all human dimensionality reflects God's glory. This process occurs through becoming sons and daughters of God through spiritual adoption.

Living for God's Glory as Adopted Sons and Daughters

Through the Father's love, the Son's model and sacrifice, and the Spirit's transformational power, believers are adopted into God's family through the Spirit's working. CSF is enacted through belonging to God. God is glorified when believers follow Jesus' example and reflect his character in living out the truth of the gospel through love and humility. The apostle Paul applies the adoption metaphor (Gk. *huiothesia*) to describe both the salvation experience and the reality of being enjoined into the family of God.[68] As Trevor Burke observes, Paul's adoption metaphor "adds nuances of meaning absent from other salvation terms and is indisputably the most intimate of Paul's metaphors because it is taken from the realm of the family in the ancient world."[69]

The word *adoption*, appearing five times in three of Paul's letters to churches under Roman rule (Rom 8:15, 23, 9:4; Gal 4:5; Eph 1:5), would have resonated with his audience.[70] The family was the foundation of human identity in the Roman world, with adoption being a legal and relational process.[71] Paul conveys that adoption into the family of God comes through faith in Christ (Gal 3:26-27), whereby freedom in Christ replaces bondage to the law.[72] "Because you are children, God has sent the Spirit of his Son into our hearts, crying, 'Abba! Father!' So you are no longer a slave but a child, and if a child then also an heir, through God" (Gal 4:6-7). Through spiritual adoption, we become heirs to all the blessings available in Christ, with the greatest inheritance being Christ himself.[73] These blessings come through being nurtured by and established in the community of faith.[74]

In speaking of life in the Spirit as children of God, Paul affirmed, "You did not receive a spirit of slavery to fall back into fear, but you have received a spirit of adoption. When we cry, 'Abba! Father!' it is that very Spirit bearing witness with our spirit that we are children of God" (Rom 8:15-16). During an ancient Roman adoption, several witnesses were required for public affirmation of the adoption, making the metaphor completely accessible to the Roman church. Noting that adoption is one of the blessings of the Spirit, James Dunn observes that "the adoption is given its existential reality by the presence and witness of the Spirit."[75] This adoptive relationship based on love (Eph 1:5) also provides the groundwork for Paul's theological discussion with the Ephesian church on what it means to be a family or household of God (Eph 4–6).[76] The Father "adopts because he loves those he adopts."[77]

As sons and daughters of the living God, we reflect the glory of God (*gloria Dei*), who made us in the *imago Dei*, redeemed us through Christ's sacrifice, and sanctifies us by the Spirit into the *imago Christi*. Thus, our adoptive relationship with Christ should be demonstrated in family likeness, clearly entailing ethical alignment.[78] Figure 3.2 illustrates the continuum of the Christian's legacy.[79]

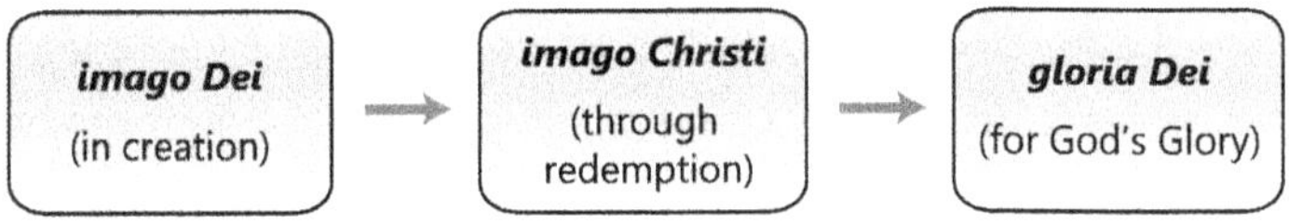

Figure 3.2. *Imago Dei, imago Christi* and *gloria Dei*

In summary, through faith we are adopted into God's family as sons and daughters, thus we have become what Dutch theologian Hendrikus Berkhof calls "respondable" to God by the Word of God through holy and abiding love.[80] As children of God, beloved of the Father through the Son and by the Holy Spirit, we are loved by God, who has created us in God's image and redeemed us through Christ. Our response to God then is to receive divine love and grace in order to be further conformed to the image of Jesus (Rom 8:29) by caring and faithful stewardship of each of the seven formation dimensions. Chapter four focuses on formation of one's spirit, the primary CSF dimension that provides the foundation for the other six dimensions and the faith journey.

4

Spirit

Our Faith

I think, if I had understood then, as I do now,
how this great King really dwells within this little palace of my soul,
I should not have left Him alone so often.

Teresa of Ávila,
The Way of Perfection

Like many young people today, Augustine was on a quest to discover his life purpose. In the process he battled intense lust and peer pressure, lived with a woman he would never marry, bore a son by her, thirsted for relational connection and desired vocational fulfillment. Reflecting on his past, Augustine submitted that his single desire was "only loving and being loved."[1] Yet a gnawing emptiness and darkness awakened him to just how futile and misdirected his pursuits had been. Challenged by the testimonies and lifestyles of other Christians and recognizing his need for Christ, Augustine made his way to a garden adjacent to his lodging, where he wept intensely over the decision to follow Christ. During this raging battle between the flesh and the Spirit, Augustine suddenly heard a voice singing, "Pick it up and read, pick it up and read."[2]

Believing that the voice announced a divine command, Augustine returned to his friend Alypius, who had been waiting for him. Picking up the Scriptures he had left there, Augustine opened to Romans 13:13-14: "let us live honourably as in the day, not in revelling and drunkenness, not in debauchery and licentiousness, not in quarrelling and jealousy. Instead, put on the Lord Jesus Christ, and make no provision for the flesh, to gratify its desires." At that moment, all doubt vanished and peace flooded his soul. Augustine's conversion to Christ was sealed. Immediately, he went inside the residence to tell his mother the good news. After many years of persevering prayer, Monica's prayers for her son's salvation were answered. Becoming a follower of Christ completely changed Augustine's life and set him on a trajectory to become one of the most influential Christian theologians in history. The detailed account of his spiritual journey, so influenced by the Scriptures, has left the Christian world a chronicle of his spiritual formation process.

God's miraculous provision for ongoing relationship with humanity through the cross creates "a story-formed community," with Jesus as the foundation.[3] As Simon Chan observes, "The Christian story is not primarily about how God in Jesus came to rescue sinners from some impending disaster. It is about God's work of initiating us into a fellowship and making us true conversational partners with the Father and the Son through the Spirit and, hence, with each other (1 Jn 1:1-4)."[4] Believers continue to live out God's story by not only continually recalling the story but also by receiving and reciprocating the love of God afresh in ongoing ways. Thus, as Gustavo Gutiérrez poignantly observes, the freedom to love comes through encounter with the Lord in a life lived according to the Spirit, "a way-faring that embraces all aspects of life and is done in community," which characterizes "every journeying in search of God."[5]

This chapter focuses on our spirit, the foundational formation dimension for the living in and telling of God's story through our ongoing faith journey. As depicted in figure 4.1, the spirit dimension comprises the most foundational of the seven formation dimensions. Starting with a discussion of restoring the human spirit, this chapter describes the how we are formed spiritually, the foundation of God's grace in being transformed from the inside out, living in communion with God by engaging in Christian spiritual practices and being shaped through suffering. Christian spiritual formation weaves through the other six holistic formation dimensions, with each being addressed in subsequent chapters. Thus, the essence of the spiritual component concerns the work of the Holy Spirit in conforming believers into the image of Jesus in order to love God and others and reflect Christ's character in the world.

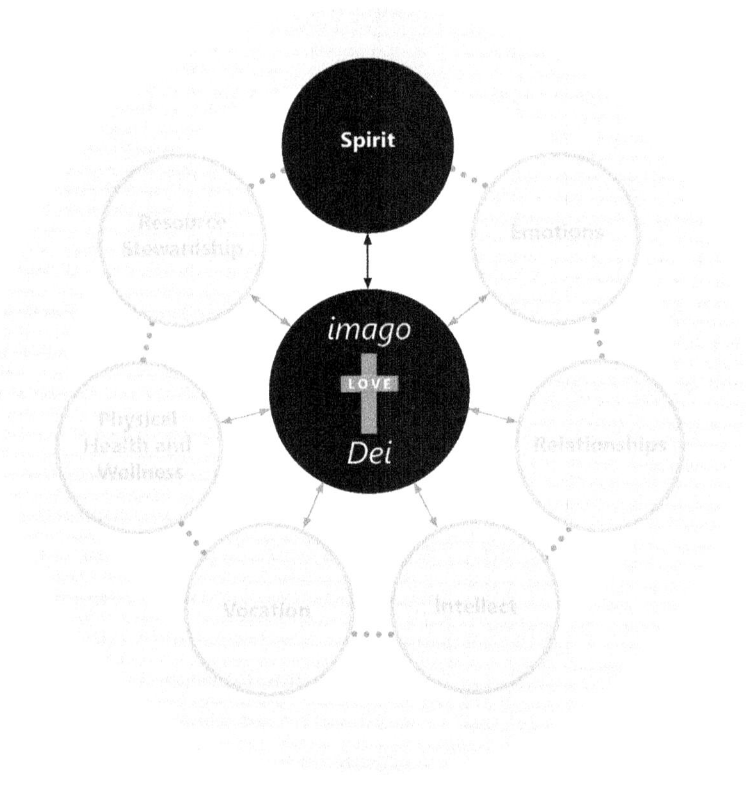

Figure 4.1. Spirit and faith formation

RESTORING THE HUMAN SPIRIT

As expressed in chapter two, it is important to understand what happened during the fall (Gen 3) in order to appreciate the purpose and process of the faith journey. Prior to the fall, Adam and Eve were tempted by the serpent, who fostered *doubt* that God was all-sufficient to meet their needs.

Doubt, then, led to *deception,* with the serpent announcing that they would not die if they partook of the tree of the knowledge of good and evil. Deception led to *illegitimate desire,* with the fruit of the tree appearing good for food, pleasing to the eye and the conduit for wisdom. The illegitimate desire of wanting to eat the fruit led to *willful disobedience;* they ate the fruit in direct contradiction to God's command.

At this point, sin entered the human heart, resulting in separation from God.[6] Adam and Eve hid in shame, were expelled from the Garden and reaped the consequences of their disobedience. As a result, the human race has dealt with temptation, sin, the sinful nature and willful separation from God ever since (Gal 5:19; Eph 2:1-3).[7] As Emil Brunner describes, humanity's apostasy from God was not an isolated occurrence, as sin continually takes persons out of the hands of God.[8] This predictable pattern of doubt, deception, illegitimate desire and willful disobedience continues to comprise the sin cycle. Thus sin, like fire, is kindled such that humankind desires to be like God apart from dependence on God.[9] Love of self replaces love of God and becomes what David Naugle calls, in Augustinian terms, disordered. Hence, the focus of love needs to be reordered to loving God with all one's heart, soul, mind and strength (Mk 12:30).[10]

With inner corruption of this magnitude, the human spirit needs to be radically restored from its sinful nature or flesh (Rom 8:5-8; Gal 5:19).[11] God made provision for this restoration by sending his Son, Jesus, to reveal God's redeeming love and pay the price to redeem humanity into right relationship through faith.[12] We must keep in mind that God is Spirit and communes Spirit to spirit. Jesus himself stated, "God is spirit, and those who worship him must worship in spirit and in truth" (Jn 4:24). Thus, this restored relationship in Christ primarily concerns God's Spirit to our spirit, designed to impact all other holistic dimensions for God's glory. How might we better understand the human spirit, which is in such need of the Spirit's inner working?

What is the human spirit? The human spirit is the core capacity and repository of one's deepest longings and desires, and it directs all of the issues of life. In other words, the human spirit serves as the "air traffic control" mechanism of all human capacity and directs the emotions, affections, thoughts, desires, will and action. Therefore, the spirit connotes the very essence or inner core of personhood, or the heart.[13] God's intention through Christ is to restore humanity's corrupted human spirit such that the people of God will share in a reciprocal love relationship with God and others. It starts with being formed spiritually.

Being Formed Spiritually

We are created in the image of God to share in a mutual love relationship with God and others, whereby the Holy Spirit spiritually shapes us into the image of Jesus. The more access God has to us, the more we begin to look like Jesus. Being formed spiritually starts with the Spirit and continues by the Spirit. I define the formation of our spirit as *the ongoing, interactive and grace-based process of being conformed to the image of Jesus through the indwelling Holy Spirit, within the community of faith, in order to bear fruit that glorifies the Father.*

First, the formation of the spirit is an *ongoing* process that reaches complete fulfillment in the age to come. However, the Spirit's work in, to and through us can increasingly demonstrate Christ's character (Mt 5:16). Second, this process is *interactive,* meaning that although it is overseen by the Holy Spirit, spiritual formation requires our cooperation and intention for maximum effect (Phil 2:12). Third, the spiritual formation process is *grace-based.* Regardless of how well-intentioned, we cannot conform ourselves into Christ's image. By continually receiving God's grace, we are able to embrace God's work in us and surrender to the multiple ways chosen to accomplish this conforming work (Rom 5:2; Jas 4:6). Fourth, the goal of this process is to become *more like Jesus* in all life dimensions (Rom 8:29; Eph 4:15). Jesus is our model for growing in grace. Fifth, this sanctifying process is driven by the *Holy Spirit* (Rom 8:14; Eph 3:16-19; 2 Thess 2:13) and is intended to be nurtured within a *faith community* (1 Cor 12:11; Eph 2:19). Sixth, the ultimate telos of our faith journey is to reflect the character of Jesus in the world, manifested in *bearing fruit* that glorifies the Father (Jn 15:16; Col 1:10), with love of God and others as the central motivation. Spiritual formation is neither to be an exclusive nor solo endeavor for one's own personal maturation process, but rather it is to be the means of extending the love of God to others in the world. In summary, Christian spiritual formation is the process of becoming more like Jesus through the power of the indwelling Holy Spirit in order to bear fruit for the Father's glory.

Foundationally, the process of spiritual formation is about the work of the Holy Spirit within the life of the believer and the community of faith as God's ambassadors in the world (2 Cor 5:20). Richard Averbeck maintains that spiritual formation concerns how the Spirit "works *in* us, *among* us, and *through* us" to achieve Christlikeness.[14] Implicit in Averbeck's statement is the notion that the Holy Spirit works deeply *in* the human spirit and *among* and *through* us to others through relationships. The Holy Spirit "searches all things, even the depths of God" (1 Cor 2:10) and communicates these deep things to the human spirit that we might understand "the gifts bestowed on us by God" (1 Cor 2:12). Further, the Spirit bears witness with our spirit that we are children of God and coheirs with Christ (Rom 8:14-17).[15]

In God's sovereignty, the Spirit uses all possible means to integratively foster spiritual formation in Christ, including our interpersonal relationships, culture, life circumstances and even nature (see chap. 10).[16] Romans 8:29 makes clear that the goal of spiritual formation is conformity to Jesus: "Those God foreknew he also predestined to be conformed to the image of his Son, that he might be the firstborn among many brothers and sisters" (NIV). This conforming process continues throughout one's life. As 2 Corinthians 3:18 affirms: "We, who with unveiled faces contemplate the Lord's glory, *are being transformed* into his image with ever-increasing glory, which comes from the Lord, who is the Spirit" (NIV). The primary impetus for spiritual formation is the Holy Spirit.

Being all-knowing, God understands our hearts (Jer 17:9; Rom 8:27) and what we need (Mt 6:8), working all things together for our good (Rom 8:28-29), including growth in Christ. However, given that we have free will,

God never coerces us into conformity but rather lovingly provides opportunities for us to freely respond to God's dealings through grace. As John Wesley (1703–1791) observed, "First, it [grace] is free in all to whom it is given. It does not depend on any power or merit in man; no; not in any degree, neither in whole, nor in part."[17] Whether or not we realize it, we are being spiritually formed by someone or something. However, receiving rather than resisting the grace of God dynamically activates the process.

Receiving God's Grace

The mother of Jesus, Mary, intimately experienced the grace of God. As a virgin engaged to be married, Mary was young, poor and unknown. She lacked experience, prestige and the credentials one might expect for such a noble role and calling. Ironically, what catapulted Mary to prominence in human history was the antithesis of what launches most people into notoriety, such as talent, gifting, ability and skill. What qualified Mary was her reception of the grace and favor of God (Lk 1:28, 30). Mary was simply humble, demonstrating that God's Kingdom is a reversal of the world's system.[18]

The often-overlooked dimension of spiritual transformation is the enabling grace of God. Without God's grace (Gk. *charis,* meaning gift), salvation, forgiveness and ongoing spiritual transformation would become impossibilities. Grace is God's gift and agency of love and enablement, which is available only by faith (Eph 2:5).[19] According to Augustine, grace is the external help of God, which does not negate free will.[20] As Thomas Oden observes, grace is both God's "divine goodwill" and "divine disposition," working in our hearts, will and actions and offered to those who can neither earn nor deserve it.[21] Fundamentally, grace is the giving of God in inexhaustible supply, intended to bless those who humbly ask for and receive it.[22]

Grace proceeds from the Father, given to us through the life of Jesus and made effective in our hearts by the Holy Spirit. The Holy Spirit, called "the Spirit of grace" (Heb 10:29), is the gift who enables grace to be fully and freely received.[23] Therefore, the Spirit applies the finished work of Christ through grace in order to transform the human spirit, emotions, relationships, thoughts and behavior for the glory of God. The Spirit, who enables and appropriates grace in complete synergy with the Father and Son, brings life and is life.[24] Interestingly, Jesus never specifically spoke of grace, yet he personified grace in all facets of his earthly and heavenly mission.[25] The apostle Paul, in particular, provided a theology of grace throughout his writings, which informs the spiritual formation process.

In his letters, Paul repeatedly recognized the goodness and effects of God's grace. Each of Paul's letters begins with a salutation of grace and peace, and concludes with extending grace to his recipients. Grace might be seen through the lens of five primary themes in Paul's writings. First, Paul emphasized that grace alone is the vehicle for *salvation* (Rom 3:24; Eph 2:8-9; Tit 3:7), a theme echoed by Martin Luther.[26] The provision of grace applies to righteousness through Christ (Rom 5:17), which could not be attained by obeying the Mosaic law (Rom 6:14; Gal 2:21). Grace alone provides the power to overcome the sinful nature (Rom 6) and is not achieved through good works (Rom 11:6).

Second, Paul was extremely conscious that divine grace was given *to him* as a minister of the gospel, as his repeated phrase "by the grace given me" attests.[27] Paul recognized that the totality of his spiritual formation, which informed his vocational calling to proclaim the gospel, directly proceeded from God's initiating and apprehending grace and resulted in the convergence of divine and human agency.[28] Grace empowered Paul to do what he was incapable of doing on his own, beginning with his conversion on Damascus Road (Acts 9:1-18), his initial Christian formation during the three years spent in Arabia (Gal 1:17) and his subsequent ministry to the Gentiles, where he "worked harder" than others in advancing the gospel.[29] As it is with us, divine grace was the architect of Paul's spiritual formation throughout his life. Receiving the grace of God in humility is the main qualification and conduit for spiritual formation (cf. Jas 4:6; 1 Pet 5:5).

Third, Paul reminded the churches of God's grace extended *to them* (Rom 5:17; 1 Cor 1:4; Eph 2:7-8; Phil 4:23; 2 Tim 2:1), through God's mighty working in their lives even in the midst of severe trials (2 Cor 8:1-2). God's grace influenced their speaking and knowledge (1 Cor 1:4-5), generous deeds (2 Cor 9:8) and prayer for others (2 Cor 9:14).[30] Fourth, Paul viewed God's grace as the overarching impetus to reach more people with the gospel, such that their spiritual formation would be eternally affected (2 Cor 4:10). Fifth, Paul was mindful that Jesus himself personified grace (2 Cor 8:9), in that Jesus gave everything for humanity's sake in light of human unworthiness (Rom 5:17). From Jesus' incarnation to his resurrection, grace from the Father as extended through the Spirit to lost humanity is the gift that continues to transform.

Grace enlightens the intellect in discovering God's truth, strengthens the will to follow the truth, and guides the emotions, appetites and passions toward greater responsiveness to God's goodness and love.[31] Thus, grace redirects the human spirit to love and obey God, while restraining sin and lust. Moreover, grace also works within each of the other six holistic formation dimensions (i.e., emotions, relationships, intellect, vocation, physical health and wellness, and resource stewardship) in order to reflect the goodness of God over time. Although spiritual growth may appear unnoticeable, grace defies timetables and works "in hidden ways that seem too slow or too quick."[32]

The enemies of God's grace are human pride, presumption and perfectionism. Pride declares, "I can do it without God." Presumption withdraws human effort in order to escape personal responsibility and is behind what German Lutheran theologian and pastor Dietrich Bonhoeffer (1906–1945) calls "cheap grace." Cheap grace results when mediocre faith fails to embrace discipleship, the cross or Jesus Christ, and is the foil of costly grace, the sobering price of following Christ. For Bonhoeffer, "It is costly because it costs a man his life, and it is grace because it gives a man the only true life. It is costly because it condemns sin, and grace because it justifies the sinner."[33] On the other hand, perfectionism advances through self-effort to achieve a desired standard of excellence and acceptance. The means to receive grace is through humble request (Jas 4:6; 1 Jn 5:14). Grace, then, is the precursor for inside-out transformation.

Being Transformed from the Inside Out

At age twenty-six in Florence, Italy, Michelangelo was commissioned to sculpt a statue of David, the biblical character. For over thirty-five years, the enormous block of Carrera marble had languished in the outdoor workshop of a notable cathedral. After two other sculptors who had previously worked on the sculpture withdrew for unknown reasons, Michelangelo was invited to continue the work. Regarding David, Michelangelo wrote,

David with his sling
And I with my bow
Michelangelo.

It is thought that Michelangelo's reference to his bow was metaphorical and referred to the sculpting instrument, a bow-shaped manual drill, used for the work. Ironically, the massive marble was referred to as "the Giant" by Florence residents. Further, it was hypothesized that Michelangelo drew parallels between himself and the historical David, related to the respective enemies they fought, which for David was Goliath and for Michelangelo was the statue that he artistically battled to sculpt.[34] Michelangelo did not use a human model but rather used his mind's eye, previous drawings and the study of other sculptures to inform the work. The colossal David turned out to be almost seventeen feet tall and weighed over six tons.

In 1550, Michelangelo's biographer, Giorgio Vasari, wrote of the resurrection of the marble into the actual sculpture as the "revival of a dead thing" and "a veritable miracle."[35] Indeed it was. In one of Michelangelo's most quoted poems, he wrote that "the best of artists" has access to the soul image within the marble block. During the Renaissance, when sculptures were representative of the highest good, beauty and virtue, the identity of Michelangelo, David and the city of Florence coalesced through an abandoned block of marble that was transformed into one of the world's greatest sculptures. Michelangelo found his own identity, as he hand-drilled, shaped and sanded away what was not the David, in order to reveal the priceless image within.

God shapes us into the image of Jesus over time, crafting an eternal identity. We are found abandoned, seemingly useless, without true identity and longing for the work of the Master to sculpt our lives into beautiful similitude that reflects God's highest good and virtue. Spiritual transformation starts with Jesus, as the Master image within the Father's eye, who through the supernatural work of the Holy Spirit sculpts us from unrecognizable masses of stone into the pliable contours of Jesus' image. The process may seem rough, conflicted or in hiatus. Yet over time, features of Jesus begin to appear, such that when others see us, they see Jesus' heart, hands, arms, mind and feet.

However, unlike the art of sculpting that works from the outside in, spiritual formation starts from the inside and works its way out.[36] The heart is the starting place, as the life of Augustine illustrates. Augustine identified the corruption of his own heart without Christ as prompting the exploration of astrology, theft of pears, adherence to various worldly philosophies and engaging in illicit sexual relationships.[37] Reflecting on his conversion to Christ, Augustine stated, "Your words are now firmly implanted in my heart of hearts, and I was besieged by you on every side."[38] He acknowledged that his conversion was not only a result of God's abundant grace but also the grace shown to him by Simplicianus, an older spiritual role model and leader. Similarly, others have a part to play in our heart transformation, which reflects God's grace.

In Scripture the human spirit has been likened to the heart.[39] The heart is often referred to as the very core of a person's life and as the source of the "springs of life" that is worthy of guarding (Prov 4:23). The heart is the seat of the will (Prov 16:9), intellect (Mk 2:6, 8), and feeling (Lk 24:32). However, the heart without God is corrupt (Jer 17:9), hard (Ezek 11:19), wicked (Ps 58:2, see ASV) and rebellious (Jer 5:23). When broken of self and sin (Ps 51:7), the heart is able to serve God. Therefore, the heart reflects the human spirit, which is the "the only thing in us that God will accept as the basis of our relationship" to God.[40] God opens the heart, as Lydia's heart was opened to respond to Paul's message (Acts 16:14), and pours love into it (Rom 5:5). The heart is where God dwells (Eph 3:17) in bringing us "the divine gifts of trust, hope, and love."[41] Spiritual practices assist to take us there.

Engaging in Spiritual Practices

Throughout the ages, Christians have engaged in spiritual practices to nurture their relationship with God. Spiritual practices are "means of grace" used by the Holy Spirit to further conform believers to the image of Jesus and sustain new life, rather than mere "tasks to accomplish or instructions to follow."[42] God created us for intimate relationship, most centrally through worship. Therefore, worship of God should be the focus of engagement in spiritual practices. We are to worship God in spirit and in truth (Jn 4:24) because, foundationally, we exist to worship God.[43] The key to worship is the movement of the Holy Spirit, who ushers worshipers into the very presence of God, where we are changed into God's likeness.[44] Therefore, worship is the response of a grateful heart in adoration of God, and spiritual practices are conduits to take us there.

Spiritual practices are what Christian philosopher James K. A. Smith describes as "thick," since they are full of meaning and are identity significant.[45] Smith argues that practices create habits that shape our identity. The formative place where this shaping occurs is worship. Smith asserts that being a disciple of Jesus is not primarily about the cognitive learning of doctrines and ideas, but rather in the affective flora of "being the kind of person who *loves* rightly—who loves God and neighbor and is oriented to the world by the primacy of that love. We are made to be such people by our immersion in the material practices of Christian worship."[46] Smith uses a creative typology in presenting these material practices of the Kingdom, which include hospitality and community as God's greeting, song as the hymning language of the Kingdom, confession as the demonstration of brokenness and grace, baptism as initiation, prayer as learning Kingdom language, Scripture as renarrating the world, and financial giving as Kingdom economics of gratitude, to name a few. Smith calls this "practicing for the Kingdom," the ultimate destination of every believer's eternal vocation (Rev 5:13).[47]

Engaging in spiritual practices takes on added significance in that they comprise the rhythms of "a story-formed community," with the narrative of Jesus as the main script. Stanley Hauerwas concludes, "Thus [Jesus'] identity is grasped not through other savior stories, but by learning to follow him, which is the necessary condition for citizenship in his Kingdom."[48] Learning to follow Jesus entails engaging in spiritual practices in order to partake in God's story and develop godly virtues that exemplify the ethics of the Kingdom.[49] However, it is crucial to keep in mind that one's culture informs engagement in spiritual disciplines. For example, Howard Thurman (1899–1981) spoke of the African American spiritual experience. Thurman addressed specific spiritual disciplines of an oppressed people that included commitment, growing in wisdom and stature, suffering, prayer and reconciliation, as well as freedom.[50] For people of color, worship of God may be closely linked with the experience of personal struggle and suffering forged through the depths of experience. Thus, culture locates worship as a spiritual discipline within various ethnic contexts that affect one's spirituality and sense of virtue.[51]

Developing godly virtues for ethical living is a byproduct of loving and worshiping God and expresses Christ's love to the world (see chap. 11).[52] I contend that following Jesus means doing what he did and following his example by engaging in spiritual practices to nurture communion with God, which in turn develops godly virtues. Just as Jesus spent time in communion with the Father (Mk 1:35; Lk 5:16), we are to imitate Jesus (Eph 5:1) by spending time in communion with God as a demonstration of worship. The Holy Spirit takes our posture of worship in orchestrating the melodies of various spiritual practices in glorifying God as a continual outpouring, in order to flourish in our faith journey.[53] As Craig Dykstra and Dorothy Bass highlight, Christian practices are rehearsals for a way of life and provide the vehicle for the shaping and healing of the community of faith.[54] With worship as the fulcrum, spiritual practices are interrelated because they make "space for God's active presence that then ripples out into other parts of life."[55]

Richard Foster and Dallas Willard provide valuable resources for nurturing one's relationship with God for inner transformation.[56] Foster identifies classical spiritual disciplines that are (1) *inward* (meditation, prayer, fasting, study), (2) *outward* (simplicity, solitude, submission, service), and

(3) *corporate* (confession, worship, guidance, celebration). Willard arranges the disciplines around those of (1) *abstinence* (solitude, fasting, frugality, chastity, secrecy where good deeds are hidden, and sacrifice) and (2) *engagement* (study, worship, celebration, service, prayer, fellowship, confession, submission related to humility and transparency). Other authors address one or more of these spiritual practices, and still others offer additional practices, including journaling, personal retreat and engaging in sabbath rest.[57] While spiritual practices are responses to God's initiating grace, God waits to be wanted. A. W. Tozer comments, "To have found God and still to pursue Him is the soul's paradox of love, scorned indeed by the too-easily-satisfied religionist, but justified in happy experience by the children of the burning heart."[58] Pursuing God through spiritual passion and obedience remains the barometer of the spiritual life (Jn 14:23-24; 15:10; 1 Jn 5:3).

Engaging in spiritual practices is not a formula for transformation but rather the ongoing experience of "the Mystery of God in its breadth and depth."[59] Indeed, there is mystery in our relationship with God, and the human mind may objectify this mystery through rote or mechanized behavior. Volition alone does not ensure communion with God. As Thomas Oden observes, "Lacking grace, the task of personal growth turns into a frantic search for innovative strategies. . . . We have tried to manufacture spiritual growth while missing the very grace that would enable it."[60] In fact, spiritual practices can become bondages of performance that miss the purpose of practicing the presence of God, if undertaken "according to the flesh" rather than "by the Spirit" (Gal 5:16-17; 6:8).[61] In Jesus' day, the teachers of the law and the Pharisees were prime examples of the former (Mt 23:13-36). When motivated by a pure heart (Mt 5:8) to commune with God, however, spiritual practices become doorways for the Spirit to work deeply in the human heart, drawing us further into worship by way of a reciprocal love relationship.

Shaping Through Suffering

Another formidable conduit of spiritual formation is suffering. Followers of Christ are shaped in their faith journeys through suffering, whether the result of one's faith, mistakes and missteps, or uncontrollable circumstances. As the apostle Paul stated, "Indeed, all who want to live a godly life in Christ Jesus will be persecuted" (2 Tim 3:12). Spiritual growth from the inside out and finding authentic identity as sons and daughters of God are fostered not only during the rhythms of life in consonance but also most dramatically when life experiences create dissonance through the inevitability of the unexpected, unwelcome transition, disappointment, interpersonal conflict, rejection, personal wounding, loss and grief, physical or emotional impairment, and unanswered prayer.[62] These situations test personal faith and can plunge even the most spiritually anchored person into deep despair, creating what Bruce Demarest describes as "painful disorientation."[63]

These unsettling times are like sharp razors, designed to strip away pride, the unessential and mundane in order to make sense of what really matters and to find God, whose ways are beyond our ways in the midst of uncertainty or trauma (Is 55:8). During times of suffering, obvious questions emerge: Where is God in this? and How can God allow this to happen? which C. S. Lewis chronicles after the extended illness and death of his wife, Joy Davidman.[64] Such helplessness in observing others suffer may have the same debilitating effect as if one suffers him- or herself, as Mother Teresa's writings reflect.[65] Identifying this as a "dark night of the soul," John of the Cross describes how after the felt presence of God dissipates, a deeper realization of the love of God and a greater knowledge of oneself through humility emerges.[66]

Even in the midst of dry or dark seasons, the apostle Paul reminds us that suffering is the shared experience of those who follow Jesus; suffering produces endurance (Rom 5:3) and enjoins believers to the living Lord through identificational fellowship (Phil 3:10-11). Through imprisonments, floggings, stoning, shipwrecks, all kinds of dangers and a thorn in the flesh, for example, Paul became intimately acquainted with suffering (2 Cor 11:25; 12:7). Although he and his companions despaired even of life itself, Paul cites one specific situation that brought consolation in the midst of dire circumstances, so that Paul could extend comfort to others (2 Cor 1:3-11). Paul likewise could affirm, "Whenever I am weak, then am I strong"

(2 Cor 12:10) and invited others to join him in suffering (Phil 1:29; 2 Tim 1:8). Paul learned that "all who want to live a godly life in Christ Jesus will be persecuted" (2 Tim 3:12), yet all who suffer for Christ will also reign with him (Rom 8:17-18).

Through the ages, men and women have been shaped into Christlikeness through suffering. For example, Amy Carmichael (1867–1951), the Irish missionary who rescued children and women from temple prostitution in India for fifty-five years, suffered from chronic pain and for the last twenty years of her life was mostly bedridden after an injury.[67] As minister and leader of the nonviolent civil rights movement, Dr. Martin Luther King Jr. (1929–1968) suffered the indignity of racism shared by other African Americans, all the while, through love and nonviolent resistance, combating the evils of discrimination and injustice that precluded equal opportunity for all Americans. Sustaining consistent misunderstanding, derision and death threats, King's suffering only strengthened his resolve to love God and to love his enemies.[68]

There can be no greater painful disorientation than suffering caused by oppression and racism, as noted by theologians of color. James Cone details suffering incurred through slavery and the racist system that perpetuates it.[69] Howard Thurman questions what Christianity can offer those who are oppressed and dispossessed, given that the slave trade was perpetrated at the hands of "Christian" slave owners, the effects of which are ongoing today. Thurman's response centers in the person of Jesus, whose suffering and overwhelming love provide the way forward.[70] Black spirituals and slave narratives bespeak this theology of suffering.[71] Through his lived experience in Latin America, Gustavo Gutiérrez nuances how an encounter with Christ brings true freedom to the poor and offers dignity to the suffering and disenfranchised as beloved sons and daughters of God.[72] Drawing from her Cuban roots, Ada Maria Isasi-Diaz grapples with the suffering of Latinas and how solidarity with the poor and oppressed accentuate God's grace, salvation and freedom.[73] Suffering caused by inhumanity stemming from poverty, racism and discrimination violates the very nature and character of God and must be boldly addressed in Christian love.

Suffering for doing good (1 Pet 3:17) contributes to spiritual formation through identification with Christ, who suffered on our behalf. Suffering for the gospel's sake produces a depth of fellowship with Christ (Phil 3:10) in light of future glory (Rom 8:18) and a sweet fragrance of hope for others (2 Cor 2:15-16). The apostle Paul expressed the effects of suffering as producing perseverance, leading to godly character and hope through love (Rom 5:3-5). Through personal trials, Paul learned that the ultimate purpose of suffering was to bring comfort to others because of the comfort he personally received directly from God (2 Cor 1:3-10). Suffering provides yet another conduit for the shaping work of the Spirit in spiritual formation.

The ultimate goal of the formation of our spirits is not the realized sense of personal growth, although this is a desired outcome, but rather the embrace of the Spirit's work in our faith journeys as we are shaped into the image of Jesus in order to love and serve God and others. This chapter focused on how God restores the human spirit, forms us spiritually through providing abundant grace in transforming us from the inside out, meets us as we engage in spiritual practices that foster communion with God, deepens our relationships and uses suffering as an identificational tool that further conforms believers into Christ's image through developing the fruit of the Spirit. With chapters one through four as a backdrop, chapter five focuses on the formation of our emotions.

5

Emotions

Our Feelings

Forgive, and you will be forgiven.

Luke 6:37

As we have seen through the preceding chapters, Christian spiritual formation originates with the Creator God, and love is the core motivation for our creation and subsequently the foundation for reciprocal relationship with God and others. Being created in the *imago Dei,* we are hardwired for love and endowed with an affective capacity through emotions in which to experience the fullness of life. Love, as expressed through acceptance and fostered through belonging, is the core catalyst for our emotional repertoire.

Christian sociologist Pitirim Sorokin, a pioneer in research on love, observes that love is the universal creative force that counteracts evil and brings harmonious unity and mutual aid.[1] When fully loved and accepted, we feel joy, happiness and delight, and are able to function with greater confidence, knowing that we are cared for and that our lives matter. In the absence of love, as when love is withheld or withdrawn through circumstance or rejection, we may evidence any number of affective reactions, such as anger, resentment, fear, hatred, envy, jealousy, grief or sorrow. In other words, "Individuals who have never experienced love or compassion may be extremely hostile and abusive in their responses to the world and may eventually reach a state of crisis."[2]

Although emotions are influenced by external and changing circumstances, such as transition, uncertainty, fear, threat or the loss of someone or something dear, psychologists inform us that our emotional makeup results from early childhood experiences that bear on biological and personality dispositions.[3] For example, we all are predisposed to experience shame when something happens for which we have little or no control or casts us in a negative light. Anyone who has ever tripped ascending a few steps in front of others or gotten caught in a misdeed can easily relate. At the same time, our affective wiring may cause us to be emotionally moved by certain music, art, film, literature or nature.[4] For instance, every time I hear composer Samuel Barber's "Adagio for Strings," I am viscerally moved. While watching certain movies, I empathize with various characters such that tears easily flow. And when I walk along the beach or watch a sunrise, I resonate in peaceful repose. Emotions are God's gifts to us that influence all life dimensions.

While the field of psychology sheds light on the diverse dynamics of human formation, some psychologists acknowledge that the various theories and perspectives have become fragmented, like a "flotsam in the widening sea of knowledge," with emotion being the missing link in the relevant approaches to personality development.[5] On one hand, secular psychological theories shed light on human emotional functioning. On the other hand, Christian psychologists have an advantage of understanding human nature on the basis of absolute truth and theology in creating a distinctively biblical anthropology.[6]

Emotional formation concerns the capacity to identify, understand, express and reflect upon one's own and others' feelings, desires and passions in healthy and God-honoring ways. The natural result is to increasingly love God and others as evidenced by the fruit of the Spirit (Gal 5:22-23). Loving God and others involves emotions that register feelings. Feelings might be seen as the experiential component of emotion, and they influence attitude, memory, motivation, behavior and survival.[7] Emotions involve automatic physiological responses, such as facial and vocal expression, and are the basis for forms of judgment, which are central to ethical thinking and behavior.[8] Emotions are not morally neutral; they frame valued judgments and decision making, being readily observed in cases of racism, war and genocide.[9] I argue that the basis for human emotion derives from the original movement of love between God and humankind at creation. As a result, the full range of human emotion is initially triggered by the felt presence of love, as upheld by acceptance, belonging and security, or the absence of love, as fostered by rejection, exclusion and insecurity.

Emotions are to the personality what a dial is to a barometer. Just as barometers indicate atmospheric conditions for weather forecasting, so too emotions indicate levels of well-being that become predictive of future functioning in light of changing life circumstances. As shown in figure 5.1, this chapter on emotional formation focuses on loving God and others in the affective or feeling domain. We begin with a brief review of the emotional components of Jesus' life, then assess the impact of childhood on emotional formation and discuss the healing of emotional wounds, including the critical component of forgiveness for overall flourishing. The chapter concludes by discussing how each of us walks with a limp, in one way or another, as tangible evidence that we all experience fragile emotions in an imperfect world.

Jesus and Emotions

As portrayed in the Gospels, the humanity of Jesus reflects the diversity of emotions he experienced and expressed in relationship with the Father and others, and provides a model for our emotional formation. Although some may argue that because of his deity Jesus was unable to fully reflect the robust nature and complexity of human emotion, we are reminded that although Jesus was without sin, he was like us in every way (Heb 2:17; 4:15), including the emotional realm. The Gospels portray Jesus' human nature as perfectly integrated with his divine nature in the fulfillment of his earthly mission.[10] Hence, the major movements of Jesus' emotions were chiefly predicated on his attachment to and love for the Father,

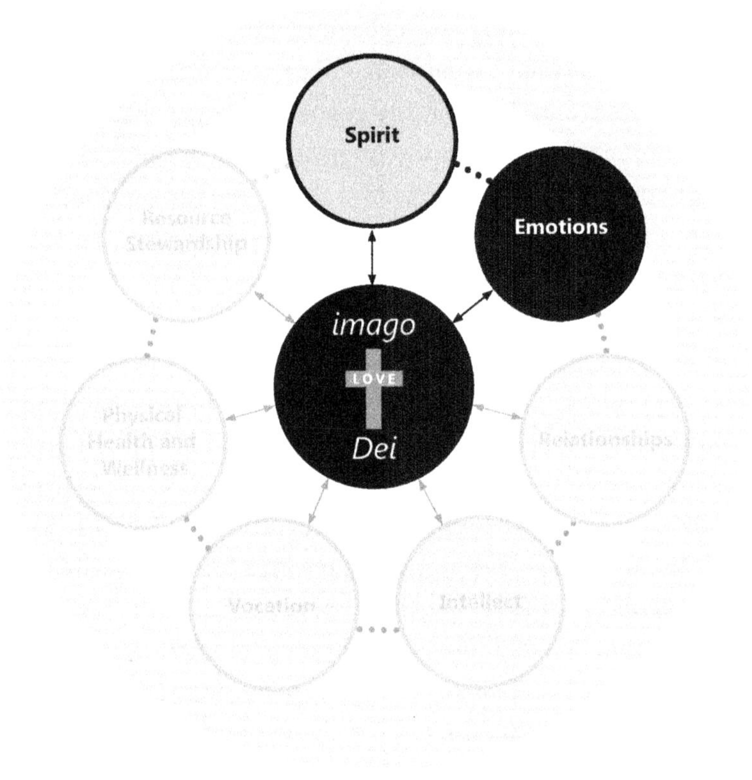

Figure 5.1. Emotional formation

readily evidenced when God's will was interrupted or compromised in others' lives.

For Jesus, love was the center point around which all other emotions, including anger, sorrow and grief, took their cue. Since God's very essence and nature is love (1 Jn 4:8, 16), Jesus' reciprocal love relationship with the Father was the source of Jesus' love for others. For example, in explaining to his disciples that he must return to the Father, Jesus declares that the ruler of this world has no power over him and that he loves the Father and does exactly what the Father has commanded him (Jn 14:31). Therefore, Jesus' self-sacrificial love and compassion for others directly flow from his love for the Father and obedience to the Father's will.

Jesus' mission of love, which perfectly aligned with mercy and compassion, resulted in his "doing good and healing all who were oppressed by the devil" (Acts 10:38).[11] B. B. Warfield asserts that because "love is the foundation of compassion," Jesus experienced compassion that interconnects intense pity with external beneficence.[12] When faced with others' spiritual, emotional and physical needs, Jesus is repeatedly moved with compassion, which resulted in acts of mercy. Jesus is deeply moved in spirit before raising his friend Lazarus from the dead (Jn 11:35). When a man with leprosy comes to him, Jesus is moved with compassion, and after touching him, the man is healed (Mk 1:41). Upon leaving Jericho, two blind men cry out to Jesus to have mercy on them. Moved with compassion, Jesus touches their eyes and heals them (Mt 20:34). In the town of Nain, Jesus has compassion on a mother who is weeping on the way to bury her son. Entreating her not to cry, Jesus touches the coffin and tells the young man to get up (Lk 7:11-15). Jesus likewise loves the rich young ruler who refuses to follow him (Mk 10:21). Whether knowing individuals well, as in the case of Lazarus, or not knowing them at all, as in the case of the rich young ruler, Jesus is moved by human need, suffering or loss. In addition, Jesus' "heart was open and readily responded to the delights of association, and bound itself to others in happy fellowship" through human attachment.[13]

In addition to individuals, Jesus' compassion extended to groups, as we see in the feeding of the five thousand (Mt 14:13-21) and the four thousand (Mk 8:1-10). Not only does Jesus respond to physical needs but he also is moved by spiritual needs: "When he saw the crowds, he had compassion for them, because they were harassed and helpless, like sheep without a shepherd" (Mt. 9:36). Jesus' weeping over the city of Jerusalem because of the people's spiritual blindness and unbelief further bespeaks his depth of love and compassion as indicative of his emotional barometer (Lk 19:41-44).

With love expressed through compassion as the primary emotional anchor in Jesus' life, it is not surprising that Jesus also expressed anger and indignation when circumstances or conditions intercepted the highest purposes for human flourishing. Incensed by inhumanity, Jesus viscerally reacts to the insensitivity and disregard of religious leaders for the hurting and disenfranchised. When the Pharisees accuse Jesus of healing the man with the withered hand on the sabbath, Jesus "looked around at them with anger" and "was grieved at their hardness of heart" (Mk 3:5). As Warfield notes, "anger always has pain at its root, and is a reaction of the soul against what gives it discomfort."[14] Jesus was pained at the spiritual condition of those the Pharisees led astray. No greater illustration can be found than at the cleansing of the temple, where Jesus' righteous indignation turns to demonstrable actions of scattering coins and overturning tables (Jn 2:13-17).

In addition to compassion, righteous anger and indignation, Jesus also experienced heart-wrenching sorrow and grief. One such situation involved the unexpected death of his friend Lazarus. When the Jews see Jesus' heartbreak, they comment, "See how he loved him!" (Jn 11:36). Jesus, who is described by Isaiah as a "man of sorrows and acquainted with grief" (Is 53:3 ESV), also comes face-to-face with personal rejection through Judas's betrayal, followed by excruciating agony in Gethsemane. In deep emotional anguish, knowing that his substitutionary death meant life for others, Jesus experiences intense despair and desolation, even crying out "My God, my God, why have you forsaken me?" (Mt 27:46). When all human attachments have dissolved, leaving him completely alone, Jesus clings to the reality of the Father's love even in death, fulfilling his mission to the very end (Lk 23:46). All of Jesus' emotions revolve around the center point of attachment to the Father's love and the threat of God's love being unrealized in others' lives. Jesus personifies that "emotions have a lot of moral importance" and indicate "the character of the one who experiences them."[15] As Christian ethicist Robert Roberts contends, "emotion virtues" such as gratitude, joy, peace, contrition and compassion are central to the fruit of the Spirit (Gal 5:22-23) and frame godly character.[16] These emotion virtues completely infused Jesus' character.

The goal of emotional formation is to move increasingly toward a fuller reception of the love of God, which results in the disabling of emotional bondages that prevent the reciprocal flow of God's love, as expressed by the fruit of the Spirit. In other words, we are to be increasingly transformed into the image of Jesus so that our emotions reflect God's character as expressed by the fruit of the Spirit. This is accomplished by remaining attached to Jesus as the true vine (Jn 15:4-5), by receiving nurture from others and by experiencing emotional healing. As we shall see in the next section, emotional formation begins through human attachment in infancy, continues in childhood and unfolds over a lifetime.

Influence of Childhood

Experiences in childhood, including in utero, greatly influence emotional formation.[17] *Two fictional characters serve as hypothetical examples. First, in J. R. R. Tolkien's fantasy epic The Lord of the Rings, the main character, Frodo, leaves the security of the Shire, home of the Hobbits, to deliver the "One Ring" that he inherited back to Mordor.*[18] *Joined by his best friend, Sam, two cousins and five others who compose the "fellowship of the ring," Frodo navigates through death-defying terrain and circumstances in order to complete his mission. I suggest that the love and security Frodo experiences through relational attachments in the Shire and throughout his journey provide the needed strength to persevere in navigating the numerous trials that awaited him.*

Second, in the classic 1939 movie The Wizard of Oz, *Dorothy finds herself in Oz, a place far from her Kansas home, where she lived with her Auntie Em and Uncle Henry. The separation from them initially invokes fear in her unknown surroundings. However, through her journey, she bonds with three unlikely characters—the scarecrow, the tin man and the lion—and develops strength and confidence to navigate the way forward with them. Dorothy's positive attachment to her Auntie Em and Uncle Henry create what psychologist Todd Hall calls "attachment filters" or "memories of relational experiences with emotionally significant people [that] are etched in our souls and become filters that shape how we feel about ourselves, God and others."*[19] *I propose that Dorothy was able to navigate her new life challenges because of the strong emotional attachments formed in Kansas.*

The quality of attachment to others in infancy and early childhood has implications for how individuals positively attach to others and also to God in later life.[20] Ongoing attachment experiences provide a sense of belonging and security essential for optimal growth and development throughout life. Therefore, emotional formation is critically influenced by significant relational attachments. Perspectives on attachment were first advanced by British psychologist John Bowlby and later developed by Bowlby's protégée, Mary Ainsworth, and her associates.[21] Their research highlights that responsiveness of a primary caregiver (usually the mother) to an infant establishes internal working models that create expectations about the world and the ability to handle ongoing loving relationships, separation and anxiety. As Bowlby argued, "Many of the most intense emotions arise during the formation, the maintenance, the disruption, and the renewal of attachment relationships."[22]

In their research, Ainsworth and her associates observed three primary infant attachment styles: (1) secure, (2) avoidant-insecure and (3) anxious/ambivalent-insecure. They found that infants with a *secure attachment* evidence confidence in the caregiver's availability to provide comfort and security. Infants with an *avoidant-insecure attachment* reflect caregivers who are emotionally distant, rejecting or abusive. Infants who demonstrate *ambivalent-insecure attachment* relate to caregivers who inconsistently interact with and neglect them. More recently, a fourth attachment style was added, labeled *disorganized/disoriented*, referring to the confusion children experience when their overtures to receive comfort result in distress for the caregiver, contributing to children's deepening uncertainty.[23]

In adulthood, attachment styles in relationships are likewise evidenced and contribute to how emotions are regulated.[24] First, adults with a *secure attachment style* retain emotionally impacting childhood memories and possess a realistic view of their primary caregivers or parents, derived from warm and supportive experiences. Generally speaking, secure adults have a positive, autonomous and forgiving attitude toward their parents. If the relationship with parents involved less-than-optimal circumstances, the secure adult has come to the place of understanding and forgiveness, while not being bound to past negativity. (Issues of forgiveness will be addressed later in this chapter.) Secure adults invest in relationships, trust others, constructively seek out others' support when under stress, appropriately self-disclose and resolve conflict, and exhibit relatively stable self-esteem.[25]

Second, adults with an *avoidant-insecure attachment style* struggle with defensiveness, cannot recall positive attachment experiences from childhood and may deny painful past memories. Avoidant adults tend to suppress feelings, fear closeness, lack trust in relationships, minimally self-disclose and emphasize work over loving relationships.[26] Avoidant adults have been shown to be either dismissing (e.g., cold, competitive and introverted) or fearful (e.g., unassertive, self-conscious and self-defeating).[27]

Third, adults with an *anxious/ambivalent-insecure style* may recall attachment events in erratic emotional bursts, where they berate primary caregivers/parents and remain upset, unforgiving and enmeshed in unresolved pain. What characterizes this style is low self-esteem, fear of rejection, excessive approval seeking, feeling unappreciated, a strong desire to attach to others for comfort, separation anxiety and an avoidance of self-disclosure.[28]

Fourth, adults with a *disorganized attachment style* may have had frightening experiences with primary caregivers or parents, which cause them to self-blame, be fearful and controlling, lack a strategy for dealing with the stress of separation, and be indiscriminate in attaching to others. Ongoing maternal depression has been mentioned as one possible contributing factor to this attachment style.[29]

Regardless of previous experiences, attachment style often reflects a natural adaptation to particular family, social and cultural circumstances, as in the case of children of a single working parent, who has limited emotional resources to invest in them, or when uncontrollable circumstances, such as war or natural disaster, intercept healthy attachment. Other disruptions to attachment, including physical and sexual abuse, marital separation or divorce, and the death of a loved one, create emotional responses laden with fear and anxiety.[30] Fear of detachment and the pain of separation explain why one marital partner may desperately try to reunite with the other in the face of a troubled marriage. Fear of attachment based on previous negative interactions with caregivers may explain why orphaned children are unable to easily bond with adoptive parents. At any rate, similarities between attachment in infancy and attachment in adult relationships reinforce that love involves not only emotions but also cognition and behavior.[31]

Although Steven Sandage notes that attachment style reflects continuity into adulthood, relational transformation does occur, as in the case of the woman who met Jesus at the well and whose human and God attachments radically changed because of this encounter (Jn 4:1-30).[32] A personal relationship with God leading to the realization that God loves us can change everything, including one's perspective of the past, present and future, and offers great hope for those whose childhoods were less than optimal. Hence, working attachment models can change over time through subsequent experiences, which can dramatically affect emotional formation.[33]

Most important, human attachment perspectives help us understand our attachment filter related to God.[34] The biblical story of Joseph illustrates that a secure attachment with a parent contributes to a secure attachment to God, even throughout sustained trials (Gen 37; 39–45). After his spitefully jealous brothers sell Joseph to Midianite traders rather than kill him, Joseph is then sold to Potiphar, the Egyptian captain of Pharaoh's guard. Having been betrayed by nine of his eleven brothers (i.e., Reuben came to his defense and Benjamin was not present) and barely escaping with his life, Joseph transitions into each subsequent life phase being fairly well-adjusted. What contributed to Joseph's emotional stability and resilience, stellar character, and uncompromising principles? I argue that Joseph's secure attachment to his loving human father contributed to his secure attachment to God, similar to Jesus' loving attachment to the Father, which sustained him during his betrayal and subsequent crucifixion.

Hence, a secure attachment filter to God contributes to a secure foundation in which to process and grow during trials.[35] As Pehr Granqvist and Lee A. Kirkpatrick observe, "It is easy to imagine how an attachment figure who is simultaneously omnipresent, omniscient, and omnipotent can provide the most secure of secure bases."[36] Psychologists acknowledge the centrality of love in religious belief systems, wherein relationship with God becomes like an attachment relationship with a parent.[37] Although attachment with God is different from attachment with people, there is a formidable correspondence.[38] One's image of God and self-image heavily draw on one's perception of and experience with other people, particularly parents or primary caregivers.[39] Thus, the goal of emotional formation relates to reconciling one's self-image with the way that God views us, as being worthy recipients of God's love.

Viewing emotional formation through an attachment lens has several advantages, including its resonance with biblical and theological perspectives of lifelong development, the range of emotions that it addresses based on the presence or absence of loving relationships, and the broad application to the human condition that is somewhat predictable based on familial and social circumstances.[40] Furthermore, the attachment perspective has universal applicability in virtually all cross-cultural settings.[41]

Essentially, human attachment in childhood, predicated on the presence or absence of positive experiences of love, belonging and security, influences emotional formation and how one views and experiences self, others and God. Fortunately, these views can change over time based on subsequent loving relationships. Love is the very fulcrum of emotional formation, influencing all other holistic formation dimensions. However, the inevitability of emotional wounds is part and parcel of being human. How we deal with these wounds further conditions our emotional formation.

Healing of Emotional Wounds

Imagine you are in your teenage years and your siblings target you for the ultimate bullying by releasing their jealousy and hatred through plotting your demise. You have been obedient to your father's request in tracking down your brothers, who are grazing the family's herd of sheep near a place called Dothan. However, their discontent because of personal insecurity heightened by intense resentment over your favored family status and seeming cockiness collides in time and space in one catalytic turning point. You find yourself at the bottom of a deep and waterless well and overhear your brothers plotting their next move. You are completely alone, defenseless, without resources and fearing for your very life.

Few of us will ever encounter what Joseph experienced on that fateful day (Gen 37:12-36). While in that pit, Joseph must have experienced a full range of emotional responses—disbelief, terror and despair—followed by the obvious question, *How could they do this to me?* Furthermore, consider the emotional rollercoaster of guilt, blame, loss and grief that Jacob must have later experienced, realizing that he unknowingly sent his favored son into a death trap. The depth of emotional wounding that Joseph experienced reverberates in the reconciliation he initiated with his brothers some twenty years later, where his past magnetized into moments of cathartic release in the present.[42] Realizing that his brothers who once wanted to destroy him now stood before him at his mercy, Joseph overflowed with emotion as expressed by intense weeping (Gen 42:24; 43:30; 45:2, 14).

It seems that after being sold into slavery Joseph had sufficiently recovered from the trauma in order to become a trusted man of integrity, a recipient of continuous favor throughout his employ in Potiphar's household and subsequent prison term, and a stellar official of the highest rank. The unthinkable led to a deep inner processing over many years, leading Joseph to an unshakeable faith in God and the culminating awareness of his God-given destiny to preserve his family and ultimately the developing nation. Most important, Joseph forgave his brothers, recognizing that what they intended for harm God had used for good (Gen 50:20). I maintain that through his emotional wounding in adolescence, Joseph drew on God's resources into adulthood, supported by the memory of a secure attachment with his father, Jacob, and the joy of connectedness with his younger brother, Benjamin.[43]

Emotional wounds are an inevitable outcome of life, and no one escapes their fury, even those with stable relational foundations and secure attachments. Being loved and accepted are universal human needs that reinforce the inextricable tie between emotional and relational formation as "social realities."[44] Emotional wounds result from myriad relational dynamics, most notably the actual or perceived absence or withdrawal of love, attachment, acceptance, security and well-being. Thus, emotional wounds result from what I identify as two equally impacting relational contexts: (1) *active wounding,* or what is done to us that should never have happened, and (2) *passive wounding,* when there are things that should have happened but never did. Active wounding relates to physical, sexual and verbal abuse, intimidation or abandonment, such as what Joseph's brothers inflicted on him. Passive wounding relates to the intentional or unintentional withholding of love, attachment, acceptance, security and protection. Examples of passive wounding include children whose parents or caregivers neglect them and those in relationships where one person lacks loving reciprocity.

Whether inflicted actively or passively, emotional wounds, if unresolved, can become so embedded that they anchor us to the past, "govern our behavior" and contribute to a distorted sense of self.[45] If leadership and ministry consultant Bobb Biehl's contention is correct, namely, that "every child has a dominant childhood feeling, resulting in a predictable emotional-motivational pattern in adulthood," then how we understand painful childhood emotions offers the first step toward personal healing.[46] In other words, naming "the deep theme" of our negative emotions is the beginning of taming them so that they do not become permanent harbors in the heart.[47] With the effects of emotional wounding so pervasive in a fallen world, as seen in the workplace, the church and the home, tracing how emotional wounds develop and recognizing the need for healing become critical for true freedom in Christ and overall emotional well-being.

Emotional wounds may develop in an instance and deepen over time. The result is a four-stage downward spiral, starting with unhealed emotional wounds.[48] *Unhealed emotional wounds* produce ungodly beliefs. *Ungodly beliefs* are lies we believe about ourselves, based on past hurts and current circumstances. Statements such as "I am worthless," "I am unloved," "I am a mistake," "I am a failure," "I am unworthy," "I am hopeless" and "My life doesn't matter" comprise ungodly beliefs, reinforced by Satan's deception that separates us from internalizing the truth of God's view of us. God views us as being worthy of love and grace

(Ps 32:10; 52:8; Lam 3:22; Rom 5:15, 17). If unaddressed, ungodly beliefs morph into emotional patterns of negative feelings. *Emotional patterns of negative feelings* relate to persistent anger, shame, fear, anxiety, inadequacy, insecurity, self-rejection, self-doubt, self-condemnation, pessimism, cynicism and despair. Persistent negative feelings provoke a repertoire of *undesirable behavior*, which may include perfectionism, withdrawal, isolation, depression, compulsiveness, addiction, blame-shifting, rebellion, aggression and underachievement or overachievement. Regardless of the cause and effects of emotional wounding, the simple truth is that we cannot heal ourselves.

Only God can heal deep wounds through the power of the Holy Spirit. The psalmist David wrote, "God is near to the broken-hearted, and saves the crushed in spirit" (Ps 34:18). In Psalm 147:3, the psalmist confirmed, "He heals the brokenhearted and binds up their wounds." When Jesus quoted Isaiah 61:1-2, he announced,

> The Spirit of the Lord is upon me,
> because he has anointed me
> to bring good news to the poor.
> He has sent me to proclaim release to the captives
> and recovery of sight to the blind,
> to let the oppressed go free. (Lk 4:18-19)

Jesus brought freedom and healing to those in deep pain and shame, including the woman caught in adultery (Jn 8:3-11), the woman with the issue of blood (Lk 8:43-48) and the ten lepers who were physically and emotionally precluded from participation in their community (Lk 17:11-19).

Emotional pain demands our attention. C. S. Lewis observed, "God whispers to us in our pleasures, speaks in our conscience, but shouts in our pain: it is His megaphone to rouse a deaf world."[49] Likewise, Lewis dismantles the faulty notion that those who suffer are bad people. The faulty logic asserts that if God were good and all-powerful, and I am good, then I should be happy. If I am unhappy, then God lacks goodness and power, and God does not love me. This punishment-retribution thinking is often at the root of the struggle in understanding why we experience pain and suffering, as Gustavo Gutiérrez addresses in his examination of the life of Job.[50] Gutiérrez asks how a good and loving God can allow such wounding among those whom Jesus so champions, including the poor, innocent and destitute, and resolves the paradox by pointing to the communion with Jesus in suffering and in hope, as reflected in the message of the cross.[51] The healing of emotional wounds unlocks inner freedom through reception of God's grace to forgive, even in the worst of situations, similar to Joseph's experience. Thus, forgiveness by grace is the essential doorway for healing emotional wounds. There is no other access road leading to true freedom in Christ.

The Grace to Forgive

On October 2, 2006, in an Amish community in Lancaster County, Pennsylvania, Charles Carl Roberts IV, a milk delivery man, entered West Nichol Mines Amish Schoolhouse with the intent to kill the innocent girls in the school, whereas the boys and adult women were released. Providentially, the sister of one of the boys was able to follow her brother out of the building. As hostages, the ten girls, ages six to thirteen, were shot at point-blank range. Five of them died. What superseded the horrendous violence of such innocents was the magnitude of the grace extended by the relatives and members of the Amish community toward the perpetrator and his family. In one interview, the grandfather of two sisters who died was asked how it was possible that he could forgive the murderer. Without hesitation, the grandfather soberly replied, "Through God's help."[52] In an Anabaptist culture deeply embedded in faith, this grandfather relinquished his right for vengeance. For the Amish, forgiveness is neither calculated nor random, but rather a way of life.[53] Forgiveness results from "sharing in divine grace."[54]

Miroslav Volf recalls lecturing in 1993 on exclusion, forgiveness and embrace, heard by renowned German theologian Jürgen Moltmann. From 1992–1995, the Bosnian War, resulting from the breakup of Yugoslavia, led to 100,000 deaths and 2.2 million people being displaced. With Orthodox Serbian forces bitterly fighting against Muslim Bosnians and Catholic Croats, rampant rape, ethnic cleansing and genocide resulted, with the Siege of

Sarajevo and the Srebrenica massacre becoming emblems of the conflict. After Volf's lecture, Moltmann asked Volf this penetrating question: "But can you embrace a četnik?"[55] *(The word* četnik *refers to a Serbian nationalist who was murdering Volf's people.) After just speaking about embracing one's enemies, Volf wrestled with the inner tension between the outrage of inhumanity to his own people and his role as a follower of Christ. He replied, "No, I cannot—but as a follower of Christ I think I should be able to."*[56] *So deep was the inner struggle within Volf that he engaged in soul-searching while wrestling through his response to Moltmann's inquiry. Volf's inability to forgive became the hammer that moved the anvil of his theology from his head to his heart.*[57]

Forgiveness is the most unnatural response to wrongdoing. Our fleshly human nature rejects, refutes and retaliates against those who incur threat or harm, while demanding that justice prevail. Retaliatory anger and vehemence tag-team between simmer and boil, by desiring to get even or get ahead, and can be internalized to the point of physical debilitation.[58] As an automatic indicator, however, anger signals a grievance or disappointment and beckons our attention before the pot explodes. If unattended, anger becomes like an aggressive cancer, monopolizing thoughts, eroding relationships and plotting vengeance. Such anger lodged in Jezebel's threats against Elijah (1 Kings 19:2), Saul's psychotic fixation on David's demise (1 Sam 18:8-11; 19:1) and Haman's rage against Mordecai (Esther 5:9-14). Nevertheless, anger need not be destructive. Coming to terms with feeling angry and acting in anger are a part of the emotional formation process. When honestly acknowledged and understood, anger and other seemingly negative emotions no longer become outlaws but rather helpful motivators for positive resolve.[59] Paying attention to angry feelings "counters the impulse to respond too quickly" and allows time to discern the appropriate and God-honoring response.[60]

Two contemporary illustrations demonstrate how anger, appropriately directed, can result in positive outcomes, regardless of one's faith conviction. First, Victor Villaseñor, a Mexican American author and Pulitzer Prize nominee who was raised in California, twice failed the third grade. Unable to read because of dyslexia, Villaseñor stewed with anger and resentment over the abuse Mexican children received for enforced "English only" mandates and other inequities. Positively channeling his anger by "writing it out," telling stories of his Mexican family and Mexican American experiences, Villaseñor became a leading author of Chicano literature.[61] His mantra "The opposite of depression is expression" eventuated into nine books and sixty-five short stories, notwithstanding 265 publisher rejections.[62] Anger against injustice produced positive expression.

Second, Mukhtar Mai, a Pakistani woman from a peasant family in southern Punjab, experienced gang rape after village council leaders decided to punish her family for unsubstantiated allegations brought against her fourteen-year-old brother.[63] As cultural consequence, such a victim would usually kill herself to ameliorate humiliation and shame. Instead thirty-year-old Mukhtar dared to report the incident to police. After one local town leader came to her defense, this injustice caught the attention of then–Pakistani president Pervez Musharraf, who provided her compensation for the crime. Mukhtar took this $8,300 and invested it in developing a school for girls in her village. Her anger and shame at the hands of her violators distilled into a national movement for girls' education and women's welfare that attracted worldwide attention. The benefits of dealing with anger appropriately are visible on all sides of the religious divide. For a follower of Jesus, Paul's exhortation is instructive: "Be angry but do not sin; do not let the sun go down on your anger, and do not make room for the devil" (Eph 4:26-27). Unresolved anger creates an access point for the enemy to exploit natural feelings. That is why Paul directs prompt action to resolve conflict. Forgiveness begins the process.

Forgiving others, as well as ourselves, not only gives God access to our hearts but also hastens God's sovereign intervention in others' lives. As long as we harbor bitter feelings against our enemies, God's hands are tied. However, if we refuse to avenge ourselves and instead bless our enemies, we surrender control to God to judge rightly (Rom 12:19-20). This is what the

Amish grandfather chose to do in the murder of his granddaughters and what Martin Luther King Jr. exemplified during the civil rights movement.[64]

Scripture offers insights into the forgiveness process. When we forgive others, God forgives us (Mt 6:14). When Peter asked Jesus how many times he should forgive his sinful brother, Jesus replied that he should forgive him seventy-seven times (Mt 18:22). In other words, keep on forgiving without keeping track. The follow-up parable tells of the actions of the unmerciful servant, who gladly received the king's merciful debt cancellation but refused to extend mercy to his fellow servant who owed him money, causing the king to reverse his benevolent decision (Mt 18:23-34). Thus, Jesus acknowledges, "This is how my heavenly Father will treat each of you unless you forgive your brother or sister from your heart" (Mt 18:35 NIV). The apostle Paul likewise had practice in both forgiving and inviting others to forgive. Paul eventually forgave John Mark, who deserted him and Barnabas early in their ministry (Acts 13:13) and called for Mark to join him at the end of his life (2 Tim 4:11). Paul appealed to Philemon to receive back Onesimus, a slave who had run away, presumably because of an unspecified offense. Paul also appealed to Euodia and Syntyche and the entire Philippian church to mend their disagreement (Phil 4:2-3). Forgiving others is the doorway to freedom in Christ and further opens the door to emotional formation.

Another vital area of forgiveness is forgiving oneself, which is often the most difficult transaction of all. With the knowledge of what we have done to dishonor and damage ourselves, God or others, we may sink into utter despair. When Peter realized that he had denied Jesus three times, he broke down and wept in agony (Mk 14:72) and returned to fishing (Jn 21:3). Peter had to come to the place where he forgave himself. Forgiveness was complete when Jesus later restored and commissioned Peter into his future ministry (Jn 21:15-19).

To ask forgiveness requires the humbling of oneself before God and others and admitting imperfections, shortcomings, misunderstandings and sin. Since God's nature is to forgive, God invites us to receive enabling grace as we are conformed in our emotions into Jesus' perfect image and reflect God's glory (Ps 86:5; 103:3; Mic 7:18; 1 Jn 1:9). As someone once said, we are most like God when we forgive. Jesus' words on the cross, "Father, forgive them; for they do not know what they are doing" (Lk 23:34) epitomize the grace to forgive as the ultimate response to betrayal. Jesus could forgive not only because it was in his nature to do so but also because Jesus knew that the Father loved him and that even in his darkest hour he could trust the Father in order to complete his earthly mission. Through the ultimate betrayal of life, Jesus serves as our model: we too can forgive. Forgiveness does not mean forgetting but rather surrendering our wounds to God so that the healing process can begin. As ministry leaders Chester Kylstra and Betsy Kylstra acknowledge, forgiveness does not equal healing. After releasing an offender, "all pain does not automatically leave one's heart."[65] Healing is a process. Freedom in Christ is the hopeful outcome.

Freedom in Christ

Suppose a small child involved in an accident sustained an injury to her arm. Over time, the rest of her body grew, with the exception of the injured arm. In adulthood, having an adult-sized body and a child-sized arm would be unusual, at best. Similarly, life circumstances may inflict such emotional pain that one area of the emotions shuts down, becomes stuck or is growth resistant. Unless there is healing intervention, these emotional wounds can become permanent fixtures that affect all formation dimensions. Many in the body of Christ have experienced deep emotional wounding, unforgiveness and bondage that preclude living the abundant life that Christ intended for us (Jn 10:10) and also loving the way Christ intended (1 Jn 3:18).

In order to gain true freedom in Christ, we need the supernatural power of the Holy Spirit to heal emotional wounds, including those that might be self-induced. We simply cannot heal ourselves. How, then, should we proceed? First, we need to acknowledge that we cannot heal ourselves and that we need God's grace and the help of others. We must believe the truth about what God believes about us, rather than the deceitful lies of the enemy that bring condemnation and keep us in darkness. Although Satan prowls around like a roaring lion seeking whom he might devour (1 Pet 5:8), we can be assured that God is for us (Rom 8:31) and that "there is therefore now no condemnation for those in Christ Jesus" (Rom 8:1). God has provided powerful spiritual weapons for pulling down strongholds (2 Cor 10:4), which we are to apprehend in the healing process. Through the Scriptures we learn that there is neither sin nor bondage that Jesus cannot heal (Ex 15:26), as God forgives all our iniquities when we genuinely repent and is able to heal all our diseases (Ps 103:3).

Second, we need to understand that healing cannot occur in a relational vacuum. We need to invite others, such as a trusted Christian leader, counselor or spiritual friend, to walk with us through the healing process. The loving support of others provides the cushion necessary to make the journey inward and the necessary objectivity to entertain key questions that unlock emotional gridlock. It is precisely this loving connectivity and community that Larry Crabb views as the essential and often-missing ingredient to wholeness.[66] For certain emotional issues, a close friend provides the needed support for the healing process to progress. However, in other cases the help of a trained Christian psychologist or spiritual director is necessary to address more complex issues.

Third, we need to receive God's grace in a posture of humility to embrace healing. Pride, arrogance and independence are obstacles to personal healing. For example, Naaman, commander of the king of Aram's army, was reluctant to follow Elisha's directive to dip seven times in the Jordan River to heal leprosy (2 Kings 5:1-15). Although leprosy is a physical issue rather than an emotional one, the general principle applies. Openness to receive is what activates God's grace: "God opposes the proud, but gives grace to the humble" (Jas 4:6).

Fourth, we need to be open to the Holy Spirit's guidance in the emotional healing process, giving God not only permission to work within us but also time to bring about the desired changes. Change does not occur overnight.[67] When surrendered to God, however, the healing process has a timetable of its own. To illustrate, some years ago a divorced woman new to our church participated in a small group. Initially, she appeared caustic, defensive and fiercely independent. Without knowing her background I sensed that she had been deeply wounded and made a concerted effort to walk alongside her throughout that year. We met outside the small group and eventually became friends. Over time, she began to open up, release her emotional defenses and share about the pain of a failed marriage and the strains of single parenthood. The bravado and self-assertion that she exhibited earlier gradually morphed into a newfound freedom and joy in Christ. Within the context of loving support and trust, healing can occur over time.

Fifth, we need to be committed to a healing approach that is completely consonant with Scripture. As the repository for all truth, the Bible is our primary resource for healing and not only provides principles for how to navigate the healing process but also offers precious promises so that we "may become participants of the divine nature" (2 Pet 1:4). Several streams of Christ-centered healing have developed over the past few decades. What they have in common is their emphasis on forgiveness as the essential doorway and the Holy Spirit as the conduit of healing.

A nonexhaustive and brief overview of selected healing approaches is offered here. In the twentieth century Swiss physician Paul Tournier (1898–1986) drew attention to the interconnectedness between the spiritual, emotional and physical life dimensions and turned his medical practice into one that focused on counseling the whole person.[68] Tournier's work influenced subsequent approaches to emotional healing. Leanne Payne's healing approach employs listening prayer through inviting the presence of the Holy Spirit into the healing context. Her books, conferences and training have enjoyed popularity, and her work focusing on gender identity issues has offered those struggling with same-sex attraction and homosexuality a safe place to address issues of sexual brokenness.[69] Payne's work paved the way for other ministries to the sexually broken.

Francis MacNutt and Judith MacNutt, founders and directors of Christian Healing Ministries, have also influenced the body of Christ through their healing ministry. Predicated on the premise that wholeness is holiness, their ministry focuses not only on emotional healing but also on physical healing. Francis has contributed substantively to the Christian literature on healing.[70] Another contributing voice is that of Neil Anderson, who emphasizes encounter with God's truth to establish personal identity in Christ and to overcome the powers of darkness that create personal bondages. His books have found their way into many church, Bible school and seminary curricula, and provide a process for working through steps to freedom in Christ on an individual or group basis.[71]

Chester and Betsy Kylstra, founders of Proclaiming His Word Ministries and the Healing House Network, advance an integrated healing approach called Restoring the Foundations (RTF). RTF addresses four problem areas: (1) sins of the fathers and resulting curses, focusing on how the sin of previous generations impact one's life; (2) ungodly beliefs, the untruths or half-truths that keep us bound; (3) soul/spirit hurts, the spiritual and emotional wounds that need to be released; and (4) demonic oppression, the direct influence of Satan to cause us to sin and to keep us bound in limitations. The Kylstras' goal is to contribute to the restoration of the biblical foundations of the individual, the local church and the church universal.[72] Another influential voice in the ministry of emotional healing is Christian psychologist Henry Cloud, whose books offer easily accessible resources for change.[73]

Regardless of the healing approach the single most important element for the healing process to occur is a loving and prayerful context supported by faith in God. Francis MacNutt comments, "Whatever else we do, it is absolutely essential that in praying for healing, we establish an atmosphere of faith and love. When love is present, I have never seen a person hurt in any way by the healing ministry."[74] To illustrate, MacNutt notes the loving and positive presence of Agnes Sanford that characterized her healing ministry.[75]

Overall, the dynamics of emotional formation remind us that we all walk with a limp and deal with a full range of emotional responses. By being students of our emotions, we can discern our emotional barometer, embrace emotions as friends and learn how to constructively deal with negative emotions. This chapter provided a brief background related to emotional formation, reviewed the emotions of Jesus as the prism for viewing emotional formation, and discussed the influence of childhood and attachment upon emotional development. Further, the chapter addressed the inevitability of emotional wounding and the power of forgiveness for healing and gaining freedom in Christ by highlighting various healing approaches. Chapter six addresses relational formation and how social interaction contributes to the process of being conformed to the *imago Dei*, through the *imago Christi*, in order to love God and others for the *gloria Dei*.

6

Relationships

Our Social Connectedness

Only in the fellowship do we learn to be rightly alone
and only in aloneness do we learn to live rightly in the fellowship.

Dietrich Bonhoeffer, *Life Together*

Allow me to introduce you to Max De Pree, the former chairman and CEO of Herman Miller, Inc., an exemplary furniture business. As an unapologetic Christian believer, De Pree incorporated biblical principles into the company's core values and business practices, fostering trust and integrity that not only resulted in profitability but also in world recognition. In one of De Pree's well-received books on leadership, he poignantly recalls the premature birth of his granddaughter, Zoe.[1]

At birth, Zoe weighed one pound, seven ounces, so small that De Pree's wedding ring could easily slip up her entire arm. Zoe was not expected to live beyond three days. Adding to the distress, Zoe's father had abandoned the family one month prior, leaving De Pree and his wife in a uniquely supportive position. Monitors, IVs and breathing and feeding tubes provided Zoe with life-sustaining connections. However, realizing the importance of relational bonding, a wise neonatal nurse advised De Pree to visit Zoe every day and to gently stroke her arms and legs with the tip of his finger. Understanding the importance of De Pree's role as a surrogate father, the nurse added, "While you are caressing her, you should tell her over and over how much you love her, because she has to be able to connect your voice to your touch."[2] This vivid illustration demonstrates how loving relationships from the onset of life contribute to overall life flourishing.[3] Relational formation involves recognizing the voice and actions of a loving God and others while navigating disappointments when human connections are damaged.

In chapter four we looked at spiritual formation and in chapter five emotional formation; in this chapter we recognize that growth in these formational dimensions occurs within the context of human relationships. By observing, interacting with and imitating others, we learn about God through relationships that intertwine with spiritual, emotional and intellectual holistic dimensions. Thus, relational formation is the glue that binds together our formation in Christ.

In the Scriptures we observe the relational dimension within the Holy Trinity, whereby the Father, Son and Holy Spirit relate intimately. Each divine member is interdependent—they are eternally involved in mutual giving and receiving. For example, Jesus announced the unity between himself and the Father as being one (Jn 10:38; 14:10-11; 17:21), and the Spirit was sent by the Father in Jesus' name (Jn 14:26). Stanley Grenz suggests, "God is best viewed as the social Trinity."[4] Hence, human relationality reflects the relationality of the Trinity.[5]

Whereas God is relational and models community as Father, Son and Holy Spirit, we who have been created in the *imago Dei* likewise reflect God's inherent relational nature. Jack O. Balswick and his colleagues affirm, "To bear the image of God is to live in reciprocating relationships with God and our fellow human beings."[6] Colin Gunton asserts, "To be human is to be created in and for relationship with divine and human others," which is at the very core of human identity.[7] Tom Smail similarly states, "As human beings made in the image of God, we are so fashioned that in our relationships with other people, we also initiate, respond, and fulfil, and so mirror the distinctive functioning of the divine persons. In that way *imago Dei* is, indeed, *imago Trinitatis*."[8] Being created in the image of God, believers are called into a relational community (1 Cor 12:13).

Catherine Mowry LaCugna refers to the trinitarian imprint in our lived faith experience: "The truth about both God and ourselves is that we were meant to exist as persons in communion in a common household, living as persons from and for others, not persons in isolation, or withdrawal, or self-centeredness."[9] Relational formation is integral within human experience. Our relationships with God and others define our personhood and identity forged by the Spirit. As Grenz avers, "Personhood, then, is bound up with relationality, and the fullness of relationality lies ultimately in relationship with the triune God. Creating this relational fullness is the work of the Spirit, who places humans 'in Christ' and thereby effects human participation in the dynamic of the divine life."[10]

As featured in figure 6.1, relational formation is the focus of this chapter. Examining how the Spirit fashions us through relationships, this chapter addresses social interactions that contribute to the process of being conformed to Jesus, the perfect *imago Dei*, in order to reciprocally love God and others through obedience as reflected in ethical living. This chapter begins by addressing the starting place of relational formation, the family, and moves to a discussion of finding safety and acceptance through trust, dealing with the inevitability of interpersonal conflict, recognizing the cry for community, and the role of the church as the family of God, as well as the influence of culture. As Max De Pree illustrated, connecting the voice to the touch in loving relationships beginning with the family contributes to life flourishing.

THE FAMILY

God's plan for humanity unfolded with Adam and Eve responding to God's directive to "be fruitful and multiply, and fill the earth and subdue it" (Gen 1:28). Composed of husband, wife and then children, this first family became a prototype for future family relationships. God's intention was clear. The family was to be an incubator of godly love and the primary conduit for Christian formation. As Ray Anderson and Dennis Guernsey highlight, love

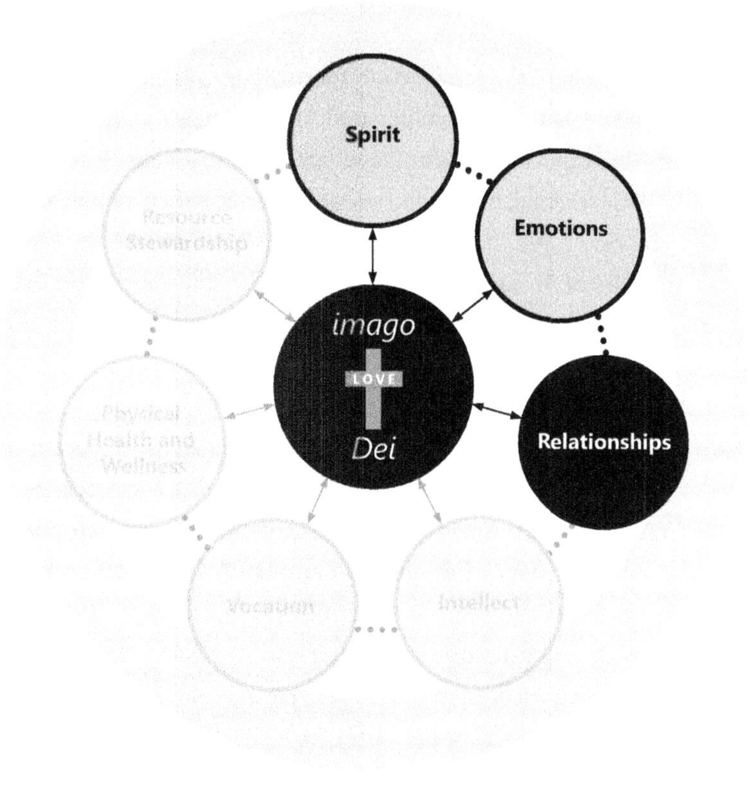

Figure 6.1. Relational formation

is rooted in God's own being as "the quintessential structure of relationship," which we see through covenantal relationships in the Old and New Testaments.[11] The divine purpose of the family generating from the very love of God contributes to its members being shaped into the image and likeness of God.[12]

Historically, the family has been the irreplaceable foundation for human development, as well as societal stability. Lisa Sowle Cahill observes that the family "has a basic and constitutive relation to biological relationship including reproductive partnership to produce the next generation, for which other relations, however valid, are analogues, not replacements."[13] Traditionally, the family, including positive interaction with parents or caregivers, provides the critical context for children's developing sense of self, including emotional and social competence.[14] Thus, Pitirim Sorokin's timeless words continue to ring true: "The family continuously controls and 'sculptures' its members by precept and example, persuasion and suggestion, constraint and punishment, and especially by abundant love in good families. It molds decisively most of the mental, moral, and social characteristics of personality."[15]

In the Hebrew Bible, the priority of family is magnified through the painful infertility of Abram and Sarai (Gen 15); the subsequent test of faith in offering their only son, Isaac, on the altar (Gen 22); the drama of Joseph providing for seventy members of his family as the nascent nation of Israel (Gen 46); Israel's continued emergence as a nation under Moses (Exodus); the story of Hannah's cry for a son (1 Sam 1); and the continuation of Israel's destiny through the line of David. Underscoring these stories, monogamous marriage between a man and a woman in fidelity emphasizes the fundamental element of the biblical family prototype around which children are to be raised (Eph 5:22-23; 6:1-4). In addition, the book of Proverbs provides instruction on training and discipling children in the appropriate fear and wisdom of the Lord (Prov 1:7), so they walk in God's ways (Prov 3:11-12; 13:24; 23:13-14; 29:15).

In the New Testament, the priority of family is magnified through Jesus' birth, as the Son of God, into a human family. Jesus obeyed his earthly parents (Lk 2:51), nurtured his calling (Lk 2:49), experienced misunderstanding from family members (Mk 3:21) and prioritized his relationship with the Father (Mt 14:23). Jesus' highest regard for marriage (e.g., "what God has joined together, let no man separate" [Mt 19:6]) and his esteem of children (e.g., "let the little children come unto me" [Mk 10:14]) affirm their supreme importance.

Additional biblical perspective flows through Paul's teaching on marriage, family, singleness and children. Paul elevates love as the zenith of godly living (Eph 5:1), evidenced in the marriage relationship (Eph 5:22-33), which he calls a great "mystery" (Eph 5:32), while upholding singleness (1 Cor 7:7, 32-35, 38). As Richard Hays observes, marriage is "a permanently binding commitment in which man and woman become one," designed to reflect the love and faithfulness of God and God's love for the church (Rev

21:2; 22:17).[16] Monogamous marriage between a man and woman is the prescribed foundation for the bearing and the raising of children, who are gifts to be cherished.[17] Hence, Christian discipleship should ideally begin in the home, where loving parents nurture their children in obedience (Eph 6:1-3) as training for obedience to God.

Building on Anderson and Guernsey's view of the family as providing love, order, stability and a place of belonging through the metaphor of covenant, Jack and Judith Balswick present a theological model for family relationships comprising (1) *commitment* based on covenant love, (2) *grace* based on acceptance and forgiveness, (3) *empowerment* of family members based on mutual support rather than control, and (4) *intimacy* based on caring, understanding, communication and communion.[18] They reinforce marriage as a covenant based on commitment as opposed to a contract that can easily be revoked. While accepting the uniqueness and differences of each family member as the ideal, the Balswicks submit that all family members move on a continuum between hurting and healing behaviors. If family members embrace healing, the family will grow. If they favor hurtful responses, the family's growth will be stymied. With trust as the basis for a nurturing environment, family members can be themselves and grow through mutual support. Without trust, family members self-protect, hide and barely survive.

Around the globe, opposing spiritual, social, cultural, economic and political forces bombard the family, causing increasing fragmentation, such that the family's cohesiveness and moral significance have plummeted.[19] In accounting for this phenomenon Stanley Hauerwas maintains, "The family has been broken because it has to carry too great a moral load."[20] Hauerwas observes that other institutions, such as local communities and churches, that once helped families stay together no longer functionally support them. While this assertion regarding the lack of appropriate accountability for the family may be true, the causes of family fragmentation are complex at best. Whereas families used to be a haven, they tragically have become the epicenter of marital and child discord, neglect and abuse through internal and external pressures involving financial strain, infidelity, abandonment, fatherlessness and violence.

As mentioned in chapter three, fatherlessness has been shown to be one factor contributing to family fracture. Addressing fatherlessness, sociologist David Blankenhorn argues, "More than any other cultural invention, fatherhood guides men away from violence by fastening their behavior to a fundamental social purpose. By enjoining men to care for their children and for the mothers of their children, the fatherhood story is society's most important contrivance for shaping male identity."[21] Although Mary Stewart Van Leeuwen notes that masculinity has been culturally under siege, Stephen G. Post argues that fatherlessness cannot be solved "until men and women achieve harmony based on equality and intimacy."[22] Regardless of cultural and sociological factors, the unfortunate reality is that the home all too often becomes a place of parental violence, violation and abandonment.

The foundation of the healthy home comprises both mother and father in loving marital relationship with each other and their children. However, even Christian families are susceptible to uncontrollable circumstances that refashion the family unit through marital separation, divorce, death, disability, health crises and any number of other mitigating circumstances. Whereas contemporary family constellations may blur this biblical ideal, neither should they be viewed as unredeemable, as Pamela Couture notes.[23] The Scriptures indicate that God uses even the most atypical family constellations to fashion us into the image of God, such as Moses living in the home of Pharaoh's daughter, Samuel growing up under Eli's supervision, and Esther being raised by her older first cousin Mordecai. God redemptively uses our family experiences to teach us about healthy and unhealthy relationships, and shapes us into the image of Jesus in order to find safety and acceptance through trust.

Finding Safety and Acceptance

Human beings have an inherent need to find safety and acceptance through relational attachment. In chapter five we saw how human attachments beginning in infancy through childhood and adulthood have a profound influence on all formation dimensions. The nuclear family or family substitute ordinarily comprises the very first social unit whereby early attachments become positively established and nurtured, or conversely, where they become dysfunctional or nonexistent.[24] Although the inner desire for acceptance and belonging is a lifelong pursuit, its genesis begins in infancy and early childhood. Sadly, finding acceptance and safety within the nuclear family is not everyone's experience, as Lisa Olson's life story conveys.

Born in Manipal, India, around September 8, 1974, Lisa remains uncertain as to the exact date of her birth. As Lisa tells her story, it is presumed that her birth parents had several children and were very poor.[25] Born without arms or legs, Lisa was abandoned at the Kasturba Medical College Hospital in Manipal. Overwhelmed by the severity of her disability, the head of pediatrics suggested to other consulting medical personnel that Lisa be euthanized by diminishing her food intake over time, such that she would become susceptible to infection and eventually die.

On moral grounds, however, the only Christian doctor among the many Hindu physicians protested and arranged for Lisa to be transferred to the Ramabai Mukti Mission in Kedgaon, outside Pune, first established by Pandita Ramabai.[26] Lisa remained there until age five and a half. With the severity of Lisa's disability, it appeared unlikely that she would be adopted. However, Marie Olson, the director of Hope Town Christian School, a year-round residential school for disabled children in Carmel, New York, learned of Lisa's plight and determined to adopt her. At fifty-one and single, Marie adopted and raised Lisa in the Christian faith, supporting her through adulthood. Eventually Lisa earned a bachelor's and a master's degree and now works as a vital staff member at a Christian university. She credits Marie's faith and care for her well-being and success.[27] Lisa's story bespeaks the need for family nurture and the benefits of finding safety and acceptance within a loving home.

One of the most basic human needs is that of belonging within the context of relationship. Positive interpersonal exchange provides the framework for belonging needs to be met, which nurtures personal identity, self-esteem, affiliation, a sense of competence, and intimacy.[28] In contrast, isolation negatively affects spiritual, emotional, mental and physical health.

For example, a Mayo Clinic report concludes, "Taking the time to build a social support network is a wise investment not only in your mental well-being but also in your physical health and longevity. Research shows that those who enjoy high levels of social support stay healthier and live longer."[29] Not only do supportive relationships deter mental health problems but they also deter physical diseases, further evidence that the seven God-given dimensions holistically interrelate.[30] For example, those lacking positive attachments to others experience increased risk for fatal heart attacks, cancer and other diseases.

When legitimate belonging needs are not met in positive ways, any number of negative results might occur. Jack Balswick and J. Kenneth Moreland contend, "The breakdown of primary groups is one of the root causes of such social ills, such as juvenile delinquency, adult crime, racial discrimination, alienation, substance abuse, poverty, and neglect of the elderly."[31] As they suggest, healthy and unhealthy relationships not only deeply affect personal holistic formation dimensions but also broader societal issues.[32] Individuals cannot be fully understood until the groups they participate in are known—be they family, friendship or work groups. We truly are known by the company we keep. Some groups we find ourselves in reflect the providential plan of God, as in the case of Ruth and Naomi.

The biblical account of Ruth and Naomi exemplifies the power of healthy relational attachment characterized by safety, acceptance and trust (Ruth 1:16-17). When Ruth was confronted with the decision to remain with or leave her mother-in-law, she insisted on remaining with Naomi, which expressed the depth of her affection, affiliation and friendship.[33] Ruth was willing to relinquish future security in order to ensure Naomi's welfare. Ruth's social identity, linked with this Israelite family, overshadowed her commitment to her Moabite culture.[34]

Next to family, friendship characterizes the most basic of human relationships. According to David Benner, spiritual friendship involves "the gift of hospitality, presence and dialogue."[35] As Elisabeth Moltmann-Wendel suggests, friendship is "helpful, necessary, and enriching" and "breaks through barriers of class, race, and gender."[36] Friendships provide valuable resources for socialization, including trying on new roles and garnering valuable feedback and support.[37] In his study of over 650 married couples, leading marriage researcher John Gottman found that when couples have a strong friendship, they are more likely to successfully respond to each other's repair attempts during conflict.[38] What determines the success of the couple's repair attempts and marriage directly corresponds to the strength of their friendship. Friendship is a married couple's secret weapon.

Friendship connects people in a bond of love and trust where mutual affirmation, encouragement, self-giving and sharing fuel individual and shared identity, a sense of belonging and the exchange of privileged information. For example, Jesus was a friend of tax collectors and sinners because he associated with them. At the same time, Jesus called his disciples "friends," revealing the deepest parts of himself, offering emotional support and sharing with them privileged information from the Father. Jesus stated, "I do not call you servants any longer, because the servant does not know what the master is doing; but I have called you friends, because I have made known to you everything that I have heard from my Father" (Jn 15:15).

Writing on friendship throughout Christian history, Liz Carmichael views Christ's love expressed on the cross, where God offered forgiveness and reconciliation to all, as the ultimate model of friendship.[39] She agrees with Jürgen Moltmann's proposal that to the three traditional titles for Jesus (i.e., prophet, priest and king) should be added a fourth—friend.[40] Friendship not only suggests unity, equality and reciprocity, but also willing obligation and hospitality.[41] Jesus' example of the individual who goes to his friend at midnight to ask for three loaves of bread on behalf of an unexpected house guest illustrates this point (Lk 11:5-8). Even in the night hour, hospitality and friendship were obliged. Authentic Christian friendship provides emotional acceptance and safety without judgment.

Other examples of the life-transforming power of friendship include the sacrificial friendship of Jonathan and David as steadfast confidants (1 Sam 20; 2 Sam 1:17-27). Their friendship typifies John Fitzgerald's assertion: "Friends are important in times of prosperity, for they sweeten life and make it more pleasant. Yet they are crucial in times of adversity."[42] More contemporary examples include the friendship of J. R. R. Tolkien (1892–1973) and C. S. Lewis (1898–1963). Despite their differences in personality, spiritual expression and literary style, Tolkien and Lewis mutually encouraged each other's literary prowess (e.g., Tolkien's Middle Earth and Lewis's Narnia), which contributed to the longevity of their friendship and the Inklings, the literary club they established.[43] Tolkien and Lewis's friendship opened the door for hospitality and made room for others. Additionally, the friendship of Elizabeth Cady Stanton (1815–1902) and Susan B. Anthony (1820–1906) not only strengthened the nineteenth-century women's rights and suffrage movements but also bonded these two inseparable advocates.[44]

Without friends, people become lonely, isolated and are more likely to contemplate and commit suicide.[45] Having at least one close friend may make the difference not only between life and death but also job satisfaction and overall well-being.[46] "Without friends, it is very difficult for us to get by, let alone thrive."[47] Although friendships, family relationships and work associations might provide safety and acceptance, they are not without interpersonal conflict, which is normal even within the closest of relationships. How we handle these conflicts reveals our character and further shapes us.

Conflict Inevitability

To be human is to experience conflict. Relational conflict results when the desires, motivations, preferences, priorities, attitudes, actions or decisions of two or more people clash, creating a lack of agreement, misunderstanding and, in some cases, irreconcilable differences. Such was the case with Paul and Barnabas, who began as solid ministry partners and ended up disassociating from each other because of contention over John Mark, their ministry helper and Barnabas's cousin (Col 4:10). After John Mark had deserted them in Pamphylia, Paul refused to give John Mark a second chance, much to Barnabas's dismay. "The disagreement became so sharp that they parted company; Barnabas took Mark with him and sailed away to Cyprus" (Acts 15:39). Few would doubt the sincerity and loyalty to Christ of either Paul or John. However, despite relational fallout, the purposes of God continued. Fortunately, later in his ministry, Paul validated John Mark as "useful in my ministry" (2 Tim 4:11). Yet we never learn whether Paul and Barnabas reconciled.

The rivalry between Cain and Abel provides another biblical example of conflict (Gen 4). Conflict begins as envy and then turns to anger, which Cornelius Plantinga Jr. calls "passionate againstness" and Miroslav Volf suggests "was the first link in a chain of exclusions."[48] Anger in rivalry then turns to exclusion. Volf notes, "From the outset, all human relations are fraught with tension between equality and difference in the context of which the relation between the self and the other has to be negotiated. Outside the Garden of Eden rivalry sets in, which drives the protagonist even farther 'east of Eden,'" a metaphor for human conflict.[49]

Conflict involves an unresolved problem between people.[50] James noted the cause of fights and quarrels: "Do they not come from your cravings that are at war within you? You want something and do not have it. . . . And you covet something and cannot obtain it; so you engage in disputes and conflicts" (Jas 4:1-2). When we feel slighted, ignored, mistreated or opposed, we develop defenses to protect ourselves and form judgments against others, which contribute to further relational rift. In writing to Philemon, Paul tried to reconcile the relational rift between Philemon and Onesimus (Philem 10-11), presumably resulting from a wrong or offense between them.[51] Conflict can also develop because of standing for truth and righteousness. Thus, righteous indignation based on love can motivate us to uphold godliness, justice, fairness and equality, as demonstrated when Jesus overturned the money changers' tables in the temple (Jn 2:12-16). As Martin Luther King Jr. exhorts, "[Humankind] must evolve for all human conflict a method which rejects revenge, aggression, and retaliation. The foundation of such a method is love."[52]

As a chief contributor to conflict, anger need not be negative and destructive, as Gary Chapman suggests. Learning how to deal with anger and conflict is a sign of maturity and can bring glory to God when handled appropriately.[53] The conflict resolution of the Council of Jerusalem mediated by Peter and James provides an anatomy of constructive group conflict resolution within the early church (Acts 15:1-35). Disagreement between Paul and Barnabas with the Jerusalem apostles and elders over requiring circumcision for Gentile believers resulted in the upholding of essential and agreed-upon moral practices without the strictures of the Mosaic law. In this case, conflict was beneficial, in that the innovative solution offered by James removed an obstacle for Kingdom expansion. Understanding conflict responses proves helpful.

Donald Palmer points out that causes of conflict relate to substantive issues concerning differences in values, beliefs, traditions, purposes, goals and leadership style, as well as emotional issues concerning lack of acceptance, recognition and appreciation, and unfair treatment.[54] Further, Palmer offers five conflict-management styles: (1) avoiding (You lose, I lose), (2) accommodating (You win, I lose), (3) collaborating (You win, I win), (4) compromising (We both win some and lose some), and (5) competing (I win, you lose).[55] Understanding one's own and others' conflict styles contributes to conflict resolution.

Ken Sande, founder of Peacemaker Ministries, identifies "the slippery slope of conflict" by proposing three basic conflict responses.[56] The first focuses on *escape* responses, which indicate conflict avoidance, such as denial, running away and the extreme act of suicide. In certain situations running away from conflict ensures appropriate physical and emotional safety. Tragically, suicide signals a complete loss of hope in resolving conflict, whether internal or external. The second conflict response is *attack*, where winning a conflict supersedes relationship preservation. Attack responses include assaults of verbal intimidation, slander, physical violence, court litigation and murder. People might move to the attack response when escape responses prove ineffective. Paul's warning that biting and devouring one another leads to destruction (Gal 5:15) applies here. The third conflict response, as in the case of the Jerusalem Council, is *peacemaking*. Peacemaking includes overlooking an offense, reconciliation and negotiation. When these three responses prove ineffective, "assisted peacemaking" may be needed, such as mediation, arbitration and accountability. Unfortunately, we have plenty of role models of the first two conflict response types and few for peacemaking. To manage conflict, Sande proposes, "Focusing on God is the key to resolving conflict constructively."[57] Those who oppose each other, however, may believe that God is on their side.

Sande provides a biblical pattern for resolving conflict by offering four principles: (1) aim to glorify God (How can I please and honor God in this conflict?), (2) remove the log from your own eye (How have I contributed to the conflict?), (3) gently restore others (How can I lovingly assist others to take responsibility for their part of the conflict?), and (4) be reconciled (How can I reflect the forgiveness of God and work toward reconciliation?).[58] Demonstrating the fruit of the Spirit (Gal 5:22-23) as we live by the Spirit sets the bar high for relational repair. When conflict rages on, the ultimate weapon is deliberate, focused love (Rom 12:20-21).[59] When tempted to react in the flesh, understanding one's own and others' conflict-management styles (Palmer's avoiding, accommodating, collaborating, compromising and competing) and conflict responses (Sande's escape, attack, peacemaking) proves helpful in seeking resolution.

Family life, whether one is single or married, provides an incubator for learning how to (or not to) resolve conflict, which in turn provides plentiful opportunities for being conformed into the image of Jesus. School playgrounds in childhood and roommate situations in young adulthood further provide such opportunities. A friend of mine once said, "I thought I was quite spiritual, until I got married." What my friend quickly learned is that marriage is not intended to make us happy but to make us holy. Similarly, Stanley Hauerwas debunks the myth that marriage is intended for self-fulfillment by noting that "we always marry the wrong person," meaning marriage does not eliminate conflict; rather husbands and wives have to work at it.[60] Gary Thomas contends that *everything* in marriage is designed to forge godly character and conform us into the image of God, including learning how to love and forgive others, respect and serve them, pray more earnestly, and build relational perseverance. Thomas further suggests, "Rather than seeing marriage as a cosmic competitor with heaven, we can embrace it as a school of faith."[61] Holding steady in times of conflict anchors us in the relationship, according to John O'Donohue.[62] The result of working through conflict in a healthy way can be termed conflict intimacy, referring to the relational resilience built through conflict resolution, if handled appropriately.[63]

How parents handle conflict through emotional responses provides shaping opportunities not only for themselves but also for their children.[64] For example, marriage researcher John Gottman examined the effects of marital discord on children.[65] Gottman found that parents clustered into one of two primary groups: (1) emotion-dismissing parents and (2) emotion-coaching parents. Emotion-dismissing parents try to protect their children from negative emotions and view negative emotions as destructive. Emotion-coaching parents see negative emotions as healthy, using them as opportunities for teaching and building intimacy. Being able to appropriately express emotion builds children's social competencies and fosters emotional intelligence.[66] Interpersonal conflict is an inevitable reality of life and one that enjoins emotional and social formation in conforming us into the image of Jesus. Through conflict, we learn about ourselves and come to appreciate the vital role of community, so crucial for relational formation.

Cry for Community and the Church

The cry for community daily confronts us in our families, friendships, churches, workplaces and news headlines. This cry manifests in the paradoxical proliferation of online social networking and the tragic rates of suicide. For example, as of October 4, 2012, Facebook, which launched in 2004, touted over one billion active users, 75 percent of whom live outside the United States, with 350 million accessing the site through mobile devices.[67] Launched in 2006, Twitter now boasts over 500 million users.[68] People want to stay connected! Conversely, suicide rates tell another story. In 2007, suicide was the third-leading cause of death for Americans ages fifteen to twenty-four and the seventh-leading cause of death for men of all ages. Over 90 percent of all suicides relate to depression or disorders connected to substance abuse.[69] Further, anxiety, hopelessness and withdrawal from friends and family serve as contributing factors.[70]

Despite various venues for human connections, loneliness has become a chronic condition. In 1982 when Mother Teresa visited the United States and spoke during a press conference at Thomas Aquinas College in California, she noted, "I think that loneliness and the feeling of being unwanted and unloved is a much greater sickness than cancer, leprosy, or TB."[71] In the West, a complex confluence of factors including individualism, economic pressures and greater mobility have resulted in the decline of social capital, according to sociologist Robert Bellah and associates.[72] Similarly, Robert Putnam awakened the American public to the fraying of traditional social bonds through the metaphor of "bowling alone," an activity traditionally done in community.[73] Paradoxically, the cry for community evidences in the dramatic emergence of self-help and small groups.[74]

What is community? Why is it so vital for our holistic growth? Community relates to the building of substantive relationships where individuals are known, accepted and embraced, and where they live in mutuality. Community forms when a group shares a common orientation, values and life goals; personally interacts; and agrees on what participation involves.[75] God's fashioning all persons to be in community is universal. However, Christian community revolves around relational formation within the body of Christ, the church, not only as the primary vehicle for God's purposes on the earth but also for transforming believers into the image of Christ.[76] In fact, God uses community as a "means of grace" to nurture faith, spirituality and moral practices within the Christian faith, in light of what Christian educator Craig Dykstra observes as social-cultural forces thwarting church communities.[77] Dykstra observes that social-cultural influences may be more powerful than the influence of faith communities, which themselves may reflect the world's values.

Simon Chan, however, emphasizes the vital role of the church in Christian formation. Rather than developing a better self-image for self-fulfillment, Christian formation concerns "developing certain qualities that enable us to live responsibly within the community that we have been baptized into," such that developing virtues reflect God's character.[78] Offering a fresh perspective of the church as a worshiping community, Chan explores the relationship between God and the church through the biblical metaphors of "the people of God," "the body of Christ" and "the temple of the Holy Spirit." He concedes that the church's role is more than "a sociological one of service provider catering to individual believers' spiritual needs"; rather it is a covenantal one with Christ as the head of the church (Eph 1:22).[79] Simply, the church is where two or three saints are gathered, with Jesus in the midst (Mt 18:20) and where the love of God reflecting the Trinity is manifest.[80] Moreover, the church is Christ's sacramental and eschatological community on the move toward the culmination of the ages, not only incorporating the traditional practices of baptism (i.e., celebrating identification with Christ) and the Lord's Supper (i.e., celebrating renewal of life) but also sharing in suffering, celebration and worship, solitude, and the life of the Spirit.[81]

The church serves as Christ's extension in the world (Eph 3:10) through the power of the Holy Spirit, who powerfully debuted at Pentecost (Acts 2:1-13). Nevertheless, the church carries a social identity, with the children of God separated from the world and called out of darkness and into God's light (1 Pet 2:9).[82] Hence, the church's role is to shine forth the "praise of his glory" (Eph 1:12), imitate Christ (Eph 5:1) and represent the loving, triune God as God's ambassadors in the world (2 Cor 5:20). As Christ embodied love for humanity on the cross, so we are to express this "cruciform love" within our community and the world.[83] Christian community, as Dietrich Bonhoeffer emphasizes, is "through and in Jesus Christ," based on what Christ has done for us.[84] Further, Bonhoeffer strips away all sentimentality related to authentic community by acknowledging the realities of relational disillusionment and crisis. Having lived among the seminary students he taught, Bonhoeffer exhorts believers to authentically love Christians rather than romanticize a perception of community.[85] Authentic Christian community embraces all people, regardless of attractiveness, similarity and compatibility.[86]

According to Joseph Hellerman, authentic Christian community comprises four values: (1) sharing our stuff, (2) sharing our hearts, (3) staying, embracing the pain and growing together, and (4) reaching out beyond the nuclear family.[87] The early church embodied these values (Acts 2:42-47; 4:32), both caring for one another but also eventually reaching out beyond its perimeter (Acts 8:1). With hospitality as an earmark of God's people,

Christian community should intentionally reach out to others through loving and listening well.[88] Henri Nouwen suggests that community must be a discipline "to create space for God among us," who "requires the constant recognition of the Spirit of God in each other."[89]

Being human involves more than basic functioning of eating and sleeping, but rather it depends on relational connectivity to reflect the transforming grace of God as we are shaped into God's image.[90] Similarly, Tom Smail contends, "In christological perspective, right relationships and the community they make possible are the measure of humanity; the state of our relationships show whether and how far we are imaging Jesus who is the image of God."[91] Likewise, Stanley Grenz affirms, "The image of God can only be expressed in human community."[92] In summary, God has hardwired us to walk through life together in family relationships and in the body of Christ, the church (Lat. *familia Dei*), in order to fashion us increasingly into the image of God through relational formation. Families and churches, however, are nested within respective cultures. The culture or cultures we live in also serve as a powerful instrument to conform us into the image of Jesus.

Culture as Formation

Culture comprises "human formation at its widest angle" and provides the backdrop for being transformed into the image of Christ.[93] The word *culture* derives from the Latin word *cultura,* a derivative of the Middle French word *colere,* meaning to till or cultivate, out of which we derive the words *agriculture* and *horticulture.* Metaphors that describe culture include "the water we swim in," "the lenses through which we see the world," "the rules of the game," "the roadmap" and a "multi-layered onion."[94]

The culture (or cultures) we live in influences implicit and explicit social norms, patterns and expectations in the framing of values, which in turn affect how we think, feel and both relate to and care for others. Generally, culture refers to one's social environment and includes ways of thinking, feeling, believing and acting that distinguish one group from another. Contributors to culture include language, tacit assumptions, beliefs, practices, religion, symbols, music and the arts, media, entertainment, play, technology, foods, traditions, celebrations, sports, and governmental structures, which are often filled with sights, sounds, tastes and experiences that imprint values, thoughts and emotions.[95] Other components of culture include gender roles, manners, use of humor, body language and the sense of right and wrong. Culture, then, becomes the canopy for the sum total of social patterns passed from one generation to another.[96] Hence, "culture and community are intertwined."[97] For better or for worse, participation in cultural experiences through relationships influences our holistic development, which may or may not foster Christlikeness.[98] Paradoxically, although we live within culture, we simultaneously create and influence it, as Jesus' life demonstrates.

Jesus navigated cultural expectations with wisdom and tact, yet also broke tacit assumptions that countered Kingdom values. For example, Jesus broke ethnic and gender mores in engaging the Samaritan woman when offering her eternal life (Jn 4:1-26). Jesus also threatened the Jewish religious establishment by repudiating the Pharisees and scribes for their hypocrisy (Mt 23), yet paid taxes to the Roman government as a good citizen (Mt 22:21). As the complete personification of the Kingdom then and now, Jesus' primary message and means of love to all cultures continue to beckon a lost world to God and to Kingdom living. According to H. Richard Niebuhr, "The virtue of love in Jesus' character and demand is the virtue of the *love of God and of the love of neighbor in God*, not the virtue of the love of love."[99] God intended that the love of God in and through Christ pervade culture, signified by God's self-giving for the world (Jn 3:16) and command to "go . . . and make disciples of all nations" (Mt 28:19).

To advance the gospel, the early church embraced many from different cultural backgrounds. For example, Philip introduced the Ethiopian eunuch to Jesus (Acts 8:26-40), Peter led the Roman centurion Cornelius and others to Christ (Acts 10:24-48), and the early church commissioned Paul and Barnabas to spread the gospel in various cultural regions (Acts 13:1-3). The grace in which the apostle Paul traversed Jewish and Gentile cultures struck a death blow to ethnocentrism and serves as a model for all believers. Even the conflict resolution evidenced at the Council of Jerusalem, which debated the requirements for Gentile membership in the church (Acts 15), demonstrated that a Kingdom culture of unity superseded cultural divides. Today, as contemporary disciples we have a cross-cultural mission that extends to all cultures.[100]

Niebuhr's influential book *Christ and Culture* offers a typology relative to Christ being "against," "of," "above," "transforming" and "paradoxical" to culture.[101] Although some take issue with Christ and culture being approached as separate entities rather than as integrative,[102] Christ through the Holy Spirit moves within culture to draw people to salvation and to fashion Kingdom values that further shape believers into the image of Jesus. In some cultures of the world extremely antithetic to the gospel, this transformation process is life threatening, with believers serving the Lord at tremendous risk.[103]

Overarching one's respective culture is God's Kingdom, where all members of the body of Christ find inclusion. Jesus personified the reality of Kingdom values as superseding those of the world when he asked the Father to protect his followers from the evil one while they were in the world (Jn 17:15). Further, Paul exhorted believers, "Do not be conformed to this world, but be transformed by the renewing of your minds" (Rom 12:2). For followers of Jesus, the ultimate cultural identity is located in God's Kingdom, not in this world.

Sherwood Lingenfelter addresses a transformational shift after conversion when people juxtapose their values, beliefs and practices with the Scriptures, such that "the power of the Holy Spirit leads to a restructuring of the forces of power in the natural and supernatural world," leading to freedom in Christ, which releases people from "culturally defined strictures."[104] Lingenfelter concludes that while followers of Christ are subject to social and cultural influences, they are empowered by the Holy Spirit and the Word of God for Kingdom living.[105] Tom Smail notes that evil forces work through culture to counter the will and nature of God and fuel "egocentricity" and a rejection of the Creator's generosity, goodness and truth.[106] Although true, Miriam Adeney takes a more proactive approach by challenging the church to go beyond its provincial thinking and take the gospel into all cultures of the world.[107] Interestingly, whether Latin, African, Asian, Middle Eastern, European, Australian, Russian or North American, Christ-followers in each culture of the world in some way reflect the beauty and character of God.[108] Through love, God works through cultural identity to draw and shape believers into the image of Jesus.

Cultural identity naturally emerges when we engage in culturally specific behaviors, are recognized and feel part of the group, but also when encountering a different culture. Acculturation into a group, whether from one's own culture or another, involves "acquiring knowledge about specific emotions and how to deal with them, for example, through the social sharing of emotions," reinforcing once again the holistic nature of CSF.[109] Cultural competence develops when the knowledge, understanding and skills needed to effectively interact with those of other cultures occurs. By respecting the values, norms and expectations of other cultures, we gain a compass for successfully navigating them and gain perspective on our own. Ultimately, cultural diversity allows us to see God's majesty through fresh eyes.[110] Paul-Gordon Chandler concludes, "Christianity worldwide is a *divine mosaic*, with each piece being a different cultural expression of the Christian faith, and the whole portraying the beauty of God's character as perhaps nothing else can."[111] God not only is the author of culture but also desires to reach people within cultures with the gospel (Mt 28:18-20).

In summary, relational formation contributes to Christian formation and shapes how we view ourselves, others and God. This chapter discussed the crucial influence of the family, the importance of finding safety and acceptance in relational connectivity in order to both give and receive love, the inevitability of relational conflict, the cry for community and the role of the church in formation, and also the often illusive but formidable role of culture. As Max De Pree's story about his granddaughter illustrates, relational formation involves connecting what we say (the voice) with our actions (the touch) in reciprocally loving God and others for God's glory and reconciling disparities when they occur. Chapter seven focuses on intellectual formation, another key dimension of CSF so crucial for loving God with all our minds.

7

Intellect

Our Minds

It is vain that we grow in riches of divine knowledge
unless by them the fire of love is increased in us.

Richard of Saint Victor,
Richard of Saint-Victor:
Selected Writings on Contemplation

In February 2011, Watson, the IBM artificial intelligence computer, competed on the popular quiz show *Jeopardy!* against the two human *Jeopardy!* champions, the winner with the top earnings and the one with the longest-running streak.[1] Led by computer science and artificial intelligence expert David Ferrucci, the IBM team spent four years empowering Watson with hardware and software, including DeepQA, a natural language processing program. With sixteen terabytes of working memory, Watson was able to process 800 trillion operations per second. Over the two-game, three-night competition, Watson trounced its human competitors and amassed $77,147, in addition to the $1 million grand prize. Despite its superior performance, Watson made a few errors, showing that even supercomputers make mistakes.[2]

Unlike its human competitors, Watson was never nervous (although the IBM team probably was!), never perspired, never was bolstered by the encouragement of the audience, and never lost sleep between videotaped programs. Watson was programmed by smart people to deliver factual answers. What Watson did not experience was the disappointment in tying on the first day of competition and the elation of winning on day three. Emotionless Watson could neither celebrate after its triumph nor hug its creators, friends or family members. Equipped with artificial intelligence, Watson was a machine without a mind, free will or the capacity to love.

Although our brains have been compared to computers, our minds are much more complex than the mere output from digital programming and information processing.[3] Equipped with between 80 and 120 billion nerve cells, the human brain is the primary organ that directs all integrative functions, including sight, sound, taste, smell and touch, and serves as the body's air traffic control mechanism for all action.[4] On the other hand, the mind not only is regarded as the intangible center of conscious and unconscious activity of thought, reason, memory, decision making, problem solving, creativity, imagination and language, but also of feeling and volition. The mind serves as the thought center while also regulating emotions.[5]

People differ from computers in that human persons are created in the image of God as multidimensional beings. Our ultimate life purpose supersedes winning on a game show but rather centers on reciprocally loving our Creator, which involves the mind. As we saw in chapter two relative to perspectives of the *imago Dei*, certain theologians through the centuries have proposed that being created in the image of God primarily derives from humankind's ability to think and reason. We saw that proponents of this view include Irenaeus, who wrote *Against Heresies*; Thomas Aquinas (1224–1274), who wrote *Summa Theologica*; and Blaise Pascal (1623–1662), a mathematician, physicist and spiritual writer who wrote *Pensées* or *Thoughts*.[6]

Quoting from the Shema, Jesus said, "Love the Lord your God with all your heart, and with all your soul, and with all your *mind*, and with all your strength," which he inseparably linked to loving one's neighbor (Mk

12:30-31, italics added).[7] Loving God, as well as others, is central to the Christian life.

In that humankind is made in the *imago Dei,* the creative potential of the human mind reflects the magnificence of Creator God. Building on the previous chapters, this chapter addresses intellectual formation (see fig. 7.1) as another dimension of Christian spiritual formation, which concerns the development of the mind with the goal of loving and glorifying God. This chapter reveals how integral the mind is in loving God by addressing the mind's capacity; the influence of learning and faith, culture and worldview upon the mind; the importance of renewing the mind; and the hindrances precluding a renewed mind.[8]

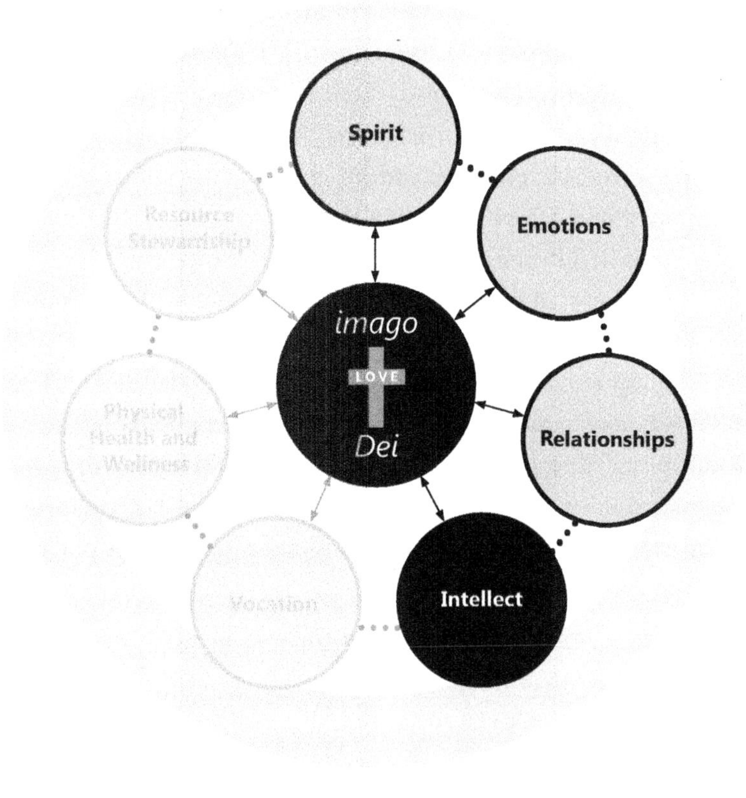

Figure 7.1. Intellectual formation

THE MIND'S CAPACITY

The capacity of the human mind is enormous, and researchers are just beginning to understand its complexity.[9] For example, we know that without a functional brain, a person's life cannot proceed normally, whereas someone can live without a limb, one kidney or parts of other vital organs.[10] The brain, however, not only reflects a unique genome or genetic inheritance, but also is affected by "external influences throughout life" that develop the brain and affect the mind's functioning.[11] The mind holistically develops through the interactive effects of genetics, social relationships, health and nutrition, education, and other environmental influences.[12]

How brain neurons composed of cell bodies, axioms and synapses prompt electrical impulses that frame thoughts, emotions and actions literally boggles the mind (no pun intended!). However, the mind supersedes René Descartes's (1596–1650) dualist notion of "I think, therefore I am."[13] Emotions and motivation have a part to play in thought processes.[14] As we have seen in chapters five and six, emotions are influenced by relational interactions. Despite all our scientific knowledge, the mind's capacity and how it fully functions remains a relative mystery.[15]

Despite the fact that much of the scientific community largely removes Creator God in explaining the mind's capacity and rejects viewing creation from a bibliocentered perspective, computer scientist Matthew Dickerson argues that human persons are integrated beings composed of body, mind, soul and spirit.[16] The complexity of the human mind reflects the Creator whose own mind is unfathomable (Is 40:13; 1 Cor 2:16). As followers of Jesus Christ who affirm that humankind is made in the image of God, we can exclaim with the psalmist,

> I praise, you, for I am fearfully and wonderfully made.
> Wonderful are your works;
> that I know very well. (Ps 139:14)

As Creator, God designed the human person to be able to love God and to explore God's wonderful works through the facility of the mind. David

Hogue contends that understanding the brain-mind connection in memory and imagination heightens attending to our souls for a living faith, because the brain reflects the *imago Dei.*[17] Interestingly, neuroscience research has shown that belief in God and accompanying spiritual practices actually change the brain.[18]

What then does it mean to love God with all our minds? Loving God with our minds means developing our intellectual capacity in pursuing God's truth in order to advance God's Kingdom and bring glory to God. In other words, we love God by using our minds to honor God.[19] Gene Edward Veith contends that loving God with the mind means that Jesus claims "every mental faculty" we have.[20] If, as A. G. Sertillanges suggests, "the mind governs everything," when we think well and act righteously through a passion for holiness and truth, we glorify God.[21] John Stott advocates for "using our minds Christianly" as a God-given responsibility for "a warm devotion set on fire by truth," not for producing a lifeless academic Christianity.[22] Stott contends Christians should use their minds, given they are created in the image of God, (1) to spread the gospel because thought shapes actions, (2) to understand the revelation of God through creation and redemption that connotes a renewing of the divine image lost during the fall, (3) to stand against the tide of secular thinking that dismisses God, the truth, the supernatural and evil, and (4) to prepare for judgment, as God will hold us responsible for the knowledge that informs our actions.[23]

Further, Stott suggests that the proper use of the mind affects six spheres of Christian living: (1) true worship, (2) Christian faith, in that faith and reason are not opposed, (3) Christian holiness, (4) Christian guidance, (5) Christian evangelism, and (6) Christian ministry.[24] If this is true, then not using our minds condemns us to spiritual superficiality.[25]As theologian and philosopher J. P. Moreland quips, "A flabby mind is no badge of spiritual honor" because a strong mind is a "crucial component in the spiritual journey."[26] Faith in God fuels an invigorated mind and passionate intellect, according to Alister McGrath, leading to a theological reflection of the nature and ways of God and worship that captures the imagination.[27]

Hence, as Wolfhart Pannenberg suggests, human reason alone cannot comprehend "the vastness of the intellectual landscape of the divine."[28] In order to tap into this landscape in the pursuit of God's truth, we need faith as the lens through which the mind understands. Anselm of Canterbury (c. 1033–1109) said it best: "I do not seek to understand so that I may believe, but I believe so that I may understand; and what is more, I believe that unless I do believe I shall not understand."[29]

Richard Hughes presents the life of the mind as involving a concerted search for truth, interaction with diverse points of view, critical thinking and analysis, and intellectual creativity. Rather than Christianity being a stumbling block for intellectual development, scholarship and teaching, Hughes asserts that Christian faith enhances them. Hughes further challenges readers to think theologically in order to deconstruct the "particularities" of their respective faith traditions in order to embrace diversity in the love of neighbor. By examining four faith traditions (Catholic, Reformed, Anabaptist and Lutheran) Hughes demonstrates how each tradition sustains the life of the mind.[30] The creeds of the Christian tradition offer yet another venue for the mind to think Christianly.[31] Thinking about God, the task of theological reflection, helps us to understand God's nature and ways as transformative conduits of faith.[32]

Accumulation of knowledge alone, however, does not comprise a living faith. Or as Diogenes Allen observes, "when intellectual inquiry is not concerned with ascent toward God" faith is not complete.[33] Without the accompanying development of godly character and virtue fueled by godly love, knowledge can become sterile, self-glorifying and antagonistic to God.[34] Sertillanges aptly concludes, "Truth visits those who love her, who surrender to her, and this love cannot be without virtue."[35] Truth through an experiential knowing and godliness go hand in hand (Tit 1:1-2). The apostle Paul affirms the notion that we can understand all mysteries and have faith and cognitive knowledge, but without love, we are nothing (1 Cor 13:2). Knowledge puffs up if unaccompanied by love (1 Cor 8:1).

Virtues such as those comprising the fruit of the Spirit (Gal 5:22-23), in addition to wisdom, honesty, humility and courage, are essential for reflecting the character of Christ through intellectual formation.[36] A proud, arrogant and boastful person with keen intellect is not a model for intellectual formation by the Spirit. Paul showed the Colossian church how to be "encouraged and united in love" so that they might have all the riches of assured understanding of the mystery of Christ, "in whom are hidden all the treasures of wisdom and knowledge" (Col 2:2-3). In that Christ has supremacy over all things (Col 1:18), he "is the Master only because he is Maestro" and unquestionably "is the smartest man who ever lived."[37] As the Logos and the source of all knowledge, Jesus is our primary role model for how to think.[38]

Two New Testament Greek words translated as "knowledge" clarify how knowledge relates not only to intellectual formation but also to love. One word is *gnosis*, meaning cognitive knowledge "between the person knowing and the object known," and denoting "an enquiry, investigation, especially of spiritual truth."[39] The word applies to the knowledge of Christ (Phil 3:8; 2 Pet 3:18). Paul reminded the Ephesians that the love of Christ surpasses *gnosis* (1 Cor 13:2; Eph 3:19). Reminding the church that knowledge of God leads to grace and peace, Peter opposed false teaching and affirmed how knowledge contributes to a vibrant faith (2 Pet 1:5-6).

The other Greek word translated as "knowledge" is *epignosis*, referring to experiential knowledge or "to observe, fully perceive, notice attentively, discern, recognize," with the idea of "special participation in the object known."[40] Paul applies this word to the knowledge of Christ leading to spiritual maturity and unity in the faith (Eph 4:13), as well as to a deeper love and depth of insight so that believers would be holy for the glory of God (Phil 1:9-11). Further, Paul prayed for the Colossian believers to be filled with the knowledge of God's will in order to live fruitful lives pleasing to God (Col 1:9-10). God has designed the human mind to receive God's truth and knowledge in order to know the Lord in a reciprocal love relationship. Faith is built on both cognitive knowledge (*gnosis*) and experiential knowledge (*epignosis*) by way of the Spirit.

The Spirit communicates knowledge that supersedes natural ability. When the armies of the Moabites and Ammonites confronted Judah, King Jehoshaphat called out to God in desperation, "We do not know what to do, but our eyes are upon you" (2 Chron 20:12). The Spirit of the Lord came upon Jahaziel, who prophesied the battle strategy to defeat Judah's enemies. God revealed strategic knowledge for victory. When Daniel and his three friends honored God by refusing to defile themselves by eating Babylonian food and wine (Dan 1:8), God gave them knowledge and skill in all kinds of literature and wisdom. They proved to be ten times better than their Babylonian counterparts. Then, after Daniel and his friends cried out to God for the interpretation of Nebuchadnezzar's dream, God supernaturally revealed its meaning to Daniel in a night vision. God gave Paul a vision of the man of Macedonia in order to direct him and Silas to Macedonia (Acts 16:6-10). God's divine revelation of knowledge superseded both Daniel's and Paul's natural abilities. The Lord influences the capacity of the human mind through natural means, such as learning venues and common sense, and supernatural means, such as prophecies, visions and dreams to reveal secrets and direction (Job 4:13). God is the source of all knowledge (Prov 2:6). For followers of Jesus, however, learning and faith align in intellectual formation.

Learning and Faith

Learning and faith are not mutually exclusive but rather are inextricably linked within intellectual formation and contribute to CSF. As seen in the introduction to this chapter, learning amounts to more than merely rote programming, as Watson on the television game show *Jeopardy!* illustrates. All things being equal, the human mind naturally develops over time, given genetic potentiality and the ability and motivation to learn, a supportive environment, and learning opportunities.

The life of the apostle Paul illustrates how learning and faith coalesce to frame a God-honoring intellectual life. Paul's pedigree without Christ was impressive. As a highly educated Jew, Paul possessed all the academic and vocational credentials for success, having been circumcised, born of the tribe of Benjamin, "a Hebrew of Hebrews," a zealous Pharisee, and a righteous legalist (Phil 3:4-6). Paul acknowledged, however, that these criteria for religious success in the Jewish world meant nothing when divorced from a vibrant faith in Christ: "I regard everything as loss because of the surpassing value of knowing Christ Jesus my Lord" (Phil 3:8). Paul regarded all his religious and academic credentials as rubbish in comparison to personally knowing Jesus and being conformed into Christ's image (Phil 3:9-11).

Prior to Paul's conversion on the Damascus Road (Acts 9:1-19), he had a finely tuned mind (Gal 1:14). However, this capacity eventuated in extreme opposition to the purposes of God, culminating in the persecution of the church and the stoning of Stephen (Acts 7:54-60). Through his natural intellectual prowess and leadership influence, Paul essentially became an enemy of the cross of Christ (cf. Phil 3:18). In Paul's case intellectual formation without faith in Christ led to tragic consequences because "the god of this world blinds the minds of unbelievers, to keep them from seeing the light of the gospel of the glory of Christ, who is the image of God" (2 Cor 4:4). Fortunately, after conversion and by God's grace, Paul set his mind on things above (Col 3:2) and applied his keen intellectual prowess to advance the gospel. For Paul, learning and faith integrally aligned.

How do we learn? And how does faith affect learning? To answer the first question, we will review four primary perspectives of human learning. Although these perspectives of learning are based on theory, research and observation, each offers a plausible perspective on how the mind learns.[41] Each perspective has obvious strengths and deficiencies. None of them fully explains the complexity of human learning and the countless contributing factors. Taken together, however, they magnify the creative genius of God in creating the human mind with learning potentiality. Four selected learning perspectives derive from the work of these developmental psychologists: (1) Jean Piaget (1896–1980), (2) Lev Vygotsky (1896–1934), (3) Albert Bandura (1925–) and (4) Howard Gardner (1943–).[42]

First, as a Swiss psychologist originally trained as a biologist, Jean

Piaget proposed that children's cognitive abilities traverse through developmental stages that subsume under *accommodation,* the adaptation in thinking to accommodate real-world realities, and *assimilation,* the interpretation of new experiences by way of previous ones.[43] Piaget broke new ground by identifying how learning relates to children's interaction within their environment. Critics counter that children may move through these stages at different rates, as influenced by social, motivational and educational factors.

Second, Russian-born Lev Vygotsky offered a different perspective, suggesting that cognitive development is better explained by factors such as language development and cultural context. Vygotsky argued that knowledge originates in socially meaningful activity, where language and actions help stimulate children's cognition. Vygotsky observed that adults can provide scaffolds for children, as temporary aides in the learning process, until they become autonomous in directing their own learning. Vygotsky termed the margin between the child's actual learning and problem-solving ability and the enhancement of having adult guidance or interaction with capable peers as the "zone of proximal development."[44] Thus, school learning with adult guidance and peer interaction can fuel a child's cognitive development. Language and cultural context alone, however, do not account for all learning.

Third, building on Vygotsky's and others' work, Albert Bandura offered a social learning approach to cognition.[45] Bandura proposed that we learn through observing others, including live role models (those we know or observe in our environment) and symbolic role models (those we do not know, such as real or fictional characters, historical figures, sports stars and media personalities). Bandura's contributions underscore the importance of observing others as role models in the process of learning. Bandura's later work focused on self-efficacy, the inner motivation to learn, a previously overlooked contributing factor.[46] Although Bandura provided a novel lens to explain learning through observing others, his approach has been criticized as being overly simplistic and ignoring biological and hormonal factors. For example, aggressive behavior may indeed be learned by observation, but it might also be a function of the sinful nature.

Fourth, Howard Gardner took a completely different approach to learning by proposing a theory of multiple intelligences that takes into account seven cognitive strengths and styles. They include (1) *linguistic intelligence,* evidenced by poets and writers, (2) *logical mathematical intelligence,* previously regarded as the gold standard of intelligence,(3) *spatial intelligence,* needed by painters and sculptors such as Michelangelo, (4) *musical intelligence,* displayed by musicians, (5) *bodily-kinesthetic intelligence,* enacted by dancers, surgeons and athletes, (6) *interpersonal intelligence,* for understanding others, and (7) *intrapersonal intelligence,* for understanding oneself.[47] Gardner proposed that all persons possess these seven intelligences in varying degrees and that different cultures reinforce particular ones. Gardner, and those influenced by him, have appealed especially to American educators since it debunks the notion that intelligence is a single entity related to IQ and that children learn in only one way. Absent from Gardner's approach is spiritual and moral intelligence, and a rigorous empirical substantiation to support his propositions.

Taken together, however, these four approaches provide windows into the probable components of learning that bear on intellectual formation. Learning (1) is a developmental process (Piaget), (2) involves social interaction and language through teaching (Vygotsky), (3) is influenced by role models and self-efficacy (Bandura), and (4) reflects multiple expressions of intelligence (Gardner). Although these four psychologists, as well as others, offer perspectives to uncover the mysteries of human learning, each provides a partial view that heightens an appreciation for the God-given capacity of the human mind to learn, imagine and create. God alone gives the capacity for learning.

Absent from these perspectives is a sense of how God opens the mind to receive divine impartation and revelation beyond natural means. When open to God, the mind becomes a conduit of divine communication. For example, intellectual processes and endowments met divine impartation in the lives of Bezalel and Aholiab, designers and craftsmen of the tabernacle furnishings (Ex 35:30-35; 36:1). We might infer that these designers (1) had developed some aptitude for the role that they were called to undertake, (2) their tasks involved a degree of interaction and language, (3) they likely benefited from role models in their environment while exercising self-efficacy, and (4) they expressed a particular kind of multiple intelligence involving design and construction acumen (e.g., logical mathematical intelligence and spatial intelligence). However, the Spirit of God filled them "with skill, intelligence, and knowledge" for their special calling (Ex 35:31). God can open the mind with special revelation and impartation in order for learning to occur and for God's purposes to advance.

This leads to the second question: how does faith affect learning? If we believe "that all things have been created through him and for him" (Col 1:16) and that in Christ "are hidden all the treasures of wisdom and knowledge" (Col 2:3), then faith in Christ is foundational for all learning. Faith anchors learning in God's purposes for coming to know God and God's created works. Echoing N. T. Wright's assertion that Christ's lordship and sovereignty bear upon "every area of human and worldly existence," I assert that for Christians all learning should be focused through the lens of the Word of God in order to glorify Christ: his creation, his person, his redemption and his Kingdom purposes.[48] Scripture, contends Gene Veith, opens up the intellectual life to the believer.[49] If, as C. S. Lewis claims, "There is no neutral ground in the universe: every square inch, every split second, is claimed by God and counterclaimed by Satan," then studying humanity and this universe in all of their finely tuned detail, intrigue and beauty through the lens of faith brings glory to God.[50]

Therefore, the various disciplines of study have extraordinary merit when illuminated by God's Word. Each discipline has "something to say about the nature of humanity," the nature of God, and God's creation.[51] According to Mark Noll, studying created things equates with "studying the works of Christ." Therefore, knowing Christ "provides the most basic possible motive for pursuing the tasks of human learning."[52] Faith in Christ gives vigor to the learning process, and study brings both "order to knowledge" and glory to God.[53]

As you look at this representative list, consider how each of these disciplines of study has extraordinary merit when illuminated by God's Word.

- *language*
- *literature*
- *education*
- *anthropology*
- *psychology*
- *sociology*
- *philosophy*
- *history*
- *archaeology*
- *mathematics*
- *science*
- *technology*
- *medicine*
- *engineering*
- *business*
- *economics*
- *communication*
- *music*
- *the arts*
- *law*
- *government*
- *theology*

The importance of education integrating learning and the Christian faith cannot be overemphasized.[54] Many in the Christian academy rigorously defend its priority for developing the whole person around the centrality of Christ and the Word of God in the pursuit of truth. Among them David Dockery envisions Christian education as the seedbed for intellectual, moral and character formation, and offers foundational components of a core curriculum within the context of community.[55] Dockery highlights the life of the apostle Paul as the model for how intellect and educational background interface in the fulfillment of vocational calling through intellectual formation.[56] Dockery holds that since we are created in the image of God, "we can creatively teach, learn, explore, and conduct research," with moral and spiritual virtues having "vital cognitive significance."[57] Similarly, Charles Malik pleads for the saving of the soul *and* the mind in order to combat Christian anti-intellectualism, to uphold the integration of mind and spirit, and to recapture the great universities for Jesus Christ within a world of disorder.[58]

George Marsden boldly proposes that Christians fully participate in the academy, where rigorous Christian scholarship melds one's faith in God with research excellence despite antagonism from various streams.[59] In concert, Richard Hughes asserts that a scholar's Christian faith "can express itself in the highest and finest kind of scholarship—a scholarship committed to search for truth, to engage a variety of conversation partners, to critique all perspectives, even one's own, and to nurture creative imagination."[60] These scholars affirm the primacy of integrating learning and faith, which takes on heightened significance when considering how contemporary culture and opposing worldview perspectives battle for truth in order to capture the mind.

Culture and Worldview

Culture and worldview shape our ways of thinking and defining reality. As mentioned in chapter six, culture relates to the external influences within one's environment that exercise a shaping effect on individual thinking, attitudes, expectations, relationships and behavior. Cultural milieus formatively contribute to intellectual functioning and development by establishing espoused values and models of acceptable behavior.[61] Worldview relates to the internal perspectives, beliefs and values that influence how one sees the world. According to James Sire, worldview "is a fundamental orientation of the heart" based on presuppositions and assumptions that legislate how "we live and move and have our being."[62] Worldview informs the answers to these questions: Who am I? Where did I come from? Why do I exist? and What is the purpose of life?[63] Moreover, one's worldview represents ways of thinking, which inform perspectives on lifestyle, morality, vocation, use of time and even environmental stewardship.[64]

Competing worldviews and moral visions in the public square vie for domination of the mind regarding perspectives on human rights, the family, education, media and the arts, law, and politics, to name a few.[65] Because cultural forces often repel any semblance of morality and religious orthodoxy associated with them, biblical truth has come under assault, resulting in unprecedented relativism.[66] Ethical standards of what is morally right and wrong have depreciated. What was once considered sacred is dismissed by competing cultural assumptions and worldviews as irrelevant.

When people do not believe that a transcendent and sovereign God created humankind in God's image and likeness (Gen 1:27) and redeemed them from original sin through Christ's atoning work on the cross (Rom

3:25; Heb 2:17), then other competing worldviews clamor mercilessly for complete allegiance in "a culture filled with empty selves."[67] J. P. Moreland notes the gradual shift from a "thick world" to a "thin world," devoid of objective value, purpose and meaning, and where absolute truth is disputed.[68] This thin world of alternative belief systems provides challenges in discerning truth from falsehood. Thus, having a biblical and ethical foundation as one's lens is essential.

In a pluralistic, contemporary culture, the main competing worldviews include deism, naturalism, humanism, nihilism, Eastern philosophies (e.g., Hinduism and Buddhism), new age philosophy, and postmodernism. Definitions of these competing worldviews bring them into focus.

Deism presents God as being revealed in nature, reflecting rationality and order, with the Almighty as a hands-off God who is neither personal nor sovereign over human affairs. Deism refutes God as being known through revelation, Scripture and the incarnation.[69]

Naturalism exalts the mind and contributed to the development of the natural sciences. This approach views matter, not God, as eternally existent in a cause-effect relationship. Naturalism purports "no god, no spirit, no life beyond the grave."[70] Scientific naturalism finds support in Darwinian evolutionists such as Carl Sagan and Stephen Hawking.[71] The vehement manifestos of atheistic writers, including evolutionary biologist Richard Dawkins, journalist Christopher Hitchens and neuroscientist Sam Harris,[72] further highlight the influence of naturalism on atheism within contemporary culture. Fortunately, other scientists engage their professions through the lens of faith. For example, physicist and theologian John Polkinghorne acknowledges the wonder of God through his exploration of science.[73] Polkinghorne aptly concludes, "Yet there is more to the mind of God than science will ever discover."[74] Pioneering geneticist Francis S. Collins, who served as the director of the international Genome Project from 1993–2008 and who became director of the National Institutes of Health in 2009, attests to his belief in God and how faith and science are not oppositional.[75]

Today, naturalism is closely connected to *humanism*, a worldview also divorced from faith in God. Proponent Paul Kurtz, the most notable among secular humanists, developed several humanist manifestos that advance what he called a moral revolution (or perhaps more fitting, an immoral one), which defends the right to complete sexual license, alternative lifestyles and euthanasia. In this view the human person becomes a god unto him- or herself in exercising complete freedom of choice. This humanistic view accounts for scientific and technological perspectives of human developments as devoid of a divine Creator.[76] Such manifestos have been countered by those such as Francis Schaeffer, who has called the church back to Judeo-Christian foundations to salvage a culture entrenched in moral decadence.[77]

Based on naturalism and humanism, *nihilism* poses a negative worldview lens that considers life as without intrinsic value or purpose, denies absolute knowledge and rejects absolute truth. Existentially insignificant, human beings become a power unto themselves since it is believed that God is dead, life is meaningless and objective truth is untenable.[78] Therefore, moral standards are irrelevant. One of the first nihilists was German philosopher Friedrich Nietzsche (1844–1900), whose themes include the "will to power" and the *Übermensch,* meaning the "Overman," who creates personal values and imposes them on others.[79] Nihilism leads to an atheistic form of existentialism, the view that one must give one's own life meaning in the midst of cosmic despair, alienation and purposelessness.

With Western traditional moorings increasingly severed, many explore *Eastern philosophies* in a search for meaning. In these pantheistic views God permeates the cosmos and exists in everything. Thus, the human soul is God. Hinduism and Buddhism derive from this worldview. Eastern philosophies served to jump start *new age philosophy,* an eclectic Western adaptation of Eastern pantheistic worldviews. Inclusive and pluralistic, the new age worldview involves various spiritualities derived from Buddhism, Hinduism, Taoism and others in attaining a higher consciousness and mystical experience, while extolling the mind and advancing various practices, including yoga, meditation and intentional communal activity. New age worldviews advocate the absence of a transcendent God and ethical standards in order to bring in a new age of enlightenment and peace.

Postmodernism has become the overarching worldview perspective in the West. After the emergence of deism, naturalism, nihilism, Eastern philosophies and new age philosophies, postmodernism entered the worldview stage on the heels of deconstructed Christianity. Postmodernism counters modernist perspectives regarding the certitude of scientific and objective realities as well as religious beliefs, and focuses on one's own subjective experiences and social constructs to define reality. Thus, postmodernists generally reject universal truth, countering that individuals determine truth from lived experience. Scholars such as Jacques Derrida, Jean-François Lyotard and Michel Foucault embraced this postmodern worldview, which refutes metanarratives in favor of individual narratives in order to define reality.[80]

The postmodern worldview lends itself to: (1) *secularism,* the resistance of any kind of religious influence or expression in public life, especially relative to ethics, and (2) *consumerism,* the attachment to material values and things as a pathway to personal fulfillment.[81] Although many bemoan postmodernism, some Christian writers call the church to a higher level of cultural sensitivity and relevance in order to be effective.[82] For example, James K. A. Smith observes, "But the church will have this countercultural, prophetic witness only when it jettisons its own modernity; in that respect postmodernism can be another catalyst for the church to *be* the church."[83]

Against the backdrop of these seven worldview approaches, a *Christian worldview* offers not simply a view of the world but rather an entire way of life predicated on the dynamic love of God and being created in God's image. James Sire advances these propositions of belief as comprising a Christian worldview: (1) the immutable nature and character of God, (2) God as trinitarian Creator, (3) persons as being created in the image of God, (4) God's creating humankind with capacity to know God and the world, (5) Christ's redemption of humanity because of the fall, (6) death as a door to eternal life, (7) ethics as based on the character of God as good, (8) history leading to the fulfillment of God's purposes for humanity, and (9) the Christian telos to enjoy and glorify God forever.[84] Although these propositions describe the

Christian belief system, they fail to fully relate the breadth and depth of the colossal love of God made available to us in Christ. Followers of Christ experience the shaping of godly character to become fully flourishing through self-giving love with the primary goal of becoming more like Christ. A Christian worldview rests on the principles and precepts of the Bible as the living Word of God and the work of the Spirit, who provides abundant grace to become ambassadors for Christ with an eternal destiny.

Moreover, with various worldviews swirling in all of society, followers of Jesus must be vigilant, while simultaneously engaging culture with the gospel rather than withdrawing in fear and isolation. Contrary to Charles Malik's view that false philosophies taught in universities are the source of societal ills, I counter that it is sin and sinful human nature as exploited by Satan that inform these false philosophies and worldviews, which in turn are ultimately responsible for the world's malaise.[85] We must keep in mind the apostle Paul's admonition, "Our struggle is not against enemies of blood and flesh, but against the rulers, against the authorities, against the cosmic powers of this present darkness, against the spiritual forces of evil in the heavenly places" (Eph 6:12). According to Alister McGrath, discipleship of the mind protects the Christian vision of reality, while being the precondition for cultural engagement.[86] Thus, for the discipleship of the mind to flourish, one's mind must be continually renewed.

Renewing the Mind

Since Paul first exhorted members of the Roman church not to conform to the world's system but rather "to be transformed by the renewing of your minds" in order to do the will of God (Rom 12:2), the challenge for doing so has never been greater.[87] Because of sin and disobedience within a fallen world, the depraved condition of the mind remains the battleground between the devil (whose arsenal includes evil and sin that lead to destruction [Rom 7:21-23]) and God (whose arsenal includes life and peace by the Spirit [Rom 8:5-6]). Whereas the depravity of the mind results in all kinds of evil (Rom 1:18-32), God transforms the mind to align with Christ through the work of the Holy Spirit. However, the enemy has a clear plan to thwart the purposes of God, starting with the mind. Spiritual warfare is real, with the powers of darkness contesting the Kingdom of light.

Beginning in the Garden, when Adam and Eve ate from the tree of the knowledge of good and evil (Gen 3:5-6), we see that knowledge apart from God opens us to evil, and that the mind must be guarded through the helmet of salvation and protected by the Spirit. As the repository for thought, the mind serves as the catalyst for action. By gaining a stronghold in the mind, the enemy deposits doubt, confusion, fear and temptation in order to shift focus away from God and to foster disobedience through any number of competing sinful allegiances and actions. These destructive patterns of thinking become strongholds that need to be torn down by taking every thought captive through obedience to Christ (2 Cor 10:4-5). As such, lack of the knowledge of God and God's ways is destructive (Hos 4:6).

We are instructed, therefore, to discipline ourselves so we do not give place to the devil, who prowls around like a roaring lion seeking someone to devour (1 Pet 5:8). As "the god of this world," the devil blinds the minds of unbelievers to keep them from receiving both Jesus, the very image of God (2 Cor 4:4), and the gospel message. Furthermore as "the father of lies" who opposes God's purposes, the devil perpetrates false beliefs (e.g., deism, naturalism, humanism, nihilism, Eastern philosophies, new age, postmodernism and other religions), since there is no truth in him (Jn 8:44).[88] Fundamentally, the enemy desires for us to believe that this world is all there is and that God either does not exist, or if God does exist, God does not love us because we are unforgiveable and without hope. However as C. E. B. Cranfield argues, we can no longer be content to allow ourselves to be stamped with the mark of this age, with its accompanying values creating internal and external pressures to conform.[89] We are able to resist conformity to the world, the flesh and the devil through Christ's merciful action made possible by the power of the Holy Spirit who lives within (1 Jn 4:4).

By renewing our minds we come to think God's thoughts by setting our minds on things above rather than on worldly things (Col 3:1-2) in order to shine like stars within "a crooked and perverse generation" (Phil 2:15).

By thinking God's thoughts, as Grant Osborne suggests, decisions are then made in the mind "that determine one's spiritual direction and destiny" and whether we live a victorious Christian life or one mired in defeat.[90] Thus, renewing the mind leads to ethical conduct that "align[s] everything into harmony," in light of God's Kingdom rather than the world's system.[91]

As John Stott concludes, the incompatibility between the world's system and God's will is so great that there is "no possibility of compromise."[92] Since believers do not belong to the world, they must anticipate that the world will hate them, just as it hated Jesus (Jn 15:18-19; 17:14). Moral transformation begins with the mind being renewed through the Word of God and the Holy Spirit, and then proceeds when we are able to discern, desire and obey the will of God in a continual cycle of transformation.[93] Paul reminded the Philippians that because their citizenship was in heaven, their minds (i.e., inner orientation) were not to be set on earthly things but rather on heavenly things in anticipating Jesus' return (Phil 3:19-20). Renewing the mind connects transformation of thought with ethical behavior for not only living in this present age but also in preparing for the one to come.[94]

How exactly is the mind renewed? Understanding that Christ gave himself to free us from this present evil age (Gal 1:4), we renew our minds by focusing on Christ, the pioneer and perfecter of our faith (Heb 12:2). The apostle Paul did not proclaim the gospel with human eloquence or wisdom; instead, his primary ambition was to "know nothing" among the Corinthians "except Jesus Christ, and him crucified" (1 Cor 2:2). Like Paul, we are to have a complete preoccupation with Christ so that we might be increasingly transformed into the *imago Dei* through the *imago Christi* for the *gloria Dei*. As Mary Stewart Van Leeuwen concludes, "we need to return to Scripture and try to understand better just what is involved in the kind of intelligence that is the *true* expression of the *imago Dei*."[95] We focus on Christ by reading and meditating on the Word of God and embracing the work of the Holy Spirit, who continually transforms us into the image of Jesus (2 Cor 3:18).

The psalmist declares that those who are blessed "delight in the law of the Lord" and meditate on it day and night (Ps 1:2). By meditating on God's precepts, we gain insight and understanding in order to obey God's Word (Ps 119:97-104). God's Word is like a lamp to our feet and a light to our path (Ps 119:105) and helps us to think aright and live a holy life. The Word of God helps us to think about what is true, honorable, just, pure, pleasing and commendable (Phil 4:8). When the Spirit of God resides within us, we have access to the mind of God. Only the Spirit, who knows the mind of God, can help us have the mind of Christ (1 Cor 2:16). Becoming aware of hindrances to a renewed mind assists us to guard against them.

Hindrances to a Renewed Mind

The mind of the twenty-first-century believer needs to be continually renewed, and for good reason. Within contemporary society, which is often characterized by economic pressures, our multiple responsibilities to family, vocation, ministry and other pursuits (all good things!) reduce margins of time, finances and life-giving relational connection. We are doing more with less, and our stress levels are soaring.[96] Furthermore, the influence of advertising, media and the arts, and technology adds to the cacophony vying for our attention. It is no wonder that our minds easily become overloaded, distracted, anxious, stressed, confused, unfocused, undisciplined and passive.

Living in the digital age where we can connect 24/7, not only by phone but also through synchronous and asynchronous venues such as Facebook, Twitter, Skype and email, we encounter any number of preoccupations. Entertainment through television, movies and video games provides further conduits of amusement that easily become habitual. Whereas some believe we are "amusing ourselves to death," others might contend that we are communicating ourselves to death.[97]

Let's start with advertising, for example. Although advertising sells products and services, it also inundates the mind and caters to materialistic inclinations. Advertising clutter is everywhere.[98] Ads on billboards, television, radio and in print through newspapers, magazines and online sources, including video ads through mobile devices, engulf us every day, to say nothing of marketing callers who try to sell us products or services. For 2014 Magna marketing company estimates that global advertising will reach $515 billion, with $164 billion projected spending in the United States alone. Digital advertising will contribute a greater share in advertising dollars.[99] Since advertising has burgeoned in the past decade, we can all agree that these billions of dollars zealously crave the mind's attention and the wallet's activity.[100]

As for online media, the explosion of mobile and online outlets creates unprecedented accessibility. For example, a 2009 study surveyed media usage of two thousand children and teens (affectionately called "screenagers" for the time they spend in front of a screen) between the ages of eight and eighteen across the United States. The data indicated that the daily average amount of time children spent on some kind of recreational media was 10 hours, 45 minutes. That broke down to roughly 4 hours, 29 minutes of television; 2 hours, 31 minutes of music/audio; 1 hour, 29 minutes on the computer; 1 hour, 13 minutes using video games; 38 minutes in a print medium, and 25 minutes watching a movie. Multitasking accounted for 29 percent of the overlap in usage.[101] These results did not account for young people's cell phone usage and text messaging. Increasingly, media creep is making its way into children's bedrooms, with 71 percent having a television, 68 percent having a DVD player, and 33 percent having full Internet access in their bedroom.[102] Mobile media through cell phones, iPods, MP3 devices and tablets increase media exposure all the more.

Media usage is not reserved for the young, as adults heavily use media too. In 2009 a video-mapping study evaluated media consumption related to television, computers, mobile devices and other outlets of adults over the age of eighteen.[103] Researchers found that the average combined daily screen time was 8.5 hours, with the 45-54 age group having the most screen time, over 9.5 hours, superseding the 18-24 age group. Television viewing trumped viewing on other outlets such as the computer, video-capable mobile phones and similar devices. Further findings revealed that television users are daily exposed to 72 minutes of television ads and promos.

The upside of digital technology, media and the arts, and entertainment in popular culture is that they provide tools not only for healthy communication and recreation but also for the gospel.[104] Young Christians especially create and engage in new media to advance the gospel. As David Kinnaman, president of the Barna Group, notes, "Access is not all negative," because young Christians comprise the earliest adopters as "digital natives."[105] When approached with discernment, wholesome technology, media and entertainment can enrich our lives and reinforce moral values.

However, the downside of popular culture is that media outlets can become seductive, addictive and all-consuming. According to Oxford neuroscientist Susan Greenfield, chronic Internet usage literally changes the microcellular structure and biochemistry of the brain.[106] With Internet addiction now a phenomenon of concern, the jury is out on whether the Internet has contributed to more expansive or more fragmented thought processes.[107] A further question relates to whether media and online content promote godly values. As communication specialists Terrance Lindvall and J. Matthew Melton suggest, "Every popular cultural medium from feature films to music videos communicates a belief or value."[108] Therefore, discernment must be applied when engaging in popular culture and its various expressions to fulfill the call to be children of light.

Additionally, time spent on text messaging and social networking sites continues to skyrocket.[109] Technology and media content can be abused for evil intent, especially when appropriate safeguards and commitments are lacking. Online pornography only adds to the devious design to capture the mind in ungodly thoughts and images.[110] In and of itself the Internet is not sinful, yet viewers can become malicious pawns in the hands of those who are dishonest, fraudulent, perverted and money mongering. On one hand, evil has full access to the Internet, demanding constant vigilance. On the other hand, the Internet is a powerful tool when used to nourish the human mind and spirit, promote godly values and foster community in Christian love.[111] Technology, along with other seemingly good things, can be our greatest friend, but it also can be our greatest foe. Regardless, the mind needs regular detoxing.

If we are bombarded with constant messages, images, advertising, media and the cares of daily life, how can the mind focus on the Lord and be renewed? When is the mind able to "think on these things" that are true, honorable, just, pure, pleasing commendable and excellent (Phil 4:8)? Detaching from what grips us in order to attach to the Lord (Jn 15:5) requires discipline. In personal time with God, we can cast all our cares on the Lord (1 Pet 5:6-7), renew our commitment to trust in God and not our own understanding (Prov 3:5), and refuse to fret or worry about life circumstances (Ps 37:3, 8). To offer our minds to God, we need to recall Paul's words, "Do not worry about anything, but in everything by prayer and supplication with thanksgiving let your requests be made known to God" (Phil 4:6). In spiritual practices of prayer, Bible reading and contemplation, the mind is offered to God to think God's thoughts such that "those of steadfast mind you [the Lord] keep in peace—in peace because they trust in you" (Is 26:3). In order to withstand the constant onslaught of possible preoccupations, we must continually exercise healthy habits of mind in order to focus on Christ in worship through the Word of God and by the Spirit and to live out of that center.

In review, this chapter on intellectual formation derives from being created in the *imago Dei*, the image of God, in order to love the Lord with all our minds as we are conformed to the *imago Christi* for the *gloria Dei*. Unlike IBM's Watson, we are integrated beings whose minds are fashioned with great capacity to reflect our Creator. By presenting how the mind learns and develops through the influence of faith, we likewise noted the impact of culture and worldview on intellectual development. By highlighting the critical importance of renewing the mind, the chapter concluded with a reminder that by detaching from the numerous lures competing for the mind's attention, we are able to continually attach to God in order to overcome hindrances to a vibrant and renewed mind. We now turn to vocational formation, which addresses how God fashions us through our life calling to express God's love and glory in the world.

8

Vocation

Our Life Purpose and Calling

Don't ask what the world needs.
Ask yourself what makes you come alive,
and go do that, because what the world
needs is people who have come alive.

Howard Thurman, quoted in
Violence Unveiled: Humanity at the Crossroads

Sojourner Truth (1797–1893) changed the course of nineteenth-century America. She rubbed shoulders with the likes of renowned abolitionist Frederick Douglass and was welcomed at the White House by President Abraham Lincoln. Born into slavery in New York as Isabelle Baumfree and later nicknamed "Bell," Truth was separated from her parents at age eleven and sold to various slave owners. However, her formative relationship with her godly mother framed Truth's spiritual sensitivities and fortified her against the cruelty of slavery.[1]

Freed from slavery in 1826, Truth then legally secured freedom for her son from an Alabama plantation owner and later became the first African American to win a slander suit against notable whites.[2] She confronted racism, sexism and social injustice at every turn.[3] Exposed to the Dutch Reformed tradition in childhood, she committed her life to Christ in 1827, joined the Methodist Episcopal Church and was later influenced by the Quakers. Life experiences of enslavement and spiritual encounter, enjoined with her unique temperament, giftings and passion, primed the way for her calling as a fearless evangelist, abolitionist and reformer. She preached the gospel and advocated for women's rights and temperance. In 1843 she changed her name to Sojourner Truth as she claimed, "The Spirit calls me, and I must go."[4]

Despite a lack of education, her skillful oratory and commanding presence attracted many diverse crowds. Following God's voice regardless of consequence, Truth engaged her life calling by overcoming barriers of race, gender and poverty, while obeying God by advocating for the marginalized.[5] How did she discover her life purpose? Simply, her God-given spiritual gifts, talents, abilities, skills and strengths uniquely converged at a singular point in history to create a formidable life purpose. In responding to natural life circumstances and God's direction, Truth's life personified loving and serving God and others in ethical congruence.

By the power of the Holy Spirit, believers are likewise called to love and serve God and others and to reflect God's glory in all of life, including their vocations. For some, the call of God gradually becomes clear, as it did for Sojourner Truth. For others, discerning life purpose is fraught with anxiety. We may not know the vocational direction we should take or may find ourselves in an uncomfortable transition because of a job loss, job change or ongoing unemployment. Underscoring this process, we want to know not only that are we significant but that what we do is significant. We want to know that we are making a difference in the world for the cause of Christ and are living in a worthwhile manner.[6]

The roles we enact and the work we do, for better or worse, provide the context in which our identities are shaped. Unfortunately, we sometimes derive too much of our sense of self-worth from what we do. Job transition and unemployment only magnify this reality. Further, we may need guidance as to how to discern our life purpose and calling and how to navigate our vocational path, not only in young adulthood but also throughout subsequent life seasons. Struggle, uncertainty and ambiguity in vocational alignment are not uncommon for many believers who earnestly desire to serve God through all of life, including work. With many interacting factors contributing to life purpose discovery, it must be noted that some may not have a choice in pursuing their life purpose, dreams or aspirations because of mitigating circumstances, which likewise frames identity. Yet like Sojourner Truth, we may find ourselves in providential hands that allow us to overcome significant hurdles and follow the pulse of our God-given passions based on a divine design.

In consonance with the preceding chapters, this chapter assesses vocational formation as integral to overall Christian spiritual formation (CSF) in order to love and serve God and others through vocational expression (see fig. 8.1). After all, the first assignment given to our original forebears related to work through tending the Garden (Gen 1:28-30; 2:15). God

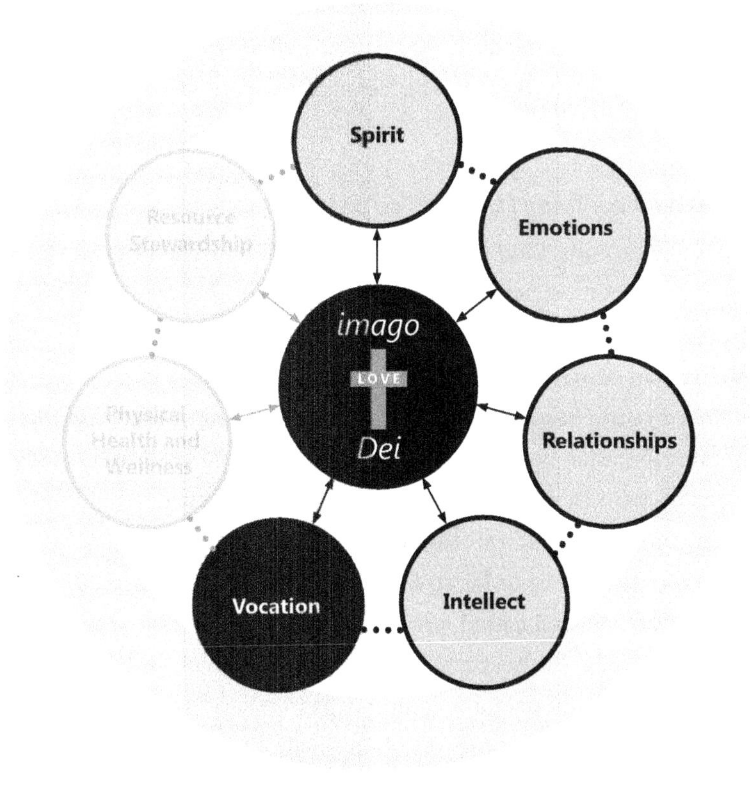

Figure 8.1. Vocational formation

blessed them and gave them dominion, or caring responsibility, over the created order. Interestingly, the temptation that ensued involved the mishandling of this prime piece of God's real estate, including what was clearly off-limits. The temptation came in the midst of their carrying out their vocational calling in response to God's stewardship directive and blessing.

Douglas John Hall argues that being created in the image of God signifies imaging our Creator.[7] If a fundamental component of our vocational calling is to image God, then Kierkegaard's summary of the *imago Dei* applies: "we can resemble God only in loving."[8] In this chapter on vocational formation, I argue that love is the primary impetus for vocation and the pursuit of one's calling, over and above all other perspectives. Further, this chapter features prominent theological perspectives regarding vocation in order to strengthen our grasp of calling and work; provides perspectives on discerning life calling and purpose, as well as understanding and discovering God-given gifting; and addresses how work provides a formative context for CSF.

Loving as the Impetus for Vocation

As the one who calls, God is the author of vocation. The English word *vocation* derives from various Latin word forms: *vocatio,* meaning "a call or summons"; *vocare,* meaning "to call"; and *vox,* meaning "voice." Fundamentally, God offers a loving invitation to receive divine grace in order to be restored in the image of Jesus through loving union with God. In the broadest sense, then, vocation relates to hearing God's call to be in loving relationship with the Father, the Son and the Holy Spirit.

Vocation begins first and foremost with a call to salvation by grace through repentance in order to love and worship God in continual fellowship. We have been called out of darkness into God's marvelous light (1 Pet 2:9) in order to become like Christ (2 Pet 1:4). In light of God's Word, the Christian's primary calling is to love God with all one's heart, soul, strength and mind, and simultaneously to love one's neighbor as oneself (Lk 10:27). According to Gary Badcock, "The Christian calling is to love," and love is the "one thing most worth living for."[9] Godly love is the north star for understanding vocation, developing character and interacting with others, within the overarching life of discipleship.[10] Recognizing godly love to be the foundation of vocation, Thérèse of Lisieux (1873–1897), a French Carmelite nun, discerned, "I understood that love comprised all vocations, that love was everything, that it embraced all times and places . . . in a word, that it was eternal! . . . MY VOCATION IS LOVE!"[11]

Godly love as the impetus for vocation is best seen through Jesus' life. From a young age, Jesus realized his primary call was to his Father's business (Lk 2:49). Early in his ministry Jesus articulated this calling when quoting Isaiah 61:1-2 (cf. Lk 4:18-19). And at the very end of his earthly life, Jesus affirmed his calling when responding to Pilate's question about kingship: "For this I was born, and for this I came into the world, to testify to the truth" (Jn 18:37). Jesus came to embody the Father's love and to carry out this calling by proclaiming the Kingdom in ethical yet grace-based teaching (Mt 5–7), caring for the poor (Mt 14:13-21; 15:29-38), healing the sick (Lk 17:11-19), doing the supernatural works of God (Jn 21:6) and offering his life to atone for the sins of humanity (Jn 19). Responding to his disciples, Jesus expressed both his and their divine calling, "We must work the works of him who sent me while it is day; night is coming when no one can work" (Jn 9:4).

The book of John traces how vocation progressed in Jesus' life as the One who was sent by the Father (Jn 16:28), did nothing on his own (Jn 5:19), spoke for the Father (Jn 12:49), did the will of the Father (Jn 6:38), accomplished the work of the Father (Jn 10:37-38; 14:31; 17:4) and obeyed the Father by remaining in his love (Jn 15:10).[12] Jesus' goal was nothing short of transformation of the world. His means for doing so was staying attached to the Father (Jn 15:1-8) and operating in the power of the Spirit (Jn 1:32-34). Vocation, then, connects our eternal relationship with God to living as God's ambassadors in this earthly life through the power of the Holy Spirit.

Responding to such a call is transformative, as highlighted through John Newton's life, which was illustrated in chapter one. After salvation, the entire trajectory of Newton's life radically changed from his earthly work as a slave trader to a writer, pastor and rector of an Anglican church. As Michael Miller observes, responding to God's call, like falling in love, changes everything.[13] Examples abound in Scripture of lives transformed through God's call, as in the case of Jesus' disciples, Nicodemus, the woman of Samaria, Mary Magdalene, the apostle Paul, Lydia and others. Their initial call was to the person of Christ, yet God had special work for them to do in reflecting God's love, grace and glory through service to others. As Gordon Smith notes, "To be a Christian is to respond to the call to know and love God and to love and serve others."[14]

Assessing Vocation in Theological Context

Like Sojourner Truth, God designed us to be ambassadors in the world (2 Cor 5:20) in order to bring glory to God. The apostle Paul observed, "For we are what he has made us, created in Christ Jesus for good works, which God prepared beforehand to be our way of life" (Eph 2:10). God created us for specific good works, such that our reciprocal love in relationship with God would be expressed to others through the power of the Holy Spirit. These good works, whereby doing flows out of being, directly connect to our vocation, which aligns with how God created us. The concept of vocation reflects a developmental trajectory, meaning that calling most often develops over time. By highlighting five primary perspectives, we will be able to assess vocational formation against the backdrop of godly love as the impetus for one's calling.

Presenting a brief overview of the theological development of the meaning and purpose of vocation is important in gaining understanding of vocation for today. Five formative perspectives are highlighted here, as drawn from these traditions: (1) ancient Greek and Roman, (2) medieval, (3) Reformed, (4) Roman Catholic and (5) three selected contemporary approaches.[15] The first perspective derives from the ancient Greeks and Romans. Like Plato and Aristotle, Greeks viewed life through the immortality of the gods and human beings as rational animals. Their vocational ideal involved contemplation, leisure and serenity. W. R. Forrester notes, "Contemplation to the Greeks and not merely to their philosophers is the highest kind of life, leisure is nobler than work."[16] Ancient Greeks associated work with mortality and what could be done by animals or slaves. Preoccupied with immortality, the ancient Greeks viewed work as servile, an irksome indignity and "an unmitigated evil to be avoided at all costs. It had no redeeming value."[17] Thus the ideal person lived a life of ease, while inferior persons worked.[18] If one did work, involvement in political life rather than economic life was prized. For example, in Plato's *Republic* those who rule are men of gold who engage in contemplation; warriors and guardians are associated with silver, whereas the artisans are made of bronze and are without citizen rights because their toil disqualifies them.[19] This ancient Roman perspective on vocation was influenced by the institution of slavery in early antiquity and then the development of guilds and wage labor in late antiquity.[20] Guilds led to the creation of apprenticeships, division of labor and business organization.

With exposure to Greek and Roman thinking and culture, the early church fathers in the premedieval era highly regarded humankind's capacity to think and reason.[21] Contemplation of the living God naturally replaced contemplation of Greek philosophy and ideas, yet active work remained of secondary importance. Augustine echoes this emphasis, "This contemplation [of God] is promised to us as the end [ultimate purpose] of all our labors and the eternal fullness of our joys."[22] In the thirteenth century Thomas Aquinas aligned his theology along similar lines when discussing the active and contemplative life: "That which belongs principally to the contemplative life is the contemplation of the divine truth, because this contemplation is the end of the whole human life."[23]

As philosophy professor Lee Hardy summarizes, "The Christian ideal of the contemplative life found its concrete manifestation in the medieval institution of the monastery. Renouncing marriage, property and related worldly entanglements, the monks abandoned their earthly occupations, withdrew to the cloister and committed themselves to the mortification of desires and the discipline of the mind, hoping that such a regimen would lead them to a mystical union with God."[24] Whereas the active life held temporal earthly value, the contemplative life was seen as being far superior, with prayer and meditation as conduits for mystical union with God. Vocation became synonymous with sacred work, and the noble goal of contemplation of God often degenerated into a merit system of religious good works, including the sale of indulgences.[25]

Medieval religious figures did not entirely dismiss work as unfavorable. For example, service to others in community characterized the Benedictine and Franciscan orders. Benedict of Nursia (c. 480–c. 550) spoke against idleness as "an enemy of the soul" in favor of manual labor so that monks would not become a burden to society.[26] The well-known Rule of St. Benedict instructed monks to live out their salvation in community through mutual service to one another. Likewise Francis of Assisi (1181–1226), who established the Franciscan order, served the poor and shared the gospel while attending to his community's needs. In the late Middle Ages, however, lay patrons of monasteries began supporting the work of those in religious orders, reinforcing what Hardy calls a "two-tiered spirituality," with laborers viewed as the distant second tier.[27] This view of vocation, which elevated love of God over love and service to others outside the monastery, continued until the Reformation in the fifteenth century.

The third perspective on vocation developed during the Reformation largely through the theology of Martin Luther and John Calvin, who challenged the medieval view.[28] With their conviction that faith alone through grace, not works, accounted for salvation, they confronted the exclusivity of the monastic view of vocation and what they perceived as a works-righteousness. Luther maintained that faith in God alone should lead to good works. Essentially, Luther viewed vocation as loving God through serving one's neighbor. Gene Veith comments, "Luther excoriated the monastic hermits who claimed that they were doing such good works in spending all of their time in prayer and devotion. These are not good works at all, he said; who are they helping?"[29] Reflecting on Luther's position, Gustaf

Wingren concludes that in vocation "one is not reaching up to God, but rather bends oneself down toward the world. When one does that, God's creative work is carried on. God's work of love takes form on earth, and that which is external witnesses to God's love."[30]

In the predominant Reformation view, vocation was not exclusive to the religious elite but rather to be embraced by all people, within what Luther called one's "station," a term meaning social location. For Luther, all the duties involving interactions with others relate to stations, which provide opportunity for believers to express the love and providence of God to others in mundane life activity, inclusive of all wholesome contexts.[31] Similar to Luther, John Calvin denied that vocation was for the religious elite within a two-tiered system. Based on his understanding of the *imago Dei,* Calvin argued for a life described as "watchful, effective, active sort, engaged in ceaseless activity."[32] With work having religious value because through it believers reflect God's image working in and through ordinary lives, Calvin viewed selfless service to others as the greatest expression of authentic love.[33] By the sixteenth century, Calvinists sought social reforms to align social institutions with God's Word. Restoring dignity to human work, the Reformed view of vocation corrected the misaligned theological bifurcation between loving God and loving and serving others. In summarizing the Reformed position, Hardy comments, "By working we affirm our uniquely human position as God's representatives on this earth, as cultivators and stewards of the good gifts of his creation, which are destined for the benefit of all."[34] Although the Reformed view of vocation realigned an imbalance, it tipped the scales in the direction of good works, which some observe framed the Protestant work ethic.[35]

A fourth noteworthy perspective of vocation connects to modern Roman Catholic theology, which developed on the heels of the medieval and Reformed perspectives. Because the Reformation challenged Catholicism's viability, coupled with the effects of the Industrial Revolution and laissez-faire economics, the Roman Catholic Church made a shift in the 1800s toward greater social thought and consciousness.[36] In 1891 Pope Leo XIII (1810–1903) published the encyclical *Rerum Novarum* (*On the New*

Things), offering a critique of the liberalism that had swept across Europe and advocating for the right to private property and the limitation of state-controlled economic intervention.[37] This encyclical essentially defined a shift from the two-tiered system, emphasizing the contemplative over the active life, to one in favor of work's integral contribution to individual and societal life.

Following *Rerum Novarum*, Catholic social teaching was reinforced by other encyclicals that addressed theologies of work. One of the most notable was *Laborem Exercens* (*On Human Work*), released in 1981 by Pope John Paul II (1920–2005).[38] Predicated on the *imago Dei* and the Genesis creation narrative, this encyclical emphasized "the fact that human work is the key, probably the essential key, to the whole social question" about "making life more human."[39] Taking a dominion perspective predicated on the creation narrative, the encyclical sets forth the centrality of work in human life as worthy of dignity, while also recognizing the toil, suffering and injustice implicitly embedded in work itself.[40] Key sections address technology, values, society, family, labor and capital, workers' rights, and the spirituality of work. Interestingly, Hardy notes how this encyclical "is remarkably Reformed in both substance and Spirit."[41]

Miroslav Volf comments that the *Laborem Exercens* is "one of the most remarkable ecclesiastical documents on the question of work ever written."[42] Although not all theologians have been so affirming, *Laborem Exercens* upheld the dignity and spirituality of human work.[43] Although this encyclical was theologically predicated on the Genesis creation narrative, it lacked grounding in a theology of love, which I argue is the primary impetus for vocation. We engage our giftings, talents, abilities, skills and strengths in vocation to express our gratitude for God's grace and mercy and to demonstrate our reciprocal love of God to others for God's glory.

A fifth perspective of vocation resonates in three selected contemporary views from Miroslav Volf, Darrell Cosden and Gary Badcock.[44] Arguing against the vocational understanding of human work related to calling evident in Protestant traditions, Volf presents a pneumatological approach to work through the prism of charisms, meaning the multiple gifts that the Spirit endows within the Christian community, which affect sacred and secular work.[45] Volf asserts, "Christian work must, therefore, be done under the inspiration of the Spirit and in light of the coming new creation."[46] Braiding eschatological and pneumatological threads, a theology of work, he maintains, must be normative, transformative and comprehensive in order to be applicable to industrial societies. Believing that the end times will result in eschatological transformation, Volf argues that work has intrinsic value because it contributes to the promised new creation rather than to a preservationist view of God's original creation. In recognizing Volf's helpful pneumatological perspective, I argue for a broader conceptualization of vocation as being predicated on the love of God and worthy to be practically discerned in order to maximize loving and serving God and others through discovering and applying one's spiritual giftings, talents, abilities, skills and strengths in service to others for the glory of God.[47]

Darrell Cosden offers a threefold model of vocation predicated on the *imago Dei*, referring to imaging God as being "humanity's primary purpose for existing."[48] Cosden posits that the threefold nature of work is (1) *instrumental*, meaning work always serves an end, including survival, (2) *relational*, referring to the way work is organized through social relationships and (3) *ontological*, referring to one's personal development at work.[49] In his helpful analysis of other views on work (i.e., from Karl Marx, Roman Catholicism, Karl Barth, Jürgen Moltmann, Alasdair MacIntyre, Oliver O'Donovan and Colin Gunton), Cosden concludes, "I am convinced that the Church of Jesus needs to provide Christ's followers with yet more encouragement to explore and to imaginatively experiment with how our daily 'normal' working activity . . . relates to the whole of our lives."[50] The strength of Cosden's presentation is that it is multidimensional and holistic in light of the *imago Dei*. However, what is absent from the presentation is a clear link between love and vocation, which this book seeks to strengthen.[51]

Gary Badcock offers another theological perspective on vocation, as introduced in the previous section. Badcock calls for love to be the foundation for understanding vocation and argues that God does not provide a blueprint for making vocational decisions but rather is removed from the particulars. Badcock maintains that God grants us freedom of choice if we get the first part of calling right (e.g., loving God and others). Asking whether "God has a tailor-made will for each individual," Badcock strongly argues against this notion of foreordination.[52] At the same time, Badcock submits that the Bible reflects "that God does have a specific plan and purpose for some individuals."[53] Although this seeming contradiction weakens Badcock's position, I find that his central premise based on love of God and others as being central to understanding vocation is compelling and aligns with the CSF model presented in this book. However, I argue for a more defined sense of calling discovery than Badcock offers and maintain that one's vocational calling, including God-given gifts, talents, abilities, skills and strengths, can be discerned and applied in order to maximize life purpose for the glory of God.

These aforementioned perspectives offer anchors for developing a theologically balanced view of vocation. All vocation is subsumed under a life of earnest discipleship through loving God in service to others. The ancient Greek view of work counters a biblical view of work as worthy and noble. The ancient Roman view involving the subjugation of slaves violates human dignity as set forth in Scripture. The medieval view of work, prioritizing the contemplative over the active life, falls shy of balanced Christian living. The Reformed view of work, emphasizing the nobility of work in loving service to others, perhaps has led to an unintentional weakening of the contemplative life so needed to sustain the active life. The Roman Catholic view of work grounded in the *imago Dei* reinforces the dignity of work as God-ordained. Contemporary views offered by Volf, Cosden and Badcock reinforce facets of vocation, namely, the importance of charisms in understanding vocation (Volf), the return to understanding the *imago Dei* and work (Cosden), and priority of love in vocational expression (Badcock). I reemphasize that love must be the central impetus for vocation that involves discerning life calling and purpose through discovery and application of God-given spiritual gifts, as well as talents, abilities, skills and strengths for the *gloria Dei*. Without love of God and others at the motivational center, vocation becomes a self-serving preoccupation. Fortunately, life calling and purpose can be discerned.

Discerning Life Calling and Purpose

Although the historical and theological perspectives surveyed provide a helpful framework for the meaning of vocation, they do not answer specific questions regarding individual life calling and purpose.[54] For example, young people especially struggle with life calling questions: Why am I here? What is my life calling? Do I have special gifts and talents, and if so, how can I discover them? What is God's purpose for my life? How can I serve God, yet make a living? What job would be most fulfilling to me? Is what I am doing significant? Responding to these questions requires time, experience, discernment, reflection, prayer and input from others. David Kinnaman notes that because many young people receive little guidance on how faith and vocational choice connect, the church would do well to proactively and relevantly address these questions.[55] Similar questions arise when adults find themselves in an unfulfilling job, a job transition or a season of unemployment, which can lead to a crisis of confidence and identity.[56]

Underscoring these questions, we must remember that vocation is not to be equated with a job. As Parker Palmer observes, "Vocation does not mean a goal that I pursue. It means a calling that I hear."[57] Vocation can be discerned. According to Gordon T. Smith, vocation first begins with (1) a general call to follow Christ, which is followed by (2) a specific call that is unique to each individual in contributing to Christ's mission in the world, and includes (3) an immediate call that involves the duties at hand, such as family roles and other obligations.[58] All three distill into our discipleship journey and reflect loving and serving God and others. A job might be associated with these second or third points, but all three frame who we are and what we do. Although one's sense of vocation unfolds developmentally through life seasons, the core of who we are, including God-given attributes, generally remains stable over time.[59]

In discovering our life calling, we see that God promises to guide us step-by-step over time through the work of the Holy Spirit (cf. Ps 23:3, 25:9; Is 48:17; Jer 10:23). Gordon Smith comments, "We should never overstate how significant one step or phase in God's providential guidance might be."[60]

For example, the character Sam in the movie version of J. R. R. Tolkien's Lord of the Rings: The Fellowship of the Ring *apprehensively announces to Frodo as they leave the safety of the shire, "If I take one more step, it will be the farthest away from home I've ever been." Neither had any idea of what awaited them. Yet Frodo knew his assignment—to take the ring to Mordor to save Middle Earth by ending Sauron's evil reign. Few of us know with certainty God's plan for our lives, but it starts and continues with a single step.*

A sense of calling might come quickly, as it did for Frodo, because of an overwhelming sense of responsibility. For others, calling develops over time when God-given desire meets aptitude and opportunity. This is true for two of my friends. One friend, whose heart of compassion met his mechanical expertise in operating industrial equipment, founded an organization that offers relief assistance after natural disasters. Another friend was so moved after watching a film on human trafficking that she established a local chapter of an international organization to end this travesty in her state. Both of their callings emerged over time when their passion and aptitude converged with opportunity to serve others.

Those with God-given passion and aptitude in various professions likewise make vocational choices based on calling. Examples include (1) *sports*—NFL coaches Tony Dungy and Joe Gibbs in football and NBA player Jeremy Lin in basketball, (2) *literature*—J. R. R. Tolkien, C. S. Lewis and Dorothy Sayers in writing, (3) *music and the arts*—J. S. Bach as classical composer, BeBe and CeCe Winans as contemporary Christian gospel artists, and Martha Williamson as Hollywood producer, (4) *business*—S. Truitt Cathy as founder of Chick-fil-A and Max De Pree as former CEO of furniture maker Herman Miller, Inc., and (5) *science*—Francis Collins as former director of the Human Genome Project and current director of the

National Institutes of Health. Calling is not relegated to Christian ministry, by any means. So how does a sense of calling develop?

In his autobiography Albert Schweitzer (1875–1965) wrote of his unfolding sense of calling in a chapter titled "I Resolve to Become a Jungle Doctor."[61] Schweitzer traced how his understanding of calling transitioned from theology and music to include becoming a medical doctor in French Equatorial Africa. Although few will be called by God to serve as a doctor in Africa, the path that Schweitzer followed is equally as relevant today as it was during his lifetime. Notice in what follows the progression that carried him along in life purpose discovery and decision making.

While engrossed in academic studies and music, Schweitzer described how he developed an increasing passion for those "struggling with sorrow and suffering."[62] *Identification of one's calling often begins with a burden of compassion to assist others.* Then at age twenty-one Schweitzer realized that he could not accept his good fortune regarding successful university study, scholarship and music proficiency as "a matter of course," but determined to "give something in return."[63] Schweitzer's calling clarity was furthered by *a sense of conviction* about what he was currently undertaking, honorable though it was. Then, determining that he "was justified" in giving himself to scholarship and the arts until age thirty, he fully committed himself "directly to serving humanity" after that time. *Commitment in decision making, although nonspecific, positions one for the faithful next step.* Then, gripped by Matthew 16:25, Schweitzer understood that by saving his life, he would lose it, but by losing his life for the gospel he would save it. *The Holy Spirit often anoints the Word of God to speak directly to our life situation in order to shape life calling.*

Not knowing quite where his next place of service would be, and equipped with only a commitment to serve humanity, Schweitzer stepped out to assist others in what he called "the experiment." First, he desired to educate abandoned and neglected children, but the organizations he approached were closed to volunteers. Next, he considered devoting himself to exconvicts and the homeless by joining with a local church pastor, but he was dissuaded because of his discomfort in soliciting finances for the work, as well as a reluctance to join an organization unless he could become "a wholly free agent." *Perceiving natural preferences through experience and trial-and-error learning provides further direction regarding life calling and purpose discovery.*

Then at the age of twenty-nine Schweitzer providentially happened upon an article titled "The Needs of the Congo Mission" in the Paris Missionary Society's publication *Journal des Missions Évangélique.* After reading the appeal for workers to carry on the work in what was then the northern province of the Congo, Schweitzer resolved to serve there as a doctor after completing medical school.[64] His decision precipitated intense opposition from relatives, friends and colleagues, who questioned his decision to leave the prestige of being the principal of a seminary, a theologian, a music scholar and an accomplished organist.[65] Appealing to his obedience to God, Schweitzer was amazed "to see them unable to perceive that the desire to serve the love preached by Jesus may sweep a man into a new course of life."[66] *Responding to a sense of life calling and purpose may be riddled with criticism and resistance by family members and close associates.* Fortunately, Schweitzer confided in one trusted and supportive friend. *In the process of discernment, it is important to secure the prayer support of a few trusted others.*

The way Schweitzer responded to this opposition revealed his godly character. He continued his own self-assessment, concluding that his "good health, sound nerves, energy, practical common sense, toughness, prudence, [and] very few wants" equipped him for the path ahead.[67] *Taking an inventory of how personal passions, gifts, abilities, talents, skills and strengths align with future plans is a worthy endeavor.* At the same time, Schweitzer humbly acknowledged that certain circumstances preclude capable and deserving people from pursuing their desired calling and dreams. Further emphasizing that strong determination must be tempered by patience and humility, Schweitzer commented, "One can save one's life as a human being, along with one's professional existence, if one seizes every opportunity, however unassuming, to act humanly toward those who need another human being. In this way we serve both the spiritual and the good."[68] *Exercising humility in one's chosen path (and all of life) reflects the character of Christ and glorifies God.*

The lives of contemporary missionaries Rolland and Heidi Baker followed a similarly circuitous path. Coming to Christ at sixteen, Heidi's early cross-cultural experiences tenderized her heart for the poor and unloved. During a five-day food fast while in college, Heidi received a prophetic word that she would be a missionary in Africa, Asia and England. Rolland was raised in China by missionary parents. After marrying and ministering in the slums of Indonesia and Hong Kong and later to the homeless in London while earning advanced theology degrees, Rolland and Heidi eventually moved to Mozambique in 1995, where they continue to care for the poor, especially orphaned and abandoned children, and plant churches.[69] Through their obedience to God's leading and varied life experiences, the Bakers dedicate all their God-given gifts and attributes to changing the nation of Mozambique, one life at a time.

From Schweitzer's and the Bakers' lives, we glean principles for discovering our own life calling and purpose. First, this process is a journey that may have many twists and turns, yet is often guided by the still small voice of the Spirit through what Christian psychologist John Neafsey calls "the inner compass."[70] Second, our sense of calling is often informed by a burden, passion, compassion, desire or sensitivity to a specific group or cause that propels us to act.[71] Third, the Holy Spirit anoints the Scriptures or sends a God-given prophetic word that guides decision making. Fourth, reflecting on how God has designed us offers life purpose clues, as we faithfully discern our God-given design to fulfill God's purposes, whatever our chosen path.[72] Socrates's wise words apply to life calling discovery: "The unexamined life is not worth living."[73] Although discerning spiritual giftings, talents, abilities, skills, strengths, life preferences, disposition and personality provides clues as to God-given design, these alone do not validate one's calling. As Os Guinness contends, "Giftedness alone should not be how you determine your calling," but you must take into consideration "your own life opportunities, God's guidance, and your willingness to do whatever God leads you to do."[74]

Fifth, God provides growth opportunities and directs our steps through experiential and trial-and-error learning.[75] Sixth, growing where we are planted in current vocational contexts prepares us for the future, remembering that we work as unto the Lord (Col 3:23). Faithfulness in little things is the prerequisite for being faithful in much (Lk 16:10-12). Seventh, responding to our sense of calling may incur criticism and resistance from family members and associates. Eighth, in the process of discernment, seeking God in prayer and enlisting the prayer support of trusted others provide needed support and encouragement.[76] We need to find those who believe in us, knowing that encouragement is an invaluable asset. Although a discussion of prayer is absent from Schweitzer's calling account, the role of prayer, worship and fasting cannot be overemphasized in gaining calling clarity. After all, it was through a time of worship and fasting that the Spirit directed Paul and Silas to the work to which they were called (Acts 13:2). Ninth, stepping out in obedience requires initiative and effort. God will not force us to take the next faithful step.

Tenth, people will recognize this sense of calling and giftedness, such as when others observed Sojourner Truth's effective oratory and passion for justice. The prophetess Deborah (Judg 4–5) likewise illustrates how stepping out in personal gifting prompts recognition from others. Many approached Deborah while she exercised leadership as a judge in settling disputes (Judg 4:4-5). Being a woman in a patriarchal society, Deborah offered her God-given gifts, talents, abilities, skills and strengths in serving her nation and thereby earned Barak's respect and confidence. Eventually she became the driving force in Israel's deliverance. Although the emergence of each individual's sense of calling varies, we can be relieved to know that we do not have to "have it altogether" and that God is more committed to our fruitfulness than we realize. Often this process involves being obedient to God's voice for each next step.[77] Then one's vision (what we are called to do) and one's mission (how we are to do it) provide further directional focus, especially when competing alternatives present themselves.[78] Another vital ingredient for calling clarification relates to gifting discovery.

Understanding and Discovering God-Given Gifting

Followers of Jesus become instruments of God's love and grace in the world through the exercising of their God-given spiritual gifts, in addition to the discovery and release of their talents, abilities, skills and strengths for God's glory. The parable of the talents (Mt 25:14-30) suggests that God expects us to put all resources to use for maximum Kingdom impact. Richard Bolles offers a simple path for fleshing out one's life purpose—"to exercise that Talent which you particularly came to Earth to use—your greatest gifts, which you most delight to use, in the places(s) or setting(s) which God has caused to appeal to you the most, and for the purposes which God most needs to have done in the world."[79] Exercising God-given gift and talents compares to an athlete who practices regularly for optimal conditioning. To do so, Bolles maintains that we need to unlearn the notion that engaging our unique life calling will result in "achievements which all the world will see," as many may be hidden from view.[80] Further, what we do is dependent on "God's Spirit breathing in us" in conjunction with our responsive efforts.[81]

Many, however, have not identified their gifts, let alone been able to intentionally exercise them. Unlike composers Mozart and Beethoven and artist Pablo Picasso, few of us are child prodigies, but each of us has gifts to be discovered and released for God's glory. The Lord uses people just like you and me to reflect God's glory in ordinary and extraordinary ways. More likely, we assume that because something comes easily for us, it is equally as easy for others. Consequently, we minimize our worth and potential contribution. Conversely, when we think that we are contributing to something bigger than ourselves, we become motivated and tap into creative energy in applying personal resources.

Discovering God-given spiritual gifts, as well as natural talents, abilities, skills and strengths, offers one step in applying them to maximize Kingdom fruitfulness because calling and spiritual gifts interface for Kingdom impact. Without spiritual gifts, our calling would be disempowered. As theologian Jürgen Moltmann affirms, "The gifts which the one or the other brings or receives are at the service of their calling; for God who calls takes people at the point *where* [God] reaches them and *as they are.*"[82] Further, Moltmann advocates that we not look at what we do not have but rather discern God's unique touch on our lives.[83] This touch comes in the form of spiritual gifts.

What are spiritual gifts, and how might we understand them?[84] Spiritual gifts are expressions of God's grace given to believers by the Spirit for building up the body of Christ for the common good and for exalting the Lord Jesus.[85] The apostle Paul refers to spiritual gifts in his letters to the New Testament churches. Paul's central unifying themes include the need for unity amid the diversity of gifts and the grace of God bestowed through gifts given to each person. Mention of spiritual gifts occurs in (1) Romans 12:6-8, (2) 1 Corinthians 12:8-11, and (3) 1 Corinthians 12:28, whereas spiritual roles identified in Ephesians 4:11 relate to the equipping positions within the church.[86] Fundamentally, spiritual gifts are endowments of God's grace, or as James Dunn expresses, "inward power coming to conscious outward expression."[87] Commentators have noted that although Paul specifies various gifts, such as those in 1 Corinthians 12, they were not intended to be exhaustive.[88]

Motivational in nature, the seven charismata mentioned in Romans 12:6-8 make clear that believers have different functions within the body of Christ. These gifts, given by grace, include (1) prophecy/perceiving, (2) ministering/service, (3) teaching, (4) exhortation/encouragement, (5) giving, (6) leading/administrating, and (7) compassion/showing mercy. As Paul explains, "so we, who are many, are one body of Christ, and individually we are members one of another" (v. 5). In other words, believers have been given different gifts, which interdependently contribute to the working of the body of Christ. After mentioning these specific gifts, Paul qualifies the motivation for exercising the gifts ("Let love be genuine" [Rom 12:9]) and the ethical requirements of the receiving gifts of grace ("love one another with mutual affection; outdo one another by showing honor" [Rom 12:10]). As a consistent theme in the CSF model, love is to be the core motivation for receiving and expressing spiritual gifts.[89] First, these spiritual gifts are most frequently discovered and released when serving others, as Miroslav Volf advocates in his pneumatological understanding of work around charisms, which he argues (and I agree) are expressed in the church *and* in the world.[90] Second, many believers benefit from taking spiritual gifts assessments in order to confirm their God-given gifts.[91]

In 1 Corinthians 12, Paul takes up similar themes to those introduced in Romans 12:6-8, including unity amid diversity of the same Spirit for church health. "Now there are varieties of gifts, but the same Spirit; and there are varieties of services, but the same Lord; and there are varieties of activities, but it is the same God who activates all of them in everyone" (1 Cor 12:4-6).[92] The ninefold manifestation gifts enumerated in 1 Corinthians 12:8-10 comprise what Gordon Fee describes as "a disclosure of the Spirit's activity" in the church's midst and include (1) the utterance or word of wisdom, (2) the utterance or word of knowledge, (3) faith, (4) gifts of healing, (5) working of miracles, (6) prophecy, (7) discernment of spirits, (8) various kinds of tongues and (9) interpretation of tongues. Paul refers to these gifts as "manifestations of the Spirit" (v. 7).[93]

Noting that the Spirit's activity can be compared to "the wind [that] blows where it chooses" (Jn 3:8), Fee argues that the Spirit distributes these gifts without qualification to "ultimately express the Spirit's sovereign action in the life of the believer and the community as a whole."[94] All become candidates for the impartation of grace through these manifestation gifts for the common good. Fee adds, "[Paul's] urgency, as vv. 8-10 show, is not that each person is 'gifted,' but rather the Spirit is manifested in a variety of ways."[95] These gifts are fluid and not exclusively possessed by any one individual within the body of Christ.

More expansive than in Romans 12, Paul in 1 Corinthians 12:12-26 metaphorically compares the working of these gifts to the working of various members of the physical body. As each part of the body (e.g., foot, hand, ear, eye) serves interdependently for overall physiological functioning, so too do all of the spiritual gifts exercised in believers' lives within the body of Christ. Paul follows up his discussion on one body with many members by reinforcing that each person is a part of the body of Christ (1 Corinthians 12:27). He then again qualifies some of the gifts that he previously mentioned (1 Cor 12:4-10), in what Fee sees as "the whole range of 'ministries' in the church," as they find expression through various persons (1 Cor

12:28): (1) apostles, (2) prophets, (3) teachers, (4) deeds of power/ workers of miracles, (5) gifts of healing, (6) assisting others, (7) forms of leadership/administration, and (8) various kinds of tongues.

After his discussion of the manifestation gifts in 1 Corinthians 12, Paul follows up his corrective on the proper manner for exercising the manifestation gifts with this challenge and assurance: "But strive for the greater gifts. And I will show you a still more excellent way" (1 Cor 12:31). Paul admonishes the Corinthians to "eagerly desire" (NIV) these gifts, while at the same time pointing out that love is the only acceptable condition for exercising them (1 Cor 13:1-13). Love is not a charism, or spiritual gift, but rather a "way of life that gives meaning and depth to any spiritual gift God grants" and heads the list of the fruit of the Spirit (Gal 5:22-23), which evidence the Spirit's indwelling presence.[96]

Life calling and purpose, then, become an opportunity to understand, discover and exercise spiritual gifts based on loving and serving God and others through grace: "Like good stewards of the manifold grace of God, serve one another with whatever gift each of you has received" (1 Pet 4:10). As Paul charged Timothy, "Do not neglect the gift that is in you, which was given to you through prophecy with the laying on of hands by the council of elders" (1 Tim 4:14). Serving others activates our spiritual gifts, in addition to God-given talents, abilities, skills and strengths. Most important, we need to pay attention to inner joy, energy and fulfillment when serving others. This is but one clue in discovering our spiritual and natural gifts and abilities.

Like spiritual gifts, natural endowments such as talents, abilities and skills are God-given and to be applied in serving others. For example, some may have natural musical, language, financial, athletic or technological abilities that can be offered to serve others and glorify God. Craig Keener points out that the apostle Paul applied all his gifts and endowments for Kingdom advance, including his Roman citizenship and language fluency.[97] Some, however, may have a dim view of their natural abilities, especially when compared to others. Although there is no universal formula for discovering natural talents, abilities, skills and strengths, there are some key contributing factors.

First, having mentors—whether parents, other relatives, teachers, ministry leaders or friends—has "both cognitive and affective appeal, offering both insight and emotional support," according to Sharon Daloz Parks.[98] Vocational formation occurs when young people are given a task to do, knowing that their contribution is meaningful to others.[99] Mentors serve as mirrors to reflect one's talents, skills and goals, as well as provide feedback in decision making. An especially tender time of identifying personal attributes is during the young adult years when competing worldviews and cultural messages circulate amid a consumer culture driven by hollow role models.[100] Emerging adults, as Parks suggests, entertain "big questions and worthy dreams," where meaning making assumes center stage. In that life discovery is a developmental process, Parks upholds the relevance of mentoring to provide the needed perspective in this shaping process.[101] Biblical examples of mentoring include Moses with Joshua, Elijah with Elisha, and Jesus with his disciples.

Second, vocational coaches and career counselors can also provide opportunity for calling clarity.[102] However, as Lee Hardy observes, "Career paths are rarely straight," and "careers decisions are rarely irrevocable."[103] Vocational exploration is part of the maturation process. Third, job skills training and higher education programs contribute to honing interests and skills where instructors and professors create mentoring environments that fuel dreams and awaken potential.[104] Fourth, taking personal assessments offers various opportunities to clarify personality, temperament, talents, abilities and strengths. For example, the DiSC Personality Assessment and the Myers-Briggs Type Indicator (MBTI) contribute to understanding personality of both self and others.[105]

Another helpful resource is the StrengthsFinder, which actually assesses talent, not strengths, according to author Tom Rath.[106] Rath suggests that a *strength* ("the ability to consistently provide near-perfect performance") is the multiplied effect of a *talent* ("a natural way of thinking, feeling, or behaving") times *investment* ("time spent practicing, developing your skills, and building your knowledge base").[107] Of the thirty-four possible resultant themes, the online report provides a profile and description of one's top five strengths, which are applicable in family, relational, educational, ministry and vocational contexts.[108] I have found the DiSC, MBTI and the StrengthsFinder especially helpful and, in some cases, confirming in each of these contexts. Understanding, discovering and releasing God-given gifts finds particular expression in the workplace, where work serves as a formational conduit for conforming believers into the image of Jesus.

WORKING AS FORMATION

For followers of Jesus, the workplace is an incubator not only for vocational formation but also for the other CSF dimensions. Work is the seedbed for what Eugene Peterson calls "vocational holiness," that quality of serving others "in a culture devoted to the Kingdom of Self."[109] The workplace is the proving ground for the fruit of the Spirit (Gal 5:22-23), giving expression to the virtues of Christ. Work not only offers continual opportunity to love and serve others but also to examine personal motives, actions and reactions for why we do what we do.

Vocational holiness is what Jesus modeled throughout his ministry, starting with his victory over the three temptations of power, prestige and compromise.[110] First, the devil tempted Jesus to use his divine power to satisfy his own needs ("If you are the Son of God, command these stones to become loaves of bread" [Mt 4:3]). Second, the devil tempted Jesus to misuse his divine power for prestige and sensationalism ("If you are the Son of God, throw yourself down; for it is written, 'He will command his angels concerning you'" [Mt 4:6]). Third, the devil tempted Jesus to compromise his primary calling for personal gain by offering Jesus all the kingdoms of the world ("All these I will give you, if you will fall down and worship me" [Mt 4:9]). These same temptations of power, prestige and compromise surface in the workplace today through the related tentacles of greed, control, manipulation and self-aggrandizement. The desire for fame and fortune in the workplace has led many to destructive ends, with endless newspaper headlines featuring these casualties. Those who withstand such temptations are increasingly rare. Joseph and Daniel offer biblical and ethical exemplars of those who did.

Contemporary voices provide practical approaches on how faith is the raison d'être for Christian living in the workplace. One need not be a pastor or missionary to be used as a vessel for the gospel with Kingdom impact.[111] The secular workplace, as the stories of Joseph and Daniel exemplify, provides abundant opportunity to love and serve others in tangible ways. Since the 1980s, various movements have legitimized the integration of faith on the job, including the "faith at work" movement with a marketplace ministry emphasis and the establishment of viable centers for studying the interconnection between faith and work in research and praxis, such as the Princeton University Faith and Work Initiative.[112] Increasingly, higher education venues are addressing faith and work integration, understanding their responsibility when preparing graduates for a successful future.[113] This trend typifies the legitimizing of influence that Christians have as salt and light in the world (Mt 5:13-16). With increasing diversity, pluralism and globalization, the workplace provides a platform for living out one's faith and demonstrating the fruit of the Spirit through genuinely serving others.

In addition to serving others, work fulfills other facets of human activity: (1) provision for life's needs and wants, (2) a means of production, (3) a vehicle for human achievement and (4) a source for deriving personal significance and satisfaction.[114] Through work, we bear the image of our Creator and further Christ's redemptive purposes in the world.[115] Simultaneously, work presents many challenges, not the least of which are inequity, injustice and inhumane practices. Those who perpetrate hypocrisy, harassment and dishonest and abusive work practices make a mockery of the biblical and ethical principles that Jesus personified (e.g., see Jesus' harsh rebuke of the Pharisees for their immoral motives cloaked within a religious veneer in Mt 23:13-36).[116] When love is absent, ethical violations are likely to erupt. The workplace provides abundant opportunity to be conformed into the image of Jesus through standing for honesty and integrity and examining one's motives, attitudes and behaviors.

The vocational holiness that Eugene Peterson refers to is especially tested in the workplace during times of (1) interpersonal conflict and misunderstanding, (2) personal failure, (3) overwork and (4) transition, each supplying opportunities for vocational and spiritual formation. First, navigating work conflict and misunderstanding supplies formational opportunity, as character is tested when values, attitudes, motives and decision making collide with those of others. We are shaped through conflict when we see ourselves as we really are and when we turn to God for help in situations that we cannot control. Sojourner Truth experienced conflict when she confronted gender and ethnic injustice, in what John Neafsey calls an "awakening from the sleep of inhumanity."[117] Similarly, abolitionist William Wilberforce (1759–1833) faced conflict when he upheld biblically moral principles to eradicate slavery in England. Both Truth and Wilberforce turned to God for strength and resolve during these social conflicts, while simultaneously speaking God's truth in love. Conflict in the workplace may also contribute to spiritual formation through a "death to self" and a dimension of suffering when noble desires and goals are misunderstood or rejected by others.

Second, personal failure offers vocational formation opportunity.[118] Parker Palmer describes his vocational journey that led to a realization of his worst fears of failure and the ensuing inner darkness that they exposed.[119] His restlessness and subsequent burnout turned to despair but eventually led to moments of truth and authenticity that shaped his future.

Dr. Ben Carson, world-renowned former director of pediatric neurosurgery at Johns Hopkins Hospital, describes how impending failure turned into success, confirming his dream of becoming a physician. Raised by a single mother in the inner city of Detroit, Carson went from being at the bottom of his fifth-grade class to graduating from Yale University and the University of Michigan medical school. Through his middle and high school years, Carson and his older brother applied themselves to their studies under the constant encouragement of their mother, who barely completed the third grade.

When faced with the final exam in chemistry during his first undergraduate semester at Yale, Carson realized his best efforts were miserably insufficient. Fighting despair and realizing that he could not cram hard enough to pass, he called out to God, as his dreams of becoming a doctor dissipated: "Either help me understand what kind of work I ought to do, or else perform some kind of miracle and help me to pass this exam."[120] *For the next two hours Carson memorized formulas and equations then went to sleep. During the night, he had a dream of a person who wrote chemistry problems on the board. When Carson awoke, he recorded those notes as best he could. Amazingly, when he sat for the chemistry exam, all of the problems from the dream appeared on the exam. He ended up with a 97 percent, which put him at the top of the class. While not being presumptuous, only desperate, Carson witnessed a miracle of God's abundant grace and vocational confirmation. This near failure led to greater personal faith and continued shaping that framed Carson's vocational future.*

Third, overwork contributes to vocational formation (or in some cases deformation, and in other cases reformation) by extending our God-given capacities beyond healthy limits. Evidence related to overwork abounds. Economist Juliet Schor highlights the steady increase of working hours and decrease in leisure time for workers in the United States and the unhealthy work rhythms of other countries.[121] Schor notes the phenomenon in Japan known as *karoshi* or "death by overwork," where perfectly healthy men in high-stress jobs die for no other known reason.[122] According to management consultant Diane Fassel, workaholism is "the cleanest of all addictions" because overwork results in socially acceptable productivity and promotion.[123]

Overwork and workaholism can lead to burnout, a debilitating erosion of personal reserves resulting in exhaustion, cynicism and ineffectiveness.[124] If sustained overwork and burnout are so debilitating, how does burnout contribute to one's formation? In some cases burnout may result in a cessation of self-effort and a complete dependence on God. For example, one qualitative study examining the outcomes of pastoral burnout found that the resultant isolation from God and others in the short-term led pastors ultimately to take needed rest, to explore unresolved issues that produced excessive overwork in the first place, and to experience God's unconditional love in deeper dependence and intimacy.[125] If unaddressed, however, excessive overwork may indicate a lack of faith, a subtle form of idolatry and pride, an inability to receive the enabling grace of God, and deeper-seated emotional and spiritual issues. Further, overwork ignores the balance of work, rest and leisure that comprises a healthy, holistic lifestyle.[126]

Fourth, various transitions related to loss and grief at work likewise influence vocational formation.[127] For example, a job loss threatening economic viability or retirement may threaten one's sense of significance. Willie Loman, protagonist in Arthur Miller's award-winning play *Death of a Salesman*, typifies how job loss affects personal identity and life purpose. Loman's identity was so tied to his job and concepts of success that his job loss precipitated his suicide. For some like Loman, the loss of job status or role or a demotion may foster similar depression. Another circumstance may include the death of someone significant in one's vocational journey, such as a family member or work associate, which results in depression, loss of vision and hopelessness. For example, after Jesus was crucified, Peter went back to fishing, reverting to his previous profession in the midst of grief and an uncertain future (Jn 21).

Another transition that is deeply shaping and connected to loss and grief relates to declining health and impending death. Crises like these cause reflection and reevaluation regarding life's priorities and interpersonal relationships. The character Ivan Ilyich in Leo Tolstoy's (1828–1910) timeless novella *The Death of Ivan Ilyich* illustrates how preoccupation with an admirable job and climbing the social ladder at the expense of meaningful relationships provide little consolation when facing imminent death.[128] A poignant contrast of how one faces death is found in the journey of Dr. Randy Pausch (1960–2008), former computer science professor at Carnegie Mellon University, whose diagnosis of terminal pancreatic cancer inspired others to fulfill their childhood dreams.[129] Vocational shaping resulting from how one deals with the imminent death of another is illustrated by Mitch Albom's experience with his former professor Morrie Schwarz. Albom's book *Tuesdays with Morrie* describes the life-changing experience of meeting with Schwarz for fourteen Tuesdays to hear insightful perspectives on the meaning of life, which influenced

Albom's subsequent life perspectives and vocational choices.[130] The workplace offers formational opportunity to be conformed to the image of Jesus through the exercise of vocational holiness during times of interpersonal conflict and misunderstanding, personal failure, overwork and transition. The workplace provides a proving ground for personal character, integrity and ethical living through expressing the fruit of the Spirit (Gal 5:22-23).

This chapter addressed love as the impetus for vocation and assessed vocation from five theological perspectives, followed by a discussion of life calling and purpose, understanding and discovering God-given gifting, and working as formation. The lives of Sojourner Truth, Albert Schweitzer, Rolland and Heidi Baker, and Ben Carson serve as powerful examples of those who have responded to God's unique calling and have left their imprint on the world. Fulfilling personal vocation and life purpose depends on the grace of God enjoined by faithful stewardship of God-given giftings, talents, abilities, skills and strengths for loving and serving God and others for God's glory. While self-effort alone is insufficient, this process requires cooperation with God through personal obedience and initiative. The Spirit anoints the work of our hands so we can say with the psalmist,

> Let the favor of the Lord our God be upon us,
> and prosper for us the work of our hands—
> O prosper the work of our hands! (Ps 90:17)

Chapter nine addresses physical health and wellness formation, another essential CSF dimension that synergistically interacts with each of the other six dimensions.

9

Physical Health

Our Bodies

Through the fact that the Word of God became flesh,
the body entered theology . . .
through the main door.

John Paul II,
Man and Woman He Created Them: The Theology of the Body

Health is not valued until sickness comes.

Dr. Thomas Fuller,
Gnomologia: Adages and Proverbs

With shoulders slumped, Stephen caught me after class.[1] We had just completed a lively session on stewarding our physical health in order not only to optimally love and serve God and others, but also to feel our best in doing so. As an assistant pastor of a church and just turning thirty-two, Stephen related how his busy lifestyle led to eating fast food twice if not three times a day. When he and his wife arrived home from their demanding jobs, they either went out for fast food or popped frozen dinners in the microwave, as neither has time for food shopping or meal preparation. Probing a bit further, I asked him to share some of what they consumed other than burgers, French fries, sodas, coffee and microwave dinners. He responded, "Little else." Realizing for the first time the possible consequences of this nutritional pattern, Stephen admitted, "We are overdue to make needed nutritional and lifestyle changes!" Armed with some new information about health, Stephen and his wife began to prepare healthy meals at home and make healthier choices when eating out.

In another setting, Valerie shared with me that she had had to quit her job as a public school teacher on the advice of her physician. At fifty-three, she had experienced congestive heart failure, aggravated by Type 2 diabetes and an overweight condition. She had moved into a pastoral role at her church, where life demands only increased. Stress related to ministry became emotionally debilitating. Valerie's doctor warned her that her health habits needed to change if she planned to make it to age sixty. After learning more about physical health and wellness, Valerie made several lifestyle changes that included improving her eating and sleeping habits, exercising four days a week for thirty minutes, and learning to say no to everyone's demands. Her health slowly began to improve.

These two examples typify what happens when people realize the benefits of informed physical health and wellness decisions not only for the care of their bodies but also as a vehicle for glorifying God.[2] Being created in the *imago Dei*, our physical bodies are masterpieces of God's creation and a critical dimension for CSF, as featured in figure 9.1.[3] Michelangelo's depiction of the creation of Adam and Eve that crowns the Sistine Chapel ceiling signifies that God created persons not only with spirits and souls but also with physical bodies. Our embodiment is not to be trivialized in favor of the spirit and soul.[4] As a conduit for God's glory, the body can be developed to maximize its purpose.

This chapter on physical health and wellness begins by addressing embodiment, or God's fashioning human bodies to reveal God's glory through the Spirit within, followed by five essential areas of physical health and wellness formation: (1) nutrition, (2) physical exercise, (3) sleep, (4) stress, rest and leisure, and (5) sexual purity. In our global culture these five areas

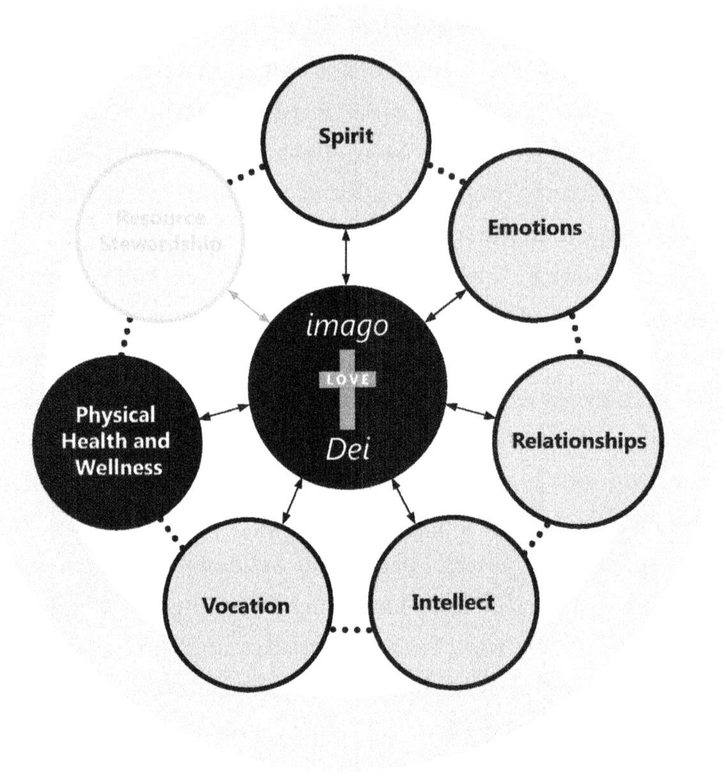

Figure 9.1. Physical health formation

are often the most ignored and yet the most crucial for physical well-being and longevity. The discussion of these five health stewardship areas, which draws upon the health sciences, is not intended to cause shame, guilt or condemnation. Quite the contrary!

With the escalation of preventable diseases, providing up-to-date research will empower readers to take reasonable and incremental steps in safeguarding their physical health in order to optimally love and serve God and others, while attending to appropriate self-care. Burnout for the cause of Christ through personal neglect or through violating physical limits is hardly a noble goal. Informed physical health stewardship, in contrast to idolatry of the body, optimizes Kingdom effectiveness. The goal of this chapter is to contribute to glorifying God through understanding God's purpose for embodiment and for the care of our bodies in practical ways toward that end. By God's grace, each of us can make incremental changes that honor God's prized creation—our bodies—because we are "fearfully and wonderfully made" (Ps 139:14). We turn to a brief overview of embodiment that lays the foundation as to why proper care of the body for physical health is so vital.

Embodiment and Holistic Alignment

The physical body made in the *imago Dei* is a conduit to be developed for the primary purpose it was designed for—to bring glory to God. According to the apostle Paul the body (not to be separated from the inner person) is to be offered to God as a living sacrifice through a spiritual lifestyle of worship (Rom 12:1) in surrender for God's service. Embodiment, then, is the practical vehicle for worship. As Stanley Hauerwas notes, worship is to be the Christian's natural bodily instinct: "Christianity is to have one's body shaped, one's habits determined, in such a manner that the worship of God is unavoidable."[5] Embodiment, therefore, lays claim to the praise of God as the common thread of the Christian's existence. The importance of embodiment manifests in the incarnation.

The Father sent Jesus, the Son of God, by the power of the Spirit to earth through physical embodiment. If human life is a gift through the breath of God, including embodiment, as Amos Yong suggests, then the body is not to be trivialized by gnostic or dualistic notions but rather needs renewing for optimal health and wellness.[6] In a holistic view of embodiment, Yong emphasizes that human life is a "gift of the breath of God that is irreducible to the body, yet life is never apart from the body."[7] Those in Christ anticipate that imperfect, broken and disabled bodies will be glorified one day by the resurrection power of the same Spirit that raised Jesus from the dead and returned him to heaven (1 Cor 15:42-44; Phil 3:21). Henri Nouwen attests to this future reality when writing about Philippe, a disabled member of the L'Arche community to whom he provided care, who "will rise from the grave with a new body."[8] Those with physical (and cognitive) disabilities are equally loved by God, reflect God's glory because they are made in God's image and are worthy of dignity as vital members of the body of Christ to be included and loved.[9] The disabled enrich our lives and have much to teach us about the love and grace of God, as well as ourselves. Regardless of disability, I intend this discussion to broaden our understanding of caring for the physical body to the extent that one is able.

According to Jürgen Moltmann the importance of embodiment evidences in the outcome of (1) *creation*, where we were made in the image of God; (2) *reconciliation*, whereby Jesus reconciled the world to God through his human body, identifying with all those who suffer; and (3) *redemption* from this world through resurrected and transfigured bodies for the Kingdom to come.[10] Moltmann affirms that "embodiment is the end of all God's works," based on "the Creator's fertile and inventive love."[11] The body has holy standing in that it expresses our "higher calling and makes its realization concrete."[12] That higher calling of worship ushers in the glory of God through one's body regardless of circumstances.

The apostle Paul expressed this higher calling when considering the impending outcome of his imprisonment: "It is my eager expectation and hope that I will not be put to shame in any way, but that by my speaking with all boldness, Christ will be exalted now as always *in my body*, whether by life or by death. For to me, living is Christ and dying is gain" (Phil 1:20-21, italics added). Paul yearned for Christ to be exalted in his body, even in the face of possible death. Gordon Fee notes that Paul's words, "now as always in my body," bespeak Paul's singular telos of praising God.[13] Similarly, F. F. Bruce comments, "Paul's constant ambition is that in his body—that is, in whatever happens to him on the physical plain, whether life or death—the glory of Christ would be promoted."[14] The Christian's body is to bring glory to God when surrendered to God. In Paul's words, the body is meant "for the Lord, and the Lord for the body" (1 Cor 6:13). In the words of theologian Adam G. Cooper, "The body of the Christian is an organic, spiritual integrated component of Christ's body."[15] Taking care of our bodies comprises a vital component of faithful formation.

As the apostle Paul stressed to the Corinthian believers, the body is a temple of the Holy Spirit within, and we are to glorify God in our bodies (1 Cor 6:19-20). Whereas Paul earlier applied the temple metaphor to the entire church (1 Cor 3:16-17), he now applies it to individual believers regarding the appropriate and holy use of their bodies in light of sexual immorality. Ben Witherington observes Paul as saying that our bodies "belong to God and therefore should glorify the one who is over them, in them, and by them in all things," including bodily behavior, and David Garland notes that the Holy Spirit marks believers' bodies "as belonging to God and set aside for God's use" and "makes their bodies a sacred place of God's presence."[16]

Stephanie Paulson of the University of Chicago Divinity School contends that our contemporary task is "to retrieve and reinterpret the practice of honoring the body for our own age."[17] Honoring the body glorifies the God who created the body in holistic alignment. Nevertheless, Paul reminds Timothy of the ultimate priority: "while physical training is of some value, godliness is valuable in every way, holding promise for both the present life and the life to come" (1 Tim 4:8). Godliness and physical health and wellness need not be in conflict. According to Christian psychologist Elizabeth Lewis Hall, glorifying God in our bodies involves decision making about our bodies, engaging in relationships in God-glorifying ways and practicing the spiritual disciplines that involve our bodies.[18] Feminist theologians focus on embodiment that regards the body as integral in all aspects of spirituality and relationship, while affirming women's personhood, which has often been debased through physical disregard and violation. These theologies of the body remind us that "Christian faith is embodied faith."[19]

The medical community is gradually realizing the interconnectedness of all holistic formation dimensions for overall health.[20] Being an ardent follower of Jesus, Dr. Harold Koenig indicates "that people who involve themselves in their religious communities, who volunteer to help others, and who regularly pray and read scriptures tend to be physically healthier than those who don't."[21] However, this does not suggest that those who are not followers of Jesus will not reap holistic health benefits if they adhere to sound health and wellness principles. Regarding physical health, Dr. Koenig reports, "The majority of the research conducted to date has found a positive relationship between religion and spirituality and both mental and physical health, whereas less than 10 percent of studies suggest the opposite and about 25 percent indicate no association."[22] We cannot, however, rest on these laurels. The body of Christ shows many signs of physical malaise.[23] Promoting healthy habits of the body is critical to offset spiritual opposition designed to deplete overall vitality.

God created the human body to rejuvenate itself through healthy physical processes for homeostasis or physiological balance. Knowing that Satan comes to steal, kill and destroy (Jn 10:10), it is not surprising that poor health is one of the many ploys to depreciate Kingdom effectiveness. Depreciating health may occur because of a lack of knowledge or inadequate resources. For example, those living in poverty have little or no access to nutritional information or sustainable food sources. In instances of affluence, depreciating health occurs because of overloaded lifestyles, willful ignorance regarding available health information and difficulty in making lifestyle changes. For instance, we know that consuming certain foods and beverages is unhealthy but may feel powerless to stop. In addition, contradictory information about health and wellness blankets news outlets, making it difficult to know what to believe about recent fad diets and nutritional studies.[24]

One thing we know for sure. Physical health is not only a personal matter but a national and global concern as well. According to the World Health Organization (WHO), high blood pressure and obesity are among the highest risk factors worldwide for disease and death. High blood pressure globally accounts for 51 percent of deaths from stroke and 45 percent from coronary heart disease.[25] Being overweight increases the risk of coronary heart disease, stroke, Type 2 diabetes and certain cancers. From 1980 to 2008, the rate of global prevalence of obesity nearly doubled, with 2.8 million deaths annually attributed to obesity and overweight issues.[26] In addition, skyrocketing health care costs in the United States continue to cut more deeply into personal finances, unless one has privileged access to affordable health care.[27] Ironically, life expectancy in the United States is rising, but chronic disabilities involving poor food choices, obesity and physical activity, among other factors, are as well.[28] In being Kingdom-minded, we have every reason to invest in the physical health and wellness of ourselves and our families in order to love and serve God and others, not only with all our hearts, souls and minds, but also with all our strength for God's glory (cf. Mk 12:30). Let's turn first to nutrition.

Nutrition

Nutrition tops the list of factors contributing to physical health and wellness. The key is consuming a balanced and nutritious diet. Dr. Rex Russell offers three nutritional principles to optimize health: (1) eat only substances God created for food and avoid everything else, (2) as much as possible eat foods as they were created—before they are changed to nutrient-deficient or toxic products, and (3) avoid food addictions.[29] Drawing from the most current nutritional research, this section amplifies these principles through discussion of some of the beverages and foods that contribute to health and those that do not.

Water. Water is the most vital nutrient for the human body. Just think—a person can survive on water alone for thirty to forty days. Composed of 60 percent water, the body requires fresh, clean water for every system from carrying nutrients to cells and flushing toxins to keeping tissues moist.[30] A recognized pioneering physician on the benefits of water, Dr. F. Batmanghelidj, lists forty-six reasons why the body daily needs water.[31] As a sampling, water (1) increases the efficiency of the immune system; (2) breaks down needed food, vitamins and minerals in the metabolism and assimilation process; (3) provides lubrication to joint spaces, preventing arthritis and back pain; (4) serves as a laxative and prevents constipation; (5) reduces the risk of heart attacks and strokes by declogging arteries; (6) keeps the body cool; (7) is needed for producing hormones, such as melatonin; (8) contributes to weight loss when water intake satisfies hunger cravings; (9) moisturizes the skin; and (10) contributes to efficient brain functioning and memory.[32] The brain is composed of 85 percent water, and lack of water contributes to fatigue. No other beverages, such as juice, soft drinks, sports drinks and coffee, substitute for water because only clean water fully hydrates the body.[33]

Considering that the body daily loses about two quarts of water through urination, perspiration and exhaling, the body requires continual hydration for optimal health.[34] So how much water should we drink? Christian physician and nutritional expert Dr. Don Colbert says, "To determine how much water your body needs, take your body weight (in pounds) and divide it by two. That's how many ounces of water you need every day."[35] For example, a person weighing 120 pounds optimally needs to drink 60 ounces of water daily, whereas a person weighing 220 pounds needs to drink 110 ounces of water. The adage of drinking eight 10-ounce glasses of water a day is fairly accurate for someone who weighs 160 pounds. Although this may seem like an inordinate amount of water intake, consider all of its benefits. Moreover, waiting to drink water until we are thirsty is an unreliable symptom, given that dry mouth is "one of the last signs of dehydration."[36] Naturally, when physical activity increases, so should water intake.[37] Deciding what water to drink is also an important decision, considering the body's need for hydration.[38]

Foods. We should consume food according to our body and nutritional needs and increase or reduce certain foods for optimal health.[39] Found at the top of the list is greater intake of vegetables and fruits, especially "dark-green and red and orange vegetables and beans and peas."[40] In other words, "eat the rainbow" of between five and thirteen servings of various vegetables and fruits every day.[41] Organic produce contains more antioxidants and beneficial minerals like zinc and iron than nonorganic produce, and it eliminates health risk from harmful chemical fertilizers.[42] All produce, whether organically or commercially grown, needs to be washed prior to eating. Produce washes made from environmentally friendly ingredients, such as grapefruit seed and lime peel extract, found at many grocery and health food stores, remove chemical sprays, waxes and soil residue.

Second, eating more whole, rather than refined, grains is recommended. Whole grain refers to the entire grain: bran, germ and endosperm, which is the starchy part. Refined grains, including white and enriched wheat flour, preserve only the starchy part, while removing beneficial nutrients. Some examples of whole grains include bulgur (cracked wheat), whole wheat flour, whole oats and oatmeal, brown rice, whole grain barley, quinoa and some cereals. Reading food labels will assist to determine food content.

Third, increasing fat-free and low-fat milk and milk products such as yogurt and cheese, in addition to soy products, helps reduce fat intake. Eradicating all good fat from the diet, however, is deleterious to health. Endocrinologist Dr. Diana Schwarzbein maintains that "fat does not make you fat" but rather the high-carbohydrate diet that people think includes "free" calories in lieu of fat.[43] Fat-free foods may be high in sugar, refined carbohydrates and calories. Although many may view carbohydrates as fat-free and low in calories, Dr. Schwarzbein maintains that "the low-fat, high-carbohydrate diet can be the most fattening" of all. Good fats, such as those found in eggs (preferably organic), avocados, olive oil, flaxseed oil and low-sodium nuts, contribute to optimal health

Fourth, eating healthy protein sources, such as lean meats, seafood (including mercury-free salmon plentiful in omega-3 fatty acids), poultry, eggs, beans and peas, unsalted nuts and seeds, and organic tofu, is also recommended. A word about red meat consumption. According to an April 2012 Harvard School of Public Health study of 121,342 participants, red meat consumption was associated with increased risk of chronic diseases, including higher rates of cardiovascular and cancer mortality because of saturated fat, charring that produces carcinogens, and meat additives. The study's authors stated, "We estimated that substitutions of 1 serving per day of other foods (including fish, poultry, nuts, legumes, low-fat dairy, and whole grains) for 1 serving per day of red meat were associated with a 7% to 19% lower mortality risk."[44] Lead author Dr. An Pan commented on abstaining from red meats: "It's better to go with unprocessed products and plant-based foods."[45] Beans and legumes provide an excellent source of protein and fiber (e.g., black, lima and pinto beans; lentils; and black-eyed and split peas). Another study found that red meat consumption (particularly processed red meat) is associated with increased risk for Type 2 diabetes.[46] These results add to a growing body of research supporting greater plant-based over animal-based protein consumption.[47]

Fifth, using oils to replace solid fats reduces cholesterol. In moderation, consuming olive and peanut oils, avocados, and unsalted nuts containing monounsaturated fat is recommended. Polyunsaturated vegetable oils found in corn, sunflower, soy and canola oil may be genetically altered, and when used at high temperatures their antioxidant properties diminish. Therefore, some disagree with the idea that polyunsaturated oils provide "good fats."[48] A healthy alternative is organic virgin coconut oil that contains no cholesterol.[49] Good fat is also found in the omega-3 fatty acids in walnuts and fish (salmon, mackerel and herring). Avoiding trans fats used in fried foods, margarine, shortening, commercially produced baked goods and candy contributes to health.[50]

A sixth area relates to consuming foods that provide more potassium, dietary fiber, calcium and vitamin D, which are often deficient in American diets. These foods include fresh vegetables, fruits, fish, whole grains, milk and milk products fortified with vitamin D. However, it should be noted that pasteurized milk is heated to 161 degrees for fifteen seconds, which affects the enzyme and protein content, making it difficult for the body to digest and assimilate.[51] Some who have milk allergies or are lactose intolerant find alternatives in goat milk, soy milk or other foods high in calcium such as red and pink salmon, cooked mustard and collard greens (minus all the fat), broccoli and spinach. Selecting organic milk and organic soy products is always optimal.

Necessary for calcium and phosphorus absorption, vitamin D, a seventh area, has come into the medical spotlight. God designed the human body to naturally synthesize vitamin D through the ultraviolet rays from appropriate sun exposure. With indoor activity increasing, especially in urban areas, however, vitamin D deficiency, attributed to 65 percent of Americans, has become an epidemic, according to Dr. Elizabeth Streeten, an endocrinologist and medical geneticist.[52] Along with others, she recommends fifteen minutes of sun exposure without sunscreen between 11 a.m. and

3 p.m. two to three times a week to reduce the risk of osteoporosis, bone fractures and various diseases such as heart disease, cancer, diabetes and other disorders. Essentially, it is believed that adequate vitamin D levels contribute to a longer, healthier life through a strengthened immune system.[53] With African Americans, older adults and babies most at risk, medical researchers are calling for greater daily minimal intake standards, since vitamin D regulates at least 10 percent of body functioning.[54] God provides this vitamin for free—if we take advantage of it!

Conversely, certain foods need to be reduced to fortify health.[55] Let's focus on salt (sodium) and sugar. First, it is no surprise that Americans consume far too much salt. Sodium consumption elevates blood pressure. Since high blood pressure increases the risk of heart disease and stroke, reducing sodium intake benefits everyone. According to the American Centers for Disease Control (CDC), "Sodium intake from processed and restaurant foods contributes to increased rates of high blood pressure, heart attack and stroke. Decreasing sodium intake to within recommended limits could prevent thousands of deaths annually."[56] High sodium levels are found in breads and rolls; cold cuts, such as deli or packaged ham or turkey; pizza; soups; sandwiches; cheeseburgers; cheese; pasta dishes; and snacks such as popcorn, chips and pretzels. Annual deaths attributed to high blood pressure total 400,000.[57] People at highest risk include those who are fifty-one or older, African Americans, and who have hypertension, diabetes or chronic kidney disease. Reducing high sodium through healthy choices in restaurants and grocery store purchases contributes to stabilizing these levels.

Second, sugar consumption is at an all-time high. Between 1970 and 2005 sugar and added sugar intake increased 19 percent, with Americans eating an average of 22.2 teaspoons per day.[58] Increased sugar and caloric sweetener consumption has been shown to increase the risk of cardiovascular disease, diabetes, blood pressure and obesity.[59] Excessive sugar intake also depresses the immune system and feeds cancer cells.[60] By 2050, researchers project, cases of diabetes may likely triple to one in three US adults; they suggest that effective strategies be implemented to reduce this likelihood.[61] As links between sugar intake and disease proliferate, one of the biggest culprits is soft drink consumption.[62] Between 2005 and 2006, sodas, energy drinks and sports drinks comprised 35.7 percent of overall sugar consumption, with an average can of soda containing the equivalent of eight to ten teaspoons of sugar. In a study of nine thousand women, those who daily drank two or more cans of soda were almost twice as likely to evidence early symptoms of chronic kidney disease.[63] Fruit juices, including natural varieties, can be deceiving too, as they often contain high levels of sugar.

In a 2012 CBS *60 Minutes* feature titled "Is Sugar Toxic?" Dr. Sanjay Gupta interviewed several leading experts on sugar, including Dr. Robert Lustig, a pediatric endocrinologist.[64] Dr. Gupta mentioned the YouTube video of Dr. Lustig's 2009 lecture titled, "Sugar: The Bitter Truth, "which went viral.[65] It highlighted how the toxic effects of sugar contribute to disease. Dr. Lustig notes that while sugar consumption has declined 40 percent since 1970, high fructose corn syrup (HFCS) has "more than made up the difference." Recent studies reveal the addictive power of sugar and HFCS, similar to drugs and alcohol, through the release of dopamine, the chemical that controls the brain's pleasure center. Dr. Eric Stice, a neuroscientist, notes overconsumption of sugary foods and beverages affects the brain's reward center, thereby creating an addictive cycle that requires more sugar to satisfy previous satisfaction levels.[66] No wonder the American Heart Association calls obesity "an epidemic of excess," with one in three American children and teens and seven in ten adults considered overweight or obese.[67]

Why is overconsumption of sugar harmful? Say, for example, someone drinks a beverage that contains ten teaspoons of sugar. After traveling to the stomach, the sugar needs to be metabolized or processed before it can be released into the bloodstream. This is the role of the pancreas, which secretes insulin to process the sugar. If insulin is unavailable to do its job, the sugar would be absorbed unmetabolized into the bloodstream and travel to the brain, causing a hyperglycemic coma and even death. Overconsumption of sugar taxes the pancreas because of the large amounts of insulin it must release. With sustained sugar consumption, the pancreas can no longer keep up with the insulin demand to maintain normal blood sugar levels. Sustained high insulin levels contribute to insulin resistance, where the cells do not respond appropriately to insulin. The bottom line: limiting sugar intake contributes to health and extends longevity.[68]

The explosive popularity of artificial sweeteners in diet and regular food products is not surprising, given the presumption that they are safe for consumption. A former colleague, for example, daily drank eight to ten cans of diet soda, not knowing the adverse effects that the chemical sweetener aspartame has on the body. What he also didn't know is that diet drinks may contribute to weight gain. Two studies conducted by the University of Texas Health Science Center San Antonio found that diet drinks may be free of calories but not the consequences. Participants who drank two or more diet sodas a day "experienced waist circumference increases that were 500 percent greater than those of non-users."[69] Other reported side effects of aspartame include headache, nausea, vision problems, abdominal pain, memory loss, seizures, fatigue and other disorders. But that's not all. One Italian study, among others, concluded that aspartame is a "multi-potential carcinogenic [cancer-causing] compound."[70]

Being a synthetic substance, aspartame is chemically composed of two amino acids (i.e., aspartic acid and phenylalanine) and methanol. Within the body, methanol converts to formic acid and formaldehyde, which is used for embalming fluid.[71] (Yes, you read this correctly.) When digested, aspartame then breaks down into (1) aspartic acid, which is considered an excitotoxin, referring to a substance that overexcites nerve cells, causing damage to the nervous system; and (2) glutamic acid or monosodium glutamate (MSG). According to neurosurgeon and biologist Russell L. Blaylock, "Both glutamate and aspartame can cause neurons to become extremely excited, and if given in large enough doses, they can cause these cells to degenerate and die."[72] Dr. Blaylock strongly recommends against consumption of aspartame and MSG.

With intense debate and governmental lobbying efforts surrounding the issue of artificial sweeteners within this global multibillion-dollar industry, we need to keep in mind Dr. Rex Russell's first diet principle: eat only substances God created for food and avoid what is not designed for food. Aspartame is not a natural food substance. Sadly, the concerns about aspartame, contained in over six thousand diet products and pharmaceuticals, remain unabated.[73] Since its highly contested approval by the US Food and Drug Administration (FDA) in 1974, medical professionals such as Dr. John Olney from the Washington University School of Medicine and Dr. Ralph Walton from the North East Ohio University College of Medicine have questioned the adequacy of the initial research that was funded by the very industry that manufactures aspartame, which eventuated in FDA approval.[74] While the FDA argues that aspartame is not a health risk, national and global efforts advocate for its ban.[75] In 2008 the Philippines completely banned aspartame from all consumable products. Although US state legislative efforts to ban aspartame in New Mexico and Hawaii have been stymied, the drive continues nevertheless.

An associated risk is believed to be found in sucralose, an artificial sweetener known as Splenda, approved by the FDA as a tabletop sweetener in 1998 and as a general-purpose sweetener in 1999. Based on one hundred research studies, Splenda manufacturers claimed that their product is noncarcinogenic and safe. The five-step chemical production process, adding three chlorine molecules to sucrose (sugar), producing a chlorocarbon substance, appears nowhere else in nature. Thus the quip "Made from sugar so it tastes like sugar" is true. Manufacturers claim that the body cannot metabolize it, so that is why it registers zero calories. However, some assert that Splenda has not been adequately proven as being safe for consumption through longitudinal human trials and caution against its use.[76] A twelve-week animal research study investigating health risks of Splenda through the Duke University Medical Center found "numerous adverse effects."[77] Dr. Don Colbert qualifies this artificial sweetener as "the dark side of the food world."[78] It is wise to keep in mind Dr. Rex Russell's first and second principles for nutrition: eating only substances God created for food and eating foods as they were created.

With concern regarding the calories in sugar and the risks of artificial sweeteners, healthy alternatives include stevia, xylitol, agave nectar and organic sucanat.[79] Stevia is an all-natural herbal sweetener grown mainly in South and Central America and Mexico. A white powder, stevia extract is two hundred to three hundred times stronger than sugar, so a little goes a long way. Xylitol is also a natural sweetener, produced from berries, fruits, vegetables and mushrooms. Agave nectar is an extract from cactus sap and is comparable to light honey, but with a lower glycemic index.[80] Organic sucanat (a short version of "sucre de canne natural") is pure dried cane juice that is not processed like white sugar.

To reiterate the three nutritional principles offered by Dr. Rex Russell for optimizing health: (1) eat only substances God created for food, and avoid everything else; (2) as much as possible, eat foods as they were created—before they are changed to nutrient-deficient or toxic products; and (3) avoid food addictions.[81] The nutritional perspectives in this section reinforce these simple principles. Christians are at liberty to eat whatever they desire, and nutritional choice will not preclude us from heaven. However, consistent consumption of unhealthy foods and beverages will undoubtedly get us there quicker. Stewarding our physical health and wellness honors the body and our Creator, who desires us to reflect divine glory. The next section discusses how physical exercise optimizes health.

Physical Exercise

God designed the human body to move. With two legs and feet, two arms, two hands, a neck, head and torso, the body works in sync to produce movement, barring disability. God also created the body to renew itself through physical activity to ensure sustained health. On a contemporary global and national scale, however, we are becoming increasingly more sedentary. As mentioned in chapter seven, work demands, the digital technology revolution and media appetites position us for lengthy periods behind computer, television, tablet, theater and mobile phone screens. Consequently, we are sitting more and moving less.

A sedentary lifestyle, however, dramatically elevates health risk.[82] In

2010 the World Health Organization warned, "Physical inactivity is now identified as the fourth leading risk factor for global mortality. Physical inactivity levels are escalating in many countries with major implications for the prevalence of noncommunicable diseases (NCDs) and the general health of the population worldwide."[83] According to the WHO, inactivity globally accounts for these incidences: 21 to 25 percent of breast and colon cancer, 27 percent of diabetes, and approximately 30 percent of heart disease.[84]

Noting that "levels of inactivity are alarming" in the United States and other nations, the American College of Sports Medicine (ACSM) observes, "Physical inactivity is a fast-growing public health problem and contributes to a variety of chronic diseases and health complications, including obesity, diabetes and cancer."[85] Inactivity heightens risk factors such as elevated blood sugar, raised blood pressure and weight gain. These risk factors also have been shown to contribute to cardiovascular disease, coronary heart disease (including atherosclerosis and arteriosclerosis), hypertension (high blood pressure), stroke, congestive heart failure, and premature death. According to the ACSM the lack of physical exercise results "in an estimated 250,000 premature deaths each year, costing $1 trillion in annual health care costs, and immense human anguish and pain."[86] The irony, as noted by ACSM, is that billions of dollars are spent annually on drug development for disease prevention, while funding for the "most potent therapeutics," namely exercise, is grossly underfunded.[87] No wonder the US surgeon general issued strong recommendations to replace sedentary habits with enjoyable aerobic activity for overall wellness.[88]

These sobering statistics prompted the ACSM, as supported by the American Medical Association, to develop a national campaign and website titled "Exercise Is Medicine," calling on health care professionals to become more informed regarding the benefits of physical exercise and to incorporate exercise into all patients' treatment plans.[89] For example, one 2005 study of 2,987 women who had been previously diagnosed with breast cancer found that regular exercise contributed to reducing the death rate among participants. The greatest benefit was for women who walked three to five hours a week at an average pace.[90] In other words, physical exercise is like natural medicine for the body.

Over the last twenty years, researchers have begun to uncover the benefits of exercise not only for physiology but also for all other aspects of human functioning, including cognition, emotional health, stress and depression reduction, and longevity enhancement. What are the benefits of physical exercise, and what are the recommended levels of exercise that are appropriate to optimize physical health?

Drawn from health and neuroscience research, the benefits of regular exercise abound.[91] First, regular exercise increases the ability of the heart muscle to pump oxygen-rich blood. A fit heart contains clear, unclogged arteries that safeguard against heart disease. Exercise increases HDL, called "good cholesterol," which prevents atherosclerosis, the deposit of materials along the walls of arteries. Second, regular exercise enhances blood circulation, which reduces the risk of a heart attack. Those who exercise build greater blood-carrying capacity in blood vessels. Third, exercise reduces high blood pressure. With one-third of all American adults having high blood pressure (and with nearly one-third of these not knowing they have it), inactivity increases the risk of hypertension by 30 to 50 percent.[92] And hypertension contributes to the onset of strokes. Fourth, regular physical exercise decreases insulin resistance by improving the body's ability to remove sugar from the blood. As mentioned previously, without proper insulin processing, diabetes, coma and even death can result.

Fifth, exercise contributes to strong muscles and bone integrity, so crucial for children and adolescents but also for men and women as they age in order to combat osteoporosis, a deterioration of bone density. Sixth, physical activity contributes to a healthy body weight in order to counter obesity. With obesity rates in US children and adolescents skyrocketing over the past thirty years, one-third of them are currently considered overweight or obese, whereas over one-third of US adults are also considered obese.[93] Seventh, regular physical activity strengthens the immune system, thus reducing the likelihood of infection while fortifying antioxidant defenses.[94] With the immune system lodged within the tissues of the small intestines, exercise improves digestion, lymphatic flow that polices against bacteria and viruses, and proper elimination.[95] Too much exercise, however, actually lowers immune function.[96] Of course, the body needs adequate recovery periods after exercise.

Eighth, regular exercise contributes to heightened cognitive functioning. A 2002 study conducted by the California Department of Education with over 884,715 student participants found that as overall physical fitness scores increased, so did academic achievement.[97] Similarly, the impact of physical exercise on academic performance is reported by Dr. John Ratey, a professor at Harvard Medical School, regarding the physical education program of Public School District 203 in Naperville, Illinois. With an exemplary fitness program, this Naperville district continuously ranks among the state's top ten in terms of academic achievement and touts a 97 percent high school graduation rate.[98] For example, on the science section of the Trends in International Mathematics and Science Study, an international test involving thirty-eight nations, students from Naperville ranked first in the world.[99] On the math section Naperville ranked sixth. Unlike other US school districts that are cutting their physical education programs because of budget constraints, Naperville wisely recognizes the interface between health fitness and academic achievement. Even in late adulthood, physical activity guards against dementia. A study by the National Institute on Aging found that older adults who walked six to nine miles weekly reduced the risk of memory loss by 50 percent.[100]

Ninth, regular exercise minimizes the effects of chronic stress and depression, and in some cases reverses them. When stress overtakes the body, heart rate and blood pressure elevate, the lungs' bronchial tubes dilate to transport more oxygen to muscles, the hormone and neurotransmitter epinephrine (also called adrenalin) prepares muscles for action, and endorphins are released to curb pain.[101] Meanwhile, cortisol, called the "stress hormone," is released, instructing the liver to make and release glucose into the bloodstream for a "fight or flight" response.

Some stress actually helps the body adapt to its environment. In chronic stress, however, too much cortisol is released, producing a surplus fuel supply. Since the brain consumes but cannot store glucose, the body stores glucose elsewhere, like the stomach, which fosters weight gain. Too much cortisol also suppresses memory.[102] Thus, a sedentary lifestyle characterized by chronic stress and poor nutrition is a formula for obesity. Aerobic exercise, which involves taking in more oxygen to elevate the heart rate, inoculates the brain against stress and depression, while also contributing to restful sleep. According to one Duke University landmark study, exercise was as effective as the drug sertraline (Zoloft) in treating depression.[103]

Tenth, exercise sparks the brain to continue to make learning connections, as Naperville School District 93 in Illinois has discovered. In an animal study on exercise and brain function, Dr. Carl Cotman, a leading neuroscientist, found that exercise sparks the master molecule of the learning process.[104] In relieving muscle tension, exercise increases levels of serotonin, a neurotransmitter, giving the brain's one hundred billion neurons heightened connectivity.[105] Finally, physical exercise contributes to longevity because people who are more physically fit live longer. "Getting older is unavoidable, but falling apart is not."[106] As Christians, we glorify God by engaging in practices that honor the body.

What are the recommended levels of exercise? Benefits of exercise vary depending on age, heredity, gender, ethnicity and current physical condition. It is always advisable to consult with a medical professional prior to initiating a fitness program. When just starting out, it is wise to gradually increase frequency, intensity and time (FIT). In 2009 the US surgeon general recommended at least 150 minutes weekly of moderate to intense exercise, or thirty minutes per day for at least five days a week for adults.[107] Examples of moderate exercise include brisk walking, biking, swimming or doing yardwork. For children and adolescents, one hour a day of vigorous activity was recommended.

Keep in mind that these are minimal recommendations. Safely increasing exercise FIT, including aerobic activity without overload, optimizes health benefits.[108] In the US surgeon general's updated 2011 publication *Physical Activity and Health,* additional guidelines were added, including resistance training for increased muscle strength and endurance (i.e., weight-bearing exercise) and appropriate stretching to prevent injury and foster flexibility before and after exercise.[109] Varying exercise activity adds fun to routines and eliminates boredom.

Regardless of one's age, exercise alone is insufficient for optimal health. Exercise and *proper nutrition are integral partners in safeguarding health. Unfortunately, this was likely not the case for jogging advocate and author Jim Fixx (1932–1984). Fixx, whose father died of a heart attack at age forty-three, was convinced that physical exercise such as jogging and refraining from smoking would ensure good health. Placing a low priority on nutrition, Fixx scoffed at those who opposed this view, such as Dr. Nathan Pritikin, who authored* Diet for Runners *and placed a high priority on nutrition. Six months after Fixx's disagreement with Dr. Pritikin regarding nutrition, Fixx tragically died of a massive heart attack at age fifty-two while running on a rural road. Nutrition in tandem with exercise and other healthy physical habits, such as sleep, honors God through health stewardship.*[110]

SLEEP

A few years ago, I passed a poster in my workplace hallway that was advertising a summer seminar series offered by an external organization. The poster read "Sleep Less, Think More." Although the poster designers hoped to appeal to intellectual engagement, they did not realize that reducing sleep to think more is counterproductive.[111] Multiple incidents indicate that lack of sleep not only impairs thinking but also puts people at great risk. For example, on March 23, 2011, before midnight, the lone air traffic controller at Reagan National Airport in Washington, D.C., had fallen asleep. When pilots of two incoming planes realized they had no guidance in approaching the airport, they communicated with another nearby air traffic control tower to ensure their planes did not collide.[112] As a result, the lives of 165 people were spared.

Other incidents partially attributed to the sleep deprivation of key decision makers did not end so well, such as the 1979 nuclear disaster at Three Mile Island, the 1986 meltdown at Chernobyl, the 1986 explosion of the US space shuttle Challenger, and the 1989 grounding of the Exxon Valdez tanker in Alaska.[113] Furthermore, the high incidence of falling asleep at the wheel contributes to avoidable vehicle crashes, injury and highway deaths. Going without sleep is hazardous to our health. God has created sleep to renew body processes.

When we sleep, the brain processes events and stores them as memories in the right places. Sleeping is to the brain what defragging is to a computer. When defragging a computer, all parts of files and directories that have been fragmented in many locations across the hard drive are arranged together in the same place in order for the computer to run more efficiently. This is similar to what happens during sleep. Various thoughts find homes in the brain. This is one reason why when we wake up in the morning we might have answers to previously perplexing questions. "Sleeping on it" actually has medical validation. During wakefulness, neurons in the brain fire randomly because of changing stimuli. During the first few stages of the sleep cycle, however, neurons fire in a "more coordinated and synchronous" fashion.[114]

Often underrated, sleep is anything but passive. According to sleep expert Dr. James Maas, "The overall level of neural activity drops only 10 percent during sleep. In fact, the 'sleeping' brain is often significantly more active than the 'awake' brain."[115] Along with healthy nutrition and physical exercise practices, sleep provides another essential component of physical health and wellness, which in turn influences the other CSF dimensions. In designing the human body, God included sleep as an essential activity for overall health, which contemporary research is just beginning to uncover.

In the early 1950s researchers discovered that sleep involves five stages.[116] Before falling asleep, breathing rate and brain waves slow down, as the precursor to light sleep in stage 1. In stage 1, muscles relax and muscle twitching may occur. In stage 2 muscle tension is reduced even more.

Breathing, heart rate and body temperature drop, and brain waves slow further. Stage 3 begins the deep sleep phase. In stage 4 blood pressure falls, blood supply to the brain recedes, and breathing and body temperature slow further. This is the deepest phase of sleep. Stage 5 is characterized by rapid eye movements (REM), as well as increased respiration and brain activity. It is also the dream phase of sleep. When REM sleep is over, the body usually returns to stage 2, initiating another sleep cycle. A complete sleep cycle of ninety to 110 minutes occurs four to six times a night.[117] Non-REM sleep accounts for roughly 75 percent of sleep, with REM sleep accounting for 25 percent.[118]

Sleep benefits the body through renewal. Just think—if a person lives to be ninety years old and sleeps eight hours a day, that individual will have slept a total of thirty years. Although some view sleep as wasted time because of lost productivity, sleep actually engages vital body processes for emotional, mental and physical health. During sleep, when metabolic activity slows, tissue repair and growth occur through energy conservation. During deep sleep, the pituitary gland releases the body's growth hormone to assist in the process. This explains why it is especially important for children and adolescents to get uninterrupted and adequate sleep. As people age, less growth hormone is released and less time is spent in deep sleep. God has designed sleep to fortify the immune system for preventing colds and disease,[119] to foster the release of important hormones such as leptin that regulate appetite, to build memory, to reduce high cortisol levels due to stress, and to slow the aging process.[120] According to Dr. William Dement, leading authority on sleep and sleep disorders, "Sleep is one of the most important predictors of how long you will live—as important as whether you smoke, exercise, or have high blood pressure or cholesterol."[121]

How much sleep do we need to maximize health, and how does our sleep time stack up to recommended levels? The "2005 Sleep in America Poll" found that the average US adult sleeps 6.8 hours on weekdays and 7.4 hours on weekends.[122] Forty-nine percent reported that they have a good night of sleep every night or almost every night, contrasting to the majority who don't. Comparative data since 1998 show that Americans are sleeping increasingly fewer hours. Individual factors such as age, gender, genetic predisposition, physical condition and life season inform recommended sleep levels. Although cautioning against a one-size-fits-all approach, the National Sleep Foundation offers the following daily sleep recommendations:

Newborns (0-2 months): 12-18 hours
Infants (3-11 months): 14-15 hours
Toddlers (1-3 years): 12-14 hours
Preschoolers (3-5 years): 11-13 hours
School-age children (5-10 years): 10-11 hours
Adolescents (11-17): 8.5-9.25 hours
Adults: 7-9 hours[123]

A graduate student once revealed to me that she only averaged about two total hours of sleep a night in order to meet the demands of family, work, church and graduate school. She sacrificed sleep in order to keep up by sleeping in a chair and doing some work after arousing every few hours. Needless to say, she was heading for an emotional, mental and physical breakdown until she realized the multiple consequences of sleep deprivation and made some lifestyle changes.

In June 2008, the CBS television program *60 Minutes* aired a two-part series titled "The Science of Sleep," hosted by Lesley Stahl.[124] Stahl interviewed four notable sleep researchers. According to sleep expert Dr. David Dinges, only four hours of sleep a night impairs attention, memory and thought processes. For example, after sleep deprivation, people often experience "micro-sleeps" during waking hours, where the craving for sleep creates a dangerous zoning out. Two to three seconds is all it takes for a driver to shift lanes and cause an accident. I will never forget the medical student I knew who had pulled two all-nighters in order to study for his board exams. Afterward, he fell asleep at the dinner table, with his head falling into his plate of spaghetti!

Another featured *60 Minutes* sleep expert was Dr. Eve Van Cauter, an endocrinologist.[125] In sleep experiments, she and her associates discovered that getting only four hours of sleep for six nights triggered a prediabetic condition where blood sugar levels escalated dramatically. During sleep deprivation, production of the regulating hormone leptin decreased. Leptin influences appetite by telling the body when it is full. With lower leptin levels, the body craves more food. Van Cauter and her colleagues have interconnected sleep loss, diabetes and obesity.[126] These research findings underscore how God has holistically created the human body such that nutrition, exercise and sleep interactively contribute to health and wellness.[127] Exercise, particularly aerobic activity, has been shown to improve sleep quality, by raising endorphin levels (i.e., the "feel-good" hormones).[128]

Because sleep loss must be repaid, returning quickly to one's regular sleep schedule helps. Going to bed earlier to retain the normal wake-up time is ideal, especially for those who experience nonoptimal sleep patterns because of family, work, educational or travel demands.[129] To ensure a good night's sleep, consider these guidelines recommended by the president of the American Academy of Sleep Medicine. First, recognize the importance of sleep on overall health. Second, adopt a healthy lifestyle, including exercise and good nutrition. Third, maintain good sleep habits. Get enough sleep. Fourth, create the optimal sleeping environment. Fifth, beware of sleep saboteurs such as watching television or using electronic devices in the bedroom, and exercising or drinking caffeinated beverages before bedtime. Sixth, seek medical help for persistent sleep problems.[130]

In 2006, George Barna polled 1,005 US adults about what they look forward to the most. The most frequent response was simply a refreshing snooze and a good night of sleep.[131] God has designed the human body to require sleep for overall renewal. One contributor to sleep is peace of mind that comes from spiritual, emotional and relational wholeness and a job well done. "Sweet is the sleep of laborers, whether they eat little or much; but the surfeit of the rich will not let them sleep" (Eccles 5:12). The writer of Proverbs assures those with sound judgment, discernment and a clean conscience that rather than being afraid, they will enjoy sweet sleep (Prov 3:24). Too much sleep, however, can be escapist and an excuse for avoiding responsibility (Prov 6:9-10; 19:15; 20:13). Getting adequate sleep is yet another way to honor God with our bodies.

Stress, Rest and Leisure

Throughout my doctoral program, I thought that I had navigated the multiple demands of family, work, ministry and studies fairly well. However, after completing my final semester, I came down with a chronic maxillary sinus infection that lasted for months. I had pushed myself to complete the final course work according to schedule but exceeded reasonable limits. The sustained stress contributed to a compromised immune system at a time when I thought I could not rest. Although the focus of my dissertation was on pastoral burnout, I had to admit that I was experiencing the very symptoms I was studying. Stress develops when internal or external demands exceed our ability to adequately cope with the physical, spiritual, emotional, relational, intellectual, vocational and resource stewardship challenges. Stress results from things we can and should control, as well as things we cannot control.[132] *No one is immune to its short- or long-term effects.*

The prophet Elijah knew something about stress. As a prophet in Israel, Elijah was commissioned by God to declare that rain would be withheld from the nation as a result of King Ahab's promotion of Baal worship. In an ironic twist, the idolatrous worship of this god of fertility was no match for the God of Israel who alone has power to give rain (1 Kings 17:1-4). On God's behalf, Elijah, not Baal, would pronounce when it would rain. After the third year of drought, the Lord instructed Elijah to speak to Ahab and offer a challenge between himself and the 450 prophets of Baal and 400 prophets of Asherah. Elijah proposed that the deity who consumed the sacrifice by fire was the true God.

After an all-day challenge with the 850 idolatrous prophets, Elijah proved before the people that his God was the only true God, the one to be worshiped. Then, after slaying these prophets four and a half miles down in the Kishon Valley, Elijah climbed back up Mt. Carmel, awaiting the rain. Likely not to have eaten all day (1 Kings 18:42), Elijah outran

Ahab's chariot to the city of Jezreel, a distance of almost nineteen miles. After learning what happened, Ahab's wife, Jezebel, issued Elijah's death sentence. Fleeing for his life ninety miles south to Beersheba, Elijah then went another day's journey into the desert. There, he asked God to take his life.

Not having eaten or slept, under such intense spiritual and physical warfare, the valiant Elijah had become completely depleted—spiritually, emotionally, mentally and physically. Further, multiple stresses converged to cripple his sense of life purpose, including vocational vision (the "what" he was to be about) and mission (the "how" he was to do it). Completely exhausted and alone, he felt hopeless (1 Kings 18:22). In today's terms, Elijah likely had a complete nervous breakdown resulting from what John A. Sanford describes as depression, burnout and ego collapse.[133] Elijah declared to God, "I have had enough, Lord. Take my life; I am no better than my ancestors." Understanding the symptoms and stages of stress due to physical, spiritual, emotional, relational, intellectual, vocational, or either resource lack or preservation may help us identify with Elijah when we approach our own danger zones.

Dr. Hans Selye (1907–1982), an endocrinology pioneer who studied the biological effects of stress, identified positive stress as "eustress" and negative stress as "distress."[134] Some stress is normal and helps us cope with everyday life, as in the case of taking a test, preparing for a new job, public speaking or getting married. However, ongoing and excessive stress has adverse effects on the body and predisposes us to various conditions and diseases. Selye identified three stages of stress: (1) alarm reaction (the flight-or-fight response), (2) resistance stage and (3) reaction stage.[135] Understanding the these stages of stress will assist us to identify and address unhealthy stress patterns.

In the first stage, the adrenal glands located atop the kidneys release epinephrine (adrenaline) and norepinephrine to enable blood pressure, heart rate and respiratory function to increase. More sugar and fat enter the bloodstream, and blood diverts to the brain and muscles. The adrenal glands also produce other hormones, including cortisol, the stress relief hormone, which was discussed earlier in the physical exercise section. In stage two, the body moves to a coping stage, where hormones continue to be released. In stage three, the body reacts through exhaustion and begins to break down. Stress affects digestion, cell growth and repair, sexual drive, reproduction, pain thresholds, sensory and memory abilities, and a sense of well-being.[136] If stress continues unabated, depression, debilitation and disease will likely occur.

In chronic stress, the adrenal glands work in overdrive to provide the needed cortisol, leading to adrenal fatigue and subsequent exhaustion. When cortisol levels are too high, they suppress the immune system, reducing body defenses to fight viral and bacterial infection, and opening the door to high blood pressure, Type 2 diabetes, and autoimmune diseases. Conversely, when cortisol levels are too low, the body reacts with inflammation, which can lead to heart disease, ulcers and some forms of cancer. Since the adrenal glands provide the body's reserve tank for releasing hormones (i.e., adrenaline and cortisol) during times of stress, inadequate supplies can led to mild to severe depression, lethargy and burnout. Individuals who experience adrenal failure may include those who spend long hours working, such as university students, ministry leaders and working professionals such as physicians and counselors, and those with inordinate personal, family or work pressures.[137] I suggest that Elijah qualified as one who most likely experienced adrenal exhaustion. Lack of recovery through adequate sleep, nutrition and relational support to balance energy expenditure during the Mt. Carmel experience caused Elijah's body and will to collapse.

Like Elijah, we may find ourselves in power-charged situations from which we cannot disengage. We feel burned out but do not know what to do next. In Elijah's case, the first step to recovery included reestablishing solid rhythms of sleeping, eating and hydration. God sent an angel to help Elijah in this process (1 Kings 19:5-7). Sleep and nutrition were vital to his restoration. When physically exhausted, we need to rest from activity. If not physical exhausted, we need to add physical exercise to reduce stress by burning off the body's stress chemicals.[138] The interplay between the spiritual, emotional, relational, intellectual, vocational and physical dimensions reflects God's holistic design for the human body.[139]

Is it possible to deal with overload in our marginless lives?[140] Can we establish healthy rhythms of rest, sabbath and leisure to provide life balance? Balance characterizes God's creation, seen through the laws of gravity and other workings of the universe. God created the human body to be resilient through internal equilibrium and stability, called homeostasis, that is predicated on adequate rest.[141]

God exemplified the practice of rest when establishing a sabbath after six days of creation (Gen 2:2). God did not do so because of exhaustion or overwork, nor was God enslaved to creation.[142] Rather God celebrated creation, declared the sabbath holy and modeled sabbath living for all humanity. As Abraham Heschel (1907–1972) wisely observed, "The Sabbath teaches all beings whom to praise."[143] The sabbath allows us to detach from things in order to focus on attachment to God. Heschel continues, "In the tempestuous ocean of time and toil there are islands of stillness where man may enter a harbor and reclaim his dignity. The island is the seventh day, the Sabbath, a day of detachment from things, instruments and practical affairs as well as of attachment to the spirit."[144] The sabbath reminds us that we are made in the image of God, who both works and rests. Dorothy Bass comments, "As God worked, so shall we; as God rested, so shall we."[145] Bass affirms that God created us for loving relationship, with the sabbath being the day "that shapes a weekly pattern."[146]

In our work-oriented and consumer-driven lives, can we afford to slow down enough to connect with God, others and ourselves through sabbath? Can we afford not to? For some, sabbath keeping is nonnegotiable and verges on legalism.[147] For others, sabbath keeping is desirable but not required. For still others, sabbath keeping is unrealistic and unnecessary because we have been delivered from the Mosaic law. Believers must determine their own convictions on sabbath living based on a careful examination of the Scriptures.[148] My own commitment is to observe a sabbath that includes ceasing work, church worship and time spent with family. Are there times on the sabbath when I've needed to attend to a work-related issue? Yes. However, these times are exceptions rather than the rule. Theologian Marva Dawn echoes the underlying assumption of sabbath keeping, where "we deliberately remember that we have ceased trying to be God and instead have put our lives back into his control."[149] Wayne Mueller aptly observes, "Sabbath rest invites us to step back, *and see that it is good.*"[150]

Rhythms of rest and sabbath allow us to enact Jesus' words, "Do not worry about tomorrow, for tomorrow will bring worries of its own" (Mt 6:34), and Paul's, "Do not worry about anything, but in everything by prayer and supplication with thanksgiving let your requests be made known to God" (Phil 4:6). Times of leisure, including vacations, help us to realize the joy of life and the multiple ways that God provides enjoyment and delight through creation, wholesome hobbies and interests. Leisure helps us to renew our spiritual, emotional, relational, intellectual and physical batteries and keep CSF in balance.[151] Vacations provide needed diversion from work that enhances productivity.[152] Actively reducing stress and attending to rest and leisure contribute to health stewardship, which in turn glorifies our Creator. Being created in the image of God, we can intentionally establish rhythms of work, rest and leisure that moderate the stresses of life and reengage us with our Creator, ourselves and others. Another area that requires intentionality is sexual purity.

Sexual Purity

In addition to nutrition, physical exercise, sleep and stress reduction that incorporates rest and leisure, sexual purity constitutes another crucial anchor for physical health and wellness formation.[153] We glorify God by how we honor the body through sexual purity, which is the telltale sign of our spiritual walk as followers of Christ. Being human, we know that sexual purity is not without temptation and struggle. For example, Augustine expressed how his desire to love and to be loved was blurred by lust. As epitomized in his candid prayer prior to surrendering his life to Christ, Augustine uttered, "Grant me chastity and continency, but not yet," hoping to extend sexual pleasure for as long as possible.[154] His cohabitation with an unnamed woman he never married and the son they bore taught him the difference between outcomes of lust and a committed marriage.[155] Augustine experienced the spiritual and physical battle articulated by the apostle Paul, "I can will what is right, but I cannot do it" (Rom 7:18).

Augustine is not alone. The area of sexual purity is an internal and external battleground fueled by contemporary culture in sexually explicit media messages from film to advertisements. Unbridled permissiveness corrupts the holiness of God's intent and purpose for sexuality—a gift of intimacy to be cherished rather than a means of self-fulfillment and exploitation. Intimacy shared in giving and receiving love is a basic human need, and sexuality plays a part in its expression. God designed both male and female to be loved and cherished by providing guidelines for sexual expression. Thus, a responsible understanding of sexuality must be grounded in the Scriptures and Christian tradition, which provide the compass for how to navigate our contemporary moral morass, rather than responding to unrestrained hormones or culturally relative values.

The apostle Paul reminded the Corinthians that for the believer the physical body belongs to Christ and must not be used to dishonor God (1 Cor 6:15) because the body is the place where the Holy Spirit dwells (1 Cor 6:19-20). Because the body's purpose is to honor and glorify God, cultivating sexual purity becomes part of the discipleship process as believers respond to the radical call to follow Christ and his ways. Discipleship reflects a new morality announced by Jesus, according to John Grabowski, which views observable actions through the moral disposition of the heart (cf. Mt 5–7).[156] Sexual purity relates to holiness: "As he who called you is holy, be holy yourselves in all your conduct; for it is written, 'You shall be holy, for I am holy'" (1 Pet 1:15-16). The apostle Paul continually exhorted believers to disassociate from sexual immorality and impropriety in self and others, which violate the holiness of God (1 Cor 5:9-11; 6:18-20).[157] Growing into Christlikeness pleases God and involves controlling one's body, which should distinguish believers from unbelievers (1 Thess 4:3-5).

While sexuality relates to physical health as male and female, it also intersects other formation dimensions involving the spirit, emotions, relationships, intellect/cognition and vocation. Both male and female were made in, as well as reflect, the *imago Dei* (Gen 1:26-27; 2:18-25).[158] From the very beginning, God's purposes for gender relate to human encounter for companionship in order to "be fruitful and multiply," implying biological capacity for reproduction and the creation of ongoing community. As God's first representatives, their relationality was to reflect the community inherent in the character of the triune God.[159] Thus, sexuality relates not only to anatomical physiology but also to "the basic datum of our existence as individuals," as we relate to God and one another.[160]

Disobedience resulting from the fall corrupted all dimensions of human nature, including sexuality (Gen 3). While expressions of sexuality have misaligned with God's purposes throughout human history, it is important to remember that procreation linked "the first human pair to the coming of the Messiah."[161] To reiterate, the value of embodiment is affirmed in that Jesus was born in a human body. By divine grace, God provides the means to bring us into alignment with divine intention through sexuality, fully expressed in monogamous marriage between a man and a woman, as Jesus affirmed when the Pharisees confronted him regarding divorce. Jesus reiterated the Genesis 2:24 passage, positioning heterosexual marriage as the prototype for human sexual expression (Mt 19:1-11). Marriage is to be upheld in honor and "the marriage bed kept pure" (Heb 13:4 NIV). As Stanley Hauerwas notes, it is in this context of monogamous, heterosexual marriage that a stable family structure contributes to stable societies through community.[162]

Sexuality reflects the deep need for human bonding, including the realization that only God can unconditionally love us. Lisa Graham McMinn asserts, "We are made in the image of God. In our fundamental longing for unity, communion, and consummation, we simultaneously reflect *imago Dei* and, whether or not we know it, we are yearning ultimately for the One who can satisfy our deepest longing to be known and loved."[163] According to Stanley Grenz, human differentiation of male and female relates to bonding. Through bonding "the unity in diversity that arises out of the bond that brings male and female together in marriage offers an obvious picture of the unity in diversity present within the triune God."[164] For Grenz, "The ultimate goal of sexuality, and hence of the impulse toward bonding, is participation in the fullness of community—namely, life together as the new humanity, as the eschatological people in relationship with God and all creation."[165]

Miroslav Volf takes it one step further by underscoring self-giving love as the basis for gender identities of male and female in order to achieve wholeness "only through the relation to the other, a relation that neither neutralizes nor synthesizes the two, but negotiates the identity of each by readjusting it to the identity of the other."[166] As the CSF model presents, love is the core catalyst for God creating humankind in the *imago Dei* infused within both genders. Cultural tides, however, dictate against a biblical view of sexuality.

How do we navigate the deep ethical void in contemporary culture, as "popular culture today teaches that one cannot be whole without . . . having sex."[167] Grenz observes, "The freedom of private decision offered by secularized culture means that persons living in contemporary Western society find themselves entrusted with unparalleled responsibility for shaping and expressing their own sexuality."[168] Grenz calls for rethinking and reasserting a sexual ethic for this generation. Duke University professor Lauren F. Winner likewise echoes this need for a relevant sexual ethic, particularly for singles regarding the virtue of chastity: "The point is that chastity, like most aspects of the Christian life, does not come naturally, and that the church might do well to think intentionally about the resources it can offer for educating people into chastity, and sustaining them in the midst of chastity."[169] Winner's comments remind me of Robert, a young, unmarried man who bravely approached me for perspective and prayer regarding his constant battle with same-sex attraction, and Arielle, a young, unmarried woman who had had two prior abortions and was pregnant with her third child. As Christians, they were looking for guidance to navigate the conflict, confusion and pain of these inner realities. Unfortunately, such guidance is often absent in the church.[170]

So where does this leave those who are single, whether adolescents, young adults or older adults? Given that sexual desire is natural and sexual purity is challenging, how do Christian singles deal with this dilemma?

Sociologist Mark D. Regnerus addressed these questions when conducting a study to assess how religion shapes understanding and expressions of sexuality among US teenagers.[171] Regnerus found that although religiosity makes a difference in sexual attitudes, it does not always follow that religion motivates sexual decision making.[172] Other factors providing supportive anchors for adolescent sexual behavior include having like-minded friends, family and authorities who teach biblical perspectives that counter permissive values and who invest relational time into teens' lives.

Regarding the college age group, religion professor Donna Freitas studied the attitudes of religion and sexuality at seven US colleges and universities reflecting Catholic, evangelical, nonreligious private, and public institutions. Freitas states, "Evidence also demonstrates that America's teens and college students are exceedingly sexually active—anywhere from 73% to 85% (depending on college institution type)."[173] She sees a correlation between the drift of college students away from traditional religion and their immersion in a sexually active college culture.

In order to assist singles in framing a moral basis for sexuality, Judith and Jack Balswick suggest that moral decision making begin with asking the right questions to frame principles rather than simply posing a do-not-do approach.[174] However, all the right questions and answers may fly in the face of raging hormones. Yet guiding principles derived from a holistic view of God, self and others must be the foundation for all moral decision making, including sexuality. In the absence of this integrated biblical approach, sexuality becomes an appendage detached from a healthy discipleship lifestyle. And discipleship prescribes chastity, as Lauren Winner contends in recounting her own past. Winner submits that "chastity is God's very best for us," although it is difficult.[175] She emphasizes that chastity, connoting moral wholeness as the counterforce to lust, can be achieved through prayer, reading of the Bible and Christian classics, and involvement in the church, which is an integral part of formation and discipleship. Although godly role models, peers and accountability relationships may reinforce chastity, the church needs to assist single adults in a relevant way that strengthens moral character.[176]

Sexual purity is for our protection, and exercising virtue provides the means, as Joseph demonstrated when he fled the seductive advances of Potiphar's wife (Gen 39:6-23) and as King David learned after his adulterous affair with Bathsheba (2 Sam 11:1-27). Alasdair MacIntyre defines virtue as "an acquired human quality the possession and exercise of which tends to enable us to achieve those goods which are internal to practices and the lack of which effectively prevents us from achieving any such goods."[177] We cannot exercise virtue to achieve "the goods" without the power of the Holy Spirit. The apostle Paul affirms, "If the Spirit of him who raised Jesus from the dead dwells in you, he who raised Christ from the dead will give life to your mortal bodies also through his Spirit that dwells in you" (Rom 8:11). The indwelling Spirit helps us discern virtuous behaviors against the competing behaviors that vie for our allegiance.

Defending sexual integrity, Caroline J. Simon offers a helpful paradigm in which to discern six contemporary worldviews regarding sexuality, incorporating both sacred and secular views. They include:

1. the *covenantal* view within the "one flesh" marriage model, reflecting God's covenant with Israel and Christ's covenant with the church (cf. Jer 3:14; Eph 5:22-33)
2. the *procreative* view upheld as the official position by the Roman Catholic Church relating to reproduction
3. the *romantic* view, which when taken on its own, supports full sexual expression within both mutual, nonmarital love relationships and loving marriages
4. the *plain sex* view, which when taken on its own, disconnects love, commitment and sex with an emphasis on sexual gratification
5. the *power* view, which views sexuality as energy, eroticism and force used for controlling, manipulating and exploiting others
6. the *expressive* view, which focuses on sex for personal development and creative self-expression, with sexual restraint seen as unnatural.[178]

Simon argues that while the covenantal lens needs to be given priority, all six perspectives provide a composite of human sexuality. For example, research on the mechanics of sexual pleasure motivated by the plain sex view has contributed to counseling married couples struggling with sexual issues. In light of the power lens, spouses may believe that as long as they are married the power dynamics within their sexual relationship do not matter. Even in Christian marriages, husbands or wives may assume that they have unlimited power over the body of their spouse. The covenantal and procreative views reflect Christian perspectives of sexuality, whereas the latter four reflect secular views. I uphold a covenantal view of sexuality that incorporates aspects of the procreative and romantic views in heterosexual marital relationships because they most clearly align with biblical principles. Of course, the decision to have children should be a personal decision between heterosexual marital partners, rather than a mandate, and marriage is certainly enlivened by romance.

It is not surprising that sexuality is the most distorted, divisive and attacked reality of human dimensionality. Referring to the immense confusion, struggle and brokenness resulting from the disordering of sexuality, David Myers asks, "Has the historical pendulum swung to a point where the pursuit of pleasure is, ironically, amplifying misery?"[179] For example in the United States in 2008, births to unmarried mothers stood at 40.6 percent, compared to 18.4 percent in 1980.[180] The US rate of chlamydia, a sexually transmitted disease (STD) caused by bacterial infection, continues to rise, with women ages eighteen to twenty-four having the highest occurrence rate.[181] According to a 2010 WHO report, approximately 34 million people were diagnosed with AIDS, with 2.7 million newly infected and with 1.8 million deaths due to AIDS, of which 250,000 were children.[182] In addition, pornography addictions continue to escalate. In 2006 it was estimated that revenue from pornography sales reached almost $100 billion through Internet websites and video sales and rentals.[183]

Neuroscientist William Struthers traces how viewing pornography actually rewires the brain's neurological circuits to create addiction much more readily in men than in women.[184] Through men's repeated visual exposures, viewing pornography develops a neurological "over-sexualized and narrowed" superhighway resulting in a mental life fixated on sex: "They have unknowingly created a neurological circuit that imprisons their ability to see women rightly as created in God's image."[185] Struthers, however, asserts that a new neurological pathway can reestablish a healthy sexual pattern leading to "holiness rather than corrupted intimacy."[186] Women likewise can be restored from the pain of misaligned emotional and sexual attachment.[187] Through forgiveness, sexual shame can be overcome through the healing power of God's grace.[188]

I would be remiss not to address homosexuality, which remains a controversial issue, causing ongoing confusion and division among Christians and within the church and society at large.[189] I am reminded of Robert, a young man mentioned earlier in this chapter who sought prayer regarding same-sex attraction. He earnestly loves Jesus and is struggling to remain sexually pure in thoughts, feelings and behavior. Regardless of the contributing causes of homosexuality (i.e., biology, childhood and adult experiences, and environmental influences), the church, according to expert Mark Yarhouse, has not provided struggling Christians like Robert an alternative to the "gay script."[190]

Yarhouse observes that for those sincerely struggling as Christians, the gay script provides a compelling message of acceptance, especially in the absence of any alternative script from the church. The gay script asserts that same-sex attractions are "intended by God," the way one discovers real personhood as an authentic self and vital for self-fulfillment. Yarhouse identifies an alternative "identity in Christ" script for Christians struggling with same-sex attraction.[191] This script observes that same-sex attraction does not define personal identity, offers decision-making opportunities surrounding gender and sexuality, and helps strugglers sort through attractions to better identify as followers of Jesus rather than embrace the gay script.[192]

Since experiencing same-sex attraction is not the same as engaging in same-sex sexual behavior, Yarhouse offers a framework for understanding same-sex attraction and meaning making. The first level relates to *description*, referring to expressing how same-sex attraction is experienced.

The second level refers to the persistent direction of homosexual or bisexual *orientation*, relating to the ongoing and intense attraction to the same gender. The third level refers to those who integrate their same-sex attraction into a *gay identity*.[193] The first two levels allow for moral scrutiny before gay identity is embraced.[194] Although those with a gay identity may relate to God, they "may have foreclosed prematurely" with respect to their identity in Christ, according to Yarhouse.[195]

Regardless of level, we need to keep in mind God's creative intention for human sexuality. As Richard Hays observes, "From Genesis 1 onward, Scripture affirms repeatedly that God has made man and woman for one another and that our sexual desires rightly find fulfillment within heterosexual marriage."[196] Based on his study of the New Testament, Hays locates homosexual conduct between Christians not primarily as a private concern between consenting adults but rather as a matter for the entire body of Christ, which highlights the power of the cross and the Spirit's empowerment to live faithfully as we anticipate the new creation where the fullness of redemption will be realized.[197]

Simultaneously, Hays identifies what he calls Paul's "homiletic sting operation" found in Romans 2:1, after Paul's diagnosis of the disordered human condition, sexual impurity and homosexuality (Rom 1:18-32).[198] Paul warns against judging others, because all believers need God's mercy. Therefore, the church must address same-sex attraction and homosexuality in a compassionate and informed way.[199] All Christians struggle with the effects of fallenness. Lust, adultery, idolatry and their multiple expressions reflect a broken image that God seeks to redeem. Expressing our sexuality in God-honoring ways conveys our discipleship walk with Christ within a sexually permissive secular world. As sexuality comes into alignment with scriptural teachings through the power of the Holy Spirit, followers of Jesus have two alternatives: disciplined abstinence for those who are single or heterosexual marriage. Sexual purity reflects the holy character of God, who made humankind in the *imago Dei*, conforms believers into the *imago Christi* and empowers us to live for the *gloria Dei*.

To review, this chapter introduced embodiment as the basis for health stewardship and described five vitals areas: (1) nutrition, (2) physical exercise, (3) sleep, (4) stress, rest and leisure and (5) sexual purity. Each of these areas contributes to overall physical health and wellness and intricately influences other CSF dimensions. As Elizabeth Lewis Hall reminds us, we honor God by making good decisions about our bodies,[200] which come under the auspices of the life-giving Spirit. By doing so, we optimize loving God and others in ways that bring God glory. Chapter ten addresses resource formation, referring to how we care for God's creation, finances, material possessions and time for God's glory.

10

Stewardship

Our Resources

To say we love God as unseen, and at the same time
exercise cruelty toward the least creature . . .
was a contradiction in itself.

John Woolman,
The Journal and Major Essays
of John Woolman

No one can serve two masters.
Either you will hate the one and love the other,
or you will be devoted to the one and despise the other.
You cannot serve both God and Money.

Matthew 6:24 niv

On December 24, 1968, three NASA astronauts of the Apollo 8 space mission orbited the moon. As they became the first humans to view the earth as a whole planet, each of them read verses from Genesis 1:1-10, humbly acknowledging God as Creator of the heavens and earth, and God's creation as good.[1] In spite of such aeronautic and technological prowess since that Apollo space flight, the world remains the signature of Creator God who spoke creation into existence. The earth is not the center of the universe but rather, like other planets in the solar system, revolves around the sun in a finely articulated cosmos created by God with structure and order.

As Creator, God alone is the originator and source of life, who gives humankind capacity for ventures like space exploration. The entire universe belongs to God: "The earth is the LORD's and all that is in it, the world, and those who live in it" (Ps 24:1). God is the owner of it all! The psalmist declares:

> Every wild animal of the forest is mine,
> the cattle on a thousand hills.
> I know all the birds of the air,
> and all that moves in the field is mine. (Ps 50:10)

Therefore, as faithful stewards, we have the responsibility to handle with care all that God has given us. Since the genesis of stewardship derives from the creation narrative, this chapter describes how we utilize the resources that God has given us (God's creation, money, possessions and time).

In creating humans in the *imago Dei*, God gave them dominion, or caring responsibility, over living creatures (Gen 1:26-27; see chap. 2 of this book). God gave them all seed-bearing plants and fruit from trees for food (Gen 1:28-30). Creation, as God's gift to all living things, is motivated by love ("For God so loved the world" [Jn 3:16]), not only to bless humankind but to reveal God's glory. If, as Kierkegaard suggests, the *imago Dei* primarily connotes resembling God in loving, then how does imaging God extend to the earth related to love?[2] Douglas John Hall answers by showing that the *imago Dei* relates to "dynamic, harmonious relationships" with God, others and nature.[3]

According to Hall, a more precise word for dominion is *stewardship*.[4] The Master Designer entrusts humanity with stewardship ability, not to dominate but rather to harmoniously take care of God's resources through delegated power. Rather than power to exploit, as J. Richard Middleton notes, God affords humankind "generous, loving power," "used to nurture, enhance, and empower others, noncoercively, for *their* benefit, rather than self-aggrandizement."[5] The notion of delegated, loving power relates to the concept of stewardship based on humility. Similarly, Anthony Hoekema asserts that the meaning of dominion relates to superintending nature as God's vice-regent to form a "God-glorifying culture" through servanthood: "We must be concerned to be stewards of the earth and all that is in it, and to promote whatever will preserve its usefulness and beauty to the glory of God."[6] As God's representatives, we are to manage all our resources as for God's glory.

For our purposes, the term *resource stewardship* refers to caring responsibility for God creation (i.e., the environment), as well as personal resources of money, possessions and time. Figure 10.1 depicts resource stewardship as integral to Christian spiritual formation (CSF) and provides another barometer of our love relationship with God.[7] In light of trends in

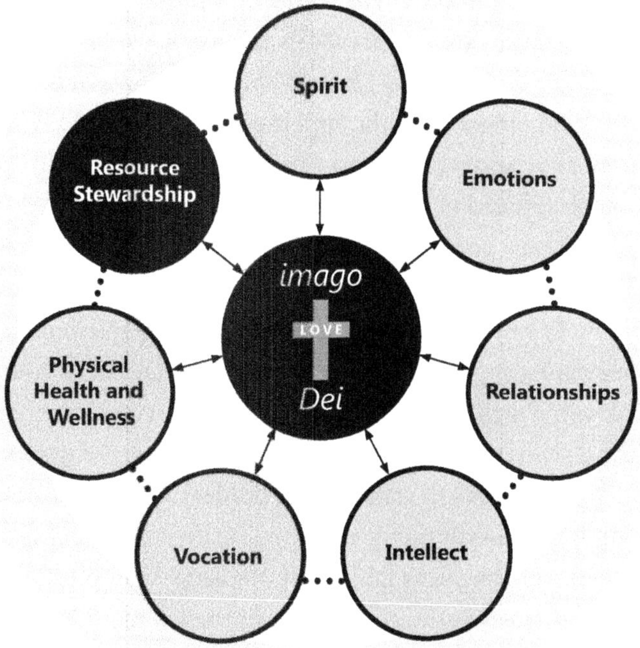

Figure 10.1. Resource formation

contemporary culture that diminish a godly approach to wise stewardship, this chapter addresses five areas integral for resource formation, a vital dimension of CSF: (1) the meaning of stewardship, (2) the care of creation, (3) money, giving and generosity, (4) handling possessions and (5) the use of time.

Meaning of Stewardship

What is stewardship? Stewardship refers to the careful oversight of what has been entrusted to one person or entity by another. Although some theologians identify the term *stewardship* as being inadequate in reference to the care of God-given resources, I will utilize this term to signify the grateful and loving response to God through what Richard Bauckham calls "caring responsibility."[8] For example, Joseph served as a steward to Potiphar, overseeing all his household affairs with caring responsibility (Gen 39:4). In the Old Testament a steward served like a supervisor. As a nation, Israel stewarded the Promised Land given to them by God (Deut 6:3), with Yahweh reminding them, "For the land is mine" (Lev 25:23). By acknowledging jealousy regarding the land (Joel 2:18), God rebuked Israel for idolatry, which resulted in disobedient stewardship that defiled the land (Jer 2:4-7). Not only does stewardship derive from creation but also from redemption in Christ through grace in all that has been given to us.

In the New Testament stewardship is a mark of discipleship, signifying the wise and caring application of God-given resources for faithful service. Three parables highlight stewardship themes, reinforcing that more will be given to those who faithfully maximize what has been entrusted to them.

First, in the parable of the faithful and prudent manager (Lk 12:42-48), Jesus responds to a question about readiness in light of the master's return (cf. Lk 12:35-41). Highlighting faithful stewardship, Jesus calls blessed the manager who is trustworthy and cares for others under his supervision. Jesus concludes, "From everyone to whom much has been given, much will be required; and from one to whom much has been entrusted, even more will be demanded" (Lk 12:48). According to Darryl Bock, Jesus evaluates good and bad stewardship in this parable, noting that a good servant "is marked by constant service to God. The Lord blesses those living faithfully as they await his return."[9] Craig Blomberg also refers to stewardship of God-given assignments, where rewards and punishments are dispensed and where "faithful stewardship requires perseverance and consistency, for the end could come at any time."[10] Leon Morris observes that accountability is part of our stewardship in fulfilling the will of God: "God's servant must make every effort to find out what God's will is and do it. We are all accountable."[11] Faithful stewardship implies responsibility.

Second, the parable of the dishonest manager, who wasted the rich man's possessions and then ingratiated himself to the rich man's debtors, also reinforces the priority of faithful stewardship (Lk 16:1-13). In that the rich man commended the dishonest manager for acting shrewdly, the exact interpretation is uncertain. Jesus commented, "If you have not been faithful with what belongs to another, who will give you what is your own?" and follows up with his exhortation that no one can serve both God and money (Lk 16:12-13). Whether the parable interpretation relates to shrewdness in the use of money or prudence in the time of crisis, Craig Blomberg offers three lessons: (1) all believers will be called to account for their service, (2) prudent use of all resources, especially finances, will contribute to giving account and (3) prudence in the context of discipleship will be rewarded.[12] Notwithstanding interpretation, Jesus himself interprets the parable by noting that stewardship is proven by what one does with little *and* with someone else's wealth (vv. 10-12).

Third, in the parable of the ten pounds (Lk 19:11-27), reminiscent of the parable of the talents in Matthew 25:14-30, Jesus conveys how a nobleman gave his servants ten pounds each in order to maximize his investment. The nobleman rewarded them according to what they earned. The first servant earned ten pounds more, the second servant earned five pounds more, and the third servant earned nothing because he failed to invest it. Thus, the nobleman took what was given to this third servant and gave it to the one who doubled his investment. Jesus commented, "I tell you, to all those who have, more will be given; but from those who have nothing, even what they have will be taken away"(Lk 19:26). Blomberg notes that all people are entrusted with a portion of God's resources for which they are to act as good stewards.[13] All three parables indicate that we will be held accountable for what God has entrusted to us.

Jesus is the perfect prototype of a faithful, caring steward who came to serve others through a pure motivation, unlike the dishonest manager in Luke 16. The dishonest manager acted shrewdly in order to defend himself against his employer's accurate accusations of mismanagement. Conversely, Jesus faithfully handled the affairs of the Father in complete obedience to the Father (Phil 2:7-8). Therefore following Jesus' example, we are "brought into a stewarding of God's grace that has already been enacted by God's chief steward."[14] Our stewardship is to proceed directly from Christ's stewardship example.[15]

Stewardship themes also appear in the Epistles. For example, Paul identified himself as a steward in his apostolic role in the church: "Think of us in this way, as servants of Christ and stewards of God's mysteries. Moreover, it is required of stewards that they should be found trustworthy" (1 Cor 4:1-2). For Paul, stewardship involved a sacred trust. Likewise, the church is to manage all of God's grace for Kingdom advance and God's glory: "Like good stewards of the manifold grace of God, serve one another with whatever gift each of you has received" (1 Pet 4:10). Such service overshadows human tendencies toward personalized power, ambition and narcissism, obvious disqualifications for the stewardship role.[16]

Invariably, we not only have stewardship responsibilities by virtue of *creation* in that God entrusted us with a stewardship mandate in the creation narrative, but also by virtue of *redemption,* in that Christ's ultimate stewardship example reconciled the world to God through grace. Ernst Conradie maintains that stewardship "cannot simply be derived from the divine command as stated in Genesis 1 and 2" but must include a Christological dimension as well.[17] Since "Christ fulfills the office of steward, redefined as servant," stewardship implies responding to God's grace in Christ as responsible inhabitants of God's house (i.e., the earth).[18] Conradie contends, "Human responsibility is best understood as a grateful response to the story of God's salvific grace epitomized in the life, ministry, death and resurrection of Jesus Christ."[19] Because Christ has redeemed us and promised us an eternal home, we cannot forfeit tending to our current home on earth, which cries out for care. In resource formation the care of creation is an essential component of our stewardship responsibility.

Caring for Creation

Creation is in crisis. Degradation of water, land and the atmosphere threatens our planet through animal extinction, global warming, deforestation, water and air pollution, and global toxification.[20] The United Nations warns that "environmental damage could pass unknown points of no return."[21] Available global resources fail to approximate demand. Like the frog in the pot of gradually heated water, the boiling point for global viability is upon us. Over time these degradation effects promise to increase. In light of this ongoing ecological crisis, I argue that creation care must become an integral part of resource formation and woven into every Christian's stewardship value, theology, commitment and practice.

Earth was created through and for Christ, and the whole creation worships God (cf. Ps 148).[22] Colossians 1:16 unequivocally identifies Christ as Creator: "all things have been created through him and for him." Thus, caring for creation is one expression of loving and glorifying our Creator. As Steven Bouma-Prediger affirms: "Authentic Christian faith includes care for the earth. Earthkeeping is integral to Christian discipleship."[23]

Paul reveals that the creation is groaning as we wait for the consummation of the Kingdom (Rom 8:19-23). Even creation is attuned to spiritual realities. In commenting on this text, James Dunn notes the "solidarity between humankind and the rest of creation," in awaiting the age to come.[24] I also wonder, however, if this groaning in expectation of the age to come might also be a groaning for healing from earth's depletion.[25] Unfortunately, care of creation is often dismissed as a secular concern and overlooked by well-meaning Christians. For example, when was the last time you heard a teaching, exhortation or sermon on creation care? Douglas John Hall's strident plea summarizes this issue:

> But if this world matters—really matters!—and if the secret for its mattering is felt in the very depths and centre of the community of the crucified one, then the stewarding of this beloved world is of the very essence of our belief, and every attempt to shove it off to the sidelines will have to be regarded as a matter of apostasy and blasphemy![26]

Strong and appropriate words! Let's briefly review how Christians have responded to the ecological crisis over the past fifty years.

In 1967, medieval historian Lynn White Jr. published a paper that became a turning point for environmental discussion among twentieth-century Christians.[27] White charged that Christian history and doctrine were to blame for endorsing a "dominion" perspective that, in his view, actually violated the earth rather than protected it. Prompted by White's paper and in the wake of Earth Day in 1970, the Greenpeace movement, an emergent ecotheology, and subsequent sacred and secular publications on environmental stewardship in the 1970s through the 1990s ushered an important wake-up call to the church.[28] Many theologians rebutted White's presuppositions, whereas others turned their attention to this overlooked issue. One such respondent was John Stott, who cautioned against deifying or exploiting nature, called for conservation of the environment for the common good, and appealed for "responsible stewardship, not a destructive domination" because care of creation reflects "our love for the Creator."[29]

It was not until 1994 that several hundred Christian leaders endorsed the "Evangelical Declaration on the Care of Creation," a brief statement in five parts that affirmed God's ownership of the earth and the church's responsibility before God to care for it.[30] In brief, the five declarations stated that (1) biblical faith is crucial to solving ecological problems; (2) Christians have responsibility for earth's degradation, which encompasses human poverty; (3) the Bible provides a tangible way forward, beginning with repentance followed by faithful response to its principles; (4) faith in God as Creator and humankind created in God's image magnify Christ's purpose to bring healing and wholeness to all of creation; and (5) with Christ being the only hope for the consequences of human sin and the church as the center of creation care, Christians should work with those dedicated to Earth's preservation.

This declaration stood on the shoulders of previous theologians such as Joseph Sittler (1904–1987), who in the 1940s and 1950s prophetically warned about the impending ecological crisis and advocated for creation care. His observation that "nature is like a fine piece of cloth; you pull a thread here and it vibrates through the whole fabric," bespeaks the fragility of God's creation.[31] Sittler drew upon the "ecological doxology" of Psalm 104, describing creation as a community of living things:

> O Lord, how manifold are your works!
> In wisdom you have made them all;
> the earth is full of your creatures. (v. 24)

In his writing and preaching, Sittler reframed environmental issues through the prism of God's love and grace. To Sittler, the beauty and dynamism of nature are manifestations of grace as gifts "pointing beyond themselves to their source in the ultimate and all-encompassing reality of the free, faithful, and self-giving love of God."[32] Acknowledging the need for creation care is the crucial first step in preserving it. The Christian community has initiated decisive steps to recast earth stewardship, which for some has become synonymous with exploitation, in terms of caring responsibility.[33]

Since 1999, Christians and Jews in the United States have jointly collaborated and advocated for creation care before Congress. Through the establishment of "Washington Week," events like the annual National Prayer Breakfast for Creation Care provide a united voice joining several faith-based entities.[34] In 2007, these entities joined together to form the National Religious Coalition on Creation Care (NRCCC) for interdenominational and interfaith collaboration.[35] Through institutional networks such as the NRCCC, it is hoped that individual awareness and efforts will increase for creation care.

What stumbling blocks prevent us from more faithful stewardship in the care of creation? Calvin DeWitt offers prevailing attitudes, such as (1) "this world is not my home, so why bother?" (2) "creation care verges on the New

Age Movement," (3) "creation care is too much like pantheism, the worship of nature," (4) "worldly people primarily participate in environmental concerns," (5) "I don't want to be viewed as alarmist," and (6) "people are more important than the environment."[36] In addition, believers may actually not know how to address such a seemingly insurmountable issue on a personal scale.[37] The converse of these prevailing attitudes should characterize followers of Christ. Although this world is not our eternal home, it is, however, the home that God created for us to faithfully care for in this earthly life. Although certain movements and worldviews such as new age, pantheism or animism extol nature, they should not dissuade believers, of all people, from active involvement in creation care. Although secular environmentalists sound the alarm regarding environmental degradation and the need for short- and long-term strategies, they do so out of concern for the created world, which frankly puts most Christians to shame. Environmental stewardship should be a part of everything we do.

If resource formation includes the care of creation, how can Christians contribute to, in Albert Schweitzer's words, "a reverence for life," which includes the environment? If godly love is the core motivational dynamic of CSF, including resource formation, how do we love God through caring for creation without *dualism* or *gnosticism* (i.e., separating the spiritual from the material), or *pantheism* (i.e., worshiping nature as divinity rather than God, who created nature)? I propose that the process begins with establishing implicit values toward our Creator and God's creation that, in turn, influence behavior. A solid starting place would be to address the question posed by James Nash on how to express godly love in an ecological context involving the protection of the planet and others against human exploitation.[38] Nash identifies five expressions of Christian love in an ecological context—reconciliation, communion, community, harmony and shalom—such that ecological harm is minimized as much as possible, the integrity of the ecosphere is upheld, and frugality characterizes consumption.[39] As Christ's ambassadors, our attitude within nature should foster these ends both ecologically and socially.

An individual and corporate Christian response to the care of creation moves from awareness to appreciation to stewardship.[40] Fred Van Dyke and his colleagues suggest this movement begins with the worship of our Creator, followed by informed study of environment issues, deliberate contact with nature (enriching outdoor activities) and acts of service that preserve the environment, such as planting trees, as well as supporting environmental lobbying efforts and community conservation projects.[41] Appreciating nature, as Steven Chase argues, can become spiritual practice through making intentional connections with nature.[42] Several years ago my husband participated in an outdoor leadership school for four months. He learned about "no-trace camping," where hikers learn to leave no trace of their presence when outdoors. In other words, "take only pictures; leave only footprints." Other ways to express creation care include participating in faith-based ecological education and developing better personal habits and practices to conserve energy, as simple as turning off lights when not needed, regulating thermostats, taking shorter showers, and recycling paper, plastic and metal. "Going green" should typify followers of Christ through using less and conserving more.[43] Resources abound to help us do so.[44]

Ways that the church might respond to enhancing creation care include biblical preaching and teaching focusing on God as Creator and Sustainer and our earth care responsibility, worshiping in outdoor settings, exercising ecologically sensitive oversight of church grounds, and even engaging in cross-cultural initiatives that meet the spiritual, physical, economic and ecological needs of the poor in developing nations.[45] As Joseph Sittler projected, "If the church will not have a theology *for* nature, then irresponsible but sensitive men will act as midwives for nature's unsilenceable meaningfulness, and enunciate a theology *of* nature."[46] The challenge is this: "The Christian community must stop being a culture in retreat, . . . it must have a great enough love for God's people and God's world, and a great enough confidence in God, to risk involvement and make an impact."[47] We can learn from Saint Francis of Assisi, whose love and respect for the created world influenced all CSF dimensions of his life.[48] A moderate lifestyle that conserves resources, money and time can become more dedicated to the service to others. As we do so, we can enjoy the beauty and wonder of God's creation as a gift to appreciate and a resource to care for. Another area of stewardship relates to money, giving and generosity.

Money, Giving and Generosity

God is the owner of everything, including our finances. Since creating us to wisely manage our God-given resources, God likewise provides principles that address motives and practices for doing so. For example, Jesus challenged his disciples to have an eternal perspective by seeking first his Kingdom over material provision (Mt 6:33). Realizing earthly temptations, Jesus cautioned the disciples against storing up earthly treasures that have no eternal value, while encouraging them to store up treasures in heaven. Knowing that the heart follows one's treasure and cannot serve two masters (Mt 6:19-21), Jesus added, "You cannot serve God and wealth" (Mt 6:24). Using direct language, Jesus posed a clear choice between two competing loyalties: loving God and loving money. The outcome of this choice reflects the quality of our spiritual lives. When Jesus is Lord, he becomes Lord over our finances. We demonstrate Christ's lordship by following his precepts and example in honesty and integrity in the handling of finances.

Early Christians Ananias and Sapphira ultimately chose money as their master (Acts 5:1-11). Being members of the first-century church, this married couple participated in a close-knit Christian community characterized by devotion to the apostles' teaching and fellowship and by breaking bread and praying together (Acts 2:42-47). Community members sold their possessions in order to give to those in need. Similarly, Ananias and Sapphira sold a piece of property and donated some of the proceeds to the apostles for distribution, keeping back a portion for themselves. After each separately lied about the amount of the sale, both collapsed and died.

The issue was not keeping a portion of the money but rather lying about it. As Philip Goodchild maintains, God and money compete as "the supreme value against which all other values are measured."[49] God, as the source of all values, provides "the ultimate criteria of power, truth, and goodness"[50] for Kingdom currency. Conversely, money offers access to power as the currency of this world. Ananias and Sapphira chose money as their master and tragically reaped the consequences. Similarly, Judas acted on his values when betraying Jesus for thirty pieces of silver (Mt 26:15).

Primary allegiance to God or money is not without tension. Goodchild states that the power of money as master is not simply in its accumulation for its own sake but rather in the way money shapes our time, attention and devotion.[51] By its very nature, money easily veils God as the source of all provision and the ultimate value on which money decisions are made. The apostle Paul observed, "But those who want to be rich fall into temptation and are trapped by many senseless and harmful desires that plunge people into ruin and destruction" (1 Tim 6:9). Money accumulation can become a singular life focus both for those who have much and desire more and for those who have little and desire to survive.

For those whose master is money, the answer to the question, How much money is enough? is "just a little more." The peasant Pahom in Leo Tolstoy's short story "How Much Land Does a Man Need?" received an offer to secure all the land he could walk around from dawn to dusk, under the condition that he end the walk at his starting place.[52] *At sunrise, Pahom began to walk quickly in order to secure as much land as possible. At sunset, he feverishly ran to his initial location. Gasping for breath, the exhausted Pahom flung himself at the starting point, only to collapse and die on the spot. Several observers dug a plot six feet by three for his burial. Tolstoy's point is clear. Material accumulation can destroy us, and six by three feet is how much land a person really needs. Is it wrong to want to own property? Of course not. However, greed may overtake us to our peril.*

Human value cannot be assessed by wealth. Ralph Moore and Alan Tang affirm, "Money does not equate to personal value. Neither can character be measured by one's wealth."[53] Jesus repeatedly affirmed through words and actions the value of the poor and disenfranchised, while chastising avarice, manipulation and the hoarding of the rich. To the poor, Jesus came to preach good news (Lk 4:18-19), to bless (Lk 6:20-21) and to give (Jn 13:29). When dining at a Pharisee's house, Jesus told his host that in order to be blessed he should invite to such events the poor and disabled rather than family, friends and rich neighbors (Lk 14:12-14). Jesus knew the power, privileges and trappings of the rich and the injustice, marginalization and exploitation of the poor.[54] In the parable of the rich man and Lazarus (Lk 16:19-31), where the pathos of the poor and the pride of the rich sharply contrast, Jesus exposes the condition of the heart, how one's values and actions have eternal consequences, and overturns the Jewish presumption that the rich are blessed merely because of their wealth.[55] In his solidarity with the poor, Jesus gave them eternal hope despite their earthly conditions.[56] Human value is based on being created in the image of God, not on wealth accumulation.

Wealth accumulation, however, is not sinful if the motive and means of caring stewardship are God-honoring. In avoiding the pitfalls of wealth accumulation the Proverbs writer asks that God would give him "neither poverty nor riches," (Prov 30:7-9), understanding that each extreme potentially causes separation from God. Riches often camouflage a false sense of security. An observer once commented to Mother Teresa, who ministered to the desperately poor in Calcutta's slums, that he would not do what she was doing for all the money in the world. She thoughtfully responded, "Neither would I."[57]

For achieving God-given goals and obligations, money should be a tool, not a tyrant. When money becomes an end in itself, it becomes idolatrous. "For the love of money is a root of all kinds of evil, and in their eagerness to be rich some have wandered away from the faith and pierced themselves with many pains" (1 Tim 6:10). The writer to the Hebrews cautioned, "Keep your lives free from the love of money, and be content with what you have; for he has said, 'I will never leave you or forsake you'" (Heb 13:5). Those who succumb to the love of money, greed and dishonest gain, like Ananias and Sapphira, do so at a great cost. For example, one of my younger brothers determined to become a millionaire by the time he was thirty through dealing illegal drugs. With money as his god, he led a fast-paced life with all of the world's perks. Yet monetary wealth could not save him when he ran a red light, collided with a semi and died instantly. For my brother, money was a tyrant, fueled by greed and dishonest gain. For Christians, money should be a tool, reflecting an eternal perspective in its use.[58]

For followers of Jesus, money, which is morally neutral in and of itself, has several purposes: (1) to glorify God when contributing to the Lord's work, (2) to do good, (3) to provide for oneself and one's family, (4) to repay debt, (5) to pay taxes, (6) to save and (7) to leave an inheritance for others.[59]

First, money glorifies God when contributed to the Lord's work. Various questions arise as to how much to give to God's work and whether tithing is the standard. As David A. Croteau observes in his historical and biblical analysis of tithing, respected Christian leaders consistently differ on this issue.[60] Croteau notes that before the Reformation church leaders generally affirmed some sort of tithing. During the Reformation, however, views on tithing began to shift because of tithing abuses. After the Reformation a diversity of opinion ensued. John Wesley's approach, "earn all you can, save all you can, and give all you can" was followed by others, such as Charles Haddon Spurgeon (1834–1892), who gave a double tithe to the work of the Lord. In the twentieth century, many advocated for a tithing renewal.[61] And today, strong stances appear on both sides of this issue.

Tithing advocates point to biblical precedents beginning with Abram's giving to King Melchizedek one-tenth of the booty after his victory over the four Mesopotamian kings (Gen 14:20; Heb 7:1-10). Jacob vowed to return to God one-tenth of God's provision (Gen 28:20-22). God gave the Levites all the Israelite tithes for serving in the tent of meeting (Num 18:20-29; Deut 14:28-29). While tithes supported the Levites, they also supported poor Israelites and needy Gentiles (Deut 14:28-29). Proverbs 3:9-10 exhorts,

> Honor the Lord with your substance
>   and with the first fruits of all your produce;
> then your barns will be filled with plenty,
>   and your vats will be bursting with wine.

Through Malachi, God chastised the returning Israelite exiles for robbing God through tithes and offerings (Mal 3:8-12). Citing this Malachi passage, Moore and Tang identify three promises of God when tithing: increased blessing, protection of one's resources and living in delight.[62] Tithing advocates observe that tithing stretches faith to believe that God will provide for financial needs when God is honored first and reinforces that money does not have control over us.

Although a tithing requirement does not appear in the New Testament, Jesus recognized the tithing of the Pharisees but condemned their neglect of mercy, justice, faith and love (Mt 23:23; Lk 11:42). In addition, the apostle Paul provided giving principles: (1) love is "the foundational motivation for giving in the new covenant" (cf. 1 Cor 13:3), (2) preachers of the gospel deserve support (1 Cor 9:13-14), (3) collections for God's people (e.g., the church in Jerusalem) should be offered by each person (1 Cor 16:2), and (4) generosity and giving result from grace (2 Cor 8:7; 9:6-10).[63] Citing traditionalism and pragmatism that frame tithing perceptions, Croteau argues that 10 percent should not be the baseline for giving but rather should result from obedience as God leads.[64] His conclusion is that although believers should not be required to give 10 percent or more of their income, their giving should not be haphazard. Croteau notes that the New Testament, in fact, sets a higher standard of giving than 10 percent, as the old covenant tithe was noted to be over 20 percent.[65]

Old Testament law required a tenth of all produce and livestock be given toward support of the Levites (Lev 27:30-33; Num 18:21-28). Every third year, additional tithes were dedicated to support for the Levites, aliens, fatherless and widows (Deut 14:28-29; 26:12). Furthermore during feast days, tithes were also collected (Deut 12:6). Craig Blomberg observes that Paul's standard "is actually a more stringent one than the traditional tithe" and that the surplus of most affluent Western Christians could easily be devoted to Christian causes.[66] Some even propose a "graduated tithe," an increase above the tithe through frugal living in order to give more to the Lord's work.[67] Tithing is to be a recognition that all we have belongs to

God. Whatever remains after tithing still belongs to God and should be stewarded wisely.

Those opposing tithing cite that it becomes legalistic, that personal debt needs to be addressed first and that tithing is a goal to attain rather than a strict requirement. There is some truth to each of these objections. Tithing can become legalistic, as in the case of a church I once visited where members were dismissed if they did not tithe. Debts may be pressing, and tithing is not a strict New Testament requirement. For instance, it is difficult to imagine parents making the choice to offer a tithe to their church rather than feeding their children, or church leaders coercing them to do so. Each person, then, must establish his or her own conviction about financial giving based on an attitude of gratitude and a clear understanding of biblical principles on giving.

Second, money is for doing good and giving to others for the glory of God. John Stott notes, "What an awesome privilege we have in helping others right across the world to give glory to God. Releasing more of the money which he has entrusted to us as stewards will end in this."[68] Typified by the widow who gave all she had into the offering, giving is a mark of godliness. God loves it when we give with a cheerful attitude (2 Cor 9:7). Paul exhorted the Corinthian church in the grace of giving (2 Cor 8:7), and even Jesus acknowledged the heart of the woman who gave two copper coins worth less than a penny (Mk 12:41-44). God promises that as we give, it will be given to us (Lk 6:38) and that we will reap what we sow (2 Cor 9:6). Caution, however, is needed. We are not to give in order to receive but rather to reflect the character of God, regardless of any return.

This principle of giving became very real for my husband and me when we prayerfully considered a significant financial gift to a worthy ministry initiative. After a time of prayer, we felt prompted to give an amount above our tithe that we honestly could not afford, yet we believed that God would somehow provide the means. After making this financial pledge, my husband was promoted to a new job with a salary that covered the exact amount of our pledge. To reiterate, giving should be motivated by reflecting on the gracious giving of Christ, rather than an expectation of return. Ministry giving should also include resources that directly minister to the poor. According to C. S. Lewis, giving to the poor is essential to Christian morality, while it tampers with human insecurity and pride. Although Lewis offers no specific amount, he advises, "I am afraid the only safe rule is to give more than we can spare."[69] By giving to worthy Kingdom purposes, we participate in God's redemptive work not only by spreading the gospel but also by caring for those in need.

Third, providing for oneself and one's family offers another purpose for money (1 Tim 5:8). Paying the rent or mortgage and other household bills are financial realities. Giving to the Lord's work while neglecting one's family obligations hardly aligns with godly character. Diligence in work, rather than idleness, to meet financial obligations reflects godly stewardship (Prov 24:30-34; 2 Thess 3:10).

Fourth, repaying debt is another purpose of money. With an ability to repay, borrowing money can advance personal goals such as owning a home or a business or furthering one's education. Not repaying what is owed is condemned (Ps 37:21; Rom 13:8). Debt accrues for many reasons. We buy what we cannot afford, lack careful budgeting practices, have not been taught how to handle finances, or experience extenuating circumstances such as a job loss or illness. When the unexpected happens, such as an economic downturn, debt can easily overtake us and become like a tightening vice. Nevertheless, borrowing makes one beholden to the lender (Prov 22:7).

Currently, the US individual debt crisis mirrors the national US economy. At this writing the US debt is heading to $17 trillion, representing a growing national economic crisis.[70] The total credit card debt in the United States stands at $962 billion.[71] Per credit card owning household, the average credit card debt is $14,750. Credit cards fees for the United States alone total $20.5 billion a year. While credit card companies depend on slick advertising, impulse buying and a "keep up with the Joneses" mentality to rake in profits, they also annually mail out five billion credit card solicitations. We are living on plastic quicksand! What is likewise alarming is the extent of student college loan defaults. Increasingly, graduates cannot find employment in order to repay college loans. The result? In 2012, the total amount on defaulted student loans totaled $76 billion.[72] With an average credit card debt of $4,100, recent college graduates find themselves in a double-debt dilemma.[73] The good news is that debt is reversible by establishing sound biblical financial values and habits. Financial expertise, like that offered by Dave Ramsey, provides a path to eliminating debt, establishing an emergency fund and getting on level financial footing.[74] Ramsey's Financial Peace University DVD series has contributed to financial freedom for many.

Fifth, paying taxes that resource our government, like it or not, is another use of money. Even Jesus paid taxes (Mt 17:24-27). Sixth, money is for saving. Every believer should have a savings plan, even if it is saving only one dollar a week. Savings provides the needed reserve for the unexpected, a cushion for peace of mind, a pool from which to provide for oneself and one's family in the future, and additional income for giving to God's work and to others (Eph 4:28). Savings reflects a wise approach regarding the future but should not supersede trust in God. Like the prodigal son who wasted away all his inheritance (Lk 15:11-32), so Proverbs 21:20 makes an insightful observation: "Precious treasure remains in the house of the wise, but the fool devours it." Savings with a godly motive reflects wisdom. Seventh, another purpose of money is to leave an inheritance. "The good leave an inheritance to their children's children" (Prov 13:22). Having left an eternal inheritance, Jesus is our stewardship model (Eph 1:14; Col 3:24; Heb 9:15; 1 Pet 1:4).

These seven purposes of money should not be confused with hoarding, which is the accumulation of money and things out of fear of loss. The purposes of money, when stewarded in God-honoring ways, further God's Kingdom purpose in the world. Money is a vehicle for godly stewardship and a key indicator of our spiritual lives. Resource stewardship also involves the wise handling of possessions.

Handling Possessions

When I was eight years old, I saw an attractive pair of mittens priced $2.99 at a local clothing store. Determined to possess them, I later rode my bike to the store. Once inside and with no one looking, I stuffed those mittens into a small paper bag that I had brought with me. Then, I quickly left the store and rode home. After becoming a follower of Christ many years later, I returned to that store and made proper restitution. I am not proud of my behavior. Yet it underscores the innate desire to possess things. Like the character Gollum in J. R. R. Tolkien's The Lord of the Rings, we may want something so desperately, like the coveted ring ("my precious"), that we will go to any length to possess it. And once we secure it, we are reluctant to release what we believe belongs to us.

The rich young ruler who asked Jesus how to inherit eternal life demonstrates the inability to release possessions (Mk 10:17-31; Lk 18:18-30). Jesus responded by restating some of the commandments, to which the rich ruler replied that he had kept them since childhood. Understanding that possessions stood in the way of his relationship with God, Jesus instructed the man to sell all he had and to give the money to the poor so as to secure treasure in heaven. "When he heard this, he was shocked and went away grieving, for he had many possessions" (Mk 10:22). Jesus commented, "It is easier for a camel to go through the eye of a needle than for someone who is rich to enter the kingdom of God"(Mk 10:25). Accumulating possessions can easily become an idolatrous preoccupation, distracting us from relationship with God. Jesus once asked his disciples, "What will it profit them to gain the whole world and forfeit their life?" (Mk 8:36). We can forfeit our spiritual lives through the allure of the world, including materialism. As Moore and Tang note, "Material things are lovely to own, but they generate personal tragedy when they own us."[75] The rich young ruler loved his possessions more than he loved God.[76]

Such was the case for others in Scripture whose desire to possess ended in theft. Jacob stole his brother's birthright (Gen 27:35), Rachel stole her father's household gods (Gen 31:19), Achan first coveted and then stole some plunder in Jericho (Josh 7:20-21), and Judas stole money from the disciples' shared coffers (Jn 12:6). A. W. Tozer observes, "There is within the human heart a tough, fibrous root of fallen life whose nature is to possess, always to possess. It covets things with a deep and fierce passion."[77]

This is exactly what James referred to when identifying the desire to possess that motivates interpersonal conflicts and disputes. James notes that we do not have because our motives are askew and because we do not ask God (Jas 4:1-3). According to Richard Foster, "we badly need a conversion in our understanding of ownership."[78] Jesus must have thought so too in that seventeen of his thirty-eight parables concerned possessions. Wesley Kenneth Willmer observes, "Possessions are mentioned 2,172 times in Scripture—three times more than love, seven times more than prayer, and eight times more than belief. About 15 percent of God's word deals with possessions—treasures hidden in a field, pearls, talents, pounds, stables, and so on."[79]

Someone once asked Jesus to instruct his brother to divide the family inheritance with him (Lk 12:13-21). Instead, Jesus addressed the issue of greed by warning, "one's life does not consist in the abundance of possessions" (v. 15). Jesus went on to share the parable of the rich fool (vv. 16-21) who planned to tear down his barns and build bigger ones in order to store his increasing bounty. Lambasting the rich fool for his cavalier attitude, Jesus drew a sharp contrast between storing up possessions for oneself and being rich toward God. In the end, earthly possessions are nontransferable. Therefore, Jesus warns not to store up treasures on earth, "For where your treasure is, there your heart will be also" (Mt 6:19-21). Jesus' priority is crystal clear.

Randy Alcorn cautions, "But every possession we hold onto presents a constant temptation that it will become our treasure."[80] Knowing this tendency, my husband and I periodically reaffirm God's ownership of everything that we possess and thank God for these blessings. In gratitude, we verbally declare that all of our material possessions come from and belong to the Lord, and that we are mere stewards of them. Regularly reaffirming God's ownership of our possessions reminds us that God is our Provider and Sustainer.

Although we frequently dedicate our belongings to God lest we forget our stewardship role, we easily become victims of our materialistic culture. Particularly in the United States where materialism and consumerism run rampant, Christians are not spared the assault. Researching the link between religious faith and economic behavior, Robert Wuthnow observes how religious Americans compartmentalize materialism and spirituality into two "separate cognitive categories." Wuthnow views this phenomenon as "a kind of mental or emotional gloss" that creates a paradox in thinking.[81] On one hand, religious Americans are deeply individualist and materialistic, while on the other they are also deeply altruistic. Yet related to actual economic decisions, Wuthnow generally finds that people of faith do not significantly differ from their secular counterparts. Therefore, Wuthnow encourages the "schooling" of the soul in fundamental stewardship values that inform a godly approach to financial responsibility: "Stewardship can engender a desire to spend money in a way that helps the needy or that preserves the environment, even without requiring that all material pleasures be forgone."[82]

To theologically evaluate the issue of material possessions, Craig Blomberg surveys the Bible to glean applicable values and offers five conclusions. First, material possessions are blessings from God to be enjoyed. Second, material possessions constitute the primary means of turning hearts away from God. Third, the tell-tale sign of being redeemed is the transformation of stewardship attitudes. Fourth, extremes of wealth and poverty are intolerable, as long as there are intolerable extremes of poverty. Fifth and most important, scriptural teaching about material possessions is inextricably intertwined with spiritual matters.[83] Blomberg insists that biblical salvation is always holistic, involving the body and the soul as well as the material and spiritual: "And a major component of the material dimension is transformation in the way God's people utilize 'mammon'—material possessions."[84]

Overconsumption, especially characteristic of US culture, has been called "affluenza" or the "painful, contagious, socially transmitted condition of overload, debt, anxiety, and waste resulting from the dogged pursuit of more."[85] This obsessive quest for more and the urge to splurge finds countless expressions, most notably in escalating debt levels. In stinging critique of materialistic attitudes evidenced in mall mania and shopping fever, filmmaker John de Graff and his colleagues observe,

> We Americans have been pursuing more—more stuff, especially—for most of our history. We've been doing it to the exclusion of other values since the "me" generation of the 80s, and like starving children at the smorgasbord during the last several years of uninterrupted economic expansion.[86]

Even our children are targets of global marketing strategies that hook them at earlier ages into the affluenza epidemic.[87] How can we escape overconsumption?

Wesley Willmer recommends taking a personal inventory designed to assess values and actions regarding possessions. For example, he suggests (1) after reviewing credit card statements, checkbooks and possessions, make a list of specific examples reflecting your priority of God's eternal Kingdom; (2) cite five ways that you leverage the use of your earthly possessions to glorify God; and (3) list examples from the past year that demonstrate generosity in extending God's Kingdom.[88] Not minimizing wealth creation, Willmer suggests living as inexpensively as possible with contentment in order to maximize resources for God's Kingdom work.[89]

In addition to the graduated tithe previously mentioned, Ronald Sider provides other specific suggestions for investing in the Kingdom while resisting consumerism. Sider suggests: (1) living a more simplified lifestyle, minus unnecessary luxuries, (2) distinguishing between legitimate and nonlegitimate expenditures related to maintaining social status, (3) resisting popular fad purchases, (4) Christian giving that supports the needs of the poor through emergency relief, development and structural change, and (5) supporting evangelism and Christian education to complement holistic social justice activity.[90]

Other suggestions that foster frugality include reducing food expenses by substituting more vegetable rather than animal protein, lowering energy consumption by keeping the thermostat a few degrees cooler in winter for heating and higher in summer for air-conditioning, regulating clothing purchases, and developing a frugal budget. To bring overspending in certain areas under control, fasting for a season from purchases such as clothes, books, CDs, DVDs, electronics and eating out may reestablish stewardship principles. In addition, praying before purchases (e.g., "Lord, do I really need this now?" and "Lord, will you guide my spending today as I shop?") invites God's presence into seeming mundanity. Developing a "theology of enough" challenges Christians in resource stewardship through CSF to establish minimum and maximum levels of expenditures that provide an economy of care for us and the earth.[91]

In discussing resource stewardship regarding the handling of possessions and money, I'm mindful that many around the world have little or no earthly belongings to manage.[92] The unemployed find it difficult to obtain work and cope with the resulting stresses of losing their homes, a sense of security and self-esteem. Furthermore, bankruptcies and loan defaults are increasing. During lean economic times, we must understand that material possessions and amounts in bank account balances do not equate with our personal value to God and others. All of our resources, whether plentiful or limited, can be applied to glorify God, including our time.

USE OF TIME

Resource formation that glorifies God includes not only caring for creation and stewarding money and possessions, but also the wise handling of our time. Time is a seemingly amorphous dimension that moves us along in life. That is, unless you are the character Phil Connors, played by Bill Murray in the movie *Groundhog Day*. In a repetitive time loop, Phil awakens every morning only to be stuck in the same day, February 2, despite his desperate attempts otherwise. For the depressed, like Connors, time is drudgery. For the ambitious, time is advancement. For the discontented, time is adversarial. For the Christian, time is opportunity—to glorify God. Time, like other stewardship areas, is a gift of God that needs to be handled through grace. Time, as Karl Barth argues, is given as a "hymn of praise to God" by the proclamation of God's mighty acts through the Holy Spirit and by God's grace through which God meets with us.[93] How we invest our lives over time has eternal potential to glorify God, change lives and conform us more deeply into the image of Jesus.

Although some of us may feel stuck in time like Connors in *Groundhog Day*, we understand that time provides the means to orient us to the past, present and future, and positions us in a lifespan continuum. Each day comprises a twenty-four-hour period where the sun comes up in the morning and sets later in the day (that is, unless you live in Alaska!). We can neither speed time up nor slow it down. No amount of money can buy time. Believers in Jesus know that time will morph into timeless eternity, the culmination of this earthly existence promised by Jesus (Jn 3:15-16; 5:24; 10:28).

Time is a resource for deepening our relationship with God and others, while giving ourselves not only to necessary mundane matters but also to activities that reflect and extend the love of God in the world. The psalmist knew about the importance of time when praying, "So teach us to count our days that we may gain a wise heart" (Ps 90:12). Time can pass, however, without a commensurate maturation of the heart. Once time passes it can never be retrieved. There is something deeply compelling about wanting to make life count and using time for good. As Gandalf told Frodo in the movie version of J. R. R. Tolkien's *The Fellowship of the Ring*, "All we have to decide is what to do with the time that is given us." We decide what to do with time, rather than time deciding what to do with us. When the tyranny of the urgent eclipses our autonomy, time becomes an unmerciful taskmaster.

On one hand, time easily drifts. On the other hand, time can become so regimented that the joy of living dissipates. Years ago, after our university commencement, I bumped into a graduate who was in tears. Having just received her diploma, she lamented, "For four years, I worked so hard to complete this joint graduate degree that I forfeited time with others. I will be moving soon and now realize what a mistake I've made. I've developed few meaningful friendships while here." Dedicating so much time to work and study in the intellectual and vocational dimensions, she forfeited life-giving relational formation. Consequently, she felt spiritually frazzled, emotionally fragile and relationally fragmented. Her CSF rhythms were so imbalanced that it took significant time to recover. Fortunately, time does provide the needed salve for change and healing.

Time brings together all aspects of CSF. Like the various string, brass, woodwind, percussion and keyboard instruments harmoniously creating music, so too the various dimensions of CSF meld into formative rhythms that declare that God, as Composer of our lives, is at work fashioning a masterpiece. Our approach to time and life's demands either artistically transpose our lives from chaos to order or indiscriminately push us from order to chaos.

Living from a harmonious, rather than a discordant, center in God is by far one of the greatest challenges of contemporary life. So much dictates against it. Life demands and interruptions involving family, work and ministry often punctuate daily living with irritations. Henri Nouwen recalls the lesson learned from a seasoned professor who rectified the reality of constant interruptions: "My whole life I have been complaining that my work was constantly interrupted, until I discovered that my interruptions were my work."[94] This reminds me that impromptu meetings and the unplanned hosting of out-of-town guests are not interruptions to an already overcrowded schedule but rather a divine distraction that reinforces that people are more important than tasks.

In a simple yet compelling way, Dorothy Bass addresses the stewardship of time and life rhythms as "receiving the day," practices that open us to God's fullest purposes.[95] At its core, receiving the day centers in worshipful praise to God as Creator who invites us to partner in divine work.[96] Stewarding time means not forgetting the Creator of time. Bass identifies how to focus attention on receiving the day through daily prayer, observing sabbath rest and enjoying nature. Recalling Christian traditions that incorporate sabbath living, she observes, "But *sabbath* is a day, a certain day that shapes a weekly pattern."[97] Since busyness and multitasking characterize much of our lives, establishing life rhythms, such as taking intentional time with God in what Howard Thurman calls "centering down" into God's presence, helps us break free from the conspiracy of overwork.[98]

Intentionally looking for the movement of the Spirit in the small and mundane as well as the big and supernatural also opens us to the gift of time. Bass recounts how one mother she knows asks her children before bedtime, "Where did you meet God today?"[99] This reflective question tunes the human spirit to recognize the move of the Spirit in daily living in order to receive the day as God's gift of time. Time allows us to attune our spirits, emotions, relationships, minds, vocations, bodies and resources, while acknowledging those of others under the provision of God's grace. Bass observes, "A life that is not well lived in time can be a source of immense grief. To squander one's life-time is tragic."[100] Grace allows us to reject the condemnation that comes from time misused, as echoed by many who, along with the prodigal son, wasted valuable resources and time on licentious living. Grace frees us to release the past and embrace the future, while living life to the fullest for God's glory. As we are reminded, God has a time for everything under heaven and desires to make everything beautiful in its time (Eccles 3:1, 11). Time is God's mechanism for transformation.

How do we deal with the thieves of time that dismantle our fruitful stewardship, including communion with God? First, we need to establish rhythms of devotion by putting God first. There is no substitute to spending time with God on a daily basis in prayer, worship and feeding on Scripture. Jesus modeled this so powerfully in his own rhythms of spending time with the Father (Mt 14:23; Mk 1:35). When struggling to put God first, it helps to set realistic goals that can be reinforced through an accountability partner. Further, learning to say no to some other things to open time for God is critical. This is one way sacred space with God can be planned and protected. M. Shawn Copeland acknowledges that believers must learn the art of saying yes to what makes space for God and no to what precludes God, similar to an athlete whose self-discipline contributes to competing for the prize (1 Cor 9:24-25).[101] Although letting our yes be yes and our no be no (cf. Mt 5:37), Copeland avers that "for a no to be effective, it must be placed in the larger context of a life-affirming yes."[102] Incorporating a sabbath, a day to cease from work, into one's weekly schedule likewise contributes to breaking free from the crush of the clock.[103]

Second, establishing life priorities helps us manage time around what is really important, including our life calling and daily responsibilities in obedience to God. Developing life rhythms provides a balance between order and spontaneity by allowing needed time margin for healthy living.[104] Establishing priorities does not connote inflexibility but rather honors the biblical values and practices that we hold dear. Priorities obviously vary according to life season, current circumstances and cultural milieu. For example, approaches to time in Latin, African, Asian and Middle Eastern cultures vary greatly from those in the West. Western conceptions of time prioritize productivity, whereas conceptions of time in these other cultures prioritize relationship.[105] Being flexible in approaches to time in deference to culture is a sign of maturity.

Third, being alert to time wasters in seemingly benign activities, such as excessive television watching, inordinate engagement with social media and compulsive shopping, helps to calibrate our inner rhythms. The extent to which we give time to them reveals whether these activities control us or we control them. Fourth, practicing simplicity and contentment counters drivenness. Paul reminded Timothy that "there is great gain in godliness combined with contentment" (1 Tim 6:6). When we are content, we cease striving and can truly receive the day. Stewarding our time in addition to God's creation, money and possessions glorifies God.

Along with the NASA astronauts who read from the Genesis creation narrative when viewing the earth from space for the first time, we acknowledge that God made the heavens and the earth. Being made in the *imago Dei* and conformed to the *imago Christi* for the *gloria Dei*, we will one day give an account for how we lived and handled the resources that were provided us (Mt 12:36; Rom 14:12; 2 Cor 5:10). How did we care for God's creation and our money, possessions and time for God's glory? How did we reciprocally love God and others through use of our resources? Resource stewardship within the sphere of CSF provides an opportunity to be further conformed into Jesus' image in order to one day hear, "Well done, good and faithful servant" (Mt 25:21 NIV).

Chapter eleven ties all seven CSF dimensions together by showing how ethical living reflects loving and serving God and others for God's glory and Kingdom effectiveness.

11

Formation Synthesis

Our Ethical Living

Love, as the ultimate principle of morality,
is always the same. Love entering the unique situation,
in the power of the Spirit, is always different.

Paul Tillich, *Morality and Beyond*

The primary purpose of Christian spiritual formation (CSF), as derived from the *imago Dei* and revealed through the *imago Christi,* relates to reflecting the *gloria Dei* in the world to others (see fig. 3.2 in chap. 3). How we live as God's ambassadors in the world matters, most notably through a lifestyle of ethical consistency by manifesting the love of God in obedience to the Scriptures as empowered by the Holy Spirit in all life dimensions. Developing in the seven CSF dimensions as described in the previous chapters (i.e., spirit in the faith journey, emotions, relationships, intellect, vocation, physical health and resource stewardship) fortifies this purpose. Followers of Jesus become mirrors, albeit imperfect, reflecting God's glory and love to others through godly character, integrity and benevolent acts. Christian ethics plays an indispensable role in the CSF process through the framing of motivations and moral behaviors evidenced in the lives of individual believers, as well as the corporate body of Christ. Being grace-based, ethical Christian living finds its highest expression in extending the love of God to others in light of the eternal Kingdom to come through holistic integration.[1]

Ethical Christian living synthesizes all seven formational dimensions together in unity, such that the way we live in obedience and holiness demonstrates our commitment to Christ. As a foundation is to a building, so are biblical ethics to the moral life. Therefore, ethics relates to the moral principles around which one establishes personal values, makes decisions and lives life. Put another way, without ethical moorings, people drift on the sea of relativism, lack conviction and have no basis for decision making.

For the Christian, ethics is more than simply a matter of determining what is right and wrong, but rather is grounded in God's love and character, producing guiding principles and virtues as presented in God's Word.[2] As N. T. Wright observes, Christian ethics has tended to inadequately focus on "an arbitrary list of instructions that God had invented," the reasons of which are unknowable, as opposed to authentic Spirit-led living.[3] Wright notes that ethical Christian living points to God's eternal Kingdom, which "consists of anticipating this ultimate reality through the Spirit-led, habit-forming, truly human practice of faith, hope, and love, sustaining Christians in their calling to worship God," reflecting God's glory to the world.[4] After all, when this age ceases, love will carry into eternity. Godly love, therefore, is the enactment of the already-but-not-yet quality of eternity. Where love is, so is eternal God.

Ethical Christian living relates to becoming like Christ—as embodied in his character, teachings and actions—in order to glorify God. As Stanley Grenz observes, "The ultimate motivation for ethical living lies beyond mere patterning one's conduct after the example of a great leader. It arises from the kind of devotion that connects disciples to the Lord at the deepest level of their person: disciples devoted to Christ. And this leads to increasing conformity to Christ."[5] Being conformed to Christ's image through the work of the Holy Spirit is implicit within the CSF process and integrates all seven holistic formation dimensions, as shown in figure 11.1. Thus, to live ethical lives, each of the seven CSF dimensions frames a holistic tandem of integrity. By way of clarification, although some may define

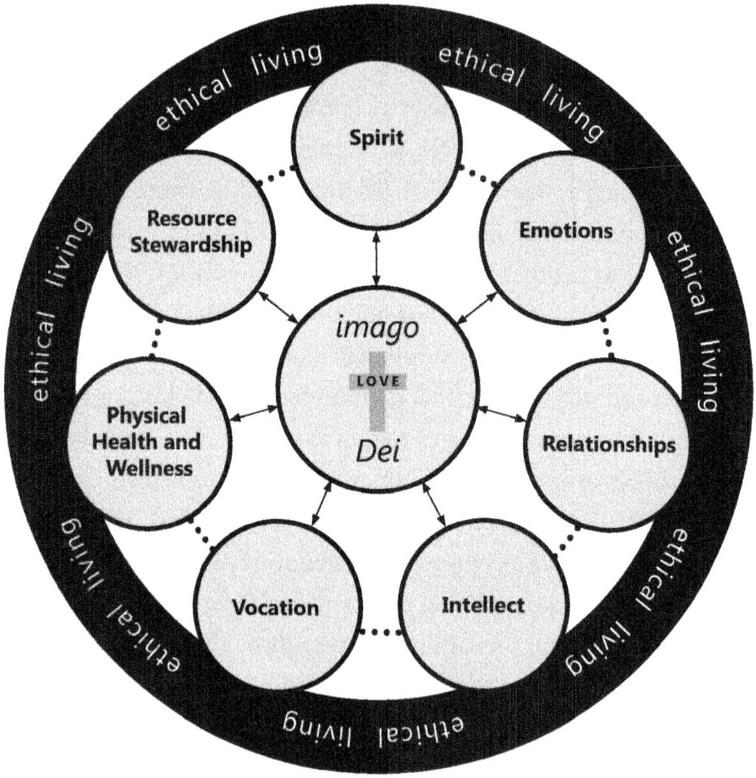

Figure 11.1. Ethical Christian living

the terms *ethics* and *morality* based on Greek and Latin traditions, with ethics relating to the study of right and good, and morality as the practical living out of them, I will use these terms interchangeably.[6]

Every approach to ethical Christian living must begin with Christ—his person, teachings and actions. As Richard Burridge contends, "First and foremost, the whole of the New Testament is about Jesus of Nazareth and what God has brought about through his deeds and words, life, death and resurrection. Without him as catalyst, there would be no New Testament, and no Christian church, let alone Christian ethics."[7] Christ must be the starting place for discussion on ethical Christian living as it relates to commitment to one's own and others' formation and well-being. When speaking of Christian ethics, we must repeatedly return to Christ as love incarnate.

Whereas chapter three introduced the love of God from a trinitarian perspective, this chapter provides an appropriate bookend to it by asserting that love *is* the primary ethic for Kingdom living. This chapter, then, begins by presenting love as the primary Kingdom ethic, arguing that authentic ethical Christian living is impossible without love as the foundation, followed by a discussion on imitating Christ as an outgrowth of godly love. Next, this chapter discusses the imperative for developing Christian character through the biblical virtues as the demonstration of godly love and how the church in a watching world is called to reflect ethical Christian living. This chapter synthesizes all seven CSF dimensions and serves as a prelude to the next and final chapter.

Love Is the Ethic

As mentioned in chapter three, love was the compelling motivation of God not only in creation but also in the redeeming work of Christ. Love prompts all of God's creation, with humanity being created in the very image of God. To reiterate, *godly love is the essence of God's character and personality, proceeding from the Father as demonstrated by the Son through the work of the Holy Spirit, which unconditionally upholds the highest good of others and fosters the same altruism and benevolence in human relationships without regard for personal sacrifice.* Jesus embodied the highest good for humanity through altruism and self-sacrifice. The CSF model illustrates the love of God in creation (*imago Dei*) and the character of Christ demonstrated through the cross (*imago Christi*) for the ultimate telos of our lives (*gloria Dei*). Our grateful response to God's unconditional love involves taking seriously the call to apply all our God-given resources for God's glory, which chapters three through ten highlighted.

As the primary Kingdom ethic, God's love is limitless. How love is positioned as the pivotal ethic in the Scriptures begins with the Genesis creation narrative and works its way through to Revelation. As Jürgen Moltmann contends, the limitless love of the Father, Son and Holy Spirit imprints all outward works of creation.[8] In addition to creation, God's love was clearly manifested in the calling of a covenant people, the issuing of the Mosaic law, working through the prophets, sending Jesus as the redeemer of the world, and preparing an eternal Kingdom. God's very nature and character is love. The Gospels reveal Jesus as love incarnate through his teachings and actions. In the Synoptic Gospels, we find what Burridge calls "the heart of Jesus'" ethic in a double love command to love God and to love one's neighbor.[9] In the greatest commandment, Jesus responded to a lawyer who asked which commandment is the most important (Mt 22:34-40; Mk 12:28-34). Jesus replied, "'You shall love the Lord your God with all your heart, and with all your soul, and with all your mind.' This is the greatest and first commandment. And a second is like it: 'You shall love your neighbor as yourself.' On these two commandments hang all the law and the prophets" (Mt 22:37-40). In Mark's account the language differs slightly by inclusion of "with all your strength" (Mk 12:30) and ends with "There is no other commandment greater than these" (Mk 12:31). *Love of God* and *love of neighbor* comprise the primary Kingdom ethic.

In Luke 10:25-37, the double command is articulated not by Jesus but by a lawyer who tried to test him. Whether this is the same scenario as in Matthew and Mark is uncertain. After asking what the lawyer must do to inherit eternal life, Jesus answers with a question, asking what is written in the law and how the lawyer understands it. The lawyer answers by citing the double love command on loving God taken from the Shema (Deut 6:5) and on loving neighbor (Lev 19:18). Responding to the lawyer's question about who his neighbor is, Jesus tells the parable of the good Samaritan, unmistakably reinforcing his point about loving one's neighbor. In the parable, a man, presumably a Jew, is stripped, robbed and beaten while traveling from Jerusalem to Jericho. Three people encounter the helpless victim. The first two, a priest and a Levite, not only do not stop to assist him but avoid him by passing to the other side. Moved with compassion, the third person, a Samaritan, comes to the victim's aid, bandages his wounds and takes him to an inn where he covers expenses incurred for the man's needs. Pointedly, Jesus asks the lawyer, "Which of the three, do you think, was a neighbor to the man who fell into the hands of the robber?" (Lk 10:36). Knowing he has no wiggle room, the lawyer identifies the Samaritan as the neighbor.

As presented in the parable, love is not limited to a specific group of close associates. The victim in the parable whom the Samaritan helped was a stranger in need. Ironically, the Jews despised the Samaritans. If we envision an Arab Muslim stopping to assist an Israeli Jew in a similar situation, then the ethics conveyed become clear. Jesus' command to love one's neighbor supersedes all religious, cultural and ethnic barriers that create division. The Samaritan applied his resources to help someone ethnically different from himself. Hence, the parable conveys not only that love mediates the moral requirements of the law but also that loving one's neighbor does not demand reciprocity but rather rejoices in meeting others' needs.

Several scholars place the love command as central to New Testament ethics. For example, Victor Paul Furnish defines the double love command as "a crucial aspect of both the literature and the life of earliest Christianity."[10] Noting how love is contextualized to specific situations, Furnish argues that "the Christian gospel of love cannot be distilled into some universal proposition or commandment, but can only be grasped in its concreteness as it impinges upon specific relationships and situations in history."[11] In other words, love is "empowered and guided, rather, by its own inherent rightness as a response to human need."[12] Edward Collins Vacek rightly argues, "Christian ethics must begin with God's love for us and it must keep this love central."[13] In every unique situation, love should be the guiding light showing us what to do. Christian spiritual formation, with love as the impetus for ethical living, prepares us to uphold the highest good of others without regard for personal sacrifice. A contemporary example involving a construction worker from Harlem illustrates this point.

On January 2, 2007, while waiting for a New York City subway with his two young daughters, Wesley Autry watched as a young man experiencing a seizure fell in between the subway tracks below the platform. With a fast-approaching train, he made a snap decision. Leaving his two young daughters in the care of a bystander, Autry jumped onto the tracks and fell on top of the young man's body to protect him, just as the subway brakes screeched to a halt. While everyone on the platform, including his daughters, screamed in horror, five subway cars passed overhead. Miraculously, both men survived unscathed, with the subway just clearing Autry's cap.

In a subsequent interview Autry, the son of a street evangelist, commented, "A voice out of nowhere said, 'Go and save that life, that life is a life worth saving and don't worry about your own.' It seemed like something just lifted me up off the platform."[14] *Autry also remarked that he felt God's presence on the tracks. As Autry's sacrificial act of genuine love for the welfare of a stranger displayed, loving one's neighbor means helping the person in need right in front of you.*

In the double love command, Jesus also refers to *loving oneself*. In order to love others, we must be able to love ourselves. How does loving one's self reconcile with biblical admonitions against self-preoccupation ("Those who love their life lose it" [Jn 12:25])? Jesus also said that if followers do not hate their own lives, they cannot become his disciples (Lk 14:26). Even the apostle Paul declared that nothing good lived in him (Rom 7:18) and warned that in the last days people would become lovers of themselves (2 Tim 3:2). To resolve this seeming paradox, Norman Geisler differentiates between self-love and selfishness: "To love one's self for the sake of loving others is definitely good."[15] For example, a pregnant mother who attends to her physical health and wellness cares for her unborn child. A pilot who gets proper sleep prior to flight time for the sake of his crew and passengers cares for them. Loving one's self derives from being created in the *imago Dei*, which is the basis for loving others. We love ourselves because we love what God loves. If self-love, however, becomes the focal preoccupation rather than others, then love becomes self-centered, selfish and potentially destructive. The challenge is to love one's self rightly in order to love others fully.

In addition to loving God, neighbor and oneself, Jesus' ethic applies to *loving one's enemies*. In the Sermon on the Mount, Jesus called his disciples to a higher ethical standard, setting his ethic apart from others (Mt 5:43-48). Luke 6:27-36 conveys doing good to one's enemies and lending to them without expectation of return. According to Furnish, loving enemies entails not ignoring them but rather being "constructively and compassionately extended" to them, such that loving does not require repentance or transformation on their part.[16] When we love our enemies, "we are participating in God's compassionate grace."[17] Through the concrete actions of prayer, doing good and lending to them without expectation, we personify Jesus' words "Do to others as you would have them do to you" (Lk 6:31). Love inextricably links God and others, not only as observable action and words but also by inner attitude, as all three intertwined when Jesus forgave those who crucified him (Lk 23:34).

Besides the Gospels, the rest of the New Testament is based on Jesus' teachings and ministry, deeds, crucifixion, death and resurrection, all of which reflect this primary love ethic.[18] Interestingly, in Paul's writings, the greatest commandment does not overtly appear, although Paul does sum up the entire law by citing the latter part of it: "For the whole law is summed up in a single commandment, 'You shall love your neighbor as yourself'" (Gal 5:14). As Furnish emphasizes, "There is no Pauline letter in which the term 'love' (almost always *agape*) does not appear and in which exhortations to love do not figure prominently."[19] For example, "more than sixty percent of the occurrences of the word 'love,' ἀγάπη, are to be found within the Pauline corpus, while Paul uses the verb 'to love' more frequently than the three Synoptic Gospels put together and only slightly less than John."[20]

Paul's unique focus is on the cross as the emblem of Christ's sacrificial love. Paul writes, "God proves his love for us in that while we still were sinners Christ died for us" (Rom 5:8; cf. 2 Cor 5:15). Paul's knowledge that Christ loved him and gave himself for Paul (Gal 2:20) motivated Paul to walk in love that was poured out through the Spirit (Rom 5:5; cf. Rom

15:30) and to teach others to do the same (1 Cor 13:1-13; 14:1; Eph 3:17-19; Col 3:14). As Michael Gorman states, "For Paul, then, the love of God that was revealed in history through Christ's one-time act is experienced in human lives through the Spirit's ongoing action."[21] Gorman concludes, "Love, then, is at the core of Paul's understanding of the experience of individuals and communities in Christ" and what puts faith into action toward others.[22] Love permeates Paul's ethics.[23] Gordon Fee summarizes Paul's ethics with its *purpose* being the glory of God, its *pattern* being Christ, its *principle* being love and its *power* being the Spirit.[24] Fee's apt summary aligns with the premises of the CSF model, which derives from the *imago Dei* and engages formation in the *imago Christi*, and then points to the ultimate telos of our lives as *gloria Dei* (cf. fig. 3.2). The way we enact this process is by imitating Christ.

IMITATING CHRIST

In the Gospels we find Jesus issuing a call to follow him: "Follow me and I will make you fish for people" (Mk 1:17). This pathway of discipleship involved spending time with Jesus, learning his ways, studying the Scriptures, obeying his teachings and following his example. Simply stated, discipleship involves *imitatio Christi* or imitating Christ.[25] Commenting on the meaning of discipleship in Jesus' time, Dallas Willard notes, "Primarily, it meant to go with him, in an attitude of study, obedience, and imitation."[26] We imitate Christ through the process of discipleship.[27] In discipleship, Jesus called his followers to be like him. Burridge notes that in the Jewish context following the rabbi meant "imitating his precedent, *ma'aseh*, and in this way learn[ing] how to imitate the Torah, and ultimately to become holy even as the Lord is holy."[28] This implicit understanding of imitation based on rabbinic tradition characterized discipleship in Jesus' time.[29] In chapter seven, we were reminded that one primary conduit of learning involves role modeling. This is precisely what Jesus hoped his followers would do through his example. As the master role model, Jesus called people to be like him.

Imitating Jesus in ethical living is a theme that begins in the Gospels and especially carries over into Paul's writings. Paul says the Thessalonians "became imitators of us and of the Lord" (1 Thess 1:6) as an example to all believers in Macedonia and Achaia of the joyful reception of the gospel despite their persecution.[30] Paul affirms their imitation of God's churches in Judea through suffering (1 Thess 2:14), which Paul was intimately acquainted with (cf. 2 Cor 1:8-9), and the resultant joy produced by the Spirit. To the Corinthians, Paul charged that they be imitators of him, who, as their father in the faith, reflected the ways of Christ that he taught in all the churches (1 Cor 4:16). To the Philippians, Paul asked that they "join in imitating me" (Phil 3:17).

Most important in Paul's view, imitating God meant living in love: "Therefore be imitators of God, as beloved children, and live in love, as Christ loved us and gave himself up for us, a fragrant offering and sacrifice to God" (Eph 5:1). Self-giving love personified in Christ's self-emptying, humility and sacrifice on the cross (Phil 2:6-8) provides the model for such imitation. As William Spohn highlights, Paul describes his own analogous journey in imitating Christ through surrendering his earthly privilege in order to gain Christ (sharing in Christ's sufferings and becoming like him [Phil 3:3-11]) in hopes of greater intimacy ("I want to know Christ" [Phil 3:10]).[31] Noting that none of the Pauline *imitatio* passages singles out specific qualities of the earthly Jesus, Furnish observes, "Rather, *it* seems always to be the humble, giving, obedient love of the crucified and resurrected Lord to which the final appeal is made."[32] Burridge puts it this way:

> To follow the example of Jesus Christ's self-giving love even to the death on the cross lies at the heart of Paul's own life as well as his theology and ethics—and must be worked out in practical ways of self-denial and concern for others, especially the weaker, through the imitation of Christ.[33]

Cruciform love, based on the cross, is the heartbeat of imitating Jesus.

For Paul, however, imitating did not convey mimicking through self-effort but rather resulted from what Christ had done in him.[34] Imitating God is not to be done blindly but rather emerges from a dynamic relationship with God.[35] Ultimately, this imitation conveys "Christ's formation in believers" (Gal 4:19), based on Christ's work on the cross as empowered by the Holy Spirit.[36] The ability to follow Christ through imitation is impossible except through this transforming work of the Spirit. The power at work within Paul was the Spirit who produces Christlikeness, and through grace the same Spirit takes shape in and among us.[37] Spohn concurs that the Spirit within is "the impetus" that reshapes the identity of every believer into Christ's image.[38] The Holy Spirit, as the source of all inner transformation by grace in Paul's ethics, is unmistakable.

As Fee contends, "the Spirit is essential to Paul's ethics *because truly Christian ethics can only be by the Spirit's empowering.*"[39] The Spirit is "the key to ethical life" because the Spirit, according to Fee, replaced the Torah by fulfilling the aim of the Torah "to create a loving community."[40] Therefore, Paul admonished believers to abstain from sin and to live in holiness in order to reproduce the life of Christ within.[41] Since imitation has holiness as its goal through a life of love, Fee then emphasizes, "The Spirit thus empowers ethical life in all its dimensions—personal, corporate, and in the world" and is "Trinitarian at its roots: the Spirit of God conforms the believer into the likeness of Christ to the glory of God."[42] This is not to say that Christian ethical living motivated by love of Christ does not require diligence and self-discipline, but rather that the power for ethical conduct comes from the Spirit, "the agent of righteous living."[43] The Spirit is the guide for "the very 'how' of right conduct."[44]

The process of imitation is not without opposition, and spiritual conflict provides a formidable context for Christ-centered ethical development. Paul describes how the Spirit opposes three enemies: (1) *the flesh* (Gal 5:17), characterized by insatiable desires (Rom 13:14; Gal 5:16-17, 24) and self-sufficiency (Phil 3:3-4); (2) *the devil,* to whom we are not to give place (Eph 4:27); and (3) *the world* with its magnetic, conforming pull (2 Cor 4:4; Col 2:8).[45] All the forces of hell are designed to oppose the imitation of Christ. This struggle, however, does not originate with people, per se, but rather through "the spiritual forces of evil in the heavenly places" (Eph 6:12). Throughout spiritual conflict, Paul proved that despite opposition an ethic of love brings about a life of imitating Christ. Imitating Christ entails the development of godly character as demonstrated by virtues and provides the means for living out Christ's life of love in the world through all seven CSF dimensions. By doing so, "we fulfill our purpose, which is to be the image of God" in the world by the power of the Holy Spirit.[46]

Christian Character and the Virtues

Through ethical living with godly love as the impetus, CSF interfaces with personal character development through the practice of godly virtues. In an age where character and integrity are wanting within all societal spheres in a relativist world, a maturing Christian character reflects Christ—his person, love, goodness and grace. In one sense, Christian character development is the divine process of engraving God's image into us through the development of virtue.[47] Thus, character conveys a sense of moral excellence, wholeness and integrity. Interestingly, the word *integrity* comes from the word *integer*, meaning "whole number," in contrast to a fraction. Character, like integrity, refers to moral wholeness.

Character and integrity, as evidenced by ethical living, serve as the common connector of all seven dimensions. If we are living for Christ, then displaying character and integrity in each of the holistic formation dimensions brings glory to God. The aim of Christian character is to develop stability and consistency across all CSF dimensions in order to please God and to reflect Christ in the world through the cultivation of godly virtue as qualities of moral excellence. As Stanley Hauerwas and Will Willimon contend, virtue is what comprises Christian ethics.[48] And Christian ethics depends on the Christian story.[49] The Christian story is dynamically lived out in us through the CSF dimensions.

Ethical Christian living derives from motives of the heart (cf. Mt 15:18; 1 Tim 1:5) as evidenced by Christian character framed by motives that precede actions, speech and reactions. For example, the 2008 global financial crisis where many US bank and business executives cheated their clients, lied about their profits and stuffed their own pockets clearly did not reflect the kind of godly character described here. Selfish motives leading to lying, cheating and "cooking the books" brought disrepute to the US financial industry. Like a vicious cancer, the underlying issue of greed coupled with the slippery slope of financial indiscretion caused deceit, coverup and law-breaking that shook the financial industry to its core. These financial indiscretions, however, exposed a greater problem: a crisis of character.

Two contrasting examples further illustrate the importance of character from a vocational formation perspective. The first involves Chesley ("Sully") Sullenberger III, the pilot of a US Airways jet who encountered a flight problem on January 15, 2009. Two minutes after takeoff from New York's LaGuardia Airport, the jet's two engines shut down when the plane flew through a flock of Canada geese. Without power and unable to safely return to the airport, Sullenberger and his copilot had to quickly decide how to navigate the plane to safety. Their best option was to land the plane in the chilly Hudson River. With Sullenberger's thirty years of commercial aviation experience, previous US Air Force fighter pilot expertise and safety consulting training, he was able to safely land the plane in the water. After the 155 passengers and crew exited the cabin onto the jet's wings awaiting rescue, Sullenberger walked through the passenger cabin twice to make sure that everyone had escaped. His aviation skill was only superseded by his sense of duty. Speaking of integrity that shaped his character, Sullenberger credited his parents for the values he enacts.[50] For the believer, moral values (sacrificial concern for others) evidenced by actions (placing others' welfare above one's own) reveal virtues—doing the right thing at the right time for the right reasons in honoring God and others.

A contrasting example evidencing a lack of character involved Francesco Schettino, who served as captain of the cruise ship Costa Concordia. As part of a stunt on January 13, 2012, Schettino sailed the ship of 4,252 passengers and crew too close to the island of Giglio in Tuscany, Italy. As a result, the ship ran aground on rocks, which knocked out power, then took on water and eventually capsized. In a follow-up report, it was determined that Schettino waited forty-five minutes to announce an evacuation. Unlike Sullenberger, Schettino evacuated the ship before all others safely escaped, claiming he tripped into a lifeboat. With maritime ethics dictating that a ship's captain must remain on a sinking vessel until all have safely escaped, Schettino then received orders from a higher command to return to his ship. All told, thirty-two people died, and sixty-four people were injured. This captain's lack of judgment exposed a severe lack of character.

What caused Sullenberger to ensure that all onboard the jet had escaped before he left the jet's cabin? And what caused Schettino to prematurely abandon his ship, leaving many in harm's way? The difference relating to character is what N. T. Wright calls "the power of right habits."[51] The term *character* is what the ancients called virtues. Virtues are traits and qualities that reflect moral excellence. Wright shows that virtue results "when wise and courageous choices have become 'second nature.'"[52]

The ancient Greek philosophers (e.g., Plato and Aristotle) identified the cardinal virtues as (1) prudence, (2) justice, (3) temperance or restraint, and (4) fortitude or courage. The word *cardinal* comes from the Latin word *cardo*, meaning hinge. The notion is that on these four virtues the moral life hinges.

To these four virtues, the early church fathers added the biblical virtues of faith, hope and love (cf. 1 Cor 13:13) and simply referred to them as the seven virtues.[53] But like learning a language or playing a musical instrument, developing godly virtues requires practice. This is exactly what James K. A. Smith asserts when speaking about habits as "love's fulcrum," being inscribed on our hearts through bodily practices.[54] As holistic beings, we are shaped by what and whom we love. What distinguishes ancient Greek virtue formation from that of Christians relates to the *telos* or goal of these virtues. For the Greeks, the *telos* of virtuous living was to become a fully flourishing person. For the Christian, the *telos* of virtuous living is becoming Christlike in order to glorify God. In both perspectives virtues require practice, just like learning to play an athletic sport.

N. T. Wright observes, "The person has to choose, again and again, to develop the moral muscles and skills which will shape and form the fully flourishing character."[55] This is a lifelong process enabled by the community we live in, the role models we aspire to and the inner work of the Holy Spirit, who lives within as our Guide. Living holy lives reflects the Lord Jesus and brings God glory. So rather than virtue being about rules and standards, virtue is about "the whole of life" since "we are called to be genuine, image-bearing, God-reflecting human beings."[56] Christian character is about evidencing this kind of whole and holy ethical consistency in our CSF journeys. Practice develops habits. Practices alone, however, do not produce godly character as displayed by the virtues, as the apostle Paul well knew.

Paul understood that to exercise virtues involved a two-pronged process. First, bad habits of the flesh—vices—had to be broken in order for godly virtues to be established. Although Paul mentions vices in other letters in order to address issues that arose in respective churches, his letter to the Galatian church contains a representative, albeit nonexhaustive, list of both vices to shun and virtues to embrace. He refers to the vices as "works of the flesh," whereas the virtues are called "fruit of the Spirit." The nine virtues mentioned are love, joy, peace, patience, kindness, generosity, faithfulness, gentleness and self-control, with love capturing priority of place. Interestingly, the nine virtues reflect not only the internal life of the believer but also the corporate life of the community. Whereas "works" suggest human effort, "fruit" suggests divine empowerment.[57] Fee notes, "Not only do people who work by the Spirit not walk in the ways of the flesh . . . but also the Spirit effectively produces in them the very character of God."[58] The Spirit and self-agency (personal self-effort) have a part to play in the practice of the virtues for ethical living.[59]

Hence, the development of Christian character through the cultivation of these virtues comprises Christian ethics and brings unity to our lives in all seven CSF dimensions. Ethical living, according to Grenz, involves the Christian vision of God through our creation to be the *imago Dei* in the world and "provides the transcendent basis for the human ethical ideal of life-in-community."[60] For we know that love received should not end there but rather should pervade in and extend through the body of Christ, the church, to others in the watching world.

Love Extended: The Church in the Watching World

As Christ's embodied presence in the world, the church is to manifest ethical consistency in holiness through living out God's story and embodying the Kingdom. As N. T. Wright rightly observes, Christian behavior is a team sport.[61] Community is the primary context where Christians develop and exhibit the virtues.[62] In response to receiving God's redeeming love, the church is not only *to live* this Kingdom story in relationship to one another (e.g., "See how they love one another," [Tertullian, *Apology* 39]), but also *to proclaim* the gospel message (Jn 3:16) by going into a lost and dying world to share the life-transforming story of God's love, mercy and grace in order to make disciples (Mt 28:18-20).[63] Making disciples relates to sharing God's story, so that God's story will be lived out in each faithful generation. In so doing, the church reflects the love of God to the watching world through godly virtues (Gal 5:22-23) as expressed in the CSF process.

Stanley Hauerwas contends that individual Christian virtues are sustained by the church over time. So the church "must, above all, be a people of virtue—not simply any virtue, but the virtues necessary for remembering and telling the story of a crucified savior. They must be capable of being peaceable among themselves and with the world, so that that the world sees what it means to hope for God's kingdom."[64] Christian virtues are necessary in order to live out the story of Jesus through our own stories within the watching world that has lost moral equilibrium. Stanley Hauerwas and Will Willimon assert, "By telling these stories, we come to see the significance and coherence of our lives as a gift . . . something we would not have known without the community of faith."[65] In all of its imperfections, the church sustains God's great narrative.

The world watches and takes note of humble and authentic Christian virtue, while readily exposing hypocrisy when character inconsistencies and violations occur. CSF forges character consistency through the core Christian ethic of love. Love reaches out. Love extends. Love acts. Love releases. Love heals. Throughout history the love of God has compelled the church to share the story of God's redeeming love through word and deed (cf. 2 Cor 6:14; Col 3:17).[66] While there are many examples of how the Christian story has become tarnished by impure motives, immorality and unethical behavior, the church continues to move forward in imperfection, with Scripture as the rudder that sets a borderless agenda of our shared story.[67] In Scripture, Jesus announced his ethical priority for ministry as being not for the healthy but rather for the sick who need a doctor (Mt 9:12; Mk 2:17; Lk 5:31). Throughout Christian history, believers have upheld this ethical priority before a watching world.

Examples of those who challenged the church to ethical excellence through godly love and service abound. Former British slave owner and clergyman John Newton, along with his contemporary William Wilberforce, worked tirelessly to abolish slavery in England. Itinerant Quaker preacher John Woolman (1720–1772) from New Jersey and former slave Sojourner Truth tirelessly advocated for abolition of slavery in the United States. Albert Schweitzer, medical doctor to Equatorial West Africa, personified meeting the felt needs of a people group as a medical missionary. Theologian Dietrich Bonhoeffer challenged the German church to sacrificial and ethical conduct by resisting Hitler's demonic regime. Martin Luther King Jr. called the church to the highest biblical ethic of love through nonviolent resistance in confronting racism.

Additionally, Mother Teresa (1910–1997) sensitized the church worldwide to care for the poorest of the poor. Through the establishment of L'Arche communities worldwide, Canadian Catholic author and theologian Jean Vanier (1928–) reminds the church to care for those with developmental disabilities. British missionary Jackie Pullinger (1944–) challenges the church to minister to drug addicts, gang members and prostitutes through her rehabilitation ministry in Hong Kong. Gary Haugen, president and CEO of International Justice Mission, reminds the church to end oppression and human trafficking worldwide. Each of these individuals has influenced the church and the watching world by upholding others in love, often through social justice, in an attitude of unselfish service, just like the Samaritan who stopped to help the man beaten and robbed on the Jericho road. The church is at its best when fulfilling its Kingdom mandate to serve the least of these: the poor, the downtrodden, the unlovely and the weak (cf. Mt 9:36; Lk 4:18; 14:13).

Moreover, average people like you and me can extend love to others every day through unselfish acts of kindness and service, such as visiting the sick, helping a friend and offering care to others in need. We do not need to establish large ministries or earn advanced degrees to love and serve others. Stephen G. Post, founder and director of the Institute for Research on Unlimited Love, maintains that love can take many forms.[68] Love can be expressed through (1) *compassion* when someone is suffering, (2) *forgiveness* when someone needs to be reconciled to another, others or the community after making mistakes, (3) *care* of others' felt needs during illness or extenuating circumstances, (4) *companionship* in friendship, active listening and the gift of time, and (5) *correction* in love for wrongdoing, even risking confrontation. Love acts through compassion and service whether little or large.

Upholding the highest good of others through serving others embodies the Christian ethic of love before the watching world. When we help others, we love our neighbor. After the terrorist attacks on September 11, 2001, several parents asked Fred Rogers (1928–2003), a Presbyterian minister and host of the children's television program *Mister Rogers' Neighborhood,* what to tell their children. Mr. Rogers thoughtfully replied, "Tell them to keep their eyes on the helpers."[69] By helping others we demonstrate the love of God. This explains why churches and their related ministries reach out after horrific natural disasters such as the 2012 Hurricane Sandy in the United States, the 2011 earthquake and tsunami in Japan, the 2010 earthquake in Haiti, and the 2005 Hurricane Katrina in the US Gulf. Sharing the love of Jesus was demonstrated in meeting felt needs of the millions of survivors. Communities once closed to the gospel are able to see the love of Jesus in action through self-sacrificial acts of helping. We embody Jesus' story when we give and serve the least of these. In so doing, we serve Jesus (Mt 25:40).

An unexpected blessing results when we give to and serve others through an ethical lifestyle generated by the love of God. When treating people with dignity, regardless of who they are, we acknowledge that they have been created in the *imago Dei*. By upholding others' highest good and fostering altruism and benevolence, we extend the unconditional love of God. Interestingly, altruism has been shown to contribute to the giver's life satisfaction, a sense of life purpose, and better overall physical and mental health over a lifetime.[70] Ultimately, the secret to a deeper and more flourishing life is self-giving love.

Interestingly, Stephen Post found a strong positive correlation between those who give to others and lower rates of depression, a greater sense of happiness and increased longevity.[71] Rather than giving in order to receive, altruism also contributes to holistic health through positive emotion and social competence. Post states, "Generous behavior shines a protective light over the entire life span" and "protects overall health twice as much as aspirin protects against heart disease."[72] Post's findings support Pitirim A. Sorokin's groundbreaking research on altruistic love as having religious, ethical, ontological, physical, biological, psychological and social aspects.[73]

By expressing the story of Jesus in word and deed, we embody the Kingdom. When love is unappreciated, scorned or rejected, we identify with Jesus, who shattered simplistic notions of love in order to embrace suffering and counter animosity, hatred and fear. Even in suffering, Jesus showed us that pain can ultimately lead to true healing and freedom.

In summary, when demonstrating godly character through the Christian virtues in the CSF process, we display the light of the gospel through divine love before a watching world. As we proclaim the love of Jesus in word and deed, we reflect the living God, who made us in the *imago Dei*, conforms us into the *imago Christi* and calls us to live for the *gloria Dei*. Ethical consistency through CSF becomes attractional. As we grow in grace in each of the seven dimensions, we mature into Christlikeness by the power of the Holy Spirit when motivated by godly love in consonance with the Scriptures. In chapter twelve we will review the preceding chapters.

12

Christian Spiritual Formation Summary

In the same way, let your light shine before others,
so that they may see your good works and
give glory to your Father in heaven.

Matthew 5:16

This book introduced and developed a Christian spiritual formation (CSF) approach with the hope that it will broaden readers' appreciation for, understanding of and growth in each formation dimension. CSF is not only a model of a fully orbed and balanced approach to Christian formation but also reinforces the ultimate telos of our lives—to humbly love and serve God and others and work toward maximum Kingdom impact for God's glory. Thus, the CSF model integrates internal formation for external effectiveness in the world regardless of gender, ethnicity, family background, education level, experience or position.

With this in mind, this final chapter begins with summary statements that capture the central themes of previous chapters. When this presentation moves from the head to the heart and then into action, real, integrated and holistic growth can occur.

Christian Spiritual Formation Summary Statements

Chapter 1. God created humankind in the* imago Dei *with potentiality for

all seven formation dimensions to reflect divine glory. Although human disobedience through sin fractured God's perfect image, God made provision for redemption and restoration of the broken image through Jesus as the perfect *imago Dei.* Since God holistically designed persons as integrated beings, the seven CSF dimensions represent the primary domains of personhood across time and culture. Each of the CSF dimensions mutually interacts with the others, which reflects the mystery of creation. The spiritual dimension related to our faith journey, however, is primary. For example, the spiritual life influences emotions, social relationships, the intellect and even vocational calling. Emotional development likewise interfaces with interpersonal relationships, one's spiritual life, the intellect, physical health and wellness, and the handling of God-given resources. Physical health influences our mental state and intersects the other CSF dimensions as well. Maximizing potential in each of the CSF dimensions not only reflects our gratitude and reciprocal love of God but also contributes to our maturation for God's glory.

Chapter 2. Within Christian theological and historical tradition, being made in the **imago Dei** ***has been seen through four primary lenses involving the human capacity for (1) thinking and reasoning, (2) interpersonal relationships, (3) dominion of the earth and (4) a divine goal and destiny.*** This book offers an integrated approach for understanding the *imago Dei* as including all four perspectives, arguing that none of them offers a fully orbed representation of humanness. Thinking and reasoning relate to intellectual formation. Interpersonal relationships tie to emotional and relational formation with God and others. Dominion connotes caring responsibility for all of creation and directly connects to vocational formation relative to one's calling and application of resource formation, along with physical health and wellness formation in which to do so. And last, the *imago Dei* represents a divine goal and destiny, which directly relates to our spiritual formation in being conformed into the *imago Christi* in this life as preparation for the eternal one to come.

Chapter 3. God is the very essence of love, deriving from the Father by the Son and communicated through the Holy Spirit. God is love, and love is of God (1 Jn 4:8). The motive for God's creating humankind in the *imago Dei* is love, as is the impetus for Christ's redeeming work on the cross, which enables our being conformed into the *imago Christi* in order to live by the Spirit for the *gloria Dei*. We first receive God's love and then love God and others as an expression of gratitude for God's unspeakable gift (2 Cor 9:15). Godly love is trinitarian in nature, flowing from the Father to the Son and through Holy Spirit in perfect unity. CSF is predicated on a clear understanding of the love of the triune God. Hence, the impetus for CSF is reciprocal love out of gratitude to God.

Chapter 4. For the Christian, formation of our spirit in the faith journey is foundational for understanding the other formation dimensions and powerfully influences each of them. Spiritual formation brings us from an *imago Dei* into an *imago Christi* relationship. Formation in Christ begins with salvation and continues throughout one's lifetime as enacted by the Holy Spirit, who superintends our being conformed into the image of Jesus through grace as the gift of God that enables ongoing transformation. Our identity as sons and daughters of God is affirmed through spiritual practices that reinforce the grand narrative of our faith through godly virtues that exemplify Kingdom ethics. As Paul wrote to Timothy, godliness has value for all things in the present life and the one to come (1 Tim 4:8). The Spirit uses many means to shape followers into Jesus' image, most notably through suffering, which follows the Lord's example. To love much is also to suffer much. The formation of the spirit in the faith journey is the primary dimension that gives purpose to the other six dimensions.

Chapter 5. Regarding emotions, the felt experience of love in childhood is the primary shaping mechanism for one's emotional repertoire. Jesus' own example of being attached to his heavenly Father and to his earthly family reveals the importance of formative relationships in one's emotional development. Although human attachments provide the primary resources for emotional formation, they likewise contribute to relational, spiritual, intellectual and vocational development. Emotional, relational, intellectual and spiritual dimensions intertwine in contributing to human flourishing. Positive and negative emotions serve as the barometer of well-being, most readily observed through interpersonal relationships. The goal of emotional formation relates to reconciling self-image with biblical truths of how God sees us. Becoming free from emotional bondages in order to experience emotional freedom is a process that most often involves forgiving and releasing others for their offenses. Forgiveness, the key to emotional formation, is illustrated through the life of Joseph with his brothers. Emotional formation contributes to the fruit of the Spirit (e.g., love, joy, peace, patience, kindness, generosity, faithfulness, gentleness and self-control [Gal 5:22-23]).

Chapter 6. God has created persons to derive their personal identity through relationship to God and others. Social relationships also serve as conduits for conforming believers into the *imago Christi*, which often involves conflict and conflict resolution. The family is the primary shaping conduit for relational formation, regardless of whether the outcomes are positive or negative. Recognizing brokenness from family fracture, relational formation also develops through other social ties that foster safety and trust. Friendships teach lessons in trust, vulnerability, mutual sharing and security. As the manifold wisdom of God (Eph 3:10), the church is designed to provide relational community reflecting the Trinity, who lives in love and unity. Composed of imperfect people, the church, as the body of Christ, is to provide nurture, safety and encouragement through relationships. Through grace manifesting in the church, the believer's identity is shaped as a child of God. For better and for worse, the culture or cultures one lives in exercise a powerful shaping effect, not only on relational formation but also on overall CSF.

Chapter 7. God has given humans an intellect in which to think, reason and understand, reflecting God's own nature. Faith does not oppose reason but rather amplifies the wonderful works of God in which thinking and reason are applied. In light of God's Word, faith invigorates the mind to learn through various contexts, including creation, culture and community. Believers are instructed to love the Lord with their entire being, including the mind. The mind is to be used for God's glory through worship, faith, holiness, guidance, daily living and Christian ministry. Believers are to seek to know truth and the source of all truth—the Father through the person of Jesus and by the work of the Spirit—as revealed in the Scriptures. Thus, a living faith is composed of intellectual inquiry with an ascent toward God, without which the mind becomes antagonistic toward God. All disciplines of study have extraordinary merit when illuminated by God's Word. Knowledge without love, however, puffs up (1 Cor 8:1). Various worldviews compete for people's minds (e.g., naturalism; humanism; nihilism; Eastern philosophies, including new age; and postmodernism with its close cousins—secularism and consumerism). Christian faith must engage these worldviews through love by living the gospel. In order to lead a victorious life and shine like stars in the world (Phil 2:15), the mind must be renewed (Rom 12:2).

Chapter 8. Vocational formation begins by responding to Jesus' call in salvation, followed by a sense of calling to engage the good work that God has designed for each believer. While calling involves the duties at hand (e.g., family roles and obligations), vocation also entails a specific call that is unique to each individual in contributing to Christ's mission in the world. Calling can be discerned through several means: (1) obedient living where God sovereignly guides; (2) a sense of burden, passion, compassion or holy desire; (3) the Scriptures, through which the Holy Spirit brings revelation; (4) evaluating our past for clues as to how God has shaped us; (5) experiential and trial-and-error learning; (6) past and current faithful service; (7) prayer and worship; and (8) input from trusted others who know and observe us. Although the ideal is for God-given calling to align with a job, this may or may not be the case. Regardless of calling alignment, love is the impetus for vocation and life purpose. As Jesus responded to the Father in love and obedience, we too can respond to our life calling through the roles that we enact (e.g., spouse, parent, son or daughter) and the sacred or secular work we undertake for God's glory (Col 3:17). Theological and historical perspectives of vocation help us to develop an informed view of vocation as part of the discipleship journey. Discovering God-given spiritual and natural gifts, as well as talents, abilities and skills, is a process that clarifies vocational formation.

Chapter 9. Since persons are made in the* imago Dei *as embodied beings, physical health formation is a critical and often neglected component of the CSF journey. Christian faith is an embodied faith. The fact that Jesus was born in a human body elevates the importance of embodiment. As the temple of the Holy Spirit (1 Cor 6:19), the body is worthy of personal care for Kingdom effectiveness. The body, therefore, should be honored to maximize its purpose, which is to worship and glorify God. In honoring the body, we honor God, who created the body. The body is not to be worshiped, trivialized, demeaned or neglected. The holistic and integrated interplay of the body with the spirit, mind, emotions, relationships, vocational expressions and resource stewardship cannot be overemphasized. The body reciprocally manifests in the other CSF dimensions when health in one area is compromised. Therefore, healthy nutritional choices, physical exercise, adequate sleep, periods of rest and leisure to release stress, and sexual purity combine to forge physical wellness practices that honor God.

Chapter 10. In resource formation, God gave humankind oversight and responsibility for created things. This oversight was issued not as a directive to abuse creation and God-given resources but rather to manage them with caring responsibility in deference to God (Gen 1:28-30). We are to be responsible stewards of our God-given resources for God's glory, not for self-aggrandizement. With creation in crisis, it behooves believers to attend to earth's degradation with a caring response, an often overlooked area of stewardship. If God owns it all, then how we use our money, possessions and time for God's glory reveals the quality of our spiritual lives. Money should be a tool, not a tyrant, for achieving God-given obligations and goals for the *gloria Dei*. Although material possessions are to be enjoyed, they also may become idolatrous and destructive by turning our heart away from God. Moreover, the value of frugality counters the seductive materialism of our age. Resource formation also includes the use of time to live harmoniously with God and others in order to maximize Kingdom impact. Making sacred space for God serves to order one's life around the highest priority—one's relationship with God.

Chapter 11. Ethical Christian living brings synthesis to all seven CSF dimensions through obedience, holiness and principled real-life application. Christian ethical living supersedes a mere discussion of right and wrong conduct but rather relates to becoming like Christ in motive and behavior in order to glorify God. Each of the CSF dimensions is to reflect moral wholeness, integrity and godly character that derive from the primary Kingdom ethic of love as embodied in Christ. From Genesis through Revelation, God demonstrates love through creation, redemption and establishing the future Kingdom. Christian ethics relates to imitating Christ, a consistent theme in the New Testament, in order for Christ's character to be reflected in the world. Developing godly character involves walking in the Spirit by demonstrating godly virtues (Gal 5:22-23). Not only do individual believers enact Christian virtues for ethical living but the church, as the body of Christ, is to proclaim the story of Jesus through biblical integrity, godly love and humble service before a watching world. When living the story of Jesus in this way of loving God and others, the watching world takes note.

In light of these summary statements, it is appropriate to comment on approaching CSF in a balanced manner.

A Balanced Approach

Having a balanced approach to CSF is the goal. Therefore, a few points are highlighted to counter imbalances based on faulty assumptions, legalism and perfectionism. First, one of the criticisms of various Christian formation approaches is that they lean too heavily on personal development, including one's spiritual life in God, to the exclusion of manifesting the love and grace of God to others through active engagement and service in the world. The CSF model is not intended to be an introverted process but rather one that focuses on personal holistic formation in order to become whole and healthy ambassadors reaching out in love and service to others. Through four arrows pointing outward, figure 12.1 connotes that the believer's aim should be focused outward in order to influence the world through reflecting a living Savior by the power of the Holy Spirit (Mt 28:19-20). In order to reflect the *imago Christi* by shining like stars in a dark world

(Mt 5:14-15), however, believers must continuously nurture loving union with God by awakening to God's presence. This centered, inner life of being "hidden with Christ in God" (Col 3:3) prompts movement into the world for the sake of others through authentic faith. This dynamic process represents Christian spiritual formation.

An exclusively inward focus in devotion may become self-serving and a withdrawal from reality. An exclusively outward focus geared toward service may become self-initiated through works righteousness and detached from the power of God. Spiritual maturity, however, balances the inward with the outward expressions of faith, such that personal devotion to God is the platform for loving, serving and blessing others. As figure 12.1

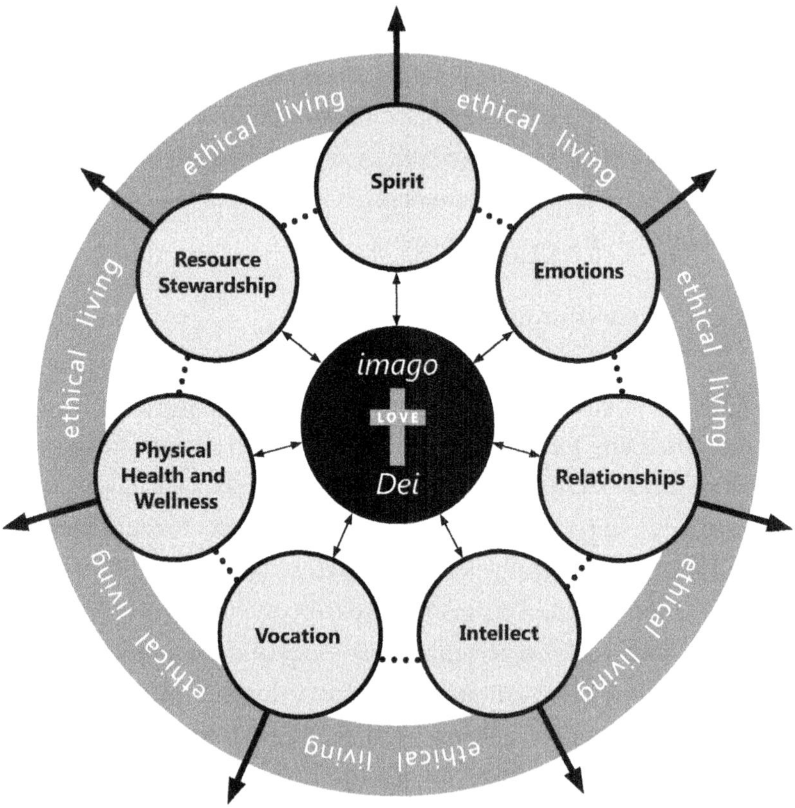

Figure 12.1. Christian spiritual formation and the world

depicts, CSF reaches full engagement when all dimensions coalesce in reaching out to others in the world for God's glory.

Second, developing in any one of the seven CSF dimensions can be taken to an extreme and become detrimental. For example, a believer might give total attention to personal communion with God to the exclusion of family relationships, without realizing that caring for one's family cannot be separated from loving God. Dedicating time to serving others outside the home to the exclusion of serving one's children in the home is reprehensible and dishonors God. In other cases, believers may spend more time in health fitness than in personal communion with God. Overemphasis on physical health to the exclusion of one's relationship with God becomes idolatrous. Others may devote so much time to their vocational calling that they burn out or become consumed with financial gain to the exclusion of interpersonal relationships. Although investing time in one's vocational calling and making money are not wrong in themselves, an inordinate focus on them causes imbalance and ultimately affects one's spiritual life. Avoiding extremes and preoccupations assists to keep life holistically healthy and balanced.

Third, seasons of life and uncontrollable circumstances may dictate an emphasis on one or more of the CSF dimensions over the others. For example, an emphasis on vocational preparation through job skills training or higher education may understandably shift one's focus and time commitment for an extended season. Losing one's job may appropriately shift focus to vocational reexamination and retooling. Seasons of parenting or caregiving naturally dictate that greater time and attention in the relational dimension be devoted to family members. During times of physical challenge, illness or disability, greater attention may need to be dedicated to physical health and wellness over other CSF dimensions. If emotional or mental instability cause disruption to daily life, then time must be devoted to regain equilibrium. Through no fault of one's own, life circumstances may inhibit the CSF process from progressing, as when believers live in disruptive familial, social, economic or political circumstances beyond their control. In none of these cases, however, should the spiritual dimension be abandoned, since our relationship with God is the cornerstone for the other six CSF dimensions and the foundation for the Christian faith.

Fourth, trying to achieve holistic balance can become legalistic and perfectionistic, stripping the joy out of living. Life can become more concerned with achieving goals than embracing the leading of the Holy Spirit. The CSF model simply illustrates a dynamic process of being conformed into the image of Jesus for ultimate Kingdom impact. In this earthly life, we will never achieve perfect holistic balance but neither are we to abandon personal initiative in the CSF process.

CONCLUSION

Chapter one opened by briefly discussing the restoration work of the frescos atop the Sistine Chapel ceiling, originally painted by Michelangelo from 1508 to 1512. Michelangelo's artistic genius captured three scenes of the creation of matter, three scenes of the creation of Adam and Eve and the subsequent fall, and three scenes from the story of Noah. Surrounding these frescoes appear other portrayals of biblical characters, including Moses and the serpent of brass, the death of Haman, David and Goliath, Isaiah, Jeremiah, Ezekiel, Joel, Jonah and Zechariah. One art commentator notes, "The wonder is that an assembly of so many forms could, in fact, be made to produce a unified impression."[1] With the vaulted ceiling sixty-five feet high from the floor and measuring 132 feet by forty-five feet, and with the painting surface an estimated 10,000 square feet, the Sistine Chapel stands as one of the greatest artistic masterpieces in history.

How did Michelangelo, at the age of thirty-four, approach such a daunting task? The truth is that he resisted. When asked by Pope Julius II to undertake this project, Michelangelo refused, asserting that he was a sculptor, not a painter. He had never previously painted frescos, which require a skillful technique of quick, precise and uninterrupted work on fresh plaster. Yet the persistent pope prevailed—but only after Michelangelo dissuaded him from requiring the painting of the twelve apostles and received the pope's permission to design the paintings as he saw fit.[2]

The preparation process was painstaking, as was the actual painting. Michelangelo first arranged for a scaffolding to be erected to support him and his assistants. Second, he had to take precise measurements and develop working drawings that began as small sketches. Once drawings were enlarged to scale, they were then ready to be applied to the wet surface of the prepared plaster and their outlines pricked in with dots to guide the brush work.[3] Third, the walls received an application of plaster, were troweled to insure a smooth surface, and then finished with a thin coat of lime and fine sand. The damp surface ensured the transfer of the drawing to the wall through a tracing process. Then the painting proceeded with color pigments mixed with lime water, which chemically bonded to the plaster.[4] At one point, after determining to work alone, Michelangelo discovered that the colors had blistered and mildewed because the plaster was too moist. After profiting from other artists' advice, Michelangelo overcame these obstacles, while others awaited him.

The actual painting process was physically demanding. Lying on his back, often bent backwards on the scaffolding, with arms elevated for hours on end and with paint dripping on his face, Michelangelo persevered. During these four years, his challenges produced formational shaping in every life dimension. He looked to God for help during the painting process and deepened in the Christian faith as he grew older.[5] In addition to physical health and wellness, other challenges came in the spiritual, emotional, relational, intellectual, vocational and resource formation dimensions. He often felt spiritually flat, emotionally distraught because of time pressures, relationally detached, mentally fatigued, vocationally insecure from believing that his work was inadequate, and financially pressured as the family breadwinner. Despite being acquainted with "the meanness of his family, the ingratitude of rulers, the hatred of rivals, [and] the loneliness of the heart," Michelangelo managed to overcome internal and external resistance because of his commitment to carry on the work.[6]

And so it is with us. With all of our imperfections, insecurities, doubts, fears and pressures, we can place ourselves on the scaffolding of divine grace, believing that God will fully restore us and holistically fashion us as unique masterpieces (*imago Dei, imago Christi*) in order to love and serve God and others for God's glory (*gloria Dei*).

Notes

1 Introduction

[1]See Pierluigi De Vecchi, ed., *The Sistine Chapel: A Glorious Restoration* (New York: Abradale Press, 1999). For a virtual tour of the Sistine Chapel ceiling, see the Vatican website at www.vatican.va/various/cappelle/sistina_vr/index.html.

[2]Supported by the US Department of Energy and the National Institutes of Health, the Human Genome Project was a thirteen-year undertaking to identify all the genes present in human DNA. Further, the goals included identifying the sequences of the three billion chemical base pairings of DNA, storing the information in databases and continuing to analyze the data. See the Human Genome Project website at www.ornl.gov/sci/techresources/Human_Genome/home.shtml.

[3]In a biblical sense, faith relates to putting one's absolute trust and belief in Christ, in God's Word and in God's promises through obedience. Faith entails relinquishing all dependence on one's own resources, trusting God alone for salvation and relying on the Holy Spirit for all aspects of life. In the broadest sense, faith conveys commitment to Christ based on God's absolute faithfulness. "Faith is the assurance of things hoped for, the conviction of things not seen" (Heb 11:1). Faith, as opposed to unbelief, connects believers to God and prompts God to move on their behalf. Without faith, it is impossible to please God (Heb 11:6).

[4]Refer to the definitions of *formation* in *Merriam-Webster's Collegiate Dictionary*, 10th ed. (Springfield, MA: Merriam-Webster, 2001), p. 458.

[5]See Jeffrey P. Greenman's essay "Spiritual Formation in Theological Perspective," in *Life in the Spirit: Spiritual Formation in Theological Perspective,* ed. Jeffrey P. Greenman and George Kalantizis (Downers Grove, IL: InterVarsity Press, 2010), pp. 34-35. Although Greenman agreeably argues for a theological approach to the discussion of spiritual formation, I maintain that a fully-orbed theology of the whole person necessitates a discussion of other formational areas as well, leading to an integrated approach as described in this book.

[6]In surveying over two dozen recognized Christian formation resources, I found very few that address the formation of the whole person. One notable exception is Dallas Willard's *Renovation of the Heart: Putting on the Character of Christ* (Colorado Springs: NavPress, 2002),

which presents six basic aspects of the human person, including thought, feeling, choice, body, social context and soul (ibid., pp. 30-31). This lacuna of theological reflection raises these questions: (1) what are the basic dimensions of human persons? and (2) from where do these dimensions derive? Therefore, this book brings together the discourses of Christian formation and biblical/theological studies from a multidisciplinary perspective to address these questions.

[7]In offering these seven dimensions, I am proposing a model in which believers in Christ might understand and grow in an integrated and purposeful manner rather than one that is simplistic, reductionist or programmatic. For example, the components of culture, creativity, personality and the psychological domain are not specified in the CSF model (see fig. 1.1). As important as these are in the development of the human person, I would place culture as an outgrowth of relational formation, as cultural identity develops within relational contexts; creativity as a confluence of spiritual, emotional, relational, intellectual and vocational formation; and personality and the psychological domain as the concourse of these seven formation dimensions.

[8]Stephen Seamands, *Ministry in the Image of God: The Trinitarian Shape of Christian Service* (Downers Grove, IL: InterVarsity Press, 2005), p. 78.

[9]Jürgen Moltmann, *The Trinity and the Kingdom: The Doctrine of God*, trans. Margaret Kohl (San Francisco: Harper & Row, 1981), p. 3.

[10]Paul S. Fiddes, "Creation Out of Love," in *The Work of Love: Creation as Kenosis*, ed. John Polkinghorne (Grand Rapids: Eerdmans, 2001), pp. 167, 169. Colin E. Gunton also affirms that creation is the product of God's eternal love, in *Father, Son and Holy Spirit: Toward a Fully Trinitarian Theology* (London: T & T Clark, 2003), p. 62.

[11]Special thanks to M. Robert Mulholland Jr. for his suggestion to include a clear definition of godly love within this chapter. See Thomas Jay Oord, *Defining Love: A Philosophical, Scientific, and Theological Engagement* (Grand Rapids: Brazos, 2010). Oord advances the following definition as a starting place for multidisciplinary dialogue: "To love is to act intentionally, in sympathetic response to others (including God), to promote overall well-being" (ibid., p. 15). Oord adds, "*Agape* is intentional sympathetic response to promote overall well-being when confronted by that which generates ill-being" (p. 43). Also see Michael J. Gorman's definition of love as "the defining characteristic of the individual in relation to others and of the community as a whole," predicated on an understanding of the cross as the supreme expression of God's love in Christ (Michael J. Gorman, *Cruciformity: Paul's Narrative Spirituality of the Cross* [Grand Rapids: Eerdmans, 2001], p. 156).

[12]For a focus on the cross as the foundation of Paul's spirituality, see Gorman, *Cruciformity*, pp. 75-95; and *Inhabiting the Cruciform God: Kenosis, Justification, and Theosis in Paul's Narrative Soteriology* (Grand Rapids: Eerdmans, 2009), pp. 161-73.

[13]Various authors offer definitions of spiritual formation. For example, Dallas Willard refers to spiritual formation as "the Spirit-driven process of forming the inner world of the human self in such a way that it becomes like the inner being of Christ himself" (*Renovation of the Heart*, p. 22). M. Robert Mulholland Jr. views spiritual formation as "a process of being conformed to the image of Christ for the sake of others" (*Invitation to a Journey: A Roadmap for Spiritual*

Formation [Downers Grove, IL: InterVarsity Press, 1993], p. 12). James C. Wilhoit defines spiritual formation as "the intentional communal process of growing in our relationship with God and becoming conformed to Christ through the power of the Holy Spirit" (*Spiritual Formation as if the Church Mattered: Growing in Christ Through Community* [Grand Rapids: Baker Academic, 2008], p. 23). Jeffrey Greenman says spiritual formation is "our continuing response to the reality of God's grace shaping us into the likeness of Jesus Christ, through the work of the Holy Spirit, in the community of faith, for the sake of the world" ("Spiritual Formation in Theological Perspective," p. 24). Greenman's definition most closely aligns with mine.

[14]For an excellent treatment of the integration of the spirit, emotions and psychology, see Mark R. McMinn, *Psychology, Theology, and Spirituality in Christian Counseling* (Wheaton, IL: Tyndale House, 1996); Mark R. McMinn and Timothy R. Phillips, eds., *Care for the Soul: Exploring the Intersection of Psychology and Theology* (Downers Grove, IL: InterVarsity Press, 2001); and F. LeRon Shults and Steven J. Sandage, *Transforming Spirituality: Integrating Theology and Psychology* (Grand Rapids: Baker Academic, 2006).

[15]See Harold G. Koenig, Michael E. McCullough and David B. Larson, *Handbook of Religion and Health* (Oxford: Oxford University Press, 2001); and Harold G. Koenig, *Medicine, Religion, and Health: Where Science and Spirituality Meet* (Conshohocken, PA: Templeton Foundation Press, 2008). For scholarly research on faith and physical wellness integration, see Duke University's Center for Spirituality, Theology, and Health, dedicated to exploring the interconnectedness between spirituality and health: www.spiritualityandhealth.duke.edu/index.html.

[16]Simon Chan, *Spiritual Theology: A Systematic Study of the Christian Life* (Downers Grove, IL: InterVarsity Press, 1998), p. 59.

[17]For more on John Newton's life, see John Newton, *The Life and Spirituality of John Newton* (Vancouver: Regent College Publishing, 1998); John Newton, *Utterance of the Heart* (Grand Rapids: Baker Books, 1979); Gerald L. Sittser, *Water from a Deep Well: Christian Spirituality from Early Martyrs to Modern Missionaries* (Downers Grove, IL: InterVarsity Press, 2007), pp. 232-40.

[18]The word *glory* derives from the Hebrew (*kabod*), which conveys "something weighty which gives importance" (Gerhard Kittel, "δόξα," *Theological Dictionary of the New Testament*, vol. 2, abridg. Geoffrey W. Bromiley [Grand Rapids: Eerdmans, 1985], p. 178). In reference to God, the word connotes that which makes God impressive. God's glory, then, reflects God's very nature, splendor and power.

[19]See the description of the Greek word for glory (*doxa*), connoting grandeur, in Gary M. Burge, "Glory," in *Dictionary of Jesus and the Gospels*, ed. Joel B. Green and Scot McKnight (Downers Grove, IL: InterVarsity Press, 1992), p. 269.

[20]Jason B. Hood, *Imitating God in Christ: Recapturing a Biblical Pattern* (Downers Grove, IL: InterVarsity Press, 2013), p. 11. Drawing on Richard Hays (*Moral Vision of the New Testament: Community, Cross, New Creation: A Contemporary Introduction to New Testament Ethics* [New York: HarperOne, 1996], p. 197), Hood argues for reclaiming the notion of imitation as being an active process of discipleship (see pp. 12, 115-16). Imitation will be further addressed in chapter eleven.

[21]Gorman, *Cruciformity*, p. 48.

[22]John R. Tyson, ed., *Invitation to Christian Spirituality: An Ecumenical Anthology* (New York: Oxford University Press, 1999), p. 3.

[23]Chan, *Spiritual Theology*, p. 80.

[24]Hood notes that imitation does not imply "passive conformity" (*Imitating God in Christ*, p. 109n6).

[25]See Thomas C. Oden's definition of grace: "Grace is an overarching term for all of God's gifts to humanity, all the blessings of salvation, all events through which are manifested God's own self-giving. . . . It is the divine disposition to work in our hearts, wills, and actions, so as actively to communicate God's self-giving love for humanity (Rom 3:24; 6:1; Eph 1:7; 2:5-8)," in *The Transforming Power of Grace* (Nashville: Abingdon Press, 1993), p. 33.

2 The Birthplace of Christian Spiritual Formation: The *Imago Dei*

[1]See also Genesis 5:1; 9:6. Psalm 8:5 exclaims, "You made them [humankind] a little lower than God, and crowned them with glory and honor."

[2]W. Lee Humphreys, *The Character of God in the Book of Genesis: A Narrative Appraisal* (Louisville: Westminster John Knox Press, 2001), p. 23.

[3]Claus Westermann, *Genesis 1–11: A Commentary*, trans. John J. Scullion (Minneapolis: Augsburg Publishing, 1984), p. 144; Claus Westermann, *Genesis: A Practical Commentary*, trans. David E. Green (Grand Rapids: Eerdmans, 1987), pp. 10-13.

[4]Gerhard von Rad, *Genesis: A Commentary*, rev. ed. (Philadelphia: Westminster Press, 1972), pp. 56-57.

[5]Ancient Christian writers known as the church fathers generally viewed God as the initiator of all of creation. For excerpts from the writings of Clement of Alexandria, Gregory of Nyssa, Chrysostom, Origen, Irenaeus, Augustine and others regarding the biblical text of Genesis 1:26-27, see Andrew Louth, ed., in collaboration with Marco Conti, *Genesis 1–11*, Ancient Christian Commentary on Scripture: Old Testament I (Downers Grove, IL: IVP Academic, 2001), pp. 27-41.

[6]von Rad, *Genesis*, p. 56; Derek Kidner, *Genesis* (Leicester, UK: Inter-Varsity Press, 1976), p. 52.

[7]Westermann, *Genesis 1–11*, pp. 144-45.

[8]Anthony A. Hoekema, *Created in God's Image* (Grand Rapids: Eerdmans, 1986), p. 12. Hoekema dismisses interpretations that identify the plurality as "plural of majesty," angelic beings or the heavenly host, or as Karl Barth contends, the Trinity. Hoekema rather advances the plausible and nonspecific interpretation that "God exists as a plurality" which hints at the Trinity further developed in the New Testament.

[9]Geoffrey W. Bromiley, ed., "Image," in *The International Standard Bible Encyclopedia* (Grand Rapids: Eerdmans, 1982), 2:803-4; Paul Niskanen, "The Poetics of Adam: The Creation of אדם in the Image of אלהים," *Journal of Biblical Literature* 129 (2009): 417-36.

[10]Gordon J. Wenham, *Genesis 1–15*, Word Biblical Commentary 1 (Waco, TX: Word, 1987), pp. 27-34, esp. p. 29.

[11]See Raymond C. Van Leeuwen, "Form, Image," in *New International Dictionary of Old Testament Theology and Exegesis* (Grand Rapids: Zondervan, 1997), 4:643-48; and Eugene H. Merrill, "Image of God," in *Dictionary of the Old Testament: Pentateuch*, ed. T. Desmond

Alexander and David W. Baker (Downers Grove, IL: InterVarsity Press, 2003), pp. 441-45.

[12]For an overview of the various views as to what *imago* and *similitude* mean, see Westermann, *Genesis 1–11*, pp. 148-52. Possible interpretations of likeness to God include (1) a distinction made between humankind's natural and supernatural likeness to God, (2) the likeness to God as spiritual only, (3) image and likeness as mainly in external form, (4) humanity as God's counterpart, and (5) humankind as God's representative on earth.

[13]Kidner, *Genesis*, p. 50.

[14]Hoekema, *Created in God's Image*, p. 13.

[15]Ibid., pp. 13-14.

[16]Van Leeuwen views the image as referring to the entire human, "not a part or property" ("Form, Image," p. 644).

[17]G. C. Berkouwer, *Man: The Image of God*, trans. Dirk W. Jellema (Grand Rapids: Eerdmans, 1962), p. 77. Emil Brunner identifies the body as being "equally a means of expression, and the instrument, of the spirit and the will" (*The Christian Doctrine of Creation and Redemption*, trans. Olive Wyon [Philadelphia: Westminster Press, 1953], p. 62).

[18]See Hoekema, *Created in God's Image*, pp. 33-65; and Richard J. Middleton, *The Liberating Image: The Imago Dei in Genesis 1* (Grand Rapids: Brazos Press, 2005), pp. 17-34.

[19]Douglas John Hall, *Imaging God: Dominion as Stewardship* (Grand Rapids: Eerdmans, 1986), p. 20.

[20]Ibid., pp. 63-64.

[21]Each of these four perspectives frames one well-established historical interpretation of the *imago Dei*. Differences of opinion abound related to the exact meaning and significance of the *imago Dei*. Hence, this CSF model includes seven primary dimensions of the human person. For those who would disagree with the CSF model, I pose this question, Where did these universal human dimensions derive from, if other than from God in creation?

[22]David Cairns, *The Image of God in Man*, rev. ed. (London: Collins, 1973), p. 110.

[23]Augustine, *The City of God*, trans. Marcus Dods (New York: Modern Library, 1950).

[24]Stanley Grenz, *The Social God and the Relational Self: A Trinitarian Theology of the Imago Dei* (Louisville: Westminster John Knox Press, 2001), p. 155.

[25]Ibid., p. 165.

[26]Ibid.

[27]Cairns, *Image of God in Man*, p. 134.

[28]Grenz, *Social God and the Relational Self*, p. 167.

[29]Karl Barth, *Church Dogmatics* 3.1, *The Doctrine of Creation*, ed. G. W. Bromiley and T. F. Torrance (London: T & T Clark, 1958), p. 196.

[30]For a synopsis of the positions of Kierkegaard, Ramsey and Brunner, see Grenz, *Social God and the Relational Self*, pp. 173-75.

[31]Hall, *Imaging God*, pp. 113-39.

[32]Middleton, *Liberating Image*, p. 29.

[33]See Hall, *Imaging God*, chap. 1, esp. p. 60.

[34]Grenz, *Social God and the Relational Self*, pp. 177-82.

[35]J. Behm, "μεταμορφόω," *Theological Dictionary of the New Testament*, abridg. Geoffrey W. Bro-

miley (Grand Rapids: Eerdmans, 1985), pp. 607-9.

[36]Hoekema, *Created in God's Image*, p. 85.

[37]Even ancient Christian writers viewed Christ as the image in which humankind is created. See Louth, *Genesis 1–11*, p. 27.

[38]See Cairns on the New Testament teachings related to the image of God (*Image of God in Man*, pp. 40-60). See esp. pp. 48, 51, where Cairns presents the image and the glory of God as being interwoven.

[39]Hoekema, *Created in God's Image*, pp. 89, 101.

[40]N. W. Porteus, "Image of God," *Interpreter's Dictionary of the Bible*, ed. George Arthur Buttrick (Nashville: Abingdon, 1962), 2:683.

[41]Robert Louis Wilken, "Biblical Humanism," in *Personal Identity in Theological Perspective*, ed. Richard Lints, Michael S. Horton and Mark R. Talbot (Grand Rapids: Eerdmans, 2006), p. 23.

[42]Stanley J. Grenz, "The Social God and the Relational Self: Toward a Theology of the *Imago Dei* in the Postmodern Context," in *Personal Identity in Theological Perspective*, ed. Richard Lints, Michael S. Horton and Mark R. Talbot (Grand Rapids: Eerdmans, 2006), p. 89.

[43]Ibid.

[44]Ibid.

[45]Hoekema, *Created in God's Image*, p. 23.

[46]Grenz, "Social God and the Relational Self," p. 83.

[47]Grenz, *Social God and the Relational Self*, p. 210.

[48]C. K. Barrett, *The Second Epistle to the Corinthians*, ed. Henry Chadwick, Harper's New Testament Commentaries (New York: Harper & Row, 1973), p. 135.

[49]F. F. Bruce, *The Epistles to the Colossians, Philemon, and the Ephesians*, The New International Commentary of the New Testament (Grand Rapids: Eerdmans, 1984), p. 57.

[50]Ibid., pp. 57-58.

[51]Arthur G. Patzia, *Colossians, Philemon, Ephesians* (Peabody, MA: Hendrickson, 1990), p. 16.

[52]W. E. Vine, *Vine's Expository Dictionary of Old and New Testament Words*, ed. F. F. Bruce (Old Tappan, NJ: Fleming H. Revell, 1981), 2:247.

[53]Ibid.

[54]Hoekema, *Created in God's Image*, p. 21.

3 The Love of God: The Starting Place

[1]Bernard of Clairvaux, *On the Love of God* (*De Diligendo Deo*), trans. A religious of C.S.M.V. (London: A. R. Mowbray, 1950), p. 24.

[2]Emil Brunner, *Dogmatics*, vol. 2, *Christian Doctrine of Creation and Redemption*, trans. Olive Wyon (Philadelphia: Westminster Press), p. 55.

[3]For more on the love that Tim Tebow shares with his parents, see Robin Roberts's interview with Tim and his mother, Pam, Jennifer Pereira and Rich McHugh, "Tim Tebow and His Mom Share Mother's Day Memories," *ABC News*, May 10, 2012, http://abcnews.go.com/US/tim-tebow-mom-share-mothers-day-memories-favorite/story?id=16316000. Roberts comments that the Tebows are "such an incredibly loving family."

[4]C. S. Lewis, *The Four Loves* (New York: Harcourt Brace, 1960), p. 127.

[5]For asserting that love is God's motivation in creation, see Karl Barth, *Church Dogmatics* 3.1, *The Doctrine of Creation*, ed. G. W. Bromiley and T. F. Torrance (London: T & T Clark, 1958), p. 331; Jürgen Moltmann, *God in Creation: A New Theology of Creation and the Spirit of God*, trans. Margaret Kohl (Minneapolis: Fortress Press, 1993), pp. 75-76; F. LeRon Shults, *Reforming the Doctrine of God* (Grand Rapids: Eerdmans, 2005), p. 242; and Paul S. Fiddes, "Creation out of Love," in *The Work of Love: Creation as Kenosis*, ed. John Polkinghorne (Grand Rapids: Eerdmans, 2001), pp. 167-91, esp. p. 168.

[6]For other perspectives on godly love, see Nygren Anders, *Agape and Eros*, trans. Philip S. Watson (New York: Harper & Row, 1969), which highlights agape love as being spontaneous, unmotivated, creative and initiated by God, creating value in the beloved; Gene Outka, *Agape: An Ethical Analysis* (New Haven, CT: Yale University Press, 1972), who contends that agape love is "an active concern for the neighbor's well-being, which is somehow independent of particular actions of the other" (p. 260). For a sociological perspective, see Pitirim Sorokin, *The Ways and Power of Love: Types, Factors, and Techniques of Moral Transformation* (Philadelphia: Templeton Foundation, 2002), who defines love as the "the drive toward unity of the separated" (p. 25); Edward Collins Vacek, *Love, Human and Divine: The Heart of Christian Ethics* (Washington, DC: Georgetown University Press, 1994), a Roman Catholic writer who contends that love is "an affective, affirming participation in the goodness of a being (or Being)" (p. 34) and views love as *agape*, *eros* and *philia*; Stephen G. Post, *A Theory of Agape: On the Meaning of Christian Love* (Lewisburg, PA: Bucknell University Press, 1990), who views Christian agape as a mutuality between God, self and others in order to share in God's divine love. In recent years the Institute for the Research on Unlimited Love, as directed by Post, and the Fetzer Institute have promoted solid scholarship on altruistic love.

[7]The doctrine of adoption, which will be addressed in the last section of this chapter, is often misinterpreted or minimized. Paul's adoption metaphor conveys the process of becoming a child of God through redemption apart from the law. Although only mentioned five times (Rom 8:15, 23; 9:4; Gal 4:5; Eph 1:5), Paul likely utilized the adoption metaphor (Gk. *huiothesia*) because these three churches, situated directly under Roman jurisdiction, would have understood the term's significance, as it conveyed the formation of a spiritual family. See Trevor J. Burke's excellent monograph *Adopted into God's Family: Exploring a Pauline Metaphor* (Downers Grove, IL: InterVarsity Press, 2006), p. 60, and Jeanne Stevenson-Moessner, *The Spirit of Adoption: At Home in God's Family* (Louisville: Westminster John Knox, 2003), p. 111.

[8]Anthony A. Hoekema, *Created in God's Image* (Grand Rapids: Eerdmans, 1986), p. 55.

[9]Donald G. Bloesch, *Spirituality Old and New: Recovering Authentic Spiritual Life* (Downers Grove, IL: InterVarsity Press, 2007), p. 29.

[10]Augustine, *The Trinity*, in *The Works of Saint Augustine* 1.5, trans. E. Hill (Brooklyn: New City Press, 1991), p. 4.9. Also see his *Answer to Maximus the Arian* 2.14.1, where Augustine asserts, "The Father then is the beginning without beginning, and the Son the beginning from the beginning . . . nor will I deny that the Holy Spirit who proceeds from each of them is the beginning. Rather, I say that these three together are one beginning just as they are one God." Augustine

explains from John 1:1 that the origin of the Son and the Holy Spirit are from the Father.

[11]Richard of St. Victor, *On the Trinity* 3, chaps. 19-20.

[12]Colin E. Gunton, *Father, Son and Holy Spirit: Toward a Fully Trinitarian Theology* (London: T & T Clark, 2003), p. 86.

[13]Fiddes, "Creation Out of Love," p. 175.

[14]Ibid., p. 177. Clark H. Pinnock and Robert C. Brow suggest that love is characterized not as what God decides to do or solely as an attribute but rather what God essentially is "as dynamic livingness, a diving circling and relating" in a "tripersonal mystery of love" (*Unbounded Love* [Downers Grove, IL: InterVarsity Press, 1994], p. 45).

[15]Czech filmmaker Matej Mináč made a documentary film of Winton's life: *Nicholas Winton: The Power of Good* (www.powerofgood.net/story.php). Those surviving rescued children, mostly grandparents now, refer to themselves as "Winton's children." Among those saved are the British film director Karel Reisz (*The French Lieutenant's Woman, Isadora,* and *Sweet Dreams*), Canadian journalist and news correspondent for CBC Joe Schlesinger (originally from Slovakia), Lord Alfred Dubs (a former minister in the Blair Cabinet), Lady Milena Grenfell-Baines (a patron of the arts whose father, Rudolf Fleischmann, saved Thomas Mann from the Nazis), Dagmar Símová (a cousin of former US Secretary of State Madeleine Albright), Tom Schrecker, (a *Reader's Digest* manager), Hugo Marom (a famous aviation consultant, and one of the founders of the Israeli Air Force), and Vera Gissing (author of *Pearls of Childhood* and coauthor of *Nicholas Winton and the Rescued Generation*).

[16]Reciprocal love often is expressed in gratitude, as in the case of one of the ten lepers who, after being healed, returned to praise God. Jesus then asked, "Were not ten made clean? But the other nine, where are they?" (Lk 17:17). Gratitude is a response to divine love.

[17]Jürgen Moltmann, "God's Kenosis in the Creation and Consummation of the World," in *The Work of Love: Creation as Kenosis*, ed. John Polkinghorne (Grand Rapids: Eerdmans, 2001), pp. 140-41.

[18]Clark H. Pinnock, *Flame of Love: A Theology of the Holy Spirit* (Downers Grove, IL: InterVarsity Press, 1996), p. 47.

[19]See also Phil 2:8; Col 1:13-20; 2 Thess 2:16.

[20]Robert Hamerton-Kelly, *God the Father: Theology and Patriarchy in the Teaching of Jesus* (Philadelphia: Fortress Press, 1979), p. 72.

[21]Thomas A. Smail, *The Forgotten Father* (Grand Rapids: Eerdmans, 1981), p. 24.

[22]Ibid., pp. 54, 57.

[23]Ibid., p. 55.

[24]For example, in 2012, over one-third of American children lived without their biological fathers in the home. For African American children this number is over one-half. See Rose M. Kreider, Table C5, *Living Arrangements of Children: 2012*, US Census Bureau, www.census.gov/hhes/families/data/cps2012.html.

[25]"Effective Parenting," US Department of Health & Human Services, http://fatherhood.hhs.gov/Parenting.

[26]Ibid. These differences were observed even after controlling for socioeconomic variables such as race and income.

[27]For more on human attachment perspectives and their influence on perceptions of God, see Jane R. Dickie et al., "Parent-Child Relationships and Children's Images of God," *Journal for the Scientific Study of Religion* 36 (1997): 24-43; Lee A. Kirkpatrick, "An Attachment-theoretical Approach to the Psychology of Religion," *International Journal for the Psychology of Religion* 2 (1992): 3-38; and Lee A. Kirkpatrick and Phillip R. Shaver, "Attachment Theory and Religion: Childhood Attachment, Religious Beliefs and Conversion," *Journal for the Scientific Study of Religion* 29 (1990): 315-34.

[28]Smail, *Forgotten Father*, p. 56.

[29]For more resources on fathering, see John Sowers, *Fatherless Generation: Redeeming the Story* (Grand Rapids: Zondervan, 2010); Carey Casey, *How to Win at Being a Dad* (Carol Stream, IL: Tyndale House, 2009); Kenneth O. Gangel and Jeffrey S. Gangel, *Fathering Like the Father* (Grand Rapids: Baker, 2003); and David Blankenhorn, *Fatherless America: Confronting Our Most Urgent Social Problem* (New York: Basic Books, 1995).

[30]Helmut Thielicke, *The Waiting Father*, trans. John W. Doberstein (San Francisco: Harper & Row, 1959), p. 29.

[31]Miroslav Volf, *Exclusion and Embrace: A Theological Exploration of Identity, Otherness, and Reconciliation* (Nashville: Abingdon Press, 1996), p. 158.

[32]Ibid., p. 159.

[33]Ibid.

[34]See Tara Parker-Pope, "Father and Son Across 1,000 Finishes," *New York Times*, August 19, 2009, http://well.blogs.nytimes.com/2009/08/19/father-and-son-across-1000-finish-lines.

[35]For a theological treatment of disability, see Amos Yong, *Theology and Down Syndrome: Reimaging Disability in Late Modernity* (Waco, TX: Baylor University Press, 2007), pp. 155-92, esp. the chapter "Reimaging the Doctrines of Creation, Providence, and the Imago Dei." Yong addresses how historical understanding of creation and providence align with contemporary experiences of intellectual and physical disabilities. He contends that "the Holy Spirit creatively enables and empowers our full humanity in relationship to our embodied selves, to others, and to God, even in the most ambiguous and challenging of situations," which in turn point us to the eschaton (ibid., p. 191).

[36]Jesus applies these particular passages to himself: (1) Matthew 21:16 and Psalm 8:1-2, related to the praise of children; (2) Luke 4 and Isaiah 61, declaring the Spirit of the Lord being upon him in his mission declaration; (3) Luke 19:10 and Ezekiel 34:16, 22, in applying the divine shepherd imagery to his mission to seek and save the lost; and (4) Luke 20:18; Isaiah 8:14-15 and Psalm 118:22-23, in identifying himself as the stone that the builders rejected but became the chief cornerstone. Paul and Peter likewise make application of Old Testament references relating the stone to Jesus (Rom 9:33; 1 Pet 2:6-8).

[37]James D. G. Dunn, *Jesus Remembered* (Grand Rapids: Eerdmans, 2003), pp. 615-704.

[38]Ibid., p. 708.

[39]Graham H. Twelftree, *Jesus: The Miracle Worker* (Downers Grove, IL: InterVarsity Press, 1999), p. 347.

[40]D. R. Bauer, "Son of God," In *Dictionary of Jesus and the Gospels*, ed. Joel B. Green and Scot McKnight (Downers Grove, IL: InterVarsity Press, 1992), p. 772.

[41]See Joachim Jeremias, *The Prayers of Jesus* (London: SCM Press, 1967), pp. 11-64.

[42]James D. G. Dunn, *Christology in the Making: A New Testament Inquiry into the Origins of the Doctrine of the Incarnation*, 2nd ed. (Grand Rapids: Eerdmans, 1998), p. 14.

[43]Jürgen Moltmann, *The Trinity and the Kingdom: The Doctrine of God* (Minneapolis: Fortress Press, 1993), p. 168.

[44]Stanley Grenz, *The Social God and the Relational Self: A Trinitarian Theology of the Imago Dei* (Louisville: Westminster John Knox Press, 2001), p. 314.

[45]Ibid.

[46]Ibid., p. 315.

[47]Bernard of Clairvaux, *On the Love of God*, p. 36.

[48]D. A. Carson, *The Difficult Doctrine of the Love of God* (Wheaton, IL: Crossway, 2000), p. 34.

[49]Brunner, *Christian Doctrine of Creation and Redemption*, p. 58.

[50]David G. Benner, *Surrender to Love: Discovering the Heart of Christian Spirituality* (Downers Grove, IL: InterVarsity Press, 2003), pp. 60-61.

[51]See the story of Zac Sunderland's journey on the DVD *Intrepid: The Zac Sunderland Story*, which culminates in his celebrative California homecoming on July 16, 2009.

[52]Anthony A. Hoekema, *Created in God's Image* (Grand Rapids: Eerdmans, 1986), p. 86.

[53]Moltmann in *The Trinity and the Kingdom* asserts that the Holy Spirit proceeds in eternity from the Father. Moltmann writes, "The Spirit is 'breathed out' (*spiratio*) not begotten (*generatio*). So the Spirit cannot be a second Son of the Father. He proceeds from the Father. He does not equally proceed from the Son. If this were so, the Son would be the second Father and there would be two different 'origins' for the divine spirit" (ibid., p. 169).

[54]Gordon D. Fee, *Paul, the Spirit, and the People of God* (Peabody, MA: Hendrickson, 1996), p. 26.

[55]Jürgen Moltmann, *The Spirit of Life: A Universal Affirmation* (Minneapolis: Fortress Press, 1992), pp. 10-14; Pinnock, *Flame of Love*, p. 25.

[56]Ralph Del Colle, "The Holy Spirit: Presence, Power, Person," *Theological Studies* 62, no. 2 (2001): 322-40, esp. p. 338.

[57]For more on the Spirit as God's personal presence, see Gordon D. Fee, *God's Empowering Presence: The Holy Spirit in the Letters of Paul* (Peabody, MA: Hendrickson, 1994), pp. 827-45.

[58]Ibid., p. 8.

[59]Ibid., p. 5.

[60]Moltmann, *Spirit of Life*, p. 51.

[61]When realizing through the Spirit the abundant love of God for us personally, we yield our lives to God in surrender and humility, knowing that our lives belong not to us but to God.

[62]Ibid., pp. 35, 40-43.

[63]Ibid., p. 61.

[64]Pinnock, *Flame of Love*, p. 40.

[65]Tom Smail, *The Giving Gift: The Holy Spirit in Person* (Lima, OH: Academic Renewal Press, 2002), p. 21.

[66]Smail, *Giving Gift*, p. 64.

[67]Peter Widdicombe, *The Fatherhood of God from Origen to Athanasius* (Oxford: Oxford University Press, 2000), p. 236.

[68]Robert J. Banks, *Paul's Idea of Community: The Early House Churches in Their Cultural Setting*, 2nd ed. (Grand Rapids: Baker, 1994), pp. 47-57.

[69]Burke, *Adopted into God's Family*, p. 45.

[70]Ibid., p. 61.

[71]James D. G. Dunn, *The Theology of Paul the Apostle* (Grand Rapids: Eerdmans, 1998), p. 436. Dunn comments that although adoption was not characteristically a Jewish practice, as it was a Greco-Roman custom, the coherence of Paul's use of adoption in Galatians 3–4 clearly points to sonship, which does align with "Jewish categories."

[72]Paul's usage of *huiothesia* negates any hint of either adoptionist theology, which proffers that Christ became the son of God as a result of his resurrection, or the ransom theory of atonement advanced by Origen, which proffers that Christ paid Satan a ransom to rescue those under Satan's dominion.

[73]Burke, *Adopted into God's Family*, p. 99.

[74]Ibid., p. 159.

[75]Dunn, *Theology of Paul the Apostle*, p. 424.

[76]Burke, *Adopted into God's Family*, p. 79.

[77]Ernest Best, *Ephesians*, International Critical Commentary (Edinburgh: T & T Clark, 1998), p. 125.

[78]John R. W. Stott, *God's New Society: The Message of Ephesians* (Downers Grove, IL: InterVarsity Press, 1980), p. 40. Living as a child of God entails living ethically in alignment with God's Word.

[79]For more on these three historical ways of viewing God's children (i.e., *imago Dei*, *imago Christi* and *gloria Dei*), see Moltmann, *God in Creation*, pp. 215-29. Also see Irenaeus, who wrote, "*Homo vivens Gloria Dei et vita hominis visio Dei est*," translated as "the living person represents the glory of God and is by nature the image of God"(*Against Heresies*, 4.20.7).

[80]Hendrikus Berkhof, *Christian Faith: An Introduction to the Study of Faith*, trans. Sierd Woudstra, 2nd ed. (Grand Rapids: Eerdmans, 1986), p. 183.

4 Spirit: Our Faith

[1]Augustine, *Confessions*, trans. Maria Boulding (Hyde Park, NY: New City Press, 1997), 2.2.2.

[2]Ibid., 8.29.

[3]Stanley Hauerwas, *A Community of Character: Toward a Constructive Christian Social Ethic* (Notre Dame, IN: University of Notre Dame Press, 1981), p. 9. Hauerwas contends that we learn about the Kingdom and Jesus' identity by following him (ibid., p. 43) and that the social ethic of living according to God's story is the task of the church (ibid., p. 52).

[4]Simon Chan, *Spiritual Theology: A Systematic Study of the Christian Life* (Downers Grove, IL: InterVarsity Press, 1998), p. 78.

[5]Gustavo Gutiérrez, *We Drink from Our Own Wells: The Spiritual Journey of a People*, trans. Matthew J. O'Connell (Maryknoll, NY: Orbis Books, 1984), p. 91.

[6]C. S. Lewis described sin as pride and self-interest: "From the moment a creature becomes

aware of God as God and of itself as self, the terrible alternative of choosing God or self for the centre is opened to it" (*The Problem of Pain* [San Francisco: Harper, 2001], p. 70).

[7]John Calvin, *Institutes of the Christian Religion*, 2.1.6, trans. Henry Beveridge (Grand Rapids: Eerdmans, 1953). Calvin states: "We must, therefore, hold it for certain that, in regard to human nature, Adam was not merely a progenitor, but, as it were, a root, and that accordingly, by his corruption, the whole human race was deservedly vitiated" (p. 215).

[8]Emil Brunner, *Man in Revolt: A Christian Anthropology*, trans. Olive Wyon (Philadelphia: Westminster Press, 1947), pp. 149, 157. Brunner observes, "Sin is the manner in which man emancipates himself from God, takes himself out of the hands of God" (ibid., p. 157). Hence, the law was given to lead humanity to Christ (Gal 3:24), in that humankind is unable to achieve obedience to God's righteous standards in the law without receiving the grace of God through Christ (cf. Rom 8:2).

[9]Emil Brunner, *The Christian Doctrine of Creation and Redemption*, trans. Olive Wyon (Philadelphia: Westminster Press, 1952), 2:92. Bernard McGinn calls sin the very essence of pride and "inflated self-assessment" (*Why Sin Matters: The Surprising Relationship Between Our Sin and God's Grace* [Wheaton, IL: Tyndale House, 2004], p. 69).

[10]David K. Naugle, *Reordered Love, Reordered Lives* (Grand Rapids: Eerdmans, 2008), p. xiii.

[11]Gordon D. Fee, *Paul, the Spirit, and the People of God* (Peabody, MA: Hendrickson, 1996). Fee notes the meaning of the word *flesh* (Gk. *sarx*) in Paul's writings as "characteristic of the whole world in its present fallenness" and that it "denotes humanity not simply in its creatureliness vis-à-vis God, but in its fallen creatureliness as utterly hostile to God in every imaginable way" (ibid., p. 129). The flesh connotes each person turning to his or her own way and living as enemies against God (Rom 5:10; 1 Cor 15:25; Gal 6:8; Phil 3:18). In Romans 7 Paul paints the picture of the struggle with the flesh (vv. 14-18). Yet he affirms that what the law was unable to do in restoring us to wholeness and holiness, Christ has done, with the Spirit enabling us to "walk in the Spirit" (Rom 8:3-4).

[12]Asserting that salvation and justification occur by faith alone through grace, Martin Luther made a clear distinction regarding the role of the Holy Spirit in salvation, arguing, "The Law and the Gospel are two quite contrary doctrines." See Philip S. Watson, ed., *Martin Luther: Commentary on St. Paul's the Epistle to the Galatians* (London: James Clarke, 1953), p. 205.

[13]The word *heart* appears 730 times in the Old Testament and 105 times in the New Testament. In various forms the words *heart, hearts, -hearted* appear a total of 955 times. See J. M. Lower, "Heart," in *The Zondervan Pictorial Encyclopedia of the Bible*, ed. Merrill C. Tenney (Grand Rapids: Regency Reference Library, 1976), 3:58-59.

[14]Richard E. Averbeck, "Spirit, Community, and Mission: A Biblical Theology for Spiritual Formation," *Journal of Spiritual Formation & Soul Care* 1, no. 1 (2008): 27-53, esp. 28 (italics added). Dunn emphasizes that "membership in God's family is defined in terms of the Spirit" (*Theology of Paul the Apostle*, p. 424).

[15]According to Gordon Fee, we are heirs "of all God's eternal glory" (*God's Empowering Presence: The Holy Spirit in the Letters of Paul* [Peabody, MA: Hendrickson, 1994], p. 569).

[16]See Steven Chase, *Nature as Spiritual Practice* (Grand Rapids: Eerdmans, 2011), esp. pp. 93-124.

[17]John Wesley, "Free Grace," in *John Wesley's Sermons: An Anthology*, ed. Albert C. Outler and Richard P. Heitzenrater (Nashville: Abingdon Press, 1991), p. 50.

[18]Bonnie J. Miller-McLemore, "'Pondering All These Things': Mary and Motherhood," in *Blessed One: Protestant Perspectives on Mary*, ed. Beverly Roberts Gaventa and Cynthia L. Rigby (Louisville: Westminster Press, 2002), pp. 97-116.

[19]See Thomas C. Oden, *The Justification Reader* (Grand Rapids: Eerdmans, 2002), pp. 81-106.

[20]Augustine, *On Nature and Grace*, ed. Philip Schaff, trans. Peter Holmes and Robert Ernest Wallis, Nicene and Post-Nicene Fathers ser. 1, vol. 5 (Grand Rapids: Eerdmans, 1971), pp. 121-55. Augustine argued against Pelagianism, which denies original sin and advocates that personal volition alone, without grace, can choose good over evil. Also in the same volume, see Augustine's *On Grace and Free Will*, which addresses how "cooperating grace" works with human will (ibid., pp. 443-65).

[21]Thomas C. Oden, *The Transforming Power of Grace* (Nashville: Abingdon, 1993), p. xii.

[22]Raniero Cantalamessa, the dynamic and Spirit-filled preacher to the papal household, calls grace "the key that will open for us the door to a whole new chamber in the treasure-house of revelation concerning the Holy Spirit" (*Come, Creator Spirit: Meditations on the Veni Creator* [Collegeville, MN: Order of Saint Benedict, 2003], p. 48).

[23]John Wesley distinguished between three operations of God's grace: (1) prevenient grace, or divine grace from birth that precedes human action in salvation; (2) justifying grace, or divine grace that extends through salvation; and (3) sustaining grace, or divine grace continually extended to live in holiness or sanctification. See John Wesley, "On Working Out Our Own Salvation," in *John Wesley's Sermons*, pp. 486-92, esp. pp. 488-89.

[24]Ambrose, *On the Holy Spirit*, 1.15.171.

[25]James Moffatt, *Grace in the New Testament* (London: Hodder & Stoughton, 1931), p. 75; and Oden, *Transforming Power of Grace*, p. 36.

[26]Martin Luther, who nailed his ninety-five theses to the Wittenberg church door and sparked the Protestant Reformation, declared that salvation was through grace alone (*sola gratia*) and contested, among other things, the sale of indulgences in the Roman Catholic Church. Based on his study of Scripture, Luther declared before the adversarial Diet of Worms in 1521, "Here I stand. I can do no other." See also Roland H. Bainton, *Here I Stand: A Life of Martin Luther* (Peabody, MA: Hendrickson, 2009) and the 2003 movie *Luther*.

[27]See Rom 12:3; 15:15-16; 1 Cor 3:10; Gal 1:15; 2:9, Eph 3:2, 7-9; 1 Tim 1:14.

[28]Thomas Aquinas viewed grace as both operative (God's gracious love) and cooperative (the gifts that infuse human nature); *Nature and Grace: Selections from the Summa Theologica of Thomas Aquinas* 12ae, Q. 111, Art. 2, trans. and ed. A. M. Fairweather, Library of Christian Classics 11 (Philadelphia: Westminster Press, 1954), pp. 166-68.

[29]Dunn, *Theology of Paul the Apostle*, pp. 319-23. Dunn observes that God's grace joins love as the centerpiece of Paul's entire theology, whereby grace breaks through human experience as "generous initiative and sustained faithfulness from start to finish." Dunn discerns five features of Paul's theology of grace as (1) derived from the Hebrew understanding of *hesed* ["gracious favour, loving kindness, covenant love"] from ancient Israel, (2) the powerful action of God, (3) originating only from God as source, (4) the reciprocity through the

imagery of overflow and abundance, and (5) "grace begetting grace," such that reception of God's grace generously extends to others.

[30]John Calvin, *Institutes of the Christian Religion*, trans. Henry Beveridge (Grand Rapids: Eerdmans, 1953), 2:119-29. John Calvin, considered the father of the Reformed tradition, agreed with Luther's emphasis on justification by faith alone through grace, as opposed to works, but also emphasized that union with Christ after salvation is evidenced through Christian good works. Also see Gordon D. Fee, *God's Empowering Presence: The Holy Spirit in the Letters of Paul* (Peabody, MA: Hendrickson, 1994), pp. 84-90.

[31]Oden, *Transforming Power of Grace*, pp. 41-44.

[32]Ibid., p. 19.

[33]Dietrich Bonhoeffer, *The Cost of Discipleship* (New York: Touchstone, 1995), p. 45.

[34]Charles Seymour Jr., *Michelangelo's David: A Search for Identity* (Pittsburgh: University of Pittsburgh Press, 1967), pp. 7-8.

[35]Ibid., p. 25; Robert S. Liebert, who examines Michelangelo's inner life through his art, notes that *David* was "hidden from public view" during sculpting (*Michelangelo: A Psychoanalytic Study of His Life and Images* [New Haven, CT: Yale University Press, 1983], p. 86).

[36]Gregory of Nyssa, bishop of Cappadocia, applied the metaphor of sculpting to Moses' wilderness and Mt. Sinai experience as an allegory of the Christian faith journey: "And when you, as a sculptor, carve in your own heart the divine oracles which you receive from God . . . then you will draw near to the goal" (*Gregory of Nyssa: The Life of Moses*, trans. Abraham Malherbe and Everett Ferguson [New York: Paulist Press, 1978], pp. 133-37).

[37]In his *Confessions* Augustine relates his struggles with lust and being in the wrong crowd (2.2.7-8), dabbling in horoscopes (4.3.5) and the hollowness of his secular ambitions (6.6.9) to a renunciation of career in order to respond to God's grace (9.2.2).

[38]Ibid., 8.1.1.

[39]Dallas Willard equates the human spirit with both the will and the heart and "as the central core of the nonphysical part of man" (*Renovation of the Heart: Putting on the Character of Christ* [Colorado Springs: NavPress, 2002], pp. 34-35). Willard defines the human spirit as "unbodily personal power" (*The Divine Conspiracy: Rediscovering Our Hidden Life in God* [San Francisco: HarperSanFrancisco, 1998], p. 81). Jürgen Moltmann views the human spirit from a Gestalt or holistic perspective, describing it as "the forms of organization and communication of all open systems of matter and life" (*God in Creation: A New Theology of Creation and the Spirit of God*, trans. Margaret Kohl [Minneapolis: Fortress Press, 1993], p. 263); and as being self-transcendently aligned toward God in *The Spirit of Life: A Universal Affirmation* (Minneapolis: Fortress Press, 1992), p. 7. John Macquarrie acknowledges that the human spirit is the "most elusive and mysterious constituent of our human nature" and is "described as a capacity for going out of oneself and beyond oneself" ("Spirit and Spirituality," in *Exploring Christian Spirituality: An Ecumenical Reader*, ed. Kenneth J. Collins [Grand Rapids: Baker, 2000], pp. 63-73, esp. pp. 66-67). Ray S. Anderson views the heart as the unity of body and soul, and explores Karl Barth's interpretation of the human spirit as being "the operation of God" upon humankind (*On Being Human: Essays in Theological Anthropology* [Grand Rapids: Eerdmans, 1982], p. 211). Barth identifies the human spirit as "the movement of God"

toward humanity (*Church Dogmatics* 3.2, *The Doctrine of Creation*, ed. G. W. Bromiley and T. F. Torrance (London: T & T Clark, 1960], p. 356). In James D. G. Dunn's view of Paul's theology, the human spirit is the means by which the person relates most directly to God, such that it is "by opening the human spirit to the divine Spirit that the human being can be whole" (*The Theology of Paul the Apostle* [Grand Rapids: Eerdmans, 1998], p. 78).

[40]Willard, *Divine Conspiracy*, p. 81.

[41]Henri Nouwen, *Finding My Way Home: Pathways to Life and the Spirit* (New York: Crossroad, 2001), p. 68.

[42]John Wesley coined the phrase *means of grace*, referring to spiritual disciplines such as prayer, searching the Scriptures and meditation, which are outward actions empowered by the Spirit ("Means of Grace," in *John Wesley's Sermons*, pp. 157-72). Regarding "tasks to accomplish," see Craig Dykstra, *Growing in the Life of Faith: Education and Christian Practices* (Louisville: Geneva Press, 1999), pp. 45-46.

[43]On union with God, see Clark H. Pinnock, *Flame of Love: A Theology of the Holy Spirit* (Downers Grove, IL: InterVarsity Press, 1996), pp. 152-55. Also see the Westminster Catechism, "The chief end of man is to glorify God and enjoy him forever"; and Ignatius of Loyola, "Man is created to praise, reverence, and serve God our Lord, and by this means to save his soul," Ignatius of Loyola, *Spiritual Exercises* (No. 23) in *Ignatius of Loyola: Spiritual Exercises and Selected Works*, ed. and trans. George E. Ganss (New York: Paulist Press, 1991), p. 130.

[44]Fee, *Paul, the Spirit, and the People of God*, pp. 152-62.

[45]James K. A. Smith, *Desiring the Kingdom: Worship, Worldview, and Cultural Formation* (Grand Rapids: Baker Academic, 2009), pp. 82-83.

[46]Ibid., p. 33.

[47]Ibid., pp. 155-214.

[48]Hauerwas, *Community of Character*, p. 43.

[49]Ibid., p. 40. According to Hauerwas, a social ethic for Christians is to become "nothing less than a community capable of forming people with virtues sufficient to witness to God's truth in the world" (ibid., p. 3), such that the believer's character becomes the ongoing telling of God's story (ibid., pp. 133-35).

[50]See Howard Thurman, *Disciplines of the Spirit* (New York: Harper & Row, 1963); and Howard Thurman, *The Inward Journey* (Richmond, IN: Friends United Press, 2007), p. 63.

[51]Pedrito U. Maynard-Reid, *Diverse Worship: African American, Caribbean and Hispanic Perspectives* (Downers Grove, IL: InterVarsity Academic, 2000).

[52]See Stanley Hauerwas, *Christian Among the Virtues: Theological Conversations with Ancient and Modern Ethics* (Notre Dame, IN: University of Notre Dame, 1997), pp. 26-30.

[53]Harold M. Best, *Unceasing Worship: Biblical Perspectives on Worship and the Arts* (Downers Grove, IL: InterVarsity Press, 2003), pp. 211-22.

[54]Craig Dykstra and Dorothy C. Bass, "Time of Yearning, Practices of Faith," in *Practicing Our Faith: A Way of Life for a Searching People*, ed. Dorothy C. Bass (San Francisco: Jossey-Bass, 1997), pp. 1-12. The practices described are (1) honoring the body, (2) hospitality, (3) household economics, (4) saying yes and saying no, (5) keeping sabbath, (6) testimony, (7) discernment, (8) shaping communities, (9) forgiveness, (10) healing, (11) dying well, and (12) singing.

[55]Ibid., p. 10. The two central practices that Dykstra and Bass contend enfold all others are prayer, as response to God's presence, and Bible intake, with both needing to be interwoven within the life of the Christian congregation (ibid., p. 202). With this I wholeheartedly agree.

[56]See Richard J. Foster, *Celebration of Discipline: The Path to Spiritual Growth*, 20th anniv. ed. (San Francisco: HarperSanFrancisco, 1998), p. 7; Richard J. Foster and Emilie Griffin, eds., *Spiritual Classics: Selected Readings for Individuals and Groups on Twelve Spiritual Disciplines* (San Francisco: HarperSanFrancisco, 2000); and Dallas Willard, *The Spirit of the Disciplines: Understanding How God Changes Lives* (San Francisco: HarperCollins, 1991). John Ortberg focuses on the practice of "slowing" to overcome hurry sickness (*The Life You've Always Wanted: Spiritual Disciplines for Ordinary People* [Grand Rapids: Zondervan, 2002], p. 83).

[57]Selected resources on spiritual practices by ancient and contemporary authors include Ignatius of Loyola, *Spiritual Exercises* in Ganss, *Ignatius of Loyola*, pp. 113-214.; Lynne M. Baab, *Sabbath Keeping: Finding Freedom in the Rhythms of Rest* (Downers Grove, IL: InterVarsity Press, 2005); James Houston, *The Transforming Power of Prayer: Deepening Your Friendship with God* (Colorado Springs: NavPress, 1999); M. Robert Mulholland Jr., *Shaped by the Word: The Power of Scripture in Spiritual Transformation* (Nashville: Upper Room, 1985); and Ruth Haley Barton, *Invitation to Solitude and Silence: Experiencing God's Transforming Presence* (Downers Grove, IL: InterVarsity Press, 2004).

[58]A. W. Tozer, *The Pursuit of God* (Harrisburg, PA: Christian Publications, 1948), p. 15.

[59]Dykstra, *Growing in the Life of Faith*, p. xii.

[60]Oden, *Transforming Power of Grace*, p. 19.

[61]Steven Sandage, Mary Jensen and Daniel Jass, "Relational Spirituality and Transformation: Risking Intimacy and Alterity," *Journal of Spiritual Formation & Soul Care* 1, no. 2 (2008): 187, 199. These authors posit that fear, anxiety and desire for approval may motivate spiritual practices rather than love of God and desire for intimacy. For a classic primer on living in awareness of God's abiding presence, see Brother Lawrence, *The Practice of the Presence of God*, ed. Hal M. Helms (Brewster, MA: Paraclete Press, 2010).

[62]Bob Sorge, *The Fire of Delayed Answers* (Canandaigua, NY: Oasis House, 1998). As a musician and worship leader, Sorge sustained severe damage to his vocal cords that prevents him from singing and speaking above hushed tones. This personal crisis drove him into deep despair through loss of personal identity, which has resulted in powerful insights into dealing with personal brokenness.

[63]Bruce Demarest, *Seasons of the Soul: Stages of Spiritual Development* (Downers Grove, IL: InterVarsity Press, 2009), pp. 39-59.

[64]See C. S. Lewis's transparent account of wrestling with God through the illness and death of his wife, Joy Davidman, which rocked his faith in *A Grief Observed* (New York: HarperOne, 2001). Calling God a "Cosmic Sadist," Lewis pleaded, "But oh God, tenderly, tenderly. Already, month by month and week by week you broke her body on the wheel whilst she still wore it. Is it not enough?" (ibid., p. 49).

[65]Mother Teresa, *Mother Teresa: Come Be My Light: The Private Writings of Mother Teresa*, ed. Brian Kolodiejchuk (New York: Doubleday, 2007), esp. pp. 149-207.

[66]For more on the seeming withdrawal of God in desolation and the benefits of seasons of

darkness, see rules 5-10 in Ignatius of Loyola, *The Spiritual Exercises of Saint Ignatius of Loyola.*

[67]Elisabeth Elliot, *A Chance to Die: The Life and Legacy of Amy Carmichael* (Old Tappan, NJ: Revel, 2005).

[68]Martin Luther King Jr., "Loving Your Enemies," chap. 5 in *Strength to Love* (Minneapolis: Fortress Press, 2010). See also King's autobiography, *The Autobiography of Martin Luther King, Jr.*, ed. Clayborne Carson (New York: Grand Central Publishing, 2001).

[69]James H. Cone takes up a discussion of theodicy in chap. 8, noting: "For some black people, slavery was clear evidence that God either does not exist or that God's existence is irrelevant to black suffering" (*God of the Oppressed*, rev. ed. [Maryknoll, NY: Orbis, 1997], p. 170).

[70]See Howard Thurman, *Jesus and the Disinherited* (Boston: Beacon, 1976).

[71]James H. Cone, *The Spirituals and the Blues: An Interpretation* (Westport, CT.: Greenwood Press, 1980). Also see Norman R. Yetman, "An Introduction to WPA Slave Narratives," Library of Congress, http://memory.loc.gov/ammem/snhtml/snintro00.html.

[72]Gutiérrez, *We Drink from Our Own Wells*, pp. 19-32.

[73]Ada Maria Isasi-Diaz, *Mujerista Theology: A Theology for the Twenty-first Century* (Maryknoll, NY: Orbis, 1996), p. 203.

5 Emotions: Our Feelings

[1]Pitirim A. Sorokin, *The Ways and Power of Love* (Chicago: Henry Regnery/Gateway, 1967), pp. 47-79.

[2]Stephen G. Post and Lynn G. Underwood, "Future Research Needs on Altruism and Altruistic Love," in *Altruism and Altruistic Love*, ed. Stephen G. Post and Lynn G. Underwood (New York: Oxford University Press, 2002), p. 383.

[3]Within the field of psychology, emotions have been viewed from a variety of perspectives: (1) as products of early attachment experiences with caregivers, (2) continued family and social experiences, (3) cognitive development and information processing, (4) neurology, (5) personality, (6) culture and the environment, (7) sexual development, and (8) moral influences, among others. A sampling of notable psychological perspectives, which offer various approaches to the study and understanding of the interplay between affective, social and cognitive development, includes (1) Abraham Maslow's hierarchy of needs, (2) Jean Piaget's theory of cognitive development, (3) Erik Erikson's stages of psychosocial development, (4) Jerome Kagan's study of temperament, (5) Lev Vygotsky's social constructivism and "scaffolding," where language and adult input contribute to children's learning, (6) Robert Kegan's adult development model, which incorporates Piaget's, Maslow's, Erikson's and others' perspectives, and (7) Silvan Tomkins' affect theory, which views nine primary emotions as having visual cues. Although Sigmund Freud's psychosexual approach and Carl Jung's dream analysis perspective influenced the field of psychology, their humanistic theories fall far short of a Bible-centered approach in understanding emotional development. For an overview of nonfaith based approaches of emotional development, see K. T. Strongman, *The Psychology of Emotion: From Everyday Life to Theory*, 5th ed. (Chichester/West Sussex, UK: Wiley, 2003); and James J. Gross, ed., *Handbook of Emotion Regulation* (New York: Guilford Press, 2007).

[4]P. N. Johnson-Laird and Keith Oatley, "Emotions, Music, and Literature," in *Handbook of Emotions*, ed. Michael Lewis, Jeannette M. Haviland-Jones and Lisa Feldman Barrett, 3rd ed. (New York: Guilford Press, 2008), pp. 102-13.

[5]Carol Magai and Jeannette Haviland-Jones, *The Hidden Genius of Emotion: Lifespan Transformations of Personality* (Cambridge: Cambridge University Press, 2002), p. 4.

[6]For viewing human development through the lens of the *imago Dei*, see Jack O. Balswick, Pamela Ebstyne King and Kevin S. Reimer, *The Reciprocating Self: Human Development in Theological Perspective* (Downers Grove, IL: InterVarsity Press, 2005), pp. 27-49; and Mark R. Talbot, "Starting from Scripture," in *Limning the Psyche: Explorations in Christian Psychology*, ed. Robert C. Roberts and Mark R. Talbot (Grand Rapids: Eerdmans, 1997), pp. 102-9.

[7]For a Christian perspective on the interplay of emotions on memory, see Keith Edwards, "The Nature of Human Mental Life," in *Christian Perspectives on Being Human: A Multidisciplinary Approach to Integration*, ed. J. P. Moreland and David M. Ciocchi (Grand Rapids: Baker, 1993), pp. 175-97. Although neurobiologists attempt to understand emotions through brain science, they have yet to fully understand the complexity of emotion, cognition and behavior. For example, while Dr. Joseph E. LeDoux notes that the human brain contains about ten billion neurons that are interconnected in highly complex ways and that emotions are biological functions of the nervous system, he acknowledges that emotions are more than stimulus-response reactions (*The Emotional Brain: The Mysterious Underpinnings of Emotional Life* [London: Weidenfeld & Nicolson, 1998], pp. 22-46).

[8]Physiological responses: Robert W. Levenson, "Autonomic Specificity and Emotion," in *Handbook of Affective Sciences*, ed. Richard J. Davidson, Klaus R. Scherer and H. Hill Goldsmith (New York: Oxford University Press, 2009), pp. 212-24. Facial expression: Carroll E. Izard, *The Face of Emotion* (New York: Appleton-Century-Crofts, 1971). Vocal expression: Jo-Anne Bachorowski and Michael J. Owren, "Vocal Expressions of Emotion," in *Handbook of Emotions*, ed. Michael Lewis, Jeannette M. Haviland-Jones and Lisa Feldman Barrett, 3rd ed. (New York: Guilford Press, 2010), pp. 196-210. Judgment: Ralph Adolphs and Antonio R. Damasio, "The Interaction of Affect and Cognition: A Neurobiological Perspective," in *Handbook of Affect and Social Cognition*, ed. Joseph P. Forgas (Mahwah, NJ: Lawrence Erlbaum, 2001), pp. 27-49. Ethical thinking: Martha C. Nussbaum, *Upheavals of Thought: The Intelligence of Emotions* (Cambridge: Cambridge University Press, 2001).

[9]Diana Fritz Cates, *Aquinas on Emotions: A Religious-Ethical Inquiry* (Washington, DC: George Washington University Press, 2009).

[10]Seldom is emotion addressed as a theological topic in the Scriptures. For a welcome exception, see Matthew A. Elliott, *Faithful Feelings: Rethinking Emotion in the New Testament* (Grand Rapids: Kregel, 2006).

[11]See Wyndy Corbin Reuschling, "Christian Moral Formation," in *Becoming Whole and Holy: An Integrative Conversation About Christian Formation*, ed. Jeannine K. Brown, Carla M. Dahl and Wyndy Corbin Reuschling (Grand Rapids: Baker Academic, 2011), pp. 125-40. Reuschling comments, "The Good is embodied, concrete, visible, and offered to us most completely in Jesus Christ" (ibid., p. 129).

[12]See Benjamin Breckinridge Warfield, "On the Emotional Life of Our Lord," *The Person and Work of Christ*, ed. Samuel Craig (Philadelphia: Presbyterian & Reformed, 1980), pp. 96-106, esp. p. 101.

[13]Ibid., p. 106.

[14]Ibid., p. 108.

[15]Robert C. Roberts, *Spiritual Emotions: A Psychology of Christian Virtues* (Grand Rapids: Eerdmans, 2007), p. 14.

[16]Ibid., p. 9. Maintaining that emotions are "concerned-based construals" of one's circumstances that result from ways that we see the world, Roberts links emotions with the ninefold fruit of the Spirit (e.g., love, joy, peace) as an outcome of one's spirituality (ibid., p. 11). Thus, emotions become expressions of character traits (ibid., p. 20).

[17]See Francis MacNutt and Judith MacNutt, who assert that experiences in utero influence later development (*Praying for Your Unborn Child* [London: Hodder & Stoughton, 1988]). Johns Hopkins developmental psychologist and researcher Janet DiPietro investigates the impact of development in utero on postnatal life, including the emotional states of mothers on their preborn children ("The Role of Prenatal Maternal Stress in Child Development," *Current Directions in Psychological Science* 13 [2004]: 71-74).

[18]J. R. R. Tolkien, *Lord of the Rings*, 50th anniv. one vol. ed. (New York: Mariner Books, 2005).

[19]Todd W. Hall, "The Person as Spirit: Human Attachment and Relationality," in *Psychology in the Spirit: Contours of a Transformational Psychology*, ed. John H. Coe and Todd W. Hall (Downers Grove, IL: IVP Academic, 2010), pp. 239-40.

[20]Attachment behavior relates to what psychologists call object relations theory, whereby we "internalize the relational dynamics that we experienced with our parents or early caregivers," which in turn become internalized object representations through which we experience other relationships. See John Coe, "A Transformational Psychology of Health and Wholeness Inside and Outside of Faith," in *Psychology in the Spirit: Contours of a Transformational Psychology*, ed. John H. Coe and Todd W. Hall (Downers Grove, IL: IVP Academic, 2010), p. 17.

[21]John Bowlby, *Attachment and Loss*, vol. 1, *Attachment* (New York: Basic Books, 1969); *Attachment and Loss*, vol. 2, *Separation, Anxiety, and Anger* (New York: Basic Books, 1973); *Attachment and Loss*, vol. 3, *Sadness and Depression* (New York: Basic Books, 1980); *The Making and Breaking of Affectional Bonds* (London: Tavistock, 1979); *A Secure Base: Parent-Child Attachment and Healthy Human Development* (New York: Basic Books, 1988). Mary D. Salter Ainsworth, Mary C. Blehar, Everett Waters and Sally Wall, *Patterns of Attachment: A Psychological Study of the Strange Situation* (Hillsdale, NJ: Erlbaum, 1978); Mary D. Salter Ainsworth, "Attachment Across the Life Span," *Bulletin of the New York Academy of Medicine* 6 (1985): 792-812.

[22]Bowlby, *Making and Breaking of Affectional Bonds*, p. 130.

[23]Mary B. Main, Nancy Kaplan and Jude Cassidy, "Security in Infancy, Childhood, and Adulthood: A Move to the Level of Representation," *Monographs for the Society for Research in Child Development* 50, nos. 1-2, serial no. 209 (1985): 66-104; and Mary B. Main and Judith Solomon, "Discovery of an Insecure-Disorganized/Disoriented Attachment Pattern," in *Af-*

fective Development in Infancy, ed. T. Berry Brazelton and Michael W. Yogman (Westport, CT: Ablex, 1986), pp. 95-124.

[24]For a formative study connecting attachment to adult love, see Cindy Hazen and Phillip R. Shaver, "Romantic Love Conceptualized as an Attachment Process," *Journal of Personality and Social Psychology* 52, no. 3 (1987): 511-24. On how threat influences attachment, see Mario Mikulincer and Phillip R. Shaver, *Attachment in Adulthood: Structure, Dynamics, and Change* (New York: Guilford Press, 2007).

[25]Phillip R. Shaver, Nancy Collins and Catherine L. Clark, "Attachment Styles and Internal Working Models of Self and Relationship Patterns," in *Knowledge Structures in Close Relationships: A Social Psychological Approach*, ed. Garth J. O. Fletcher and Julie Fitness (Mahwah, NJ: Lawrence Erlbaum, 1996), pp. 25-61.

[26]Cindy Hazen and Phillip R. Shaver, "Love and Work: An Attachment Perspective," *Journal of Personality and Social Psychology* 59, no. 2 (1990): 270-80.

[27]Shaver, Collins and Clark, "Attachment Styles and Internal Working Models," p. 37.

[28]Mario Mikulincer and Phillip R. Shaver, "Adult Attachment and Affect Regulation," in *Handbook of Attachment: Theory, Research, and Clinical Applications*, ed. Jude Cassidy and Phillip R. Shaver (New York: Guilford Press, 2008), pp. 503-31.

[29]Karlen Lyons-Ruth and Deborah Jacobvitz, "Attachment Disorganization," in Cassidy and Shaver, *Handbook of Attachment*, pp. 666-97.

[30]Phillip Shaver, Cindy Hazan and Donna Bradshaw, "Love as Attachment: The Integration of Three Behavioral Systems," in *The Psychology of Love*, ed. Robert J. Sternberg and Michael L. Barnes (New Haven, CT: Yale University Press, 1988), pp. 68-99.

[31]Ibid., pp. 73-77, 93.

[32]Steven J. Sandage, "Spirituality and Human Development," in *Transforming Spirituality: Integrating Theology and Psychology*, ed. F. LeRon Shults and Steven J. Sandage (Grand Rapids: Baker Academic, 2006), p. 181.

[33]Judith Feeney and Patricia Noller, *Adult Attachment* (Thousand Oaks, CA: Sage, 1996), p. 15; and Everett Waters et al., "Attachment Security in Infancy and Early Adulthood: A Twenty Year Longitudinal Study," *Child Development* 71, no. 3 (2000): 684-89.

[34]Hall, "Person as Spirit: Human Attachment and Relationality," p. 247.

[35]Ibid.

[36]Pehr Granqvist and Lee A. Kirkpatrick, "Attachment and Religious Representations and Behavior," in Cassidy and Shaver, *Handbook of Attachment*, p. 911.

[37]Ibid., pp. 907-8.

[38]Todd W. Hall et al., "Attachment to God and Implicit Spirituality: Clarifying Correspondence and Compensation Models," *Journal of Psychology and Theology* 64, no. 4 (2009): 227-42.

[39]Similar to psychological perspectives of attachment, the concept of "God image" serves as a bridge between biblical-theological concepts and psychological perspectives. God image refers to one's emotional experience of God. Connected to object relations theory, which refers to developing in relationship to others ("objects in one's environment"), a genre of God image research has developed. See Ana-Maria Rizzuto, *The Birth of the Living God: A Psychoanalytic*

Study (Chicago: University of Chicago Press, 1979); and Glendon L. Moriarty and Louis Hoffman, eds., *God Image Handbook for Spiritual Counseling and Psychotherapy: Research, Theory, and Practice* (Binghamton, NY: Haworth Pastoral Press, 2007).

[40]Bowlby, *Making and Breaking of Affectional Bonds*, pp. 28-29.

[41]For an Australian perspective see Feeney and Noller, *Adult Attachment*. For an Israeli perspective see Mario Mikulincer and Orna Nachson, "Attachment Styles and Patterns of Self-Disclosure," *Journal of Personality and Social Psychology* 61, no. 2 (1991): 321-31. For volumes on cross-cultural attachment research, see Patricia McKinsey Crittenden and Angelika Hartl Claussen, eds., *The Organization of Attachment Relationships: Maturation, Culture, and Context* (Cambridge: Cambridge University Press, 2000); and Phyllis Erdman and Kok-Mun Ng, eds., *Attachment: Expanding the Cultural Connections* (New York: Routledge, 2010).

[42]Joseph was seventeen when his brothers sold him into slavery, thirty when he became Pharaoh's second-in-command, and between thirty-seven and forty-four when he reconciled with his brothers (Gen 37:2; 41:46, 53-54).

[43]Joseph's affection for Benjamin, the only other son of his mother, Rachel, is shown by Benjamin receiving five times the food servings as compared to his brothers (Gen 43:34) and Joseph embracing Benjamin first before his other brothers when revealing his identity (Gen 45:14).

[44]Evelyn Eaton Whitehead and James D. Whitehead, *Transforming Our Painful Emotions: Spiritual Resource in Anger, Shame, Grief, Fear, and Loneliness* (Maryknoll, NY: Orbis, 2010), p. 8.

[45]Robert S. McGee, *The Search for Significance: See Your True Worth Through God's Eyes* (Nashville: Thomas Nelson, 2003), p. 7. McGee offers a biblical approach to dealing with the performance trap, approval addiction, blaming others and shame.

[46]Bobb Biehl, *Why You Do What You Do: Answers to Your Most Puzzling Emotional Mysteries* (Nashville: Thomas Nelson, 1993), p. 18.

[47]Whitehead and Whitehead, *Transforming Our Painful Emotions*, pp. 20-23. The Whiteheads note that the positive outcome of negative emotions includes the opportunity for (1) self-examination, (2) action and change, and (3) greater appreciation of life's mystery of feelings (ibid., p. 7). They contend that negative emotions give rise to positive outcomes, if directed appropriately.

[48]This four-stage model is based on my observations of Scripture and human nature, as well as the reading of literature on emotional healing, psychology and human behavior.

[49]C. S. Lewis, *The Problem of Pain* (New York: HarperSanFrancisco, 1996), p. 91.

[50]Gustavo Gutiérrez, *On Job: God-Talk and the Suffering of the Innocent*, trans. Matthew J. O'Connell (Maryknoll, NY: Orbis, 1987).

[51]Ibid., p. 100.

[52]Ann Curry, "The Amish Display the True Meaning of Forgiveness," NBCNews.com, October 4, 2006, www.msnbc.msn.com/id/15134030/ns/nightly_news/t/amish-display-true-meaning-forgiveness.

[53]For an account of the tragedy from the perspective of Amish culture and spirituality, written by three professors of small colleges with Anabaptist roots, see Donald B. Kraybill, Steven M. Wolf and David L. Weaver-Zercher, *Amish Grace: How the Forgiveness Transcended Tragedy*

(San Francisco: Jossey-Bass, 2007). For a poignant documentary on forgiveness that transcends religion and culture, see Martin Doblmeier, *The Power of Forgiveness,* Journey Films, 2007, www.thepowerofforgiveness.com.

[54]F. LeRon Shults, "Forgiveness as Sharing in Divine Grace," in *The Faces of Forgiveness: Searching for Wholeness and Salvation,* ed. F. LeRon Shults and Steven J. Sandage (Grand Rapids: Baker Academic, 2003), pp. 168-221.

[55]Miroslav Volf, *Exclusion and Embrace: A Theological Exploration of Identity, Otherness, and Reconciliation* (Nashville: Abingdon, 1996), p. 9.

[56]Ibid.

[57]Similar to Volf, Everett L. Worthington Jr. recounts his personal experience with forgiveness resulting from the brutal murder of his mother (*Forgiveness and Reconciliation: Theory and Application* [New York: Routledge, 2008], pp. x-xi). Worthington offers a decisional approach to forgiveness involving five phases, using the acronym REACH: (1) *recall* the hurt, (2) *empathize* with the one who hurt you, (3) give the *altruistic* gift of forgiveness, (4) *commit* to emotional forgiveness, and (5) *hold* on to forgiveness (ibid., pp. 171-86).

[58]Alex H. S. Harris and Carl E. Thoresen, "Forgiveness, Unforgiveness, Health, and Disease," in Worthington, *Handbook of Forgiveness,* pp. 321-33.

[59]According to Everett L. Worthington Jr., "Forgiveness is defined as the emotional replacement of (1) hot emotions of anger or fear that follow a perceived hurt or offense, or (2) unforgiveness that follows ruminating about the transgression, by substituting positive emotions" and can move from an unending unforgiveness loop to a forgiveness loop (*Five Steps to Forgiveness: The Art and Science of Forgiving* [New York: Crown, 2001], pp. 32, 113).

[60]Whitehead and Whitehead, *Transforming Our Painful Emotions,* p. 51.

[61]See Victor Villaseñor, *Rain of Gold,* 2nd ed. (New York: Delta, 1992).

[62]See "Biography," on Victor Villaseñor's website at http://victorvillasenor.com/about.

[63]For Mukhtar's story, see Nicholas D. Kristof and Sheryl WuDunn, *Half the Sky: Turning Oppression into Opportunity for Women Worldwide* (New York: Vintage Books, 2009), pp. 70-79. As a married couple, Kristof and WuDunn, both Pulitzer Prize–winning journalists, advocate for women's empowerment in order to combat global oppression and poverty, and redeem shame-inducing treatment. The title of the book derives from the Chinese proverb "Women hold up half the sky." For a strong biblical treatment on how shame can draw us to God, see Jill McNish, *Transforming Shame: A Pastoral Response* (New York: Haworth Press, 2004).

[64]See Martin Luther King Jr., *Strength to Love* (Minneapolis: Fortress Press, 2010); and Clayborne Carson, ed., *The Autobiography of Martin Luther King, Jr.* (New York: Warner Books, 1998).

[65]Chester Kylstra and Betsy Kylstra, *Biblical Healing and Deliverance: A Guide to Experiencing Freedom from the Sins of the Past, Destructive Beliefs, Emotional and Spiritual Pain, Curse and Oppression* (Grand Rapids: Chosen, 2005), p. 40.

[66]Larry Crabb, *Connecting: Healing Ourselves and Our Relationships* (Nashville: W Publishing Group, 1997), pp. 23-55.

[67]Francis MacNutt highlights the impact of extended times of prayer for physical as well as emotional and spiritual healing in what he refers to as "soaking prayer" (*The Prayer That Heals: Praying for Healing in the Family* [Notre Dame, IN: Ave Maria Press, 1981], p. 57).

[68]Paul Tournier, *The Meaning of Persons*, trans. Edwin Hudson (New York: HarperCollins, 1997). This book was selected by *Christianity Today* in 2006 as one of the top fifty books that have shaped evangelicals. Tournier's other influential works include *The Healing of Persons*, 3rd ed. (New York: Harper & Row, 1965); *The Whole Person in a Broken World* (New York: Harper & Row, 1981); and *Guilt and Grace: A Psychological Study* (New York: HarperCollins, 1982).

[69]Leanne Payne, *The Broken Image: Restoring Personal Wholeness Through Healing Prayer* (Grand Rapids: Baker, 1981); *Crisis in Masculinity* (Grand Rapids: Baker, 1985); *Listening Prayer: Learning to Hear God's Voice and Keep a Prayer Journal* (Grand Rapids: Baker, 1994); and *Restoring the Christian Soul: Overcoming Barriers to Completion in Christ Through Healing Prayer* (Grand Rapids: Baker, 1996).

[70]Francis MacNutt, *Healing: The Power to Heal* (Notre Dame, IN: Ave Maria Press, 1992) and *The Healing Reawakening: Reclaiming Our Lost Inheritance* (Grand Rapids: Chosen Books, 2005).

[71]Neil T. Anderson, *The Steps to Freedom in Christ*, 3rd ed. (Ventura, CA: Gospel Light, 2004); *The Bondage Breaker: Overcoming Negative Thoughts, Irrational Feelings, and Habitual Sins*, 3rd ed. (Eugene, OR: Harvest House, 2000); and *Victory Over the Darkness: Realizing the Power of Your Identity in Christ*, 2nd ed. (Ventura, CA: Gospel Light, 2000).

[72]Kylstra and Kylstra, *Biblical Healing and Deliverance*.

[73]Henry Cloud, *Changes That Heal: How to Understand Your Past to Ensure a Healthier Future* (Grand Rapids: Zondervan, 1992); *How People Grow: What the Bible Says About Personal Growth* (Grand Rapids: Zondervan, 2001); and *The Law of Happiness: How Spiritual Wisdom and Modern Science Can Change Your Life* (New York: Howard Books/Simon & Schuster, 2011).

[74]Francis MacNutt, *Healing*, rev. ed. (Notre Dame, IN: Ave Maria Press, 1999), p. 120.

[75]Ibid., p. 119. Agnes Sanford (1897–1982) was engaged in the ministry of healing, as is her son, John Sanford. John and his wife, Paula Sanford, cofounders of Elijah House, a healing ministry, are coauthors of *The Transformation of the Inner Man* (Tulsa, OK: Victory House, 1982), among other books.

6 Relationships: Our Social Connectedness

[1]Max De Pree, *Leadership Jazz* (New York: Doubleday, 1992), pp. 1-3.

[2]Ibid., p. 2.

[3]Max De Pree honors the gift of relationship through his granddaughter's life in celebrating her sixteenth birthday in *Dear Zoe: Letters to My Miracle Grandchild* (New York: HarperCollins, 1999).

[4]Stanley J. Grenz, *The Social God and the Relational Self: A Trinitarian Theology of the Imago Dei* (Louisville: Westminster John Knox Press, 2001), p. 5.

[5]For more on a relational/social view of God, see Stanley J. Grenz, *Rediscovering the Triune God: The Trinity in Contemporary Theology* (Minneapolis: Fortress Press, 2004), pp. 117-62; Jürgen Moltmann, *God in Creation: A New Theology of Creation and the Spirit of God*, trans. Margaret Kohl (Minneapolis: Fortress Press, 1993), pp. 234-45; Ray S. Anderson, *On Being Human: Essays in Theological Anthropology* (Grand Rapids: Eerdmans, 1982), pp. 69-87; and

Miroslav Volf, *After Our Likeness: The Church as the Image of the Trinity* (Grand Rapids: Eerdmans, 1998), pp. 209-10.

[6]Jack O. Balswick, Pamela Ebstyne King and Kevin S. Reimer, *The Reciprocating Self: Human Development in Theological Perspective* (Downers Grove, IL: InterVarsity Press, 2005), p. 40.

[7]Colin E. Gunton, *One, the Three and the Many: God, Creation, and the Culture of Modernity* (Cambridge: Cambridge University Press, 1993), p. 222.

[8]Tom Smail, *Like Father, Like Son: The Trinity Imagined in Our Humanity* (Grand Rapids: Eerdmans, 2006), p. 158.

[9]Catherine Mowry LaCugna, *God with Us: The Trinity and the Christian Life* (New York: HarperOne, 1993), p. 383.

[10]Stanley J. Grenz, "The Social God and the Relational Self: Toward a Theology of the *Imago Dei* in the Postmodern Context," in *Personal Identity in Theological Perspective*, ed. Richard Lints, Michael S. Horton and Mark R. Talbot (Grand Rapids: Eerdmans, 2006), p. 92.

[11]Ray S. Anderson and Dennis B. Guernsey, *On Being Family: A Social Theology of the Family* (Grand Rapids: Eerdmans, 1985), p. 18.

[12]For Scott Hahn, the Trinity reveals the very notion of family: "God is . . . a family" (*First Comes Love: Finding Your Family in the Church and the Trinity* [London: Darton, Longman, & Todd, 2002], p. 43).

[13]Lisa Sowle Cahill, *Sex, Gender, and Christian Ethics* (Cambridge: Cambridge University Press, 1996), p. 106.

[14]Deborah Liable and Ross A. Thompson, "Early Socialization: A Relationship Perspective," in *Handbook of Socialization: Theory and Research*, ed. Joan E. Grusec and Paul D. Hastings (New York: Guilford, 2007), pp. 181-207.

[15]Pitirim Sorokin, *The Ways and Power of Love: Types, Factors, and Techniques of Moral Transformation* (Philadelphia: Templeton Foundation, 2002), p. 193.

[16]Richard B. Hays, *The Moral Vision of the New Testament: A Contemporary Introduction to New Testament Ethics* (San Francisco: HarperCollins, 1996), p. 361.

[17]Bonnie J. Miller-McLemore, *Let the Children Come: Reimagining Childhood from a Christian Perspective* (San Francisco, CA: Jossey-Bass, 2003), p. 88. Also see John Chrysostom, "Homily 21 on Ephesians 6:1-4," in *On Marriage and Family Life*, trans. Catherine P. Roth and David Anderson (Crestwood, NY: St. Vladimir's Seminary Press, 1986), pp. 56-72.

[18]Anderson and Guernsey, *On Being Family*, pp. 36, 40-45. Jack O. Balswick and Judith K. Balswick, *The Family: A Christian Perspective on the Contemporary Home*, 3rd ed. (Grand Rapids: Baker Academic, 2007), pp. 17-35.

[19]For an analysis of the complex factors contributing to family fragmentation, see Brenda Almond, *The Fragmenting Family* (Oxford: Oxford University Press, 2006); and Mitch Pearlstein, *From Family Collapse to America's Decline: The Educational, Economic, and Social Costs of Family Fragmentation* (Lanham, MD: Rowman & Littlefield, 2011).

[20]Stanley Hauerwas, *A Community of Character: Toward a Constructive Christian Social Ethic* (Notre Dame, IN: University of Notre Dame, 1981), p. 167. In the same book, see also chapter eight: "The Moral Value of the Family," pp. 155-66, and chapter nine: "The Family: Theological and Ethical Reflections," pp. 167-74.

[21]David Blankenhorn, *Fatherless in America: Confronting Our Most Urgent Social Problem* (New York: Basic Books, 1995), p. 65.

[22]Mary Stewart Van Leeuwen, *My Brother's Keeper: What the Social Sciences Do (and Don't) Tell Us About Masculinity* (Downers Grove, IL: InterVarsity Press, 2002), pp. 15-31. Stephen G. Post, *More Lasting Unions: Christianity, the Family, and Society* (Grand Rapids: Eerdmans, 2000), p. 107.

[23]According to 2012 federal US statistics, children lived within the following family constellations in 2011: (1) 69% with both parents (65% of them with married parents), (2) 27% with one parent and (3) 4% with neither parent, with half of those living with grandparents. One parent living in a cohabiting relationship accounted for 7%. In 2010, 40.8% of all births were to unmarried women. In "America's Children in Brief: Key National Indicators of Well-Being, 2012," p. 3, www.childstats.gov/pdf/ac2012/ac_12.pdf. Pamela D. Couture, *Seeing Children, Seeing God: A Practical Theology of Children and Poverty* (Nashville: Abingdon Press, 2000), pp. 48-70.

[24]Laura E. Brumariu and Kathryn A. Kerns, "Parent-Child Attachment in Early and Middle Childhood," in *The Wiley-Blackwell Handbook of Childhood Social Development*, ed. Peter K. Smith and Craig H. Hart, 2nd ed. (Malden, MA: Wiley-Blackwell, 2011), pp. 319-36.

[25]Lisa Olson told her compelling story on May 17, 2011, at a chapel gathering hosted by Regent University. For her written testimony, see Lisa Olson, "Testimony: Lisa Manyata Olson," February 16, 2012, www.lovefeast.net/2012/testimony-lisaolson.

[26]Pandita Ramabai (1858–1922) was a committed Christian, brilliant scholar and social advocate against oppression of women and girls who challenged patriarchal norms (Keith J. White, "Jesus Was Her Guru," *Christian History*, July 1, 2005, www.ctlibrary.com/ch/2005/issue87/5.12.html). Offering vocational training, the Mukti Mission, which included a school and hospital, was open to all needy women (e.g., child widows, orphans and famine victims).

[27]For more on a biblical theology of disability, see Amos Yong, *The Bible, Disability, and the Church: A New Vision of the People of God* (Grand Rapids: Eerdmans, 2011); Amos Yong, *Theology and Down Syndrome: Reimagining Disability in Late Modernity* (Waco, TX: Baylor University Press, 2007); and Larry J. Waters and Roy B. Zuck, eds., *Why, O God? Suffering and Disability in the Bible and the Church* (Wheaton, IL: Crossway, 2011).

[28]For a social science perspective regarding interpersonal relationships, see Henri Tajfel, *Social Identity and Group Relations* (Cambridge: Cambridge University Press, 2010); Michael A. Hogg, "Social Identity," in *Handbook of the Self and Identity*, ed. Mark R. Leary and June Price Tangney (New York: Guilford Press, 2003), pp. 462-79. Intimacy is viewed as the outcome of mutual verbal and nonverbal communication and actions with another that leads to feeling accepted, supported and cared for. See Harry T. Reis, "Relational Experiences and Emotional Well-Being," in *Emotion, Social Relationships, and Health*, ed. Carol D. Ryff and Burton H. Singer (Oxford: Oxford University Press, 2001), pp. 57-86; and Harry T. Reis and Phillip Shaver, "Intimacy as an Interpersonal Process," in *Handbook of Personal Relationships: Theory, Research and Interventions*, ed. Steve Duck (New York: John Wiley, 1988), pp. 367-89.

[29]"Social Support: Tap this Tool to Combat Stress," Mayo Clinic, August 1, 2012, www.mayoclinic.com/health/social-support/SR00033.

[30]Bert N. Uchino, *Social Support and Physical Health: Understanding the Health Consequences of Relationships* (New Haven, CT: Yale University Press, 2004); Lyla M. Hernandez and Dan G. Blazer, eds., *Institute Brief: Genes, Behavior, and the Social Environment: Moving Beyond the Nature/Nurture Debate* (Washington, DC: National Academies Press, 2006), pp. 1-14.

[31]Jack O. Balswick and J. Kenneth Morland, *Social Problems: A Christian Understanding and Response* (Grand Rapids: Baker, 1990), p. 57.

[32]For an African perspective, see Mpyana Fulgence Nyengele, *African Women's Theology, Gender Relations, and Family Systems Theory* (New York: Peter Lang, 2004), p. 173. This Congolese author and associate professor focuses on healthy family relationships based on gender and relational justice and healing for both genders.

[33]Cf. Agneta H. Fischer and Antony S. R. Manstead, "Social Functions of Emotions," in *Handbook of Emotions*, ed. Michael Lewis, Jeannette M. Haviland-Jones and Lisa Feldman Barrett, 3rd ed. (New York: Guilford Press, 2008), pp. 456-58. Fischer and Manstead contend that the degree of expressed emotion is related to the nature of the relationship in order to promote intimacy, closeness and harmony, and thus avoid social isolation (ibid., p. 458). Ruth certainly expressed such emotion to Naomi.

[34]Cf. See Michael A. Hogg, "Social Identity and the Sovereignty of the Group: A Psychology of Belonging," in *Individual Self, Relational Self, Collective Self*, ed. Constantine Sedikides and Marilynn B. Brewer (Philadelphia: Psychology Press, 2001), pp. 123-24. Hogg asserts that proximity and similarity are strong determinants of interpersonal relationships. Ruth found both proximity and similarity in her relationship with Naomi, producing a bond of trust despite their diverse ethnic backgrounds.

[35]David G. Benner, *Sacred Companions: The Gift of Spiritual Friendship and Direction* (Downers Grove, IL: InterVarsity Press, 2002), p. 46.

[36]Elisabeth Moltmann-Wendel, "Friendship: The Forgotten Category for Faith in Christian Community," trans. Marianne M. Martin, in Jürgen Moltmann and Elisabeth Moltmann-Wendel, *Passion for God: Theology in Two Voices* (Louisville: Westminster John Knox Press, 2004), pp. 37, 38.

[37]Robert B. Hays, "Friendship," in Duck, *Handbook of Personal Relationships*, p. 407.

[38]John M. Gottman, *The Seven Principles for Making Marriage Work* (New York: Three Rivers Press, 1999), pp. 22-23.

[39]Liz Carmichael, *Friendship: Interpreting Christian Love* (New York: T & T Clark, 2004), p. 6.

[40]Ibid., p. 2.

[41]Luke Timothy Johnson, "Making Connections: The Material Expression of Friendship in the New Testament," *Interpretation* 58, no. 2 (2004): 158-71.

[42]For a biblical comparison of Christian friendship in the writings of John and Paul, see John Fitzgerald, "Christian Friendship: John, Paul, and the Philippians," *Interpretation* 61, no. 3 (2007): 284-96.

[43]Colin Duriez, *Tolkien and C. S. Lewis: The Gift of Friendship* (Mahwah, NJ: Hidden Springs/Paulist Press, 2003).

[44]See the obituary of Elizabeth Cady Stanton, in which Susan B. Anthony is quoted: "I cannot express myself at all as I feel. I am too crushed to say much, but, if she had outlived me, she

would have found fine words with which to express our friendship" ("Elizabeth Cady Stanton Dies at Her Home," *New York Times*, October 27, 1902, www.nytimes.com/learning/general/onthisday/bday/1112.html).

45Peter S. Bearman and James Moody, "Suicide and Friendships Among American Adolescents," *American Journal of Public Health* 94, no. 1 (2004): 89-95, esp. p. 93.

46See Tom Rath, *Vital Friends: The People You Can't Afford to Live Without* (New York: Gallup, 2006), p. 54. Gallup research findings indicate that having one best friend at work contributes to job satisfaction by 50%, despite the lack of other incentives, and increases work engagement by as much as seven times (ibid., pp. 53-54). Survey participants who had "at least three close friends at work were 96% more likely to be extremely satisfied with their life" (ibid., p. 55). Having friends contributes not only to relational formation but also to emotional and vocational formation, supporting the basic premise of this book that Christian spiritual formation is holistic and integrated among seven primary dimensions.

47Ibid., p. 15.

48Cornelius Plantinga Jr., *Not the Way It's Supposed to Be: A Breviary of Sin* (Grand Rapids: Eerdmans, 1995), p. 165. Miroslav Volf, *Exclusion and Embrace: A Theological Exploration of Identity, Otherness, and Reconciliation* (Nashville: Abingdon, 1996), p. 95.

49Volf, *Exclusion and Embrace*, p. 95.

50For an ironic account of the interpersonal conflict between two coauthors while writing a book on women as peacemakers, see Tara Klena Barthel and Judy Dabler, *Peacemaking Women: Biblical Hope for Resolving Conflict* (Grand Rapids: Baker, 2005), pp. 322-28.

51Ralph P. Martin, *Colossians and Philemon* (London: Oliphant, 1974), p. 144; and Peter T. O'Brien, *Colossians, Philemon*, Word Biblical Commentary 44 (Waco, TX: Word, 1982), p. 266.

52James Melvin Washington, ed., *A Testament of Hope: The Essential Writings of Martin Luther King, Jr.* (San Francisco: Harper & Row, 1986), p. 225.

53Gary Chapman, *Anger: Handling a Powerful Emotion in a Healthy Way* (Chicago: Northfield, 2007).

54Donald C. Palmer, *Managing Conflict Creatively: A Guide for Missionaries and Christian Workers* (Pasadena, CA: William Carey Library, 1990), pp. 11-13.

55Ibid., pp. 26-31.

56Ken Sande, *The Peacemaker: A Biblical Guide to Resolving Conflict* (Grand Rapids: Baker, 2004), pp. 22-29.

57Ibid., p. 20.

58Ibid., pp. 263-69. Sande offers helpful, reflective questions to engage when in conflictual situations.

59Kevin Johnson and Ken Sande, *Resolving Everyday Conflicts* (Grand Rapids: Baker, 2011), pp. 106-7.

60Hauerwas, *Community of Character*, p. 172.

61Gary Thomas, *Sacred Marriage: What If God Designed Marriage to Make Us Holy More Than to Make Us Happy?* (Grand Rapids: Zondervan, 2000), p. 266.

62"When the gentleness between you hardens, / And you fall out of your belonging with each other, / May the depths you have reached hold you still" (John O'Donohue, "For Love in a

Time of Conflict," in *To Bless the Space Between Us: A Book of Blessings* [New York: Doubleday, 2008], p. 32).

[63]See John M. Gottman, *The Science of Trust: Emotional Attunement for Couples* (New York: W. W. Norton, 2011), esp. chaps. 4, 8. Gottman focuses on building trust that sustains marital conflict through repairing negativity and addressing what he calls "the four horsemen of the apocalypse": criticism, defensiveness, contempt and stonewalling (ibid., pp. 121-23).

[64]For a compelling and fictional story of an Arab and a Jew who overcome conflict related to the deaths of their fathers and seek peace, see Arbinger Institute, *The Anatomy of Peace: Resolving the Heart of Conflict* (San Francisco: Berrett-Koehler, 2008).

[65]John Gottman, "Meta-Emotion, Children's Emotional Intelligence, and Buffering Children from Marital Conflict," in *Emotion, Social Relationships, and Health*, ed. Carol D. Ryff and Burton H. Singer (Oxford: Oxford University Press, 2001), pp. 23-40.

[66]Ibid., p. 36.

[67]Geoffrey A. Fowler, "Facebook: One Billion and Counting," *Wall Street Journal*, October 4, 2012, http://online.wsj.com/article/SB10000872396390443635404578036164027386112.html.

[68]Lauren Dugan, "Twitter to Surpass 500 Million Registered Users on Wednesday," Media Bistro.com, February 21, 2012, www.mediabistro.com/alltwitter/500-million-registered-users_b18842 (accessed August 27, 2012).

[69]For suicide statistics, see "Suicide in the US: Statistics and Prevention," National Institute of Mental Health, www.nimh.nih.gov/health/publications/suicide-in-the-us-statistics-and-prevention/index.shtml. For every suicide death, it is estimated that there are eleven nonfatal suicide attempts. Over 90% of all suicides relate to depression or substance abuse–related disorders.

[70]See "Suicide Risk Factors," National Suicide Prevention Hotline, www.suicidepreventionlifeline.org/Learn/RiskFactors; "Suicide: Risk and Protective Factors," US Center for Disease Control, www.cdc.gov/violenceprevention/suicide/riskprotectivefactors.html. Anecdotally, as a child growing up in a lower-middle-class neighborhood, I recall with anticipation our annual summer block parties, enjoyed by all families on the street. Fun events entertained children, and bedtimes were always extended. The demise of the neighborhood block party reflects the weakening of neighborly ties.

[71]Mother Teresa, press conference at Thomas Aquinas College, June 5, 1982, YouTube, www.youtube.com/watch?v=ybv9TDC0-B4.

[72]Robert N. Bellah, Richard Madsen, William M. Sullivan and Ann Swidler, *Habits of the Heart: Individualism and Commitment in American Life*, 3rd ed. (Berkeley: University of California Press, 2007).

[73]Robert Putnam, *Bowling Alone: The Collapse and Revival of American Community* (New York: Simon & Schuster, 2000), pp. 93-115.

[74]Robert Wuthnow, *Sharing the Journey: Support Groups and America's Quest for Community* (New York: Free Press, 1994), p. 16.

[75]Evelyn Eaton Whitehead and James D. Whitehead, *Community of Faith: Crafting Christian Communities Today* (Mystic, CT: Twenty-Third Publications, 1992), pp. 42-47.

[76]Tod E. Bolsinger, *It Takes a Church to Raise a Christian: How the Community of God Transforms Lives* (Grand Rapids: Brazos Press, 2004). In arguing that the single end result of

Christian community is to "become like Christ," Bolsinger maintains, "Christian community is an ontologically irreducible organism. It is a living reality that is imbued with the Spirit of God" (ibid., p. 25).

[77]Craig Dykstra, *Growing in the Life of Faith: Education and Christian Practices* (Louisville: Geneva Press, 1999), p. 83.

[78]Simon Chan, *Spiritual Theology: A Systematic Study of the Christian Life* (Downers Grove, IL: InterVarsity Press, 1998), pp. 102-3.

[79]Simon Chan, *Liturgical Theology: The Church as Worshiping Community* (Downers Grove, IL: InterVarsity Press, 2006), p. 24.

[80]Volf, *After Our Likeness*, pp. 135-36. Colin Gunton, "The Church on Earth: The Roots of Community," in *On Being the Church: Essays on the Christian Community*, ed. Colin E. Gunton and Daniel W. Hardy (Edinburgh: T & T Clark, 1989), p. 49.

[81]Gunton, "The Church on Earth," pp. 112-21.

[82]For how the apostle Paul addressed the issue of social identity and community within the Corinthian church in the Greco-Roman world (1 Cor 1–4), see J. Brian Tucker, *You Belong to Christ: Paul and the Formation of Social Identity in 1 Corinthians 1–4* (Eugene, OR: Pickwick, 2010). Tucker predicates the book on Henri Tajfel's social identity theory and John Turner's self-categorization theory.

[83]Michael J. Gorman, *Cruciformity: Paul's Narrative Spirituality of the Cross* (Grand Rapids: Eerdmans, 2001), pp. 214-15.

[84]Bonhoeffer, *Life Together*, pp. 24-25.

[85]Ibid., pp. 26-27.

[86]Henri Nouwen, *Making All Things New: An Invitation to the Spiritual Life* (San Francisco: Harper & Row, 1981), pp. 82-83.

[87]Joseph H. Hellerman, *When the Church Was a Family: Recapturing Jesus' Vision for Authentic Christian Community* (Nashville: B & H Academic, 2009), p. 162.

[88]Ana María Pineda, "Hospitality," in *Practicing Our Faith: A Way of Life for a Searching People*, ed. Dorothy C. Bass (San Francisco: Jossey-Bass, 1997), pp. 29-42. See James C. Wilhoit, *Spiritual Formation as if the Church Mattered: Growing in Christ Through Community* (Grand Rapids: Baker Academic, 2008), p. 150. Peter Scazzero discusses how to live incarnationally in *The Emotionally Healthy Church: A Strategy for Discipleship That Actually Changes Lives* (Grand Rapids: Zondervan, 2003), pp. 172-93.

[89]Nouwen, *Making All Things New*, p. 81.

[90]Karl Barth, *Church Dogmatics* 3.1, *The Doctrine of Creation*, ed. G. W. Bromiley and T. F. Torrance (Edinburgh: T & T Clark, 1960), p. 249.

[91]Smail, *Like Father, Like Son*, p. 281.

[92]Stanley J. Grenz, *Created for Community: Connecting Christian Belief with Christian Living* (Wheaton, IL: Victor Books, 1996), p. 79.

[93]Michael Warren, *Faith, Culture, and the Worshiping Community: Shaping the Practice of the Local Church* (Washington, DC: Pastoral Press, 1993), p. 1.

[94]Brian M. Howell and Jenell Williams Paris, *Introducing Cultural Anthropology: A Christian Perspective* (Grand Rapids: Baker Academic, 2011), pp. 38-40.

[95]On religion, see Almond, *Fragmenting Family*, pp. 180-81. Religion is a cultural identity marker. Regarding music, black spirituals, for example, have characterized the music of African Americans churches as they capture the story and experience of slavery and suffering. See James Earl Massey, "Faith and Christian Life in African-American Spirituals," in *God the Holy Trinity: Reflections on Christian Faith and Practice*, ed. Timothy George (Grand Rapids: Baker, 2006), pp. 57-68; and James Cone, *The Spirituals and the Blues: An Interpretation* (Westport, CT: Greenwood Press, 1972). On play, see Wolfhart Pannenberg's chapter titled "Foundations of Culture," in *Anthropology in Theological Perspective*, trans. Matthew J. O'Connell (Philadelphia: Westminster Press, 1985). Pannenberg develops the notion of play as the "free and creative activity of individuals" (ibid., pp. 321-22), along with language, as formidable contributors to cultural identity and precursors to imagination and reason.

[96]For a helpful approach to culture and human development from an ecological systems perspective, see Urie Bronfenbrenner, *The Ecology of Human Development: Experiments by Nature and Design* (Cambridge, MA: Harvard University Press, 1979). Bronfenbrenner proffers that the nested environment, like a set of Russian dolls, influences the development of the person in four primary levels: (1) *microsystem*, including the immediate environment such as the family, school, peers, neighborhood and church group, (2) the *mesosystem*, including the interaction of two or more microsystems such as the family and school, (3) the *exosystem*, including the extended family, neighbors, media, friends of the family, and (4) the *macrosystem*, the overarching and complex ideological system.

[97]Katherine Van Wormer and Fred H. Besthorn, *Human Behavior and the Social Environment: Groups, Communities, and Organizations*, 2nd ed. (Oxford: Oxford University Press, 2011), p. 165.

[98]Barbara Rogoff, *The Cultural Nature of Human Development* (Oxford: Oxford University Press, 2003), pp. 37-62.

[99]H. Richard Niebuhr, *Christ and Culture* (New York: HarperSanFrancisco, 2001), p. 16.

[100]The Greek word *ethne*, which appears in Matthew 28:19 and is translated as "nations," refers to people groups, as opposed to specific nations. For a comprehensive overview of global Christianity highlighting gospel advance in the global South, see Philip Jenkins, *The Next Christendom: The Coming of Global Christianity*, 3rd ed. (Oxford: Oxford University Press, 2011).

[101]Niebuhr, *Christ and Culture*. Although the book deals with these five types, a summary of them appears on pages xliii-lv.

[102]Howell and Paris, *Introducing Cultural Anthropology*, p. 40.

[103]For more on the persecuted church, see Brother Andrew and Al Janssen, *Secret Believers: What Happens When Muslims Believe in Christ* (Grand Rapids: Revell, 2007); Anneke Companjen, *Singing Through the Night: Courageous Stories of Faith from Women in the Persecuted Church* (Grand Rapids: Revell, 2007); and Caroline Cox and Benedict Rogers, *The Very Stones Cry Out: The Persecuted Church: Pain, Passion, and Praise* (London: Continuum, 2011).

[104]Sherwood G. Lingenfelter, "Mind, Emotion, Culture, and the Person: Perspectives from Cultural Anthropology and Scripture," in *Christian Perspectives on Being Human: A Multidisciplinary Approach to Integration*, ed. J. P. Moreland and David M. Ciocchi (Grand Rapids: Baker, 1993), p. 131.

[105]Ibid., p. 137.

[106]Smail, *Like Father, Like Son*, p. 232.

[107]Through stories, Miriam Adeney shows how the gospel has been shared throughout diverse cultures and nations (*Kingdom Without Borders: The Untold Story of Global Christianity* [Downers Grove, IL: InterVarsity Press, 2009], pp. 274-75).

[108]Paul-Gordon Chandler, *God's Global Mosaic: What We Can Learn from Christians Around the World* (Downers Grove, IL: InterVarsity Press, 2000), pp. 16-17.

[109]Brian Parkinson, Agneta H. Fischer and Antony S. R. Manstead, *Emotion in Social Relations: Cultural, Group, and Interpersonal Processes* (New York: Psychology Press, 2005), p. 45.

[110]Howell and Paris, *Introducing Cultural Anthropology*, p. 41.

[111]Chandler, *God's Global Mosaic*, p. 17.

7 Intellect: Our Minds

[1]Joab Jackson, "IBM Watson Vanquishes Human Jeopardy Foes," *PC World*, February 17, 2011, www.pcworld.com/businesscenter/article/219893/ibm_watson_vanquishes_human_jeopardy_foes.html.

[2]Ibid. For example, under the category of US cities, the clue was "Its largest airport is named for a World War II hero; its second largest, for a World War II battle." Watson responded "Toronto," a Canadian city, rather than Chicago, the correct response.

[3]Implying the work of Creator God, John Polkinghorne rhetorically says, "*If the brain were a computer*, one would have to ask the question of what had programmed it" (*Science and Theology: An Introduction* [Minneapolis: Fortress Press, 1998], p. 59).

[4]See Ronald Kotulak, *Inside the Brain: Revolutionary Discoveries of How the Mind Works* (Kansas City, MO: Andrews McMeel, 1997), p. 5.

[5]For the association between feeling and knowing, see Antonio R. Damasio, *The Feeling of What Happens: Body and Emotion in the Making of Consciousness* (New York: Harcourt Brace, 1999), pp. 67-71.

[6]On Irenaeus, see Anthony A. Hoekema, *Created in God's Image* (Grand Rapids: Eerdmans, 1986), p. 34. Hoekema comments that Irenaeus's emphasis on rationality in interpreting the *imago Dei* is not surprising, given the supreme emphasis placed on reason by Greek philosophers and Roman culture. On Thomas Aquinas, see *The Summa Theologica of Saint Thomas Aquinas*, 1.93.2, ed. Fathers of the English Dominican Province, Great Books of the Western World 19 (Chicago: William Benton, 1952), p. 493. Aquinas describe three stages of knowing and loving God, beginning with an aptitude, then in an actual disposition, then in actual reality. Also see Hoekema, *Created in God's Image*, p. 36; Blaise Pascal, *Pensées*, trans. W. F. Trotter (Grand Rapids: Christian Classics Ethereal Library, n.d.), p. 69, www.ccel.org/ccel/pascal/pensees.pdf. Referring to humankind as a "thinking reed" (#347), Pascal proffered: "Thoughts constitute the greatness of man," (#346) and "All dignity consists of thought" (#347).

[7]The Shema, taken from Deuteronomy 6:4-5, became the Jewish declaration of faith, recited by pious Jews at the beginning of every synagogue service.

[8]Although the phrase *faith and learning* is the more common semantic order in Christian academic circles and literature, I have intentionally inverted the order to present perspectives of

learning common to all persons. By doing so, however, I do not relegate faith as of secondary importance in the learning process.

[9]David Parks, "The Vulnerability of Persons: Religion and Neurology," in *From Cells to Souls—and Beyond: Changing Portraits of Human Nature*, ed. Malcolm Jeeves (Grand Rapids: Eerdmans, 2004), pp. 34-57, esp. p. 43. In asking the question, Who moves the mover?, Parks contends that despite scientific knowledge and understanding, we cannot answer this question by scientific knowledge alone.

[10]D. Gareth Jones, "The Emergence of Persons," in Jeeves, *From Cells to Souls*, pp. 11-33, esp. p. 14.

[11]Ibid., p. 25. For more on the functions of the human brain, see Ronald Kotulak, *Inside the Brain: Revolutionary Discoveries of How the Mind Works* (Kansas City, MO: Andrews McMeel, 1997).

[12]On social relationships, see Daniel J. Siegel, *The Developing Mind: How Relationships and the Brain Interact to Shape Who We Are*, 2nd ed. (New York: Guilford Press, 2012); and Louis Cozolino, *The Neuroscience of Human Relationship: Attachment and the Developing Social Brain* (New York: W. W. Norton, 2006), esp. pp. 11-19. Regarding nutrition, D. Gareth Jones states, "Malnutrition interferes with a child's motivation as well as the ability to concentrate and learn," in *Our Fragile Brains: A Christian Perspective on Brain Research* (Downers Grove, IL: InterVarsity Press, 1981), p. 181. In addition to nutrition, other external factors affecting cognitive development include the influence of (1) prenatal care, (2) family and caregiving environments, (3) enriching learning experiences and schooling, (4) infectious diseases, and (5) environmental toxins. See Robert J. Sternberg and Elena L. Grigorenko, *Environmental Effects on Cognitive Abilities* (Mahwah, NJ: Lawrence Erlbaum, 2001).

[13]René Descartes, "Discourse 4," in *Discourse on Method and the Meditations*, trans. F. E. Sutcliffe (Harmondsworth, UK: Penguin, 1968), p. 53.

[14]On how feeling, emotion and cognition work in tandem, see Antonio Damasio, *Descartes' Error: Emotion, Reason, and the Human Mind* (New York: Penguin, 2005). Based on his work as a neuroscientist with brain-damaged patients, Damasio argues that feelings, as derived from emotions, serve as "internal guides" to direct thoughts and communication (ibid., p. xiii). With many other scientists, Damasio attributes this complexity to evolution. However, his discoveries acknowledge the limits of science in understanding the human mind. See also David Yun Dai and Robert J. Sternberg, "Beyond Cognitivism: Toward an Integrated Understanding of Intellectual Functioning and Development," in *Motivation, Emotion, and Cognition: Integrative Perspectives on Intellectual Functioning and Development*, ed. David Yun Dai and Robert J. Sternberg (Mahwah, NJ: Lawrence Erlbaum, 2004), pp. 3-38. Dai and Sternberg call for "a multidimensional approach to understanding intellectual functioning," including affect, neurobiology, psychology, personal agency, levels of learning, and social/cultural factors (ibid., p. 8). Despite an absence of a faith-based worldview, their writings bear witness to God's genius in designing the human mind.

[15]Susan A. Greenfield, *The Human Brain: A Guided Tour* (New York: Basic Books, 1998). Oxford neuroscientist Greenfield acknowledges that the regions of the brain are organized

as a cohesive system "for the most part in a mysterious way" (ibid., p. 31). Despite all scientific research prowess, we are still unable to plumb the depths of God's miraculous creation of the human body and the workings of the mind.

[16]Matthew T. Dickerson, *The Mind and the Machine: What It Means to Be Human and Why It Matters* (Grand Rapids: Brazos, 2011), pp. 189-207. Dickerson argues that humans are more than mere computers, as the *Matrix* film trilogy (1999–2003) suggests; they are integrated beings fashioned by Creator God. He counters the writings of atheistic scientists and naturalists such as Richard Dawkins in order to further a biblical defense of faith and science, noting that some of the world's most prominent scientists, such as Nicholas Copernicus and Sir Isaac Newton, believed in God as Creator of the universe (ibid., pp. 181-82).

[17]David A. Hogue, *Remembering the Future, Imaging the Past: Story, Ritual, and the Human Brain* (Cleveland: Pilgrim Press, 2003), p. 196.

[18]Andrew Newberg and Mark Robert Waldman, *How God Changes Your Brain: Breakthrough Findings from a Leading Neuroscientist* (New York: Ballantine Books, 2008), pp. 43-44.

[19]Clifford Williams, *The Life of the Mind: A Christian Perspective* (Grand Rapids: Baker Academic, 2002), p. 37.

[20]Gene Edward Veith Jr., *Loving God with All Your Mind: Thinking as a Christian in the Postmodern World*, rev. ed. (Wheaton, IL: Crossway, 2003), p. 150.

[21]A. G. Sertillanges, *The Intellectual Life: Its Spirit, Conditions, Methods*, trans. Mary Ryan (Washington, DC: The Catholic University of America Press, 1987), p. vii. See also James W. Sire, *Habits of the Mind: Intellectual Life as a Christian Calling* (Downers Grove, IL: InterVarsity Press, 2000), pp. 10, 89.

[22]John R. W. Stott, *Your Mind Matters: The Place of the Mind in the Christian Life* (Downers Grove, IL: InterVarsity Press, 1972), pp. 10, 11.

[23]Ibid., pp. 12-24.

[24]Ibid., pp. 29-55.

[25]See Os Guinness, *Fit Bodies, Fat Minds: Why Evangelicals Don't Think and What to Do About It* (Grand Rapids: Baker, 1994); and Mark A. Noll, *The Scandal of the Evangelical Mind* (Grand Rapids: Eerdmans, 1994).

[26]J. P. Moreland, *Love Your God with All Your Mind: The Role of Reason in the Life of the Soul* (Colorado Springs: NavPress, 1997), pp. 16, 65.

[27]Alister E. McGrath, *The Passionate Intellect: Christian Faith and the Discipleship of the Mind* (Downers Grove, IL: InterVarsity Press, 2010), pp. 19-21.

[28]Addressing the tension between faith and reason, in that faith looks forward to an eschatological future whereas reason looks to the present, Wolfhart Pannenberg concludes that "faith cannot stand in opposition to reason," in *Basic Questions in Theology*, Collected Essays 2, trans. George H. Kehm (Philadelphia: Fortress Press, 1971), p. 64.

[29]Anselm of Canterbury, *The Prayers and Meditations of the St. Anselm with the Proslogion*, trans. Benedicta Ward (London: Penguin, 1973), p. 244.

[30]Richard T. Hughes, *How Christian Faith Can Sustain the Life of the Mind* (Grand Rapids: Eerdmans, 2001), pp. 2-8, 57-96. For example, the Roman Catholic tradition provides a "stunning array of intellectual resources" (ibid., p. 59) for over nearly two thousand years,

drawing from the works of Irenaeus, Origen, Augustine, Anselm, Aquinas and Bernard Lonergan, to name a few. In the Reformed tradition, the works of John Calvin, who advanced that all truth is God's truth, have directly influenced a more holistic view of learning and faith integration. In the Anabaptist or Mennonite tradition, the life of the mind is balanced with an emphasis on ethics, involving hands and heart. Martin Luther's works, representing the Lutheran tradition, assert the sovereignty of God and the propensity of the human mind to be wrong, which opens the door for honest inquiry and engagement. Each of these four traditions contributes to the life of the mind by higher educational initiatives that have furthered their vision and values.

[31]For how creeds provide foundations for the Christian faith, see Mark Noll, *Jesus Christ and the Life of the Mind* (Grand Rapids: Eerdmans, 2011), pp. 11-22; and Jaroslav Pelikan, *Credo: Historical and Theological Guide to Creeds and Confessions of Faith in the Christian Tradition* (New Haven, CT: Yale University Press, 2003).

[32]Noll, *Jesus Christ and the Life of the Mind*, p. 19.

[33]Diogenes Allen, "Intellectual Inquiry and Spiritual Formation," in *Essentials of Christian Community*, ed. David F. Ford and Dennis L. Stamps (Edinburgh: T & T Clark, 1996), p. 255.

[34]The building of the Tower of Babel provides a classic illustration of knowledge being misappropriated in opposition to God's purposes (Gen 11:1-9). Through their mental capacity and one common language, the people united to build a tower to reach heaven. Realizing their motivations, God confused their language and scattered them. Mary Stewart Van Leeuwen refers to this disposition as "self-glorifying and consequently blasphemous" (*The Person in Psychology: A Contemporary Christian Appraisal* [Grand Rapids: Eerdmans, 1985], pp. 142-43).

[35]Sertillanges, *Intellectual Life*, p. 19.

[36]Moreland, *Love Your God with All Your Mind*, pp. 106-11; and Sertillanges, *Intellectual Life*, pp. 24-25.

[37]Dallas Willard, *The Divine Conspiracy: Rediscovering Our Hidden Life in God* (San Francisco: HarperSanFrancisco, 1998), p. 95.

[38]Sertillanges, *Intellectual Life*, 184.

[39]W. E. Vine, "Ginōskō" and "Gnōsis," in *Vine's Expository Dictionary of Old and New Testament Words* (Old Tappan, NJ: Revell, 1981), pp. 298, 301.

[40]See "Epiginōskō" and "Epignōsis," in ibid., pp. 299, 301.

[41]Some readers may criticize my inclusion of secular learning theories to account for human learning because they are based on nonbiblical material. Each approach, however, provides a plausible explanation regarding how the human mind works. It would seem evident that the human mind learns through (1) precept (teaching through information), (2) example (role modeling), (3) observation (perception), (4) rehearsal (practice and interaction), and (5) trial and error (experience and engagement), which these four selected learning perspectives are based on.

[42]Perspectives not addressed here but nonetheless noteworthy include the seminal work of linguist and cognitive scientist Noam Chomsky in *Language and the Mind* (Cambridge, MA: Cambridge University Press, 2006). Chomsky advanced the notion that children are born with the innate capacity for learning language and that children's brains naturally learn rules

of grammar. See also the influential work of Urie Bronfenbrenner, who highlighted an ecological systems approach to understanding children's development. See his *Making Human Beings Human: Bioecological Perspectives on Human Development* (Thousand Oaks, CA: Sage, 2005). Bronfenbrenner highlighted the importance of social environments in childhood cognitive development and the consequences of the breakdown of the family that lead to various negative outcomes in American youth. His many programs, including "Head Start," aim to maximize children's early learning potential for future academic success and well-being.

[43]The Piagetian stages include (1) sensorimotor, ages 0-2, where learning occurs through senses and movement; (2) preoperational, ages 2-7, where language and motor skills further develop cognitive skills through cause and effect relationships; (3) concrete operations, ages 7-11, where logical and abstract thinking begins to develop; and (4) formal operations, ages 11-12 onward, where deductive reasoning emerges. See Jean Piaget and Bärbel Inhelder, *The Psychology of the Child*, trans. Helen Weaver (New York: Basic Books, 2000).

[44]Lev Vygotsky, *Mind in Society: The Development of Higher Psychological Processes* (Cambridge, MA: Harvard University Press, 1978), pp. 85-86; and *Thought and Language* (Cambridge, MA: MIT Press, 1962).

[45]Albert Bandura, *Social Learning Theory* (Englewood Cliffs, NJ: Prentice Hall, 1977); and *Social Foundations of Thought and Action: A Social Cognitive Theory* (Englewood Cliffs, NJ: Prentice Hall, 1986).

[46]Albert Bandura, *Self-Efficacy: The Exercise of Control* (New York: W. H. Freeman, 1997), esp. pp. 212-58.

[47]Howard Gardner, *Frames of Mind* (New York: Basic Books, 1983); and *Multiple Intelligences: The Theory in Practice* (New York: Basic Books, 1993), pp. 5-12. Subsequent scholars have expanded these original seven.

[48]N. T. Wright, *The Epistle of Paul to the Colossians and to Philemon: An Introduction and Commentary*, Tyndale New Testament Commentaries (Grand Rapids: Eerdmans, 1986), pp. 79-80.

[49]Veith, *Loving God with All Your Mind*, p. 94.

[50]C. S. Lewis, "Christianity and Culture," in *Christian Reflections*, ed. Walter Hooper (Grand Rapids: Eerdmans, 1967), p. 33.

[51]Polkinghorne, *Science and Theology*, p. 49. As both a theologian and a scientist, Polkinghorne discusses the nature of humanity and the relationship between the brain and the mind, which he submits is an "unresolved dispute" (ibid., p. 56).

[52]Noll, *Jesus Christ and the Life of the Mind*, pp. 25, ix-x.

[53]Sire, *Habits of the Mind*, pp. 65, 89.

[54]See Noll's reference to Os Guinness's assertion that "Evangelicals need to repent of their refusal to think Christianly and to develop the mind of Christ" (*Scandal of the Evangelical Mind*, p. 23). Noll puts forth a clarion call for rigorous intellectual pursuit in Christian colleges, universities and seminaries (ibid., pp. 15-27).

[55]David S. Dockery, *Renewing Minds: Serving Church and Society Through Christian Higher Education* (Nashville: B & H Academic, 2008), pp. 38-39.

[56]Ibid., pp. 77-82.

[57]Ibid., p. 75.

[58]Charles Malik, "The Two Tasks," in *The Two Tasks of the Christian Scholar: Redeeming the Soul, Redeeming the Mind*, ed. William Lane Craig and Paul Gould (Wheaton, IL: Crossway, 2007), pp. 55-65; see esp. p. 59.

[59]George M. Marsden, *The Outrageous Idea of Christian Scholarship* (Oxford: Oxford University Press, 1997), pp. 44-58.

[60]Hughes, *Life of the Mind*, p. 11.

[61]David Yun Dai and Robert J. Sternberg, "Beyond Cognitivism: Toward an Integrated Understanding of Intellectual Functioning and Development," in Dai and Sternberg, *Motivation, Emotion, and Cognition*, p. 28.

[62]James W. Sire, *The Universe Next Door: A Basic Worldview Catalog*, 5th ed. (Downers Grove, IL: InterVarsity Press, 2009), p. 20. See also Sire's *Naming the Elephant: Worldview as a Concept* (Downers Grove, IL: InterVarsity Press, 2004), pp. 121-36. Sire updates his definition of worldview to "A worldview is a commitment, a fundamental orientation of the heart, that can be expressed as a story or in a set of presuppositions (assumptions which may be true, partially true or entirely false) which we hold (consciously or subconsciously, consistently or inconsistently) about the basic constitution of reality, and that provides the foundation on which we live and move and have our being" (*Naming the Elephant*, p. 122).

[63]Dockery, *Renewing Minds*, pp. 92-99.

[64]Sire, *Universe Next Door*, pp. 21-23. Sire poses seven questions, the answers to which define a person's worldview: (1) What is the prime reality—the really real? (2) What is the nature of external reality (the world around us)? (3) What is a human being? (4) What happens to a person at death? (5) Why is it possible to know anything at all? (6) How do we know what is right from wrong? and (7) What is the meaning of human history? Questions 1-4 and 7 are ontological, question 5 is epistemological, and question 6 is ethical.

[65]James Davison Hunter, *Culture Wars: The Struggle to Define America* (New York: Basic Books, 1991), pp. 107-35.

[66]Ibid., pp. 322-23. See Williams, *Life of the Mind*, p. 79.

[67]J. P. Moreland, *Kingdom Triangle: Recover the Christian Mind, Renovate the Soul, Restore the Spirit's Power* (Grand Rapids: Zondervan, 2007), p. 24. Moreland focuses on scientific naturalism and postmodernism in his analysis of worldview, while calling for the recovery of knowledge of faith and reason.

[68]Ibid., pp. 26-32.

[69]Sire, *Universe Next Door*, pp. 47-65.

[70]Ibid., p. 85.

[71]Carl Sagan, *Cosmos* (New York: Random House, 1980); Stephen Hawking, *A Brief History of Time* (New York: Bantam, 1996).

[72]Richard Dawkins, *The God Delusion* (New York: Mariner Books, 2008) and *The Blind Watchmaker* (New York: W. W. Norton, 1986). Christopher Hitchens, *God Is Not Great: How Religion Poisons Everything* (New York: Hatchet, 2007). Sam Harris, *End of Faith: Religion, Terror, and the End of Reason* (New York: W. W. Norton, 2005).

[73]See John Polkinghorne, *Beyond Science: The Wider Human Context* (Cambridge: Cambridge University Press, 1998); *Science and Theology*; and John Polkinghorne and Michael Welker,

Faith in the Living God: A Dialogue (Minneapolis: Fortress Press, 2001).

[74]John C. Polkinghorne, *Belief in God in an Age of Science* (New Haven, CT: Yale University Press, 2003), p. 19.

[75]Francis S. Collins, "Introduction," in *Belief: Readings on the Reason for Faith* (New York: HarperOne, 2010), pp. vii-xviii; and *The Language of God: A Scientist Presents Evidence for Belief* (New York: Free Press, 2006), pp. 11-56.

[76]See Paul Kurtz, *Humanistic Manifesto I and II* (Amherst, NY: Prometheus Books, 1973) and *Humanist Manifesto 2000: A Call for a New Planetary Humanism* (Amherst, NY: Prometheus Books, 2000), pp. 31-34.

[77]Francis Schaeffer, *A Christian Manifesto* (Wheaton, IL: Crossway, 2005), esp. chaps. 2-3.

[78]Sire, *Universe Next Door*, pp. 94-119.

[79]Friedrich Nietzsche, *Thus Spoke Zarathustra*, trans. R. J. Hollingdale (London: Penguin, 2011).

[80]For an introduction to postmodern thought, see James K. A. Smith, *Who's Afraid of Postmodernism: Taking Derrida, Lyotard, and Foucault to Church* (Grand Rapids: Baker Academic, 2006). Smith proposes viewing postmodern thought as an opportunity to recover ancient Christian themes and traditions (pp. 109-46).

[81]See Moreland, *Love Your God with All Your Mind*, pp. 32-38; and Juliet Schor, *The Overspent American: Why We Want What We Don't Need* (New York: Basic Books, 1999).

[82]Christian writers Brian McLaren, Leonard Sweet and Robert E. Webber embrace the challenge of calling the church to cultural relevance and engagement with postmodernity.

[83]Smith, *Who's Afraid of Postmodernism*, p. 30. Smith takes his cues from Francis Schaeffer's *The God Who Is There*, 30th anniv. ed. (Downers Grove, IL: InterVarsity Press, 1998); and *Escape from Reason* (Downers Grove, IL: InterVarsity Press, 2006).

[84]Sire, *Universe Next Door*, pp. 28-47.

[85]Malik, "The Two Tasks," p. 64.

[86]McGrath, *Passionate Intellect*, p. 13.

[87]The Greek verb for "be transformed" *is metamorphoo*, similar to the English word *metamorphosis*. The few occurrences of the word in the New Testament include (1) the transfiguration narratives (Mt 17:2; Mk 9:2), where Jesus' appearance was completely changed before Peter, James and John; and (2) Paul's reference to believers ongoing change into Christlikeness (2 Cor 3:18). See F. F. Bruce, *The Epistle of Paul to the Romans: An Introduction and Commentary* (Leicester, UK: Inter-Varsity Press, 1963), pp. 226-27.

[88]Jesus shows us how to oppose the enemy of our souls. In the desert Jesus confronts the devil's three temptations to compromise the purposes of God with a confident belief in and declaration of the Word of God (Mt 4:1-11).

[89]C. E. B. Cranfield, *Romans: A Shorter Commentary* (Grand Rapids: Eerdmans, 1985), p. 296.

[90]Grant R. Osborne, *Romans* (Downers Grove, IL: InterVarsity Press, 2004), p. 321.

[91]Anders Nygren, *Commentary on Romans*, trans. Carl C. Rasmussen (Philadelphia: Fortress, 1949), pp. 419-20.

[92]John R. W. Stott, *The Message of Romans* (Downers Grove, IL: InterVarsity Press, 2001), pp. 323-24.

[93]Ibid., p. 324.

[94]Karl Barth, *The Epistle to the Romans*, 6th ed., trans. Edwyn C. Hoskyns (Oxford: Oxford University Press, 1968), p. 436; and James D. G. Dunn, *The Theology of Paul the Apostle* (Grand Rapids: Eerdmans, 1998), p. 74.

[95]Van Leeuwen, *Person in Psychology*, p. 174.

[96]Richard A. Swenson claims we are "breaking life's speed limit" because of chronic hurry and overload (*The Overload Syndrome: Learning to Live Within Your Limits* [Colorado Springs: NavPress, 1998], p. 124).

[97]Neil Postman, *Amusing Ourselves to Death: Public Discourse in the Age of Show Business*, 20th anniv. ed. (New York: Penguin, 2005).

[98]Caitlin Johnson, "Cutting Through Advertising Clutter," CBS News, February 11, 2009, www.cbsnews.com/stories/2006/09/17/sunday/main2015684.shtml.

[99]Wayne Freidman, "Global TV Ad Growth Forecast at 3% for 2013, 6% Next Year," *Media Daily News*, June 14, 2013, www.mediapost.com/publications/article/202434/global-tv-ad-growth-forecast-at-3-in-2013-6-nex.html#axzz2WI6IJDaI.

[100]"How Many Advertisements Is a Person Exposed to in a Day?" *4A's*, August 2011, www.aaaa.org/agency/pubs/NewEssentials/Documents/Ad%20Marketing%20and%20Media/Ad%20exposure%20%20PDF%20version%202011-08.pdf.

[101]Victoria J. Rideout, Ulla G. Goehr and Donald F. Roberts, "GENERATION M^2: Media in the Lives of 8- to 18-Year-Olds: A Kaiser Family Foundation Study," Kaiser Family Foundation, January 1, 2010, www.kff.org/entmedia/upload/8010.pdf, p. 2. This is the third Kaiser Family Foundation study evaluating media usage trends in children. The others were in 1999 and 2004.

[102]Ibid., p. 9.

[103]See the summary of "Key findings" in "Ground-Breaking Study of Video Viewing Finds Younger Boomers Consume More Video Media Than Any Other Group," Council for Research Excellence, March 26, 2009, www.prnewswire.com/news-releases/ground-breaking-study-of-video-viewing-finds-younger-boomers-consume-more-video-media-than-any-other-group-61955592.html.

[104]For a redemptive comparison of human artistry and spirituality, see Steven R. Guthrie, *Creator Spirit: The Holy Spirit and the Art of Becoming Human* (Grand Rapids: Baker Academic, 2011), p. 209.

[105]David Kinnaman, *You Lost Me: Why Young Christians Are Leaving Church . . . and Rethinking Faith* (Grand Rapids: Baker, 2011), p. 42. For a sociological perspective, see also Robert Wuthnow, *After the Baby Boomers: How Twenty- and Thirty-Somethings Are Shaping the Future of American Religion* (Princeton, NJ: Princeton University Press, 2007).

[106]Susan A. Greenfield, *Tomorrow's People: How 21st Century Technology Is Changing the Way We Think and Feel* (London: Penguin, 2009), pp. 265-72.

[107]Kimberly S. Young, *Caught in the Net: How to Recognize the Signs of Internet Addiction—and a Winning Strategy to Recover* (New York: John Wiley, 1998); and Kimberly S. Young, Xiao Dong Yue and Li Yung, "Prevalence Estimates and Etiological Models of Internet Addiction," in *Internet Addiction: A Handbook and Guide to Evaluation and Treatment*, ed. Kimberly S. Young and Cristiano Nabuco de Abreu (Hoboken, NJ: John Wiley, 2011), pp. 3-18. See Nicholas Carr, *The Shallows: What the Internet Is Doing to Our Brains* (New York: W. W.

Norton, 2011), who argues that habits of surfing the Net foster interruption and distraction that intercept good habits of mind.

[108]Terrance Lindvall and J. Matthew Melton, "The Entertainment Media Culture," in *Elements of a Christian Worldview*, ed. Michael D. Palmer (Springfield, MO: Legion Press, 1998), pp. 378-410.

[109]According to a 2011 study of 799 teens, the average number of texts sent daily by teens rose from fifty in 2009 to sixty in 2011. See Amanda Lenhart, "Teens, Smartphones and Texting," Pew Internet and American Life Project, March 19, 2012, www.pewinternet.org/Reports/2012/Teens-and-smartphones.

[110]William M. Struthers, *Wired for Intimacy: How Pornography Hijacks the Male Brain* (Downers Grove, IL: InterVarsity Press, 2009).

[111]Gene Edward Veith and Christopher L. Stamper, *Christians in a .com World: Getting Connected Without Being Consumed* (Wheaton, IL: Crossway, 2000), p. 146. These authors explain, "The key to a Christian appropriation of the Internet is to apply what Christianity has always taught about liberty, community, and gatekeeping" (ibid., p. 104). They see the need for Christian love as the foundation for online community and discernment for filtering voluminous information and ungodly material. Websites such as the Christian Classics Ethereal Library (ccel.org) operated by Calvin College provide one example of how the Internet contributes to Christian formation by making published Christian materials accessible for free.

8 Vocation: Our Life Purpose and Calling

[1]Margaret Washington, ed., *Narrative of Sojourner Truth* (New York: Vintage Books, 1993), pp. 6-7; and Margaret Washington, *Sojourner Truth's America* (Chicago: University of Illinois Press, 2009), pp. 16-17.

[2]Hertha Pauli, *Her Name Was Sojourner Truth* (New York: Avon Books, 1962), p. 11.

[3]See Washington, *Narrative of Sojourner Truth*, p. xxxii.

[4]Ibid., pp. 147-48.

[5]For example, Truth's efforts led to the desegregation of Washington, D.C., streetcars and to women's rights involvement. For example, see her infamous "Ar'n't I a Woman" speech delivered in 1851 at the Ohio Women's Rights Convention (Washington, *Narrative of Sojourner Truth*, pp. xii, 117-18).

[6]For excellent anthologies that address perspectives on vocation from diverse writers, see Mark R. Schwehn and Dorothy C. Bass, eds., *Leading Lives That Matter: What We Should Do and Who We Should Be* (Grand Rapids, Eerdmans, 2006); William C. Placher, ed., *Callings: Twenty Centuries of Christian Wisdom on Vocation* (Grand Rapids: Eerdmans, 2005); and Gilbert C. Meilaender, ed., *Working: Its Meaning and Its Limits* (Notre Dame, IN: University of Notre Dame Press, 2000).

[7]Douglas John Hall, *Imaging God: Dominion as Stewardship* (Eugene, OR: Wipf & Stock, 1986), p. 108.

[8]Søren Kierkegaard, *Works of Love* (Princeton, NJ: Princeton University Press, 1946), p. 52.

[9]Gary D. Badcock, *The Way of Life: A Theology of Christian Vocation* (Grand Rapids: Eerdmans, 1998), p. 108.

[10]Douglas J. Schuurman, *Vocation: Discerning Our Callings in Life* (Grand Rapids: Eerdmans,

2004), p. 79. Dietrich Bonhoeffer, "The Place of Responsibility: Vocation," in *Ethics* (New York: Touchstone, 1995), p. 251. For a supporting view of vocation as discipleship, see Mark Jensen, *Shattered Vocations* (Nashville: Broadman, 1990), pp. 114-39. Jenson states, "One of the things that life as a disciple means is that we can be delivered from a vocation that is too narrowly conceived" (ibid., p. 138).

[11]Thérèse of Lisieux, *The Story of a Soul: The Autobiography of Thérèse of Lisieux,* trans. John Clarke (Washington, DC: ICS Publications, 1976), p. 194. See also Thomas Looney, "Vocation as Proclamation of Love," in *Doing More with Life: Connecting Christian Higher Education to a Call to Service,* ed. Michael R. Miller (Waco, TX: Baylor University Press, 2007), pp. 35-48.

[12]For more on Jesus as a model of vocation, see Urban C. von Wahlde, "'My Food Is to Do the Will of the One Who Sent Me' (John 4:34): Jesus as Model of Vocation in the Gospel of John," in *Revisiting the Idea of Vocation: Theological Explorations,* ed. John C. Haughey (Washington, DC: Catholic University Press, 2004), pp. 53-76.

[13]Michael R. Miller, "Introduction: A Vision of Vocation," in Miller, *Doing More with Life,* p. 13.

[14]Gordon T. Smith, *Courage and Calling: Embracing Your God-Given Potential* (Downers Grove, IL: InterVarsity Press, 1999), p. 9.

[15]These five perspectives on vocation by no means offer a developmental history of the concept of vocation. Other worthy foci that are beyond the scope of this chapter include (1) an expanded Roman view of work, (2) the development of Protestantism and the Puritan work ethic during the sixteenth and seventeenth centuries, (3) the work of Scottish economist and philosopher Adam Smith (1723–1790), and (4) the theories of German economist and philosopher Karl Marx (1818–1883). Also see Max Weber's influential essay "The Protestant Ethic and the Spirit of Capitalism," in *The Protestant Ethic and the "Spirit" of Capitalism and Other Writings,* trans. Peter Baehr and Gordon C. Wells (New York: Penguin, 2002), pp. 1-202; Adam Smith, *An Inquiry into the Nature and Cause of the Wealth of Nations,* ed. Edwin Cannon (Chicago: University of Chicago Press, 1976); and Karl Marx, *Capital: A Critique of Political Economy,* 3 vols. (New York: Penguin, 1993).

[16]W. R. Forrester, *Christian Vocation* (New York: Charles Scribner's, 1953), p. 126.

[17]Lee Hardy, *The Fabric of This World: Inquires into Calling, Career Choice, and the Design of Human Work* (Grand Rapids: Eerdmans, 1990), p. 7. Hardy provides a commendable overview of human work (see pp. 3-75).

[18]Forrester, *Christian Vocation,* p. 122.

[19]Ibid., pp. 123-24.

[20]Sandra R. Joshel, *Slavery in the Roman World* (Cambridge: Cambridge University Press, 2010), pp. 29-76; Steven A. Epstein, *Wage Labor and Guilds in Medieval Europe* (Chapel Hill: University of North Carolina Press, 1991), pp. 10-49.

[21]See chapter two on the four perspectives of the *imago Dei.* The first perspective on humankind's ability to think and reason aligns with this view of vocation, whereas the third perspective aligns with a dominion perspective, in that Adam and Eve were given dominion to work and take care of the Garden.

[22]Augustine, *The Trinity,* 1.8, trans. Stephen McKenna (Washington, DC: Catholic University of America Press, 1963), p. 25.

[23]Thomas Aquinas, *Summa Theologica* 2, Q.2.180, art. 4., trans. Fathers of the English Dominican Province (Chicago: Encyclopedia Britannica/University of Chicago, 1952), p. 611.

[24]Hardy, *Fabric of This World*, p. 19.

[25]During the Middle Ages, people who desired to escape judgment for confessed and forgiven sin purchased indulgences, believing that through specific good works and prayers their sins would be absolved. Sale of indulgences by the Catholic Church became an abusive, profit-generating practice, which Martin Luther condemned.

[26]Benedict of Nursia, *The Rule of St. Benedict*, trans. Anthony C. Meisel and M. L. dei Mastro (New York: Image Books, 1975), p. 86.

[27]Hardy, *Fabric of This World*, p. 24.

[28]See Forrester, *Christian Vocation*, pp. 146-51.

[29]Gene Edward Veith Jr., *God at Work: Your Christian Vocation in All of Life* (Wheaton, IL: Crossway, 2002), pp. 39-40.

[30]Gustaf Wingren, *Luther on Vocation*, trans. Carl C. Rasmussen (Eugene, OR: Wipf & Stock, 2004), p. 10.

[31]Hardy, *Fabric of This World*, p. 46.

[32]John Calvin, *Institutes of the Christian Religion*. 1.16.3, ed. John T. McNeill, trans. Philip Schaff, Library of Christian Classics 1 (Philadelphia: Westminster Press, 1960), p. 200.

[33]Ibid., 3.7.5-7, pp. 695-98.

[34]Hardy, *Fabric of This World*, p. 48.

[35]Weber, "Protestant Ethic and the Spirit of Capitalism," pp. 1-202. As a German sociologist and economist, Weber (1864–1920) explored the sociology of religion with the rise of capitalism, specifically the impact of Protestantism on economics.

[36]For a history of this shift see A. R. Vidler, *A Century of Social Catholicism* (London: SPCK, 1964).

[37]Leo XIII, *Encyclical Letter of His Holiness Pope Leo XIII on the Condition of the Working Classes: Rerum Novarum* (Boston: Pauline Books, 2000). An encyclical is an open papal letter circulated worldwide on an important Catholic Church issue or doctrine.

[38]John Paul II, *On Human Work: Encyclical Laborem Exercens* (Washington, DC: United States Catholic Conference Publishing, 1981).

[39]Ibid., p. 7.

[40]Based on Genesis 1:26-28, the dominion perspective, highlighted in chapter two, relates to interpreting the *imago Dei* as humankind's "dominion" or caring responsibility over the earth as God's representatives.

[41]Hardy, *Fabric of this World*, p. 71.

[42]Miroslav Volf, *Toward a Theology of Work* (New York: Oxford University Press, 1991), p. 5.

[43]For a critique of *Laborem Exercens*, see Stanley Hauerwas's chapter titled "Work as Co-Creation: A Critique of a Remarkably Bad Idea," in *In Good Company: The Church as Polis* (Notre Dame, IN: University of Notre Dame Press, 1995), pp. 109-24. Hauerwas faults the encyclical for being theologically deficient and presenting social and economic theory that "distorts the nature and significance of work in most people's lives" (ibid., p. 109). Hauerwas refutes the premise that the *imago Dei* relates to being cocreators with God, arguing instead that we are

God's representatives who should not dominate the created order but "learn to live in a covenant with God's good creation" (ibid., p. 113). This cocreator perspective is supported by feminist author Dorothee Söelle, *To Work and to Love: A Theology of Creation*, with Shirley A. Cloyes (Philadelphia: Fortress Press, 1984).

[44]Other worthy views of vocation include those of Emil Brunner and Karl Barth.

[45]Volf, *Toward a Theology of Work*, pp. 79-122, esp. pp. 110-13.

[46]Ibid., p. 79. Volf's view of work in light of the eschatological new creation excludes creation and redemption as influencing a fully orbed theology of work.

[47]Volf offers two reasons why human beings work: (1) God created us to work, and (2) God gifts and calls us to work. The purpose of work, Volf poses, relates to obtaining necessities, providing for the needy, developing culture and cooperating with God (Miroslav Volf, "Work," in *Elements of a Christian Worldview*, ed. Michael D. Palmer [Springfield, MO: Logion Press, 1998], pp. 222-29). However, work at its very core is a God-given capacity and provision based on God's love for humanity in fulfilling God's redemptive plan.

[48]Darrell Cosden, *The Heavenly Good of Earthly Work* (Peabody, MA: Hendrickson, 2006), p. 89.

[49]Darrell Cosden, *A Theology of Work: Work and the New Creation* (Eugene, OR: Wipf & Stock, 2006), pp. 10-12.

[50]Ibid., p. 187.

[51]The closest Cosden comes to discussing love and work is in an analysis of Moltmann's theological anthropology, where love takes center stage. See Jürgen Moltmann, *The Coming of God: Christian Eschatology*, trans. Margaret Kohl (London: SCM Press, 1996), p. 53.

[52]Gary D. Badcock, *The Way of Life: A Theology of Christian Vocation* (Grand Rapids: Eerdmans, 1998), p. 81.

[53]Ibid., p. 82.

[54]Emil Brunner bemoans the perception of calling as being relegated only to "earning a living" (Emil Brunner, *The Divine Imperative: A Study in Christian Ethics*, trans. Olive Wyon [London: Lutterworth Press, 1937], p. 205).

[55]David Kinnaman, *You Lost Me: Why Young Christians Are Leaving Church . . . and Rethinking Faith*, with Aly Hawkins (Grand Rapids: Baker, 2011), p. 29.

[56]For an integrated approach to life purpose discovery, see Tony Stoltzfus, *A Leader's Life Purpose: Calling and Destiny Discovery Tools for Christian Life Coaching* (Virginia Beach, VA: Coach22, 2009).

[57]Parker J. Palmer, *Let Your Life Speak: Listening for the Voice of Vocation* (San Francisco: Wiley, 2000), p. 4.

[58]Smith, *Courage and Calling*, p. 10. In a similar vein, Karl Barth identifies two aspects of vocation around the themes of human freedom and obedience that include (1) divine calling to Christ as Savior, and (2) calling in a "technical sense" referring to everyday work or "sphere of operation" (Karl Barth, *Church Dogmatics* 3.4, ed. G. W. Bromiley and T. F. Torrance [Edinburgh: T & T Clark, 1961], pp. 595-647).

[59]Barth notes, "Man must allow his divine calling to determine that particularity of his vocation on the various stages of his way through life, and not *visa versa*" (ibid., p. 610).

[60]Smith, *Courage and Calling*, p. 109.

[61]Albert Schweitzer, "I Resolve to Be a Jungle Doctor," in *Leading Lives That Matter: What We Should Do and Who We Should Be*, ed. Mark R. Schwehn and Dorothy C. Bass (Grand Rapids: Eerdmans, 2006), pp. 29-36. This excerpt is taken from Schweitzer's autobiography, first published in 1933 and titled *Out of My Life and Thought: An Autobiography*.

[62]Ibid., p. 30.

[63]Ibid.

[64]Schweitzer pursued medical studies for seven years.

[65]Of the many books Schweitzer wrote, including scholarship on J. S. Bach, perhaps his best-known publication is *The Question of the Historical Jesus: A Critical Study of Its Progress from Reimarus to Wrede*, trans. W. Montgomery (New York: Macmillan, 1968). It was originally published in German in 1905.

[66]Schweitzer, "I Resolve to Be a Jungle Doctor," p. 33.

[67]Ibid., p. 34.

[68]Ibid., p. 35. As a humanitarian protesting colonialism and nuclear proliferation, Schweitzer went on to win the Nobel Peace Prize in 1953 and lived out his credo that he termed "a reverence for life."

[69]Rolland Baker and Heidi Baker, *Always Enough: God's Miraculous Provision Among the Poorest Children on Earth* (Grand Rapids: Chosen Books, 2002), esp. pp. 23-52. Through their leadership in Iris Ministries, the Bakers have planted thousands of churches in Mozambique and around the world, and ministered to the poorest of the poor through the supernatural power of the Holy Spirit.

[70]John Neafsey, *A Sacred Voice Is Calling: Personal Vocation and Social Conscience* (Maryknoll, NY: Orbis, 2006), pp. 36-37. Parker Palmer would describe this inner voice as "'something I can't not do, for reasons I'm unable to explain to anyone else and don't fully understand myself but that are nonetheless compelling'" (*Let Your Life Speak*, p. 25).

[71]John Eldredge's popular books highlight the importance of paying attention to our God-given desires (John Eldredge, *The Journey of Desire: Searching for the Life We've Only Dreamed of* [Nashville: Thomas Nelson, 2000], p. 13).

[72]Badcock, *Way of Life*, p. 126. Badcock asserts that "it does not matter greatly" about one's career choice because God gives us freedom to choose (ibid., pp. 126-27). Although I maintain that God does have specific works for us to do (Eph 2:10), I concur with Badcock that God offers us choice in career decision making.

[73]Plato, *Apology*, 38a.

[74]Os Guinness, "How to Build a Successful Life and Career," in Joe Gibbs, *Game Plan for Life: Your Personal Playbook for Success*, with Jerry B. Jenkins (Carol Stream, IL: Tyndale House, 2009), p. 179.

[75]Recounting the clinical depression and midlife crisis he experienced regarding calling clarity, Parker Palmer honestly acknowledged personal limitations where his "vocational reach had exceeded" his grasp (Palmer, *Let Your Life Speak*, p. 22).

[76]For a helpful resource on developing prayer support see C. Peter Wagner, *Prayer Shield: How to Intercede for Pastors, Christian Leaders, and Others on the Spiritual Frontlines* (Ventura, CA: Regal Books, 1992).

[77]For a delightfully illustrated book on vocation and following the voice of God, see R. W. Metlen, *The Voice: A Story of Faith and Trust* (Mahwah, NJ: Paulist Press, 2001).

[78]I thank my colleague Dr. Mara Crabtree for clearly differentiating vision and mission in this way.

[79]Richard Nelson Bolles, *How to Find Your Mission in Life* (Berkley, CA: Ten Speed Press, 2000), p. 12.

[80]Ibid., p. 15.

[81]Ibid.

[82]Jürgen Moltmann, *The Spirit of Life: A Universal Affirmation* (Minneapolis: Fortress Press, 1993), p. 180. Asserting that all of life is discipleship, Moltmann argues that the charisms of the Spirit cannot be restricted to the church context alone but rather operate in all of life and should be "practiced in family, profession and society" to preclude artificial separation (ibid., p. 183). I affirm Moltmann's position.

[83]Ibid., pp. 180-81.

[84]The expansive and controversial topic of spiritual gifts is only briefly introduced here. I argue that the Spirit of God did not surrender the spiritual gifts after the first century but rather continues to globally release gifts for the building up of the body of Christ. For more on the growth of the Pentecostal and charismatic movements, the fastest-growing segment of global Christianity, see the Pew Forum on Religion and Public Life, "Spirit and Power: A 10-Country Survey of Pentecostals," October 5, 2006, www.pewforum.org/Christian/Evangelical-Protestant-Churches/Spirit-and-Power.aspx, where it is estimated that out of the world's two billion Christians, at least one-quarter of them are Pentecostals or in related charismatic movements. See also David Barrett, *World Christian Encyclopedia* (New York: Oxford University Press, 1982), pp. 815-48.

[85]Gordon D. Fee notes, "The ultimate criterion of the Spirit's activity is the exaltation of Jesus as Lord" (*God's Empowering Presence: The Holy Spirit in the Letters of Paul* [Peabody, MA: Hendrickson, 1994], p. 158). Further, Fee is uncomfortable with "spiritual gifts" terminology, favoring instead "*gifts of God which are effectively brought into the life of the community by the Spirit*" (p. 607). Nevertheless, I will use the term *spiritual gifts* to mean gifts (charisms) of God for the benefit of the body of Christ.

[86]Ephesians 4:11 identifies equipping roles as gifts within the body of Christ: (1) apostles, (2) prophets, (3) evangelists, (4) pastors and (5) teachers. Not addressing them here does not imply that they are of secondary importance, only that to do so is beyond the scope of this discussion.

[87]James D. G. Dunn, *Jesus and the Spirit: A Study of the Religious and Charismatic Experience of Jesus and the First Christians as Reflected in the New Testament* (Grand Rapids: Eerdmans, 1975/1999), p. 205. Dunn highlights that charisma through spiritual gifts is always an expression of grace (Gk. *charis*), typically an experience, and should not be confused with natural talent and ability (ibid., pp. 253-56).

[88]D. A. Carson, *Showing the Spirit: A Theological Exposition of 1 Corinthians 12–14* (Grand Rapids: Baker, 1987), p. 35. Additionally, in making his argument related to the specific Corinthian situation, Gordon Fee observes that Paul listed these nine spiritual gifts "entirely ad hoc," or offered on the spot, as representative and not exhaustive (*God's Empowering Presence*, p. 160).

[89]Moltmann comments, "The power of unity is *love.* The power of diversity is *freedom*" (*Spirit of Life*, p. 194).

[90]Volf, *Work in the Spirit*, pp. 156, 199.

[91]For resources to discover one's motivational spiritual gifts, see Don Fortune and Katie Fortune, *Discover Your God-Given Gifts*, 2nd ed. (Grand Rapids: Chosen Books, 2009); C. Peter Wagner, *Discover Your Spiritual Gifts*, updated and expanded (Ventura, CA: Regal Books, 2012); and Erik Rees, *S.H.A.P.E.: Finding and Fulfilling Your Unique Purpose for Life* (Grand Rapids: Zondervan, 2006). While spiritual inventories are helpful, as Craig S. Keener observes, "we should not limit God's gifts to those discovered in such inventories" (Craig S. Keener, *Gift Giver: The Holy Spirit for Today* [Grand Rapids: Baker Academic, 2001], p. 113).

[92]Paul addresses an apparent issue in the Corinthian church related to the misuse of the gift of tongues and the minimizing of the other gifts. This notion is reinforced by Paul's reference in 1 Cor 13:1 to speaking in the tongues of men and of angels and not having love. See C. K. Barrett, *The First Epistle to the Corinthians* (Peabody, MA: Hendrickson, 1993), p. 296.

[93]Fee, *God's Empowering Presence*, p. 164.

[94]Ibid., p. 174. Fee emphasizes that Paul's purpose in explicating the spiritual gifts in 1 Corinthians 12 was not so much instructional as corrective.

[95]Ibid., p. 164.

[96]Carson, *Showing the Spirit*, p. 57.

[97]Keener, *Gift Giver*, p. 113.

[98]Sharon Daloz Parks, *Big Questions, Worthy Dreams: Mentoring Emerging Adults in Their Search for Meaning, Purpose, and Faith*, 10th anniv. ed. (San Francisco: Jossey-Bass, 2011), pp. 105-6.

[99]Laurent A. Parks Daloz, Cheryl H. Keen, James P. Keen and Sharon Daloz Parks, *Common Fire: Leading Lives of Commitment in a Complex World* (Boston: Beacon Press, 1996), p. 41.

[100]Typical role models for young people include media personalities and sports figures who often reflect weak or nonexistent moral anchors. Emerging adults between ages eighteen and twenty-three "are sorting out what their purpose in life might be" (Christian Smith with Patricia Snell, *Souls in Transition: The Religious and Spiritual Lives of Emerging Adults* [New York: Oxford University Press, 2009], p. 53).

[101]Parks, *Big Questions, Worthy Dreams*, pp. 165-202.

[102]Hardy, *Fabric of This World*, p. 88. The burgeoning coaching movement, both secular and sacred, testifies to this reality.

[103]Ibid., p. 87.

[104]Parks, *Big Questions, Worthy Dreams*, pp. 203-23.

[105]Versions of the DiSC Personality Assessment are often available in paper and online formats at college and university career centers. The DiSC that I recommend is offered through the Institute for Motivational Living, a faith-based institute that offers training certification. See their website at www.motivationalliving.com. The publisher of the MBTI is CPP, Inc. See their website at www.cpp.com/products/mbti/index.aspx. This assessment is also available through various consulting companies.

[106]See Tom Rath, *StrengthsFinder 2.0* (New York: Gallup Press, 2007), p. 17. Also see the Clifton Strengths Finder website at www.strengthsfinder.com/home.aspx.

[107]Ibid., p. 20.

[108]See Marcus Buckingham, *Go Put Your Strengths to Work: 6 Powerful Steps to Achieve Outstanding Performance* (New York: Free Press, 2007); Tom Rath and Barry Conchie, *Strengths Based Leadership: Great Leaders, Teams, and Why People Follow* (New York: Gallup Press, 2008); and Marcus Buckingham, *StandOut: The Groundbreaking New Strengths Assessment from the Leader of the Strengths Revolution* (Nashville: Thomas Nelson, 2011).

[109]Eugene H. Peterson, *Under the Predictable Plant: An Exploration in Vocational Holiness* (Grand Rapids: Eerdmans, 1992), p. 50. With the book of Jonah as a compelling backdrop, Peterson traces his own journey in vocational holiness as a pastor and writer.

[110]Smith, *Courage and Calling*, pp. 102-4.

[111]Rare is the church that equips its congregants for effective influence in the workplace. For a rare exception see the Center for Faith and Work website of Redeemer Presbyterian Church located in New York City led by Senior Pastor Tim Keller: www.faithandwork.org.

[112]David W. Miller, *God at Work: The History and Promise of the Faith at Work Movement* (Oxford: Oxford University Press, 2007), esp. pp. 125-42. For a sampling of faith at work resources, see John D. Beckett, *Loving Monday: Succeeding in Business Without Selling Your Soul* (Downers Grove, IL: InterVarsity Press, 1998); Os Hillman, *The 9 to 5 Window: How Faith Can Transform the Workplace* (Ventura, CA: Regal Books, 2005); Laura Nash and Scotty McLennan, *Church on Sunday, Work on Monday: The Challenge of Fusing Christian Values with Business Life* (San Francisco: Jossey-Bass, 2001); Doug Sherman and William Hendricks, *Your Work Matters to God* (Colorado Springs, CO: NavPress, 1987); Ed Silvoso, *Anointed for Business: How to Use Your Influence in the Marketplace to Change the World* (Ventura, CA: Regal Books, 2002); and Jeff Van Duzer, *Why Business Matters to God (and What Still Needs to Be Fixed)* (Downers Grove, IL: IVP Academic, 2010). A related movement, Reclaiming Seven Mountains, highlighted by Os Hillman, Lance Wallnau, Kent Humphries and Henry Blackaby, among others, focuses on influencing the seven mountains of culture: (1) arts and entertainment, (2) business, (3) education, (4) family, (5) government, (6) media and (7) religion.

[113]For example, after launching the grant awards initiative Programs for the Theological Exploration of Vocation (PTEV), aimed at assisting college students with career issues, the Lilly Endowment awarded 88 grants to church-related colleges and universities and renewed grants to 40 of the original 88, with a total investment of $217 million. See the Lilly Endowment's PTEV's website at http://lillyendowment.org/religion_ptev.html. In 2009 in the Netherlands, the European Chapter of the International Association for the Promotion of Christian Higher Education published conference proceedings and essays in Bram de Muynck, Johan Hegeman and Pieter Vos, eds., *Bridging the Gap: Connecting Christian Faith and Professional Practice* (Sioux Center, IA: Dordt College Press, 2011). Sample essay topics include: "Connecting Christian Faith and Professional Practice in a Pluralistic Society," by Sarota Nagy (pp. 25-37); "The Personal Character of Worldview and Its Meaning for Professional Practices," by Peter Blokhuis (pp. 109-15); and "Vocation and Inspiration in Education," by Bram De Muynck (pp. 385-94).

[114]Leland Ryken, *Work and Leisure in Christian Perspective* (Portland, OR: Multnomah Press, 1987), pp. 22-26.

[115]Hardy, *Fabric of this World*, pp. xvi-xvii.

[116]On the effects of the fall and sin on work, see Sherman and Hendricks, *Your Work Matters to God*, pp. 97-107.

[117]Neafsey, *Sacred Voice Is Calling*, pp. 146-60, esp. p. 146.

[118]Lest we think that failure alone is formational, see how success can feed the human dark side in John R. O'Neil, *The Paradox of Success: When Winning at Work Means Losing at Life* (New York: Penguin, 2004), pp. 52-115.

[119]Palmer, *Let Your Life Speak*, pp. 17-30.

[120]Ben Carson, *Gifted Hands*, with Cecil Murphey (Grand Rapids: Zondervan, 1990), pp. 75-76. In 1987, Dr. Carson was the first surgeon to successfully separate Siamese twins joined at the back of their heads.

[121]Juliet B. Schor, *The Overworked American: The Unexpected Decline of Leisure* (New York: Basic Books, 1992), pp. 28-41.

[122]Ibid., pp. 153-54.

[123]Diane Fassel, *Working Ourselves to Death: The High Cost of Workaholism and the Rewards of Recovery* (Lincoln, NE: iUniverse.com, 2000), p. 2.

[124]Christina Maslach and Michael P. Leiter, *The Truth About Burnout: How Organizations Cause Personal Stress and What to Do About It* (San Francisco: Jossey-Bass, 1997), pp. 17-18.

[125]Diane J. Chandler, "The Impact of Pastors' Spiritual Practices on Burnout," *Journal of Pastoral Care & Counseling* 64, no. 2 (2010): 1-9.

[126]See Ryken, *Work and Leisure*, pp. 181-206.

[127]Mark Jensen, "The Pain of Lost Vocation," in *Shattered Vocations* (Nashville: Broadman, 1990), pp. 28-61.

[128]Leo Tolstoy, *The Death of Ivan Ilyich*, trans. Lynn Solotaroff (New York: Bantam Dell, 2004). Tolstoy published this novella in 1886, after experiencing his own crisis of faith in the 1870s.

[129]Randy Pausch, *The Last Lecture*, with Jeffrey Zaslow (New York: Hyperion, 2008). Pausch gave his last lecture on September 18, 2007, titled "Really Achieving Your Childhood Dreams." The lecture can be viewed on YouTube at www.youtube.com/watch?v=ji5_MqicxSo.

[130]Mitch Albom, *Tuesdays with Morrie: An Old Man, A Young Man, and Life's Greatest Lessons* (New York: Doubleday, 1997). A TV movie by the same title is based on this book.

9 Physical Health: Our Bodies

[1]The names mentioned in this chapter have been changed to honor confidentiality.

[2]The information presented in this chapter is based on my personal research over several years. However, I am not a medical doctor, nutritionist or endocrinologist. Readers are advised to undertake their own research related to the information presented here and consult with their personal physician for medical, nutritional and lifestyle advice before making any health-related changes.

[3]For an illustrated volume that explains how the body works and how to keep it healthy, see Patricia Daniels et al., *Body: The Complete Human* (Washington, DC: National Geographic Society, 2007).

[4]For a holistic perspective on body and soul, see John W. Cooper, *Body, Soul and Life Everlasting: Biblical Anthropology and the Monism-Dualism Debate*, 2nd ed. (Grand Rapids: Eerdmans, 1989).

[5]Stanley Hauerwas, "The Sanctified Body: Why Perfection Does Not Require a 'Self,'" in *Embodied Holiness: Toward a Corporate Theology of Spiritual Growth*, ed. Samuel M. Powell and Michael E. Lodahl (Downers Grove, IL: InterVarsity Press, 1999), p. 22.

[6]Amos Yong, *Theology and Down Syndrome: Reimagining Disability in Late Modernity* (Waco, TX: Baylor University Press, 2007), pp. 248-59.

[7]Ibid., p. 248.

[8]Henri J. M. Nouwen, *The Road to Daybreak: A Spiritual Journey* (New York: Doubleday, 1990), pp. 162-63.

[9]I concur with Jürgen Moltmann, who argues that regardless of disability all are valuable and useful and that the body of Christ "needs weak and handicapped members as well as strong ones," for "the strength of Christ is also powerful in the disablement" (Jürgen Moltmann, *The Spirit of Life: A Universal Affirmation* [Minneapolis: Fortress Press, 1992], pp. 192-93).

[10]Jürgen Moltmann, *God in Creation: A New Theology of Creation and the Spirit of God* (Minneapolis: Fortress Press, 1993), pp. 245-47.

[11]Ibid., p. 244. Moltmann takes this quote from theologian Friedrich Christoph Oetinger. For more on embodiment, see Karl Barth, *Church Dogmatics* 3.2, *The Doctrine of Creation*, ed. G. W. Bromiley and T. F. Torrance (London: T & T Clark, 1960), pp. 366-94; G. C. Berkouwer, *Man: The Image of God*, trans. Dirk W. Jellema (Grand Rapids: Eerdmans, 1962), p. 203; and Emil Brunner, *Man in Revolt: A Christian Anthropology* (Philadelphia: Westminster Press, 1947), p. 108.

[12]Emil Brunner, *The Christian Doctrine of Creation and Redemption*, vol. 2, *Dogmatics*, trans. Olive Wyon (Philadelphia: Westminster Press, 1952), p. 62.

[13]Gordon D. Fee, *The First Epistle to the Corinthians* (Grand Rapids: Eerdmans, 1987), p. 137.

[14]F. F. Bruce, *Philippians* (Peabody, MA: Hendrickson, 1989), p. 49.

[15]Adam G. Cooper, *Life in the Flesh: An Anti-Gnostic Spiritual Philosophy* (Oxford: Oxford University Press, 2008), p. 43.

[16]Ben Witherington III, *Conflict and Community in Corinth: A Socio-Rhetorical Commentary on 1 and 2 Corinthians* (Grand Rapids: Eerdmans, 1995), p. 169. David E. Garland, *1 Corinthians*, Baker Exegetical Commentary on the New Testament (Grand Rapids: Baker Academic, 2003), pp. 238-39.

[17]Stephanie Paulsell, "Honoring the Body," in *Practicing Our Faith: A Way of Life for a Searching People*, ed. Dorothy C. Bass (San Francisco: Jossey-Bass, 1997), p. 18.

[18]Elizabeth Lewis Hall, "What Are Bodies For? An Integrative Examination of Embodiment," *Christian Scholar's Review* 39, no. 2 (2010): 159-75, esp. p. 171.

[19]Mary Timothy Prokes, *Toward a Theology of the Body* (Grand Rapids: Eerdmans, 1996), p. 25. Also see Elisabeth Moltmann-Wendell, *I Am My Body: New Ways of Embodiment*, trans. John Bowen (London: SCM Press, 1994), pp. 103-5.

[20]Harold G. Koenig appeals to the healthcare community not to dismiss the spiritual component of medical interventions (Harold G. Koenig, *The Healing Power of Faith: Science Explores Medicine's Last Great Frontier* [New York: Simon & Schuster, 1999], p. 169).

[21]Harold G. Koenig, *The Healing Connection: A World-Renowned Medical Scientist Discovers the Powerful Link Between Christian Faith and Health*, with Gregg Lewis (Nashville: Word, 2000), p. 177.

[22]Harold G. Koenig, *Spirituality and Health Research: Methods, Measurement, Statistics, and Resources* (West Conshohocken, PA: Templeton Press, 2011), pp. 13-27. For a comprehensive volume, see Harold G. Koenig, Dana E. King and Verna Benner Carson, eds., *Handbook of Religion and Health*, 2nd ed. (Oxford: Oxford University Press, 2012), esp. pp. 317-556.

[23]Koenig, *Spirituality and Research*, p. 23. For example, the majority of religion/spirituality and health research studies indicate an association between weight gain and those who are more religious.

[24]In response to the fat scare over the past twenty-five years, one popular fad diet promotes a "low-carb diet," high in protein, meat and fat. However, the intake of sugary foods has more than made up for the loss of calories. The truth is that vegetables, fruits, grains and dietary fiber contain needed complex carbohydrates. Overindulgence in refined, simple carbohydrates (i.e., doughnuts, cookies, cakes and pies) presents nutritional concerns.

[25]World Health Organization, "World Health Statistics 2012: A Snapshot of Global Health," p. 5, http://apps.who.int/iris/bitstream/10665/70889/1/WHO_IER_HSI_12.1_eng.pdf.

[26]Ibid.

[27]Health care costs continue to rise in the United States, which spends more of its gross national product (GNP) on health care than any other industrialized nation. For example, the cost of health care in the United States comprised 17.6 percent of the GNP in 2009, compared to 13.4% in 1990. See World Health Organization, "Global Health Indictors 2012, Part III, Global Health Indicators," www.who.int/healthinfo/EN_WHS2012_Part3.pdf.

[28]Christopher Murray et al., "The State of US Health, 1990-2010: Burden of Diseases, Injuries, and Risk Factors," *Journal of the American Medical Association*, August 14, 2013, http://jama.jamanetwork.com/article.aspx?articleid=1710486.

[29]Rex Russell, *What the Bible Says About Healthy Living* (Ventura, CA: Regal Books, 1996), p. 53.

[30]"Water: How Much Should You Drink Every Day?," Mayo Clinic, www.mayoclinic.com/health/water/NU00283.

[31]Fereydoon Batmanghelidj, *Water for Health, for Healing, for Life: You're Not Sick, You're Thirsty!* (New York: Warner Books), pp. 32-35.

[32]Melatonin is a hormone produced in the brain's pineal gland that controls sleep and waking cycles.

[33]For example, coffee is a dehydrating diuretic that increases the rate of urination (Batmanghelidj, *Water for Health*, p. 17). Limiting coffee intake to no more than one to two cups daily is advisable because coffee is a mildly addictive stimulant and incurs cardiovascular effects. See Harvard Health Publications, "Coffee Health Risks: For the Moderate Drinker, Coffee Is Safe, Says Harvard Women's Health Watch," August 2004, www.health.harvard.edu/press_releases/coffee_health_risk.

[34]Don Colbert, *The Seven Pillars of Health: The Natural Way to Better Health for Life*, with Mary Colbert (Lake Mary, FL: Siloam, 2007), p. 7.

[35]Ibid., p. 31.

[36]Ibid., p. 33. In dehydration, the body loses "a number of essential amino acids that are used to manufacture neurotransmitters" (Batmanghelidj, *Water for Health*, p. 21).

[37]Colbert, *Seven Pillars of Health*, pp. 33-34. It has been suggested that water intake should occur throughout the day for optimal hydration, but minimally during meal time because fluids interrupt the digestion process by diluting necessary enzymes and digestive juices in the stomach and intestines. However, if water is desired during a meal, consider smaller quantities at room temperature. Depending on one's weight, this flexible water intake plan is recommended: (1) eight to sixteen ounces of water as the first beverage of the day and at least thirty minutes before breakfast to rehydrate the body after a night's sleep; (2) a few hours after breakfast, another eight to sixteen ounces of water; (3) thirty minutes prior to lunch, eight to sixteen ounces of water; (3) two hours after lunch, eight to sixteen ounces of water; (4) thirty minutes prior to dinner, eight to sixteen ounces of water; (5) two hours after dinner, another eight ounces of water; and (6) before bed, if possible, drink eight ounces of water, unless this interferes with sleep.

[38]Colin Ingram, *The Drinking Water Book: How to Eliminate Harmful Toxins from Your Water* (Berkeley, CA: Celestial Arts, 2006), pp. 4, 6-21. Since drinking quality water is critical to health, giving care to the source of water becomes important. For example, avoid drinking tap water because of the chemical content in most municipal water. Drinking only distilled water may increase carbon dioxide absorption, causing the body to become more acidic, which can contribute to inflammation. Although distillation removes impurities from water, including pesticides, herbicides, chlorine, fluoride and bacteria, even beneficial minerals are removed. The reverse osmosis process also removes all impurities but adds back needed minerals, which is a viable option. Another option is using water filters, whether carbon filters or alkaline filters. Carbon filters provide "entry-level" filtration by the pitcher or by being connected to a faucet. Alkaline water filters change the pH of water to make it less acidic. Installed near the kitchen sink, alkaline filters use an electromagnetic process to separate acidic water from alkaline water. Alkaline water is then used for drinking, whereas the acidic water may be used for other purposes (e.g., washing clothes and showering).

[39]US Department of Agriculture and US Department of Health and Human Services, Center for Nutrition Policy and Promotion, "Dietary Guidelines for Americans, 2010: Executive Summary," www.cnpp.usda.gov/Publications/DietaryGuidelines/2010/PolicyDoc/ExecSumm.pdf. These guidelines supply the discussion points in this section. Although they focus on the United States, these guidelines also apply cross-culturally.

[40]Ibid., p. 4.

[41]Harvard School of Public Health, "Vegetables and Fruits: Get Plenty Every Day," *The Nutrition Source*, www.hsph.harvard.edu/nutritionsource/what-should-you-eat/vegetables-full-story.

[42]Danny K. Asami et al., "Comparison of the Total Phenolic and Ascorbic Acid Content of Freeze-Dried and Air-Dried Marionberry, Strawberry, and Corn Grown Using Conventional, Organic, and Sustainable Agricultural Practices," *Journal of Agricultural Food Chemistry* 51, no. 5 (2003): 1237-41. These researchers found 58% more antioxidants in organically rather than conventionally grown produce.

[43]Diana Schwarzbein and Nancy Deville, *The Schwarzbein Principle: The Truth About Losing Weight, Being Healthy and Feeling Younger* (Deerfield Beach, FL: HCI, 1999), p. 127.

[44]An Pan et al., "Red Meat Consumption and Mortality," *Archives of Internal Medicine* 172, no. 7 (2012): 555-63, http://archinte.jamanetwork.com/article.aspx?articleid=1134845.

[45]An Pan, quoted in Ann Harding, "Too Much Red Meat May Shorten Life Span," CNN Health, March 13, 2012, www.cnn.com/2012/03/12/health/red-meat-shorten-lifespan/index.html.

[46]An Pan et al., "Red Meat Consumption and Risk of Type 2 Diabetes: 3 Cohorts of US Adults and an Updated Meta-Analysis," *American Journal of Clinical Nutrition* 94, no. 4 (2011), pp. 1088-96, www.ncbi.nlm.nih.gov/pubmed/21831992.

[47]See T. Colin Campbell and Thomas M. Campbell II, *The China Study: Startling Implications for Diet, Weight Loss and Long-term Health* (Dallas: BenBella Books, 2006). Based on twenty-seven years of funded research through the National Institutes of Health, the American Cancer Society and the American Institute for Cancer Research, Dr. Colin Campbell argues that "eating right can save your life" (ibid., p. 2). Through laboratory studies and the China study, the most comprehensive nutritional study, involving 6,500 adults, Dr. Campbell concluded "that people who ate the most plant-based foods were the healthiest and tended to avoid chronic disease," whereas those who ate mostly an animal-based diet incurred the most chronic disease (ibid., p. 7). However, not everyone agrees with Dr. Campbell that a pure vegan diet provides the essential nutrients available from lean meat and animal products. See Jordan S. Rubin, *The Maker's Diet: The 40-day Health Experience That Will Change Your Life Forever* (New York: Penguin, 2004), pp. 99-105.

[48]Joseph Mercola, "Coconut Oil Benefits: When Fat Is Good for You," *Huffington Post*, February 14, 2011, www.huffingtonpost.com/dr-mercola/coconut-oil-benefits_b_821453.html.

[49]Ibid.

[50]Because of public outcry, many fast food chains have changed from frying French fries in trans fat to other saturated fats. Although butter contains saturated fat, it is a natural product, whereas margarine is a processed product with more omega-6s than omega-3s, which contributes to inflammatory diseases (David Servan-Schreiber, *Anti-Cancer: A New Way of Life* [New York: Viking, 2009], pp. 75-76). When in a more solid state, such as in sticks, margarine is more hydrogenated, composed of unsaturated oils and trans fatty acids, both of which are unhealthy. Margarine may also contain highly processed rancid vegetable oils and additives for color. Butter contains healthy properties such as lecithin, antioxidants and vitamins A and E. See Sally Fallon and Mary G. Enig, "Why Butter Is Better," Weston A. Price Foundation, January 1, 2000, www.westonaprice.org/food-features/why-butter-is-better.

[51]Colbert, *Seven Pillars of Health*, pp. 106-7.

[52]Elizabeth A. Streeten, "Vitamin D and Bone Health 1 and 2," University of Maryland Medical Center, www.umm.edu/media/video/vitamind_bonehealth_streeten_1.htm. According to Dr. Michael Holick, director of the General Clinical Research Unit and professor of medicine, physiology and biophysics at Boston University Medical Center, vitamin D deficiency is the most common global health challenge (Michael Holick, *The Vitamin D Solution: A Three-fold Strategy to Cure Our Most Common Health Problem* [New York: Hudson Street Press, 2011], chap. 1).

[53]Edward Giovannucci, "Can Vitamin D Reduce Total Mortality?" *Archives of Internal Medicine*

167, no. 16 (2007): 1709-10, http://archinte.jamanetwork.com/article.aspx?articleid=412953. This meta-analysis indicated a 7% reduction in mortality rates regardless of cause for those with adequate vitamin D levels. For the linkage between vitamin D deficiency and numerous conditions and diseases, see endocrinologist Dr. Sarfraz Zaidi, *Power of Vitamin D* (Parker, CO: Outskirts Press, 2010).

[54]Bruce W. Hollis, "Circulating 25-Hydroxyvitamin D Levels Indicative of Vitamin D Sufficiency: Implications for Establishing a New Effective Dietary Intake Recommendation for Vitamin D," *Journal of Nutrition* 135, no. 2 (2005): 317-22, http://jn.nutrition.org/content/135/2/317.long.

[55]Center for Nutrition Policy and Promotion, *Dietary Guidelines for Americans, 2010*.

[56]US Centers for Disease Control and Prevention, "Americans Consume Too Much Sodium (Salt)," February 24, 2011, www.cdc.gov/Features/dsSodium. This website presents recommended levels of sodium consumption.

[57]US Centers for Disease Control and Prevention, "Sodium: The Facts," June 2010, www.cdc.gov/salt/pdfs/Sodium_Fact_Sheet.pdf.

[58]Rachel K. Johnson et al., "Dietary Sugars Intake and Cardiovascular Health: A Scientific Statement from the American Heart Association," *Circulation* 120 (2009): 1011-20, http://circ.ahajournals.org/content/120/11/1011.full.pdf.

[59]Jean A. Welsh et al., "Caloric Sweetener Consumption and Dyslipidemia Among US Adults," *Journal of the American Medical Association* 303, no. 15 (2010): 1490-97, www.ncbi.nlm.nih.gov/pmc/articles/PMC3045262. Johnson et al., "Dietary Sugars Intake and Cardiovascular Health," *Circulation*, pp. 1013-15.

[60]Colbert, *Seven Pillars of Health*, p. 80; Nancy Appleton and G. N. Jacobs, *Suicide by Sugar: A Startling Look at Our #1 National Addiction* (Garden City Park, NY: 2009), pp. 96-99; and Servan-Schrieber, *Anti-Cancer*, pp. 67-72.

[61]James P. Boyle et al., "Projection of the Year 2050 Burden of Diabetes in the US Adult Population: Dynamic Modeling of Incidence, Mortality, and Prediabetes Prevalence," *Population Health Metrics* 8, no. 29 (2010): 1-12, www.pophealthmetrics.com/content/pdf/1478-7954-8-29.pdf.

[62]Johnson, "Dietary Sugars Intake and Cardiovascular Health," p. 1012; Cynthia L. Ogden et al., "Consumption of Sugar Drinks in the United States, 2005-2008," *National Center for Health Statistics Data Brief* 71 (2011), www.cdc.gov/nchs/data/databriefs/db71.pdf.

[63]David A. Shoham et al., "Sugary Soda Consumption and Albuminuria: Results from the National Health and Nutrition Examination Survey, 1999-2004," *PLoS ONE* 3, no. 10 (2008): e3431, www.plosone.org/article/info:doi%2F10.1371%2Fjournal.pone.0003431#.

[64]Sanjay Gupta, "Is Sugar Toxic?" *60 Minutes*, April 1, 2012, www.cbsnews.com/video/watch/?id=7403942n.

[65]Robert H. Lustig, "Sugar: The Bitter Truth," YouTube, July 30, 2009, www.youtube.com/watch?v=dBnniua6-oM. See also table 1 of Robert H. Lustig, Laura A. Schmidt and Claire D. Brindis, "Public Health: The Toxic Truth About Sugar," *Nature* 482 (2012), pp. 27-29, www.nature.com/nature/journal/v482/n7383/fig_tab/482027a_T1.html.

[66]Gupta, "Is Sugar Toxic?"

[67]"Understanding Childhood Obesity: 2011 Statistical Sourcebook," American Heart Association, www.heart.org/idc/groups/heart-public/@wcm/@fc/documents/downloadable/ucm_428180.pdf.

[68]In an effort to curb obesity, in 2012 New York City mayor Michael Bloomberg and the NYC Health Department created quite a stir when they proposed limiting the size of sugary drinks served in restaurants, theaters, ballparks and streetcars to sixteen ounces. Many objected, claiming that their civil liberties would be violated. The soft-drink industry then sponsored a multimillion-dollar campaign to defeat the ban. Educating the public on the hazards of sugar consumption is a formidable challenge. While the ban was initially approved by the New York City Board of Health, it was later contested, with a judge blocking the ban's implementation. After an appeal by Mayor Bloomberg to the appellate division of the NY State Supreme Court, the unanimous decision supported the lower court's ruling against the ban. See E. C. Gogolak, "Appeals Court Rules Against Bloomberg Beverage Restriction," *New York Times*, July 30, 2013, www.nytimes.com/2013/07/31/nyregion/appeals-court-rules-against-bloomberg-beverage-rules.html.

[69]"Related Studies Point to the Illusion of the Artificial: Waistlines in People, Glucose Levels in Mice Hint at Sweeteners' Effects," University of Texas Health Science Center at San Antonio, June 27, 2011, www.uthscsa.edu/hscnews/singleformat2.asp?newID=3861.

[70]Morando Soffritti et al., "First Experimental Demonstration of the Multipotential Carcinogenic Effects of Aspartame Administered in the Feed to Sprague-Dawley Rats," *Environmental Health Perspective* 114, no. 3 (2005): 379-85, http://ehp03.niehs.nih.gov/article/info:doi/10.1289/ehp.8711.

[71]Colbert, *Seven Pillars of Health*, pp. 82-83.

[72]Russell L. Blaylock, *Excitotoxins: The Taste That Kills* (Santa Fe: Health Press, 1997), p. 39.

[73]For an overview of the controversial approval of aspartame by the US Food and Drug Administration (FDA), see Mike Wallace, "How Sweet It Is," *60 Minutes*, December 29, 1996, www.youtube.com/watch?v=yCoBuTroOro; Joseph Mercola, *Sweet Deception: Why Splenda, NutraSweet, and the FDA May Be Hazardous to Your Health* (Nashville: Thomas Nelson, 2006), pp. 36-67.

[74]Mike Wallace, "How Sweet It Is." Dr. Ralph Walton reports on the 164 research studies on aspartame that he evaluated. Seventy-four of these studies funded by the aspartame industry supported its safety, suggesting a conflict of interest. Of the other ninety independently conducted studies, eighty-three reported a problem with aspartame.

[75]See one internist's strident cautions in H. J. Roberts, *Aspartame (NutraSweet): Is It Safe?* (Philadelphia: Charles Press, 1990), pp. 266-80.

[76]Mercola, *Sweet Deception*, pp. 68-123; Janet Starr Hull, *Splenda®: Is It Safe or Not?* with Lynn Townsend Dealy (Dallas: Pickle Press, 2005), p. 5.

[77]M. B. Abou-Donia et al., "Splenda Alters Gut Microflora and Increases Intestinal P-Glycprotein and Cytochrome P-450 in Male Rats," *Journal of Toxicology and Environmental Health* 71, no. 21 (2008): 1415-29.

[78]Colbert, *Seven Pillars of Health*, pp. 83-84.

[79]Ibid., p. 83.

[80]Servan-Schreiber, *Anticancer*, p. 71. Developed in 2002 by the University of Sydney in Australia, the glycemic index is the measurement of the effect of carbohydrates on the body's blood sugar levels.

[81]Russell, *What the Bible Says About Healthy Living*, p. 53.

[82]Mark Stephen Tremblay et al., "Physiological and Health Implications of a Sedentary Lifestyle," *Applied Physiology, Nutrition, and Metabolism* 35, no. 6 (2010): 725-40. First coined by Dr. Frank Booth of the University of Missouri-Columbia, "Sedentary Death Syndrome," or SeDS, regards sedentary living as a matter of life and death.

[83]World Health Organization, *Global Recommendations on Physical Activity for Health* (Geneva, Switzerland: WHO Press, 2010), pp. 1-60, esp. p. 7, http://whqlibdoc.who.int/publications/2010/9789241599979_eng.pdf.

[84]Ibid., p. 10.

[85]"Exercise Is Medicine: 2012 Fact Sheet," American College of Sports Medicine, 2012, p. 1, www.exerciseismedicine.org/documents/EIMFactSheet2012_all.pdf.

[86]American College of Sports Medicine, *ACSM's Health-Related Physical Fitness Assessment Manual*, 3rd ed. (Philadelphia: American College of Sports Medicine, 2010), p. 30.

[87]Ibid.

[88]Dean A. Haycock, "Exercise Recommendations from the Surgeon General," March 6, 2011, www.livestrong.com/article/397644-exercise-recommendations-from-the-surgeon-general. In 2013 the surgeon general, Regina Benjamin, announced the health fitness program "Every Body Walk!" www.surgeongeneral.gov/initiatives/walking/index.html. And the US Department of Health and Human Services still affirms their 2008 exercise guidelines, www.health.gov/paguidelines/guidelines/summary.aspx.

[89]For the "Exercise Is Medicine" website, see www.exerciseismedicine.org.

[90]Michelle D. Holmes et. al., "Physical Activity and Survival After Breast Cancer Diagnosis," *Journal of the American Medical Association* 293, no. 20 (2005): 2479–86, http://jama.jamanetwork.com/article.aspx?articleid=200955.

[91]For the benefits of physical exercise, see Charles B. Corbin et al., *Concepts of Physical Fitness: Active Lifestyles for Wellness*, 16th ed. (New York: McGraw-Hill, 2011), pp. 65-84; Brian J. Sharkey and Steven E. Gaskill, *Fitness and Health*, 6th ed. (Champaign, IL: Human Kinetics, 2007), pp. 13-45; and Werner W. K. Hoeger and Sharon A. Hoeger, *Lifetime Physical Fitness and Wellness: A Personalized Program*, 11th ed. (Belmont, CA: Wadsworth, 2009), pp. 1-32.

[92]Corbin, *Concepts of Physical Fitness*, p. 72.

[93]"Childhood Obesity Facts," US Center for Disease Control and Prevention, July 10, 2013, www.cdc.gov/healthyyouth/obesity/facts.htm; and "Adult Obesity Facts," US Center for Disease Control and Prevention, August 16, 2013, www.cdc.gov/obesity/data/adult.html.

[94]Georg Kojda and Rainer Hambrecht, "Molecular Mechanism of Vascular Adaptations to Exercise: Physical Activity as an Effective Antioxidant Therapy?" *Cardiovascular Research* 67, no. 2 (2005): 187-97.

[95]Jordan, *Maker's Diet*, p. 60.

[96]Corbin, *Concepts of Physical Fitness*, p. 76.

[97]James B. Grissom, "Physical Fitness and Academic Achievement," *Journal of Exercise Physiology* 8, no. 1 (2005): 11-25, www.asep.org/files/Grissom.pdf.

[98]John J. Ratey, *Spark: The Revolutionary New Science of Exercise and the Brain*, with Eric Hagerman (New York: Little, Brown, 2008), p. 13.

[99]Ibid., p. 14.

[100]K. I. Erickson et al., "Physical Activity Predicts Gray Matter Volume in Late Adulthood," *Neurology* 75, no. 16 (2010): 1415-22, www.ncbi.nlm.nih.gov/pmc/articles/PMC3039208.

[101]Ratey, *Spark*, p. 64.

[102]Ibid., pp. 65-67.

[103]Michael Babyak et al., "Exercise Treatment for Major Depression: Maintenance of Therapeutic Benefit at 10 Months," *Psychosomatic Medicine* 62 (2000): 633-38. www.uppity sciencechick.com/babyak_dep_exercise.pdf.

[104]Carl W. Cotman and Nicole C. Berchtold, "Exercise: A Behavioral Intervention to Enhance Brain Health and Plasticity," *Trends in Neurosciences* 25, no. 6 (2002): 295-301, http://resulb .ulb.ac.be/facs/ism/docs/behaviorBDNF.pdf.

[105]Ratey, *Spark*, p. 36.

[106]Ibid., p. 221.

[107]Dean Haycock, "Exercise Recommendations from the Surgeon General," Livestrong.com, May 6, 2011, www.livestrong.com/article/397644-exercise-recommendations-from-the-surgeon-general.

[108]Corbin, *Concepts of Physical Fitness*, pp. 86-88.

[109]"Executive Summary," *Physical Activity and Health: A Report of the Surgeon General* (Rockville, MD: US Department of Health and Human Services, Office of the Surgeon General, 2011), pp. 12-13, www.cdc.gov/nccdphp/sgr/summary.htm. For more in-depth recommendations, see Carol Ewing Garber et al., "Quantity and Quality of Exercise for Developing and Maintaining Cardiorespiratory, Musculoskeletal, and Neuromotor Fitness in Apparently Healthy Adults: Guidance for Prescribing Exercise," *Medicine & Science in Sports & Exercise* 43, no. 7 (2011): 1334-59, http://journals.lww.com/acsm-msse/Fulltext/2011/07000/Quantity_and_Quality_of_Exercise_for_Developing.26.aspx.

[110]Jim Fixx's story is recounted in John Robbins, *Healthy at 100: The Scientifically Proven Secrets of the World's Healthiest and Longest-Lived Peoples* (New York: Ballantine Books, 2007), pp. 183-85.

[111]"The longer, more continuously, and later at night you work, the less efficient and more mistake-prone you become" (Jim Loehr and Tony Schwartz, *The Power of Full Engagement: Managing Energy, Not Time, Is the Key to High Performance and Personal Renewal* [New York: Free Press, 2003], p. 56).

[112]Ashley Halsey III and Debbi Wilgoren, "Control Tower Supervisor Suspended at National After Failing to Respond to Planes," *Washington Post*, March 23, 2011, www.washingtonpost .com/local/tower-at-reagan-national-goes-silent-as-planes-attempt-to-land/2011/03/23/AB9aslKB_story.html.

[113]"Sleep, Performance, and Public Safety," Harvard Medical School, Division of Sleep Medicine,

December 18, 2007, http://healthysleep.med.harvard.edu/healthy/matters/consequences/sleep-performance-and-public-safety.

[114]Stephen Shea, "The Characteristics of Sleep," *Healthy Sleep*, December 18, 2007, http://healthysleep.med.harvard.edu/healthy/science/what/characteristics.

[115]James B. Maas, *Power Sleep: The Revolutionary Program That Prepares Your Mind for Peak Performance* (New York: Harper Perennial, 1998), p. 26.

[116]In 1951 University of Chicago researcher Nathaniel Kleitman oversaw the sleep research of doctoral students Eugene Aserinsky and William Dement, who attached electrodes to study participants' faces to record their brain waves. Their pioneering research opened the floodgates for what we currently know about the importance of sleep. Tragically, Eugene Aserinsky died at age seventy-seven in 1998 after falling asleep behind the wheel.

[117]Maas, *Power Sleep*, pp. 30-33.

[118]Mary Carskaden and William C. Dement, "Normal Human Sleep: An Overview," in *Principles and Practices of Sleep Medicine*, ed. Meir H. Kryger, Thomas Roth and William C. Dement, 5th ed. (St. Louis: Elsevier Saunders, 2011), pp. 16-25, esp. p. 22.

[119]Sheldon Cohen et al., "Sleep Habits and Susceptibility to the Common Cold," *Archives of Internal Medicine* 169, no. 1 (2009): 62-67, http://archinte.jamanetwork.com/article.aspx?articleid=414701.

[120]Colbert, *Seven Pillars of Health*, pp. 37-39.

[121]"Exploring New Frontiers in Human Health," Stanford Center for Sleep Sciences, p. 2, http://neuroscience.stanford.edu/research/programs/program_info/Sleep%20Science_011609B_compress.pdf.

[122]"2005 Sleep in America Poll: Summary of Findings," National Sleep Foundation, March 29, 2005, p. 7, www.sleepfoundation.org/sites/default/files/2005_summary_of_findings.pdf.

[123]"How Much Sleep Do We Really Need," National Sleep Foundation, 2013, www.sleepfoundation.org/article/how-sleep-works/how-much-sleep-do-we-really-need.

[124]For this recommended two-part series online, see (1) Lesley Stahl, "The Science of Sleep," part 1, *60 Minutes*, June 15, 2008; and (2) Lesley Stahl, "The Science of Sleep," part 2, *60 Minutes*, June 15, 2008, www.cbsnews.com/video/watch/?id=4181994n&tag=contentBody;storyMediaBox.

[125]Stahl, "Science of Sleep," part 2.

[126]Eric C. Hanlon and Eve Van Cauter, "Quantification of Sleep Behavior and of Its Impact on the Cross-talk Between the Brain and Peripheral Metabolism," *Proceedings of the National Academy of Sciences* 108, supp. 3 (2011): 15609-16, www.ncbi.nlm.nih.gov/pmc/articles/PMC3176603; Esra Tasali et al., "Slow-wave Sleep and the Risk of Type 2 Diabetes in Humans," *Proceedings of the National Academy of Sciences* 105 (2008): 1044-49, www.ncbi.nlm.nih.gov/pmc/articles/PMC2242689.

[127]"Diet, Exercise, and Sleep," National Sleep Foundation, December 2009, www.sleepfoundation.org/article/sleep-topics/diet-exercise-and-sleep.

[128]Abby C. King et al., "Moderate-Intensity Exercise and Self-Rated Quality of Sleep in Older Adults: A Randomized Controlled Trial," *Journal of the American Medical Association* 277, no. 1 (1997): 32-37, jama.jamanetwork.com/article.aspx?articleid=412611#; Kathryn J. Reid et al., "Aerobic Exercise Improves Self-Reported Sleep and Quality of Life in Older Adults with In-

somnia," *Sleep Medicine* 11, no. 9 (2010), pp. 934-40, www.ncbi.nlm.nih.gov/pmc/articles/PMC2992829/pdf/nihms234497.pdf. Maas, *Power Sleep*, p. 85.

[129]Maas, *Power Sleep*, p. 79.

[130]Lawrence Epstein with Steven Mardon, *The Harvard Medical School Guide to a Good Night's Sleep* (New York: McGraw-Hill, 2007), pp. 55-68.

[131]George Barna, "Americans Just Want a Good Night of Sleep," *Barna Update*, October 16, 2006, www.barna.org/barna-update/article/13-culture/145-americans-just-want-a-good-night-of-sleep.

[132]Colbert, *Seven Pillars of Health*, p. 231.

[133]John A. Sanford, *Ministry Burnout* (Louisville: Westminster John Knox Press, 1982), p. 86.

[134]See Hans Selye, *The Stress of Life*, 2nd ed. (New York: McGraw-Hill, 1978); and *Stress Without Distress* (New York: Signet, 1995).

[135]Also see Don Colbert, *Stress Less* (Lake Mary, FL: Siloam, 2005), pp. 19-28.

[136]Robert M. Sapolsky, *Why Zebras Don't Get Ulcers: A Guide to Stress, Stress-Related Diseases, and Coping*, 3rd ed. (New York: Henry Holt, 2004), pp. 8-11.

[137]Colbert, *Stress Less*, p. 257.

[138]Ibid., pp. 204-14; Colbert, *Seven Pillars of Health*, p. 121.

[139]Harold G. Koenig, *Medicine, Religion, and Health: Where Science and Spirituality Meet* (West Conshohocken, PA: Templeton Foundation Press, 2008), pp. 37-53.

[140]Dr. Richard A. Swenson argues that progress is the culprit for marginless living (Richard A. Swenson, *Margin: Restoring Emotional, Physical, Financial, and Time Reserves to Overloaded Lives*, 2nd ed. (Colorado Springs: NavPress, 2004), pp. 21-33. However, are the inescapable realities of progress in technology, information access and Internet connectivity the real culprits, or is it our own inability to establish personal life rhythms and set healthy boundaries that honor God?

[141]Richard A. Swenson, *In Search of Balance: Keys to a Stable Life* (Colorado Springs: NavPress, 2010), pp. 19-20. Swenson provides other examples of the importance of balance: balance of weight on a plane, balance of power in government, a balanced diet and balancing of checkbooks.

[142]Margaret Diddams et al., "Implications of Biblical Principles of Rhythm and Rest for Individual and Organizational Practices," *Christian Scholar's Review* 33, no. 3 (2004): 311-44, esp. p. 314.

[143]Abraham Joshua Heschel, *The Sabbath: Its Meaning for Modern Man* (New York: Farrar, Straus & Giroux, 1951), p. 24.

[144]Ibid., p. 29.

[145]Dorothy C. Bass, *Receiving the Day: Christian Practices for Opening the Gift of Time* (San Francisco: Jossey-Bass, 2000), p. 48.

[146]Ibid., p. 55.

[147]"To refuse the sabbath is to close the world in upon ourselves, by making it yield to our (often self-serving) desires and designs, and to cut ourselves off from God's presence and purpose" (Norman Wirzba, *Living the Sabbath: Discovering the Rhythms of Rest and Delight* [Grand Rapids: Brazos, 2006], p. 34).

[148]For divergent approaches on the sabbath, see Christopher Donato, ed., *Perspectives on the Sabbath: Four Views* (Nashville: B & H, 2011).

[149]Marva J. Dawn, *Keeping the Sabbath Wholly: Ceasing, Resting, Embracing, Feasting* (Grand Rapids: Eerdmans, 1989), p. 76.

[150]Wayne Muller, *Sabbath: Finding Rest, Renewal, and Delight in Our Busy Lives* (New York: Bantam Books, 1999), p. 41.

[151]Annalyn Censki, "Vacation: No Thanks, Boss," *CNN Money*, May 18, 2012, http://money.cnn.com/2012/05/18/news/economy/unused_vacation_days/index.htm. From one study, Censki cites that 57% of working Americans had an average of eleven unused vacation days at the end of 2011. Known as the "no-vacation nation," the United States has much to learn from its European peers.

[152]Derek Thompson, "The Case for Vacation: Why Science Says Breaks Are Good for Productivity," *The Atlantic*, August 6, 2012, www.theatlantic.com/business/archive/2012/08/the-case-for-vacation-why-science-says-breaks-are-good-for-productivity/260747.

[153]Sexuality purity could easily have been addressed in the chapters on spiritual, emotional, relational, intellectual or vocational formation because sexuality influences each of these dimensions.

[154]Augustine, *Confessions* 8.2.17, trans. Henry Chadwick (Oxford: Oxford University Press, 2008), p. 145.

[155]Ibid., 4.2.2, p. 53.

[156]John S. Grabowski, *Sex and Virtue: An Introduction to Sexual Ethics* (Washington, DC: Catholic University of America Press, 2003), pp. 49-70.

[157]Cf. Gal. 5:19; Eph. 5:3-5; Col. 3:5.

[158]Phyllis A. Bird, "'Male and Female He Created Them': Genesis 1:27b in the Context of the Priestly Account of Creation," *Harvard Theological Review* 74, no. 2 (1981): 129-59, esp. p. 147.

[159]As highlighted in chapter three, several theologians advance this relational perspective in interpreting the *imago Dei*, including Karl Barth, Dietrich Bonhoeffer, Søren Kierkegaard, Paul Ramsey and Emil Brunner. For a succinct overview of their positions, see Stanley J. Grenz, *The Social God and the Relational Self: A Trinitarian Theology of the Imago Dei* (Louisville: Westminster John Knox Press, 2001), pp. 162-77.

[160]Stanley J. Grenz, *Sexual Ethics: An Evangelical Perspective*, 2nd ed. (Louisville: Westminster John Knox, 1997), pp. 20, 47.

[161]Grenz, *Sexual Ethics*, p. 19. For a historical analysis of sexuality from antiquity to the modern era, see Stephen Garton, *Histories of Sexuality* (New York: Routledge, 2004).

[162]Stanley Hauerwas supports the moral value of the family based on heterosexual marriage by stating that "the family is integral to the entire culture" ("The Moral Value of the Family," in *A Community of Character: Toward a Constructive Christian Social Ethic* [Notre Dame, IN: University of Notre Dame Press, 1981], pp. 165). Cultural and moral challenges to traditional definitions of the family and gender abound. For example, see Ted Olson, "The Conservative Case for Gay Marriage," *Newsweek*, January 8, 2010, www.thedailybeast.com/newsweek/2010/01/08/the-conservative-case-for-gay-marriage.html. Further, sexual reassignment treatments to change the gender of children as young as seven, and surgery on

adolescents with diagnosed gender identity disorder (GID), are being performed in transgender clinics like the one at the Boston Children's Hospital, led by Dr. Norman Spack. See the alarm this has evoked in Den Trumbull, "Sex Change Therapy: Not Best for Children," *American College of Pediatrics*, February 28, 2012, www.acpeds.org/category/press-release/page/3.

[163]Lisa Graham McMinn, *Sexuality and Holy Longing: Embracing Intimacy in a Broken World* (San Francisco: Jossey-Bass, 2007), p. 7.

[164]Grenz, *Social God and the Relational Self*, p. 302.

[165]Ibid., p. 279.

[166]Miroslav Volf, *Exclusion and Embrace: A Theological Exploration of Identity, Otherness, and Reconciliation* (Nashville: Abingdon Press, 1996), p. 186.

[167]Ronald Rolheiser, *The Holy Longing: The Search for a Christian Spirituality* (New York: Doubleday, 1999), p. 195.

[168]Grenz, *Sexual Ethics*, p. 11. This deep ethical void is reflected in theological scholarship of those who dismantle the biblical basis for sexuality that frames heterosexual marriage and subsequent family relationships. They include feminist Judith Butler, who deconstructs the binary nature of sexuality; Mary Daly, who reconstructs female realities; and liberal ethicist Mark M. Ellison. Many postmodern theologies take their cues from the writings of French philosopher Michel Foucault (1926–1984), who died of AIDS at fifty-eight. For one critique, see Lisa Sowle Cahill, *Sex, Gender, and Christian Ethics* (Cambridge: Cambridge University Press, 1996), pp. 21-25.

[169]Lauren F. Winner, *Real Sex: The Naked Truth About Chastity* (Grand Rapids: Brazos, 2005), p. 22.

[170]Judith K. Balswick and Jack O. Balswick, *Authentic Human Sexuality: An Integrated Christian Approach* (Downers Grove, IL: InterVarsity Press, 1999), p. 108. These authors observe that many churches and parents have two inadequate responses to the dilemma of sexual intimacy and singleness: (1) "don't ask, don't tell" and (2) "just say no."

[171]Mark D. Regnerus conducted a study of 3,370 adolescents who completed a phone survey with 267 in-depth personal interviews. He reports on the findings in *Forbidden Fruit: Sex and Religion in the Lives of American Teenagers* (Oxford: Oxford University Press, 2007).

[172]Ibid., pp. 203-7.

[173]Donna Freitas, *Sex and the Soul: Juggling Sexuality, Spirituality, Romance, and Religion on America's College Campuses* (Oxford: Oxford University Press, 2008), p. 10. The study on which her book is based, "Sexuality and Spirituality in American College Life," was inspired by twenty-one students in Freitas's class who wanted to address their dismay with the "hookup" culture at St. Michael's College. Where hooking up in sexual activity has replaced the first date on college campuses, Freitas observes, "The hookup culture, though pervasive, does not appeal to the average student" (ibid., p. 217).

[174]Balswick and Balswick, *Authentic Human Sexuality*, pp. 113-28.

[175]Winner, *Real Sex*, pp. 15, 22-24. Chastity is the godly virtue that combats lust, as presented by Aurelius Prudentis Clemens (348–c. 410) in his epic poem titled *Psychomachia*, meaning "spiritual combat." The seven deadly sins include lust, gluttony, greed, sloth, wrath, envy and pride. Guarding against the deadly sins, the seven heavenly virtues include chastity, tem-

perance, charity, diligence, patience, kindness and humility.

[176]Christine A. Colón and Bonnie E. Field, *Singled Out: Why Celibacy Must Be Reinvented in Today's Church* (Grand Rapids: Brazos, 2009), pp. 54-76; Doug Rosenau and Michael Todd Wilson, *Soul Virgins: Redefining Single Sexuality* (Grand Rapids: Baker, 2006).

[177]Alasdair MacIntyre critiques the emotivism characteristic of contemporary moral philosophy, indicts the individualism fostered during the Enlightenment, and bemoans the current lack of virtue in individual and public life (*After Virtue*, 3rd ed. [Notre Dame, IN: Notre Dame University Press, 2007], p. 191).

[178]Caroline J. Simon, *Bringing Sex into Focus: The Quest for Sexual Integrity* (Downers Grove, IL: IVP Academic, 2012), pp. 30-39. The four secular views offered by Simon regarding sexuality correlate with humanism and postmodernism, two of the worldviews presented in chapter seven on intellectual formation.

[179]David D. Myers, *The American Paradox* (New Haven, CT: Yale University Press, 2000), p. 32. See chapter two on "The Sexual Swing," pp. 13-35.

[180]Joyce A. Martin et al., "Births: Final Data for 2008," National Vital Statistics Reports 59, no. 1 (2010), www.cdc.gov/nchs/data/nvsr/nvsr59/nvsr59_01.pdf. Percentages of mothers who are unmarried include 72 percent for African Americans, 52.7 percent for Hispanics, and 35.7 percent for Caucasians. Dr. Natalie Carroll, an African American gynecologist who practices in Houston, has emphasized that black children deserve both a father and mother (Jesse Washington, "Blacks Struggle with 72 Percent Unwed Mothers Rate," November 11, 2010, NBC News, www.msnbc.msn.com/id/39993685/ns/health-womens_health/t/blacks-struggle-percent-unwed-mothers-rate.

[181]The three most prevalent STDs are chlamydia, gonorrhea and syphilis. Often undetected, STDs cause pelvic inflammatory disease in women, a major cause of infertility; ectopic pregnancy; and pelvic pain. See "Sexually Transmitted Disease Surveillance 2010," Centers for Disease Control and Prevention, November 2011, www.cdc.gov/std/stats10/surv2010.pdf.

[182]"Global Summary of the HIV/AIDS Epidemic," World Health Organization, December 2010, www.who.int/hiv/data/2011_epi_core_en.png. See also Hoeger and Hoeger, "Preventing Sexually Transmitted Infections," in *Lifetime Physical Fitness and Wellness*, pp. 447-56.

[183]Jerry Ropelato, "Internet Pornography Statistics," *Top Ten Reviews*, http://internet-filter-review.toptenreviews.com/internet-pornography-statistics-pg8.html.

[184]William M. Struthers, *Wired for Intimacy: How Pornography Hijacks the Male Brain* (Downers Grove, IL: InterVarsity Press, 2009), pp. 83-111.

[185]Ibid., p. 85. The release of hormones and regulation of neurotransmitters—such as dopamine (known as the pleasure chemical), norepinephrine and epinephrine that contributes to sexual arousal—and the lowering of serotonin that contributes to emotional euphoria converge to produce sexual addiction. See also Stephen Arterburn and Fred Stoeker, *Every Man's Battle: Winning the War on Sexual Temptation One Victory at a Time*, with Mike Yorkey (Colorado Springs: Waterbrook, 2009), esp. pp. 83-124.

[186]Struthers, *Wired for Intimacy*, p. 106.

[187]See Paula Rinehart, *Sex and the Soul of a Woman: How God Restores the Beauty of Relationship from the Pain of Regret*, 2nd ed. (Grand Rapids: Zondervan, 2010); and Shannon Ethridge,

Every Woman's Battle: Discovering God's Plan for Sexual and Emotional Fulfillment (Colorado Springs: Waterbrook, 2003).

[188]Karen A. McClintock, *Sexual Shame: An Urgent Call for Healing* (Minneapolis: Fortress Press, 2001), esp. pp. 121-45.

[189]Within church networks and denominations, the controversy over ministerial ordination of those in the lesbian, gay, bisexual, transgender (LGBT) community magnifies this debate. In order to legitimize homosexual behavior and same-sex marriage, strident advocates announce that the Bible is outdated, arguing that passages about homosexuality have been misinterpreted. In framing theology, Christian ethics have traditionally drawn from John Wesley's quadrilateral of (1) Scripture, (2) Christian tradition, (3) reason and (4) personal experience. Those advocating for ordination of LGBTs and same-sex marriage weight reason and personal experience over scriptural prohibition and Christian tradition. Dan O. Via and Robert A. J. Gagnon provide a helpful discussion on relevant biblical passages related to homosexual practice and orientation in *Homosexuality and the Bible: Two Views* (Minneapolis: Fortress Press, 2003).

[190]Mark A. Yarhouse, *Homosexuality and the Christian: A Guide for Parents, Pastors, and Friends* (Bloomington, MN: Bethany House, 2011), pp. 48-53.

[191]Mark A. Yarhouse et al., "Listening to Sexual Minorities on Christian College Campuses," *Journal of Psychology and Theology* 37, no. 2 (2009): 96-113; Stanton L. Jones and Mark A. Yarhouse, *Ex-Gays? A Longitudinal Study of Religiously Mediated Change in Sexual Orientation* (Downers Grove, IL: IVP Academic, 2007); and Stanton L. Jones and Mark A. Yarhouse, *Homosexuality: The Use of Scientific Research in the Church's Moral Debate* (Downers Grove, IL: InterVarsity Press, 2000).

[192]See Alan Chambers, *Leaving Homosexuality: A Practical Guide for Men and Women Looking for a Way Out* (Eugene, OR: Harvest House, 2009). Various ministries that reinforce this identity-in-Christ approach include Desert Streams Ministries and their Living Waters program, Homosexuals Anonymous, and Leanne Payne's Pastoral Care Ministries, among other independent ministries and support groups. Christian counselors, however, are rethinking reparative conversion and change therapy approaches. See Patrick Condon, "Exodus International, 'Ex-Gay' Christian Group, Backs Away from Reparative Therapy," *Huffington Post*, June 26, 2012, www.huffingtonpost.com/2012/06/27exodus-international-ex-gay-christian-group-reparative-therapy_n_1630425.html.

[193]Yarhouse, *Homosexuality and the Christian*, pp. 41-42.

[194]Mark A. Yarhouse and Lori A. Burkett, *Sexual Identity: A Guide to Living in the Time Between the Times* (Lanham, MD: University Press of America, 2003), p. 31.

[195]Ibid., p. 32.

[196]Richard B. Hays, *The Moral Vision of the New Testament: A Contemporary Introduction to New Testament Ethics* (San Francisco: HarperSanFrancisco, 1996), p. 390.

[197]Ibid., pp. 391-94. Hays presents a sensitive and biblical analysis of homosexuality based on (1) Genesis 19:1-29; (2) Leviticus 18:22; 20:13; (3) Acts 15:28-29; (4) 1 Corinthians 6:9-11; (5) 1 Timothy 1:10; and (6) Romans 1:18-32 (ibid., pp. 381-89).

[198]Ibid., p. 389.

[199]Andrew Marin calls evangelicals to build bridges of dialogue with the LGBT community: "The Christian community has only ever known one way to handle same-sex behavior: take a stand and keep a distance. Productive dialogue comes from cognitive insight and can only be accomplished through an incarnational posture of humility and living as a learner" (Andrew Marin, *Love Is an Orientation: Elevating the Conversation with the Gay Community* [Downers Grove, IL: InterVarsity Press, 2009], p. 37). Also see Joe Dallas and Nancy Heche, *The Complete Christian Guide to Understanding Homosexuality: A Biblical and Compassionate Response to Same-Sex Attraction* (Eugene, OR: Harvest House, 2010).

[200]Hall, "What Are Bodies For?" p. 171.

10 Stewardship: Our Resources

[1]Astronauts Frank F. Borman II, James A. Lovell Jr. and William A. Anders, who comprised the *Apollo 8* crew, read portions of Genesis, as recorded by the National Space Science Data Center. For a written excerpt of this message, see "The Apollo 8 Christmas Eve Broadcast," NASA, September 25, 2007, http://nssdc.gsfc.nasa.gov/planetary/lunar/apollo8_xmas.html.

[2]Søren Kierkegaard, *Works of Love* (Princeton, NJ: Princeton University Press, 1946), p. 52.

[3]Douglas John Hall, *Imaging God: Dominion as Stewardship* (Eugene, OR: Wipf & Stock, 2004), p. 179.

[4]Ibid., p. 49.

[5]J. Richard Middleton, *The Liberating Image: The* Imago Dei *in Genesis 1* (Grand Rapids: Brazos, 2005), p. 295.

[6]Anthony A. Hoekema, *Created in God's Image* (Grand Rapids: Eerdmans, 1986), pp. 79-80.

[7]Other areas that involve stewardship, such as vocation and interpersonal relationships, have been addressed in previous chapters and will not be addressed here.

[8]Richard Bauckham prefers *caring responsibility* over the term *stewardship*, since he views the term *stewardship* as associated with domination and human exploitation rather than a biblical view of dominion as supported by God-given delegation (Richard Bauckham, *Living with Other Creatures: Green Exegesis and Theology* [Waco, TX: Baylor University Press, 2011], pp. 2-7, 61-62; and *The Bible and Ecology: Rediscovering the Community of Creation* [Waco, TX: Baylor University Press, 2010], pp. 1-36).

[9]Darryl L. Bock, *Luke*, IVP New Testament Commentary (Downers Grove, IL: InterVarsity Press, 1994), pp. 232-33.

[10]Craig Blomberg, *Interpreting the Parables*, 2nd ed. (Downers Grove, IL: IVP Academic, 2012), p. 237.

[11]Leon Morris, *The Gospel According to St. Luke: An Introduction and Commentary* (Leicester, UK: Inter-Varsity Press, 1974), p. 219.

[12]Blomberg, *Interpreting the Parables*, p. 237.

[13]Ibid., p. 271.

[14]Douglas John Hall, *The Steward: A Biblical Symbol Come of Age* (Grand Rapids: Eerdmans, 1990), p. 44. From historical, sociological, ethological and ecclesiastical perspectives, Hall retrieves a biblical view of stewardship often overlooked in the contemporary church.

[15]Ibid., pp. 44-45.

[16]Ibid., p. 45.

[17]Ernst M. Conradie, *An Ecological Christian Anthropology: At Home on Earth?* (Aldershot, UK: Ashgate, 2005), p. 202.

[18]Ibid., p. 208.

[19]Ibid., p. 202.

[20]One report indicates that extinction threatens many animal species: (1) 30 percent of amphibians, (2) 21 percent of birds and (3) 25 percent of mammals (Jeff Tollefson and Natasha Gilbert, "Earth Summit: Rio Report Card," *Nature* 486 [2012]: 20-23, www.nature.com/news/earth-summit-rio-report-card-1.10764. "Planet's Tougher Problems Persist," *Global Environmental Outlook (GEO-4)*, October 24, 2007, pp. 1-8, www.unep.org/geo/GEO4/media/media_briefs/Media_Briefs_GEO-4%20Global.pdf.

[21]Ibid., p. 2. For example, Arctic temperatures are rising twice as rapidly as the rest of the world, with sea levels likewise rising. Global chemical production is projected to increase by 85 percent through 2027, while consumption exceeds available resources.

[22]Bauckham, *Living with Other Creatures*, p. 221.

[23]Steven Bouma-Prediger, *For the Beauty of the Earth: A Christian Vision for Creation Care*, 2nd ed. (Grand Rapids: Baker Academic, 2010), p. xii.

[24]James D. G. Dunn, *The Theology of Paul the Apostle* (Grand Rapids: Eerdmans, 1988), pp. 100-101.

[25]Bouma-Prediger, *For the Beauty of the Earth*, pp. xii, 24, 55.

[26]Hall, *Steward*, p. 121.

[27]Lynn White Jr., "The Historical Roots of Our Ecological Crisis," *Science* 155 (1967): 1203-7. This article is reprinted in R. J. Berry, ed., *The Care of Creation: Focusing Concern and Action* (Leicester, UK: Inter-Varsity Press, 2000), pp. 31-42.

[28]Greater appreciation emerged for the secular work of John James Audubon (1785–1851), ornithologist and inspiration for the National Audubon Society; Henry David Thoreau (1817–1862), author of *Walden*; John Muir (1838–1914), preservationist and founder of the Sierra Club; Aldo Leopold (1887–1948), ecologist and author of *A Sand County Almanac*; and Rachel Carson (1907–1964), marine biologist and conservationist who wrote the influential book *Silent Spring* on the harmful effects of pesticides. Also feminist ecotheologians associate the domination of women with the domination of nature. See Rosemary Radford Ruether, "Ecofeminism: The Challenge to Theology," in *Christianity and Ecology: Seeking the Well-Being of Earth and Humans*, ed. Dieter T. Hessel and Rosemary Radford Ruether (Cambridge, MA: Harvard University Press, 2000), pp. 97-112; Sallie McFague, *The Body of God: An Ecological Theology* (Minneapolis: Augsburg Fortress Press, 1993); and McFague, *Super, Natural Christians: How We Should Love Nature* (Minneapolis: Fortress Press, 1997), esp. pp. 150-75.

[29]John Stott, foreword in *The Care of Creation: Focusing Concern and Action*, ed. R. J. Berry (Downers Grove, IL: IVP Academic, 2000), pp. 8-9.

[30]Evangelical Environmental Network, "An Evangelical Declaration on the Care of Creation," in Berry, *The Care of Creation*, pp. 17-22.

[31]Joseph Sittler, *Gravity and Grace* (Minneapolis: Augsburg, 1985), p. 22.

[32]Peter W. Bakken, "Nature as a Theater of Grace: The Ecological Theology of Joseph Sittler,"

in Joseph Sittler, *Evocations of Grace: The Writings of Joseph Sittler on Ecology, Theology, and Ethics*, ed. Steven Bouma-Prediger and Peter Bakken (Grand Rapids: Eerdmans, 2000), p. 18.

[33]In addition to Richard Bauckham, other theologians who beckon Christians to active engagement in creation care include Larry L. Rasmussen, *Earth Community, Earth Ethics* (Maryknoll, NY: Orbis, 1996), who calls for religious and social reformation for a sustainable moral, spiritual, moral and environmental future to counter the degradation of the earth and the anthropomorphism that sustains it (ibid., pp. 1-19); Michael S. Northcott, *The Environment and Christian Ethics* (Cambridge: Cambridge University Press, 1996), who asserts the created order gives humanity a moral responsibility for its care (ibid., pp. 164-98); H. Paul Santmire, *Nature Reborn: The Ecological and Cosmic Promise of Christian Theology* (Minneapolis: Augsburg Fortress, 2000), who argues that Christians need to reclaim and reenact the Christian story beyond anthropomorphic interpretations to advance creation care values. For a historical account tracing Christian thought relative to nature, see H. Paul Santmire, *The Travail of Nature: The Ambiguous Ecological Promise of Christian Theology* (Minneapolis: Fortress Press, 1985).

[34]Entities collaborating include the Evangelical Environmental Network, Christians Caring for Creation, the National Council of Churches, the American Baptist Churches USA, the Roman Catholic Franciscan Order, the Religious Society of Friends (Quakers), the United Methodist Church, the Episcopal Church, Au Sable Institute of Environmental Studies in Michigan, the Social Action Committee of Reformed Judaism, and the Central Conference of American Rabbis, among others.

[35]See the National Religious Coalition on Creation Care website at www.nrccc.org.

[36]Calvin DeWitt, "Creation's Environmental Challenge to Evangelical Christianity," in Berry, *Care of Creation*, pp. 68-71.

[37]In answering who is in charge of nature and the world, Douglas John Hall cites two positions: (1) As sovereign, God is in control, and human wisdom is to be distrusted, and (2) human autonomy and responsibility. Hall sees danger in both positions. An overemphasis on divine sovereignty and intervention may cause resignation and withdrawal of culpability (e.g., "Whatever God wills . . ." and "I cannot do anything to change this"). An overemphasis on human responsibility exaggerates human wisdom and goodness, which can lead to deception and stewardship abuse (*Imaging God*, pp. 43-48).

[38]James A. Nash, *Loving Nature: Ecological Integrity and Christian Responsibility* (Nashville: Abingdon, 1991), p. 106.

[39]Ibid., pp. 139-61, esp. pp. 145, 147.

[40]DeWitt, "Creation's Environmental Challenge," pp. 72-73.

[41]Fred H. Van Dyke et al., *Redeeming Creation: The Biblical Basis for Environmental Stewardship* (Downers Grove, IL: InterVarsity Press, 1996), pp. 142-61, 168.

[42]Steven Chase, *Nature as Spiritual Practice* (Grand Rapids: Eerdmans, 2011).

[43]For one family's stewardship journey, see J. Matthew Sleeth, *Serve God, Save the Planet: A Christian Call to Action* (White River Junction, VT: Chelsea Green, 2006). For more practical "green" suggestions, see Nancy Sleeth, *Go Green, Save Green: A Simple Guide to Saving Time, Money, and God's Green Earth* (Carol Stream, IL: Tyndale House, 2009).

[44]See Kim McKay and Jenny Bonnin, *True Green: 100 Ways You Can Contribute to a Healthier*

Planet (Washington, DC: National Geographic, 2006); and Nicky Scott, *Reduce, Reuse, Recycle: An Easy Household Guide* (White River Junction, VT: Chelsea Green, 2007). For the film documentary *Renewal*, on interfaith initiatives to steward the environment by Marty Ostrow and Terry Kay Rockefeller, producers of PBS and NOVA specials, see the Renewal Project website at www.renewalproject.net.

[45]Van Dyke et al., *Redeeming Creation*, p. 149.

[46]Joseph Sittler, "A Theology of the Earth," in *Evocations of Grace: The Writings of Joseph Sittler on Ecology, Theology, and Ethics*, ed. Steven Bouma-Prediger and Peter Bakken (Grand Rapids: Eerdmans, 2000), p. 25.

[47]Van Dyke et al., *Redeeming Creation*, pp. 147-48.

[48]Francis of Assisi, "The Canticle of Brother Sun," in *Francis and Clare: The Complete Works*, trans. Regis J. Armstrong and Ignatius C. Bradley (New York: Paulist Press, 1982), pp. 37-39. See also Roger D. Sorrell, *St. Francis of Assisi and Nature: Tradition and Innovation in Western Christian Attitudes Toward the Environment* (New York: Oxford University Press, 1988), p. 79.

[49]Philip Goodchild, *Theology of Money* (Durham, NC: Duke University Press, 2009), p. 218.

[50]Ibid., p. 7.

[51]Ibid., p. 6.

[52]Leo Tolstoy, "How Much Land Does a Man Need?" *Literature Network*, www.online-literature.com/tolstoy/2738.

[53]Ralph Moore and Alan Tang, *Your Money* (Ventura, CA: Regal Books, 2003), p. 16.

[54]Cf. Eduard Schweizer, *The Good News According to Luke*, trans. David E. Green (Atlanta: John Knox Press, 1984), p. 262.

[55]On eternal consequences see Bock, *Luke*, pp. 274-78; Morris, *Gospel According to St. Luke*, p. 253. On the mistaken notion that wealth prompts God's blessing, see Blomberg, *Interpreting the Parables*, p. 259.

[56]Gustavo Gutiérrez, *We Drink from Our Own Wells: The Spiritual Journey of a People*, 2nd ed., trans. Matthew J. O'Connell (Maryknoll, NY: Orbis, 2003), pp. 19-32.

[57]This quote of Mother Teresa is found in Randy C. Alcorn, *Money, Possessions and Eternity*, 2nd ed. (Carol Stream, IL: Tyndale House, 2003), p. 223.

[58]Larry Burkett, *How to Manage Your Money*, 3rd ed. (Chicago: Moody Press, 1991), p. 13.

[59]Ron Blue, *Master Your Money: A Step-by-Step Plan for Financial Freedom*, 2nd ed. (Nashville: Thomas Nelson, 1991), pp. 27-28.

[60]David A. Croteau, *You Mean I Don't Have to Tithe? A Deconstruction of Tithing and a Reconstruction of Post-Tithe Giving* (Eugene, OR: Pickwick, 2010), pp. 9-82.

[61]See Albert C. Outler and Richard P. Heitzenrater, eds., *John Wesley's Sermons: An Anthology* (Nashville: Abingdon, 1991), pp. 636-46.

[62]Moore and Tang, *Your Money*, pp. 56-59.

[63]Regarding point 1, see Croteau, *You Mean I Don't Have to Tithe*, p. 249. See also ibid., pp. 254-56 for an excellent New Testament summary regarding the foundation, details, amount, motivation, attitude and results of giving.

[64]Ibid., p. 264.

[65]Ibid., pp. 205, 258.

[66]Craig L. Blomberg, *Neither Poverty Nor Riches: A Biblical Theology of Material Possessions* (Grand Rapids: Eerdmans, 1999), pp. 198-99.

[67]See Ronald J. Sider, *Rich Christians in an Age of Plenty: Moving from Affluence to Generosity*, 5th ed. (Nashville: Thomas Nelson, 2005), pp. 187-90.

[68]John R. W. Stott, *The Grace of Giving: 10 Principles of Christian Giving*, 2nd ed. (South Hamilton, MA: Lausanne Movement, 2008), p. 18.

[69]C. S. Lewis, *Mere Christianity* (New York: Macmillan, 1960), pp. 82-83.

[70]"The Debt to the Penny and Who Holds It," *TreasuryDirect*, June 22, 2013, www.treasurydirect.gov/NP/debt/current.

[71]"Credit Card Debt in the USA," US Trade and Development Agency, 2012, www.usdta.org/credit-card-debt-in-the-usa.php.

[72]Andrew Martin, "A Big Default Problem, but How Big?" *New York Times*, September 8, 2012, www.nytimes.com/2012/09/09/business/a-big-student-loan-default-problem-but-how-big.html. Also see Alissa F. Cunningham and Gregory S. Kienzel, "Delinquency: The Untold Story of Student Loan Borrowing," Institute for Higher Education Policy, March 2011, www.ihep.org/assets/files/publications/a-f/Delinquency-The_Untold_Story_FINAL_March_2011.pdf.

[73]US Trade and Development Agency, "Credit Card Debt in the US."

[74]See Dave Ramsey, *Dave Ramsey's Complete Guide to Money: The Handbook of Financial Peace University* (Brentwood, TN: Lampo Press, 2012); and *The Total Money Makeover: A Proven Plan for Financial Fitness*, 3rd ed. (Nashville: Nelson Books, 2009).

[75]Moore and Tang, *Your Money*, pp. 41-42.

[76]See Robert H. Stein, *Mark*, Baker Exegetical Commentary on the New Testament (Grand Rapids: Baker Academic, 2008), p. 470; and William L. Lane, *The Gospel According to Mark* (Grand Rapids: Eerdmans, 1974), p. 368.

[77]A. W. Tozer, *The Pursuit of God* (Harrisburg, PA: Christian Publications, 1958), p. 22.

[78]Richard J. Foster, *The Challenge of the Disciplined Life: Christian Reflections on Money, Sex & Power* (New York: HarperSanFrancisco, 1989), p. 35.

[79]Wesley Kenneth Willmer, *God and Your Stuff: The Vital Link Between Your Possessions and Your Soul*, with Martyn Smith (Colorado Springs: NavPress, 2002), p. 9.

[80]Randy C. Alcorn, *Money, Possessions and Eternity*, 2nd ed. (Carol Stream, IL: Tyndale House, 2003), p. 98.

[81]Robert Wuthnow, *God and Mammon in America* (New York: Free Press, 1994), pp. 166, 150-51, 157.

[82]Ibid., p. 263.

[83]Blomberg, *Neither Poverty Nor Riches*, pp. 243-53.

[84]Ibid., p. 246.

[85]John de Graff, David Wann and Thomas H. Naylor, *Affluenza: The All-Consuming Epidemic*, 2nd ed. (San Francisco: Berrett-Koehler, 2005), p. 2. This book is based on two PBS documentaries produced by De Graff: (1) "Affluenza" in 1997, and (2) "Escape from Affluenza" in 1998.

[86]Ibid.

[87]See Juliet B. Schor, *Born to Buy: The Commercialized Child and the New Consumer Culture* (New York: Scribner, 2005). As an expert on consumerism and economics and as a Boston College professor, Schor provides guidelines for parents and teachers on combating consumerism in order to enhance the well-being of children.

[88]Willmer, *God and Your Stuff*, pp. 18-19.

[89]Ibid., p. 35.

[90]Sider, *Rich Christians in an Age of Hunger*, pp. 191-94.

[91]See Bob Goudzwaard and Harry de Lange, *Beyond Poverty and Affluence: Toward an Economy of Care*, 4th ed. (Grand Rapids, Eerdmans, 1994).

[92]For example, in 2008, the world's population that lived on less than $1.25 per day, about the cost of a cup of coffee, was 22.2 percent ("World Development Indicators, 2012," World Bank, April 14, 2012, http://data.worldbank.org/news/world-development-indicators-2012-now-available.

[93]Karl Barth, *Church Dogmatics* 3.2, *The Doctrine of Creation*, ed. G. W. Bromiley and T. F. Torrance (London: T & T Clark, 1960), p. 527.

[94]Henri Nouwen, *Reaching Out: The Three Movements of the Spiritual Life* (New York: Image/Doubleday, 1975), p. 52.

[95]Dorothy C. Bass, *Receiving the Day: Christian Practices for Opening the Gift of Time* (San Francisco: Jossey-Bass, 2000).

[96]Ibid., p. 18.

[97]Ibid., p. 55.

[98]Howard Thurman, *For the Inward Journey: The Writings of Howard Thurman*, ed. Anne Spencer Thurman (San Diego: Harcourt Brace Jovanovich, 1984), pp. 93-94.

[99]Bass, *Receiving the Day*, p. 15. Also see Lynne Baab's *Sabbath Keeping: Finding Freedom in the Rhythms of Rest* (Downers Grove, IL: InterVarsity Press, 2005). Baab addresses sabbath as a gift and a celebration.

[100]Bass, *Receiving the Day*, p. 112.

[101]M. Shawn Copeland, "Saying Yes and Saying No," in *Practicing Our Faith: A Way of Life for a Searching People*, ed. Dorothy C. Bass (San Francisco: Jossey-Bass, 1997), pp. 59-73, esp. p. 60.

[102]Ibid., p. 66.

[103]For a helpful resource that presents four views on sabbath keeping from diverse theological and biblical perspectives, see Christopher John Donato, ed., *Perspectives on the Sabbath: 4 Views* (Nashville: B & H Academic, 2011). Differing viewpoints from Seventh-day Adventist (Skip MacCarty), Presbyterian (Joseph A. Pipa), Lutheran (Charles P. Arand) and Baptist (Craig L. Blomberg) perspectives deal with the meaning of sabbath, biblical and historical precedents regarding sabbath, the applicability of sabbath observance for today, and the benefits of sabbath taking. As with tithing, sabbath keeping is a sensitive issue that requires believers to examine the Scriptures and determine their own convictions without condemning others who may disagree.

[104]Richard A. Swenson, *Margin: Restoring Emotional, Physical, Financial, and Time Reserves to Overloaded Lives*, 2nd ed. (Colorado Springs: NavPress, 2004), pp. 109-29.

[105]A Western perception of time has been called *monochronic*, where things are done systematically through scheduling. Perceptions of time characterized by Latin, African, Asian and

Middle Eastern culture have been called *polychronic* in that several things can be done at the same time in a more fluid manner.

11 Formation Synthesis: Our Ethical Living

[1]Jesus summons all to repentance, to reorder priorities and to seek the Kingdom. As the trilogy of parables of the lost sheep, the lost coin and the lost son convey (Lk 15:1-32), God's grace, mercy and forgiveness coalesce under the rule of God's love. Love is the primary ethic of the Kingdom.

[2]Scott B. Rae, *Moral Choices: An Introduction to Ethics*, 3rd ed. (Grand Rapids: Zondervan, 2009), pp. 24, 40.

[3]N. T. Wright, *After You Believe: Why Christian Character Matters* (New York: HarperOne, 2010), p. 67.

[4]Ibid., p. 69.

[5]Stanley J. Grenz, *The Moral Quest: Foundations of Christian Ethics* (Downers Grove, IL: InterVarsity Press, 1997), p. 115.

[6]Ibid., p. 23.

[7]Richard A. Burridge, *Imitating Jesus: An Inclusive Approach to New Testament Ethics* (Grand Rapids: Eerdmans, 2007), p. 31.

[8]Jürgen Moltmann, "God's Kenosis in the Creation and Consummation of the World," in *The Work of Love: Creation as Kenosis*, ed. John Polkinghorne (Grand Rapids: Eerdmans, 2001), pp. 137-51, esp. pp. 40-41.

[9]Burridge, *Imitating Jesus*, p. 50.

[10]Victor Paul Furnish, *The Love Command in the New Testament* (London: Abingdon, 1972), p. 18.

[11]Ibid., p. 23.

[12]Ibid., pp. 60-61.

[13]Edward Collins Vacek, *Love, Human and Divine: The Heart of Christian Ethics* (Washington, DC: Georgetown University Press, 1994), p. 136.

[14]Wesley Autry, quoted in Kimberly Winston, "Wesley Autry: New York City's Subway Hero," *Beliefnet*, January, 2007, www.beliefnet.com/Inspiration/Most-Inspiring-Person-Of-The-Year/2007/Wesley-Autrey.aspx.

[15]Norman Geisler, *The Christian Ethic of Love* (Grand Rapids: Zondervan, 1973), pp. 41-42.

[16]Furnish, *Love Command in the New Testament*, p. 67.

[17]Glen Harold Stassen and David P. Gushee, *Kingdom Ethics: Following Jesus in Contemporary Context* (Downers Grove, IL: InterVarsity Press, 2003), p. 340.

[18]Although not addressed in this section but equally as important, John's Gospel and John's three epistles focus on love as a major theme, which reinforces love as the primary New Testament ethic. See Furnish, *Love Command in the New Testament*, pp. 132-58; and Burridge, *Imitating Jesus*, pp. 285-346.

[19]Furnish, *Love Command in the New Testament*, p. 91.

[20]Raymond F. Collins, *Christian Morality: Biblical Foundations* (Notre Dame, IN: University of Notre Dame Press, 1986), p. 137.

[21]Michael J. Gorman, *Cruciformity: Paul's Narrative Spirituality of the Cross* (Grand Rapids: Eerdmans, 2001), p. 72.

[22]Ibid., p. 156.

[23]Wolfgang Schrage, *The Ethics of the New Testament*, trans. David E Green (Philadelphia: Fortress, 1988), pp. 212-17; Furnish, *Love Command in the New Testament*, pp. 68-69; Burridge, *Imitating Christ*, pp. 107-10. Burridge argues against Richard B. Hays's contention that love is not central to Paul's ethics based on Hays's noting that the term *love* is misused in contemporary discourse. (See Richard B. Hays, *The Moral Vision of the New Testament: A Contemporary Introduction to New Testament Ethics* [San Francisco: HarperSanFrancisco, 1996], pp. 200-203.) Hays's portrayal of Paul's ethics relates to community, the cross and the new creation (ibid., pp. 193-205). What connects these three themes is arguably the love of God. My view aligns with that of Schrage, Furnish and Burridge.

[24]Gordon D. Fee, *God's Empowering Presence: The Holy Spirit in the Letters of Paul* (Peabody, MA: Hendrickson, 1994), p. 879.

[25]Jason B. Hood reclaims the theme of imitation of God as central in discipleship (*Imitating God in Christ: Recapturing a Biblical Pattern* [Downers Grove, IL: IVP Academic, 2013], esp. pp. 28-48).

[26]Dallas Willard, *The Spirit of the Disciplines* (San Francisco: HarperSanFrancisco, 1990), pp. 259-60.

[27]Stanley Hauerwas, *The Peaceable Kingdom: A Primer in Christian Ethics* (Notre Dame, IN: University of Notre Dame Press, 1983), p. 80.

[28]Burridge, *Imitating Jesus*, pp. 77-78.

[29]Noting how imitation is "thoroughly Jewish," see Frank J. Matera's book *New Testament Ethics: The Legacies of Jesus and Paul* (Louisville: Westminster John Knox, 1996), pp. 221-22.

[30]Fee, *God's Empowering Presence*, p. 46.

[31]William C. Spohn, *Go and Do Likewise: Jesus and Ethics* (New York: Continuum, 1999), pp. 147-49.

[32]Victor Paul Furnish, *Theology and Ethics in Paul* (Nashville: Abingdon, 1982), p. 223.

[33]Burridge, *Imitating Jesus*, p. 148.

[34]Gorman, *Cruciformity*, p. 48.

[35]Vacek, *Love, Human and* Divine, p. 40.

[36]Ibid.

[37]Ibid, pp. 52-53.

[38]Spohn, *Go and Do Likewise*, p. 149.

[39]Fee, *God's Empowering Presence*, p. 878.

[40]Ibid., p. 426.

[41]Ibid., p. 881.

[42]Ibid., p. 898.

[43]Grenz, *Moral Quest*, p. 126.

[44]Ibid., p. 127.

[45]Ibid., p. 122.

[46]Ibid., p. 10.

[47]Over the past four decades, philosophers and theologians have recaptured the emphasis of the virtues in the development of character. For example, see Scottish Roman Catholic phi-

losopher Alasdair C. MacIntyre, who identified the loss of Aristotelian ethics as the reason for moral decline in Western societies (*After Virtue: A Study in Moral Theory*, 3rd ed. [Notre Dame, IN: University of Notre Dame Press, 2007]). MacIntyre argued that virtue brings unity to our lives. See also Stanley Hauerwas, *Vision and Virtue: Essays in Christian Ethical Reflection* (Notre Dame, IN: University of Notre Dame Press, 1986); and Joseph J. Kotva, *The Christian Case for Virtue Ethics* (Washington, DC: Georgetown University Press, 1996).

[48]Stanley Hauerwas and William H. Willimon, *Resident Aliens: A Provocative Christian Assessment of Culture and Ministry for People Who Know That Something Is Wrong* (Nashville: Abingdon Press, 1989), p. 62.

[49]Ibid., p. 63. Hauerwas is noted for his narrative approach to Christian ethics, namely, that the Christian story and set of stories from the Scriptures comprise the Christian tradition and frame the ongoing faith community. Hauerwas, therefore, dismisses an emphasis on rules or principles, claiming that even doctrine is intended to help tell the story better (*Peaceable Kingdom*, pp. 24-26).

[50]For more on how his entire lifetime was preparation for that harrowing episode, see Chesley Sullenberger, *Highest Duty: My Search for What Really Matters*, with Jeffrey Zaslow (New York: HarperCollins, 2009), p. 388.

[51]Wright, *After You Believe*, p. 20.

[52]Ibid., p. 21.

[53]These seven virtues are contrasted with the seven deadly sins of lust, gluttony, greed, sloth, wrath, envy and pride.

[54]James K. A. Smith, *Desiring the Kingdom: Worship, Worldview, and Cultural Formation* (Grand Rapids: Baker Academic, 2009), p. 55.

[55]Wright, *After You Believe*, p. 35.

[56]Ibid., p. 71.

[57]Fee, *God's Empowering Presence*, p. 444.

[58]Ibid.

[59]Wright, *After You Believe*, pp. 142-43.

[60]Grenz, *Moral Quest*, p. 238.

[61]Wright, *After You Believe*, p. 144.

[62]Matera, *New Testament Ethics*, p. 220.

[63]James M. Gustafson, *Christ and the Moral Life* (New York: Harper & Row, 1968), p. 270.

[64]Hauerwas, *Peaceable Kingdom*, pp. 102-3. Hauerwas maintains that the story of Jesus is not only told but enacted as a social witness through the sacraments such as baptism, communion, preaching and prayer, which in turn prepare believers to more effectively tell the story (ibid., pp. 106-11).

[65]Hauerwas and Willimon, *Resident Aliens*, p. 55.

[66]Hauerwas argues that through the church "the world is given a history" by its story-formed community that enables the acquisition of moral and intellectual skills as individuals and a community in order to be effective in the world. Rather than the task of the church in a divided world being to deny the reality of other stories or to force the many stories into unity, the church's task "is to be faithful to the story of God that makes intelligible the divided

nature of the world" (Stanley Hauerwas, *A Community of Character: Toward a Constructive Christian Social Ethic* [Notre Dame, IN: University of Notre Dame Press, 1981], pp. 91, 96).

[67]Hauerwas, *Peaceable Kingdom*, p. 98.

[68]Stephen G. Post, *Unlimited Love, Altruism, Compassion, and Service* (Radnor, PA: Templeton Foundation Press, 2003), p. 5.

[69]Ibid., p. 3.

[70]For more on the connection between altruism and health, see the various chapters in Stephen G. Post, ed., *Altruism and Health: Perspectives from Empirical Research* (Oxford: Oxford University Press, 2007).

[71]Stephen G. Post and Jill Neimark, *Why Good Things Happen to Good People: How to Live a Healthier, Happier Life by the Simple Act of Giving* (New York: Broadway Books, 2007), p. 2. Post and Neimark identify four domains where giving and love are expressed: the family, friends, community and humanity. Also see Post's personal story of how he and his family developed a helping lifestyle: Stephen G. Post, *The Hidden Gifts of Helping: How the Power of Giving, Compassion, and Hope Can Get Us Through Hard Times* (San Francisco: Jossey-Bass, 2011), esp. pp. 23-87.

[72]Ibid., pp. 2, 7.

[73]Pitirim A. Sorokin, *The Ways and Power of Love* (Chicago: Henry Regnery, 1967), esp. pp. 15-35. Sorokin's research explores five dimensions of love: (1) intensity, (2) extensity, related to the extent of love for all humankind, living creatures and the whole universe, (3) duration, (4) purity, and (5) adequacy, referring to love aligning with truth and knowledge for inner transformation. Sorokin provides an example of inadequate love: when a parent spoils children to the extent that children become weak and lazy (ibid., pp. 17-18).

12 Christian Spiritual Formation Summary

[1]Heinrich Wölfflin, quoted in Charles Seymour Jr., *Michelangelo: The Sistine Chapel Ceiling* (New York: W. W. Norton, 1972), p. 178.

[2]John Addington Symonds, *The Life of Michelangelo Buonarroti* (New York: Random House, 1893/1928), pp. 126-28.

[3]Ibid., p. 130.

[4]Georg Brandes, *Michelangelo: His Life, His Times, His Era*, trans. Heinz Norden (New York: Frederick Ungar, 1963), pp. 256-57.

[5]Howard Hibbard, *Michelangelo* (New York: Harper & Row, 1974), p. 118. Michelangelo once wrote his father, "But I have good hopes God will help me." Maria Luisa Rizzatti, *The Life and Times of Michelangelo*, trans. Arnoldo Mondadori Editore (Philadelphia: Curtis Books, 1966), p. 62.

[6]Rizzatti, *Life and Times of Michelangelo*, p. 50.

Subject Index

Author Index

Scripture Index

Romans

1 Corinthians

2 Corinthians

Galatians

Ephesians

Philippians

About the Author

Diane J. Chandler (PhD, Regent University; MDiv, Regent University; MS, Canisius College) is associate professor of spiritual formation and leadership at Regent University School of Divinity in Virginia Beach, Virginia. She frequently publishes on leadership topics related to pastor care, burnout, women and ethics. With a passion for equipping the body of Christ, including emerging and seasoned leaders, Diane speaks at seminars, retreats and conferences. Having a love for the nations, she and her husband, Doug, both minister cross-culturally.

Connect with Diane online, where she shares her thoughts on spiritual formation, discipleship, holistic health, women in leadership, pastor care and many other areas of life and ministry.

On Facebook: www.facebook.com/ChristianSpiritualFormation

On Twitter: @DianeJChandler